3rd Edition Extra

with business skills lessons and self-assessment

Advanced

MARKET LEADER

Business English Course Book

with MyEnglishLab

Iwonna Dubicka   Margaret O'Keeffe

FT Publishing
FINANCIAL TIMES

GLOBAL SCALE
of English

Contents

Introduction

What is *Market Leader,* and who is it for?

Market Leader is a multi-level business English course for businesspeople and students of business English. It has been developed in association with the *Financial Times*, one of the leading sources of business information in the world. It consists of 12 units based on topics of great interest to everyone involved in or studying international business.

This third edition of the Advanced level features completely updated content and a significantly enhanced range of authentic resource material, reflecting the latest trends in the business world. If you are in business, the course will greatly improve your ability to communicate in English in a wide range of business situations. If you are a student of business, the course will develop the communication skills you need to succeed in a professional environment and will broaden your knowledge of the business world. Everybody studying this course will become more fluent and confident in using the language of business in a variety of contexts and should further their career prospects.

The authors

Margaret O'Keeffe (*left*) has over 20 years' teaching experience. Based in Barcelona, she is a freelance teacher-trainer, course designer and in-company English language teacher. Her background is in research and planning, working for both British Airways and British Telecom before becoming a teacher. She has taught at the Universitat Pompeu Fabra, and the Servei Extern d'Idiomes, Universitat de Barcelona, Spain. She also writes materials for coursebooks and multimedia, and co-authored the English language modules for the Universitat Oberta de Catalunya.

Iwonna Dubicka (*right*) has over 20 years' experience as a Business English trainer in Barcelona, including six years as Director of Studies of English at In Company Languages. She has also taught for SEI, Universitat de Barcelona, as an online tutor for the Universitat Oberta de Catalunya, and is currently a freelance teacher for ESADE's Executive Language Center in Barcelona. Together with Margaret O'Keeffe, she has co-authored various titles published by Pearson Education, such as *English for International Tourism* (Pre-intermediate) and *Lifestyle* (Intermediate).

What is in the units?

VOCABULARY

You are offered a variety of discussion questions as an introduction to the theme of each unit. You will hear authentic interviews with businesspeople. You will develop listening skills, such as listening for key information, note-taking and summary writing. In this section, you will also extend your vocabulary by learning useful new words and phrases. A good business dictionary such as the *Longman Business English Dictionary* or a monolingual dictionary for advanced learners such as the *Longman Dictionary of Contemporary English* will also help you to increase your business vocabulary.

READING AND LANGUAGE

You will read authentic articles on a variety of contemporary topics from the *Financial Times* and other newspapers and books on business management. You will develop your reading skills. You will also be able to discuss and respond to the issues in the articles. There is a language review after each article and related exercises in the Language reference section for each unit. You will be able to revise language and structures which are common problem areas for advanced learners. You will become more accurate in your use of English at an advanced level.

BUSINESS SKILLS

You will develop essential business communication skills, such as giving presentations, dealing with questions, taking an active part in meetings, negotiating, strategies for telephoning and teleconferences, English for networking, as well as using the language for a variety of business writing tasks. Each Business skills section contains a Useful language box which provides you with the language you need to carry out the realistic tasks in the Course Book.

CASE STUDY

The *Market Leader* case studies are linked to the business topics of each unit. They are based on business problems or situations and allow you to use the language and communication skills you have developed while working through each unit. They give you the opportunities to practise your speaking, listening, reading and writing skills in realistic contexts. Each case study ends with a follow-up writing task. A full writing syllabus is provided in the *Market Leader* Practice File.

WORKING ACROSS CULTURES

These four units focus on different aspects of international communication. They help to raise your awareness of potential problems or misunderstandings that may arise when doing business with people from different cultures.

REVISION UNITS

Market Leader Advanced third edition also contains four review units which recycle and revise material covered in the preceding three Course Book units. Each review unit is designed so that it can be completed in two sessions or on a unit-by-unit basis.

EXTRA BUSINESS SKILLS

The new Business Skills lessons offer the learner a task-based, integrated skills approach to the development of core business skills such as Presentations, Negotiations, Meetings, and Small Talk. These lessons appear at the end of every three units and incorporate performance review, suggestions for professional development and goal setting. They are based on the Global Scale of English Learning Objectives for Professional English. These objectives are signposted at the top of each new lesson in the Student's book and the carefully scaffolded activities are crafted around each objective, creating a clear sense of direction and progression in a learning environment where learners can reflect on their achievement at the end of the lesson.

First impressions

'You don't get a second chance to make a first impression.'
Anonymous

LISTENING AND DISCUSSION
First impressions in presentations

Anneliese
Guérin-LeTendre

A **Discuss these questions.**

1 What reasons can you think of for giving a presentation to an audience?

2 What is the hardest part of giving a presentation?

3 How can you secure your audience's attention at the start of a presentation? Think of three useful techniques.

4 Have you ever heard a speaker who you felt was truly inspirational? What techniques did they use to engage the audience?

5 What, for you, are the ingredients of a great presentation?

6 What impact do you think body language can have on a presenter's success? Think of some examples of good and bad body language.

B ◀)) CD1.1 **Anneliese Guérin-LeTendre is an intercultural communications expert who works with Communicaid, a culture and communication-skills consultancy. Listen to the first part of the interview and answer these questions.**

1 What percentage of communication is said to be non-verbal?

2 How do audiences form a first impression of a presenter?

C ◀)) CD1.2 **Listen to the second part of the interview. What four aspects of verbal and non-verbal communication does Anneliese talk about?**

6

D ◀)) CD1.2 **Listen again and complete these tips with one word in each gap. Which tip do you find the most useful?**

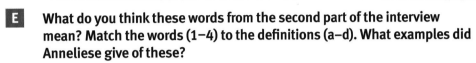

- The way you stand, known as ....^{1}, is important. Try to be ....^{2} but not rigid. Take ....^{3} of the space and don't hide behind the table or ....^{4}. Use a remote to 'liberate you from your laptop'.
- Use eye contact to ....^{5} the whole room, not just the first few rows.
- The way you use ....^{6} and intonation can produce all sorts of light and dark ....^{7} in your voice that add interest and get the audience paying attention. Avoid shouting. Try out the microphone beforehand.
- Control your gestures so that they don't become a ....^{8} to the audience.

Watch the interview on the DVD-ROM.

E **What do you think these words from the second part of the interview mean? Match the words (1–4) to the definitions (a–d). What examples did Anneliese give of these?**

1   mannerism   a) keep moving your hands or feet because you are bored or nervous

2   flick   b) slight movement of something you are wearing so that it is neater or more comfortable

3   fidget   c) way of speaking or moving that is typical of a particular person

4   adjustment   d) make something move with a sudden, quick gesture

F **What other examples of distracting gestures and behaviour have you noticed in presentations? What else can distract you?**

G **What do the verbs in this box mean? Use them in the correct form to complete the advice below.**

| lean   lean towards   nod   nod off   slouch   stare   wander |

Decoding the silent signals

You can also improve your presentation by noticing the messages your audience sends back to you through their own body language. Check out their reactions to what you're saying. Are people ....^{1} their heads in agreement or are they ....^{2}? If they look puzzled, stop and allow them to ask questions.

Watch for signals of boredom or misinterpretation. Are they ....^{3} you to listen or are they ....^{4} back with their arms folded? When members of your audience are ....^{5} in their seats letting their eyes ....^{6}, it usually means they're uninterested in what you're saying. But if they're sitting with their arms folded across their chest, ...^{7} at you, they may have been offended by something you've said. If you're paying close attention, you can catch this and clarify your statement without any negative feelings.

H **Is this advice true for audiences in your country? What other types of behaviour indicate an audience's reaction to a presentation?**

I **Prepare a two-minute introduction to a presentation on one of these topics.**

A passion of mine   What I love about ...

My ideal weekend   A memorable business trip

A special occasion   Three important moments in my life

J **Watch your colleagues' presentations. Make a note of two positive aspects of each presentation and one possible distraction.**

READING AND LANGUAGE

A What do you understand by the expression *It's not what you know, but who you know that counts*? Do you think networking is more important in some of these professions than others?

> accountancy banking the civil service law
> the media medicine politics teaching

B What are your views on networking? To what extent do you agree with these statements? Compare and discuss your answers.

		strongly agree	partially agree	disagree
1	Networking just means socialising with my colleagues and friends.			
2	Networking is all about finding lots of useful business contacts.			
3	Networking with business contacts is insincere and manipulative.			
4	Online social networking is as useful as face-to-face networking.			
5	Networking involves getting lots of help from others.			

C Read the article on the opposite page and compare the writer's views on networking with your own. What points does he make in relation to the five statements in Exercise B?

D Read the article again and find words or expressions which mean the following.

1 met someone you know when you were not expecting to (paragraph 2)

2 develop and use fully (paragraphs 3 and 5)

3 morally doubtful (paragraph 3)

4 not related to anything previously mentioned (paragraph 5)

5 when you recommend someone to another person for work (paragraphs 6 and 7)

6 move from one place to another in large amounts (paragraph 10)

7 caring about other people more than about yourself (*two expressions*) (paragraph 10)

E Look at these extracts from the article and indicate where the adverbs in brackets should go. Sometimes more than one answer is possible.

1 We have enough friends and contacts. (*already*)

2 You have more than 150 close contacts. (*probably*)

3 The dilemma is how to leverage existing contacts. (*successfully*)

4 It is important to determine how well your contacts understand what you do. (*also*)

5 One investment bank had a system for asking for two referrals. (*merely*)

6 The chances of receiving a referral are increased if they understand what you do. (*greatly, exactly*)

7 High-level networking is a face-to-face activity. (*primarily*)

8 If you connect with your network on this beneficial basis, the financial rewards will flow. (*mutually*)

➡ *Language reference: Adverbs page 126*

FT

It's not what you know

by Mike Southon

It is often said that your personal value is not what you know, but who you know. This is powerful motivation for recent graduates to build their personal networks. But some of us may conclude that we already have enough friends and contacts – the challenge is making the best use of those that we already have.

Mathematics supports this argument. If you have been in business more than 20 years, you probably have more than 150 close contacts – people you like and respect and would recognise if you bumped into them out of their work context. If you add to this all the people in *their* close networks, this aggregates to potentially more than 20,000 agreeable and interesting people.

It is not a problem to identify other networking prospects. We all have a drawer full of business cards and often a large number of online connections. The dilemma is how to successfully leverage existing contacts without appearing sleazy and manipulative.

The most important lesson to learn from the best-connected individuals is that little of their networking activity is carried out with any specific business goal in mind. They concentrate their effort on people they most like and who seem to like them back.

Even for the shyest individual, all that is required to leverage their network is to generate a list of people whose company they enjoy and invite them to a private dinner. This would be apropos of nothing in particular other than the pleasure of good company.

The tools for engineering a mutually successful outcome of such events are well explained by one of Europe's leading business networking strategists, Andy Lopata. His website explains that connecting is not enough; it is important also to determine how well your contacts understand what you do and then

Andy Lopata, Networking Strategist

how inspired they might be to provide a referral.

Lopata provides networking training and is always amazed to discover how few companies have an effective referral strategy. One investment bank merely had a system for asking for two referrals at the end of every meeting, regardless of whether they had built up any trust with the client. Lopata says the chances of receiving a referral are greatly increased if they understand exactly what you do and the problems you solve, have a high level of trust and understand how you help people. Your chances of receiving a referral are increased if you are also perceived to have a wider purpose to your working life.

Lopata recommends making a detailed assessment of your best contacts, the people they know, their willingness to refer you to them and how you might inspire them to make

that introduction, for free. While some people offer direct financial rewards for referrals, seasoned networkers mostly make introductions on the basis that everyone gains a benefit, including the prospect of referrals in return.

While high-level networking is primarily a face-to-face activity, Lopata agrees that online tools accelerate the process.

Expert networkers work on the basis that if you connect with your network on this mutually beneficial basis, the financial rewards will flow. Successful networking should be selfless and altruistic, giving referrals without remembering your simple favour, and receiving them without forgetting their kind gift.

F **Which of the networking strategies mentioned in the article do you find most useful? Which do you think you will probably never use? Why? / Why not?**

BUSINESS SKILLS
Networking

A Work in pairs. Look at these tips on networking with people you don't know, or don't know very well. Which of them are essential, desirable or best avoided in your culture? What other useful tips can you think of?

- Tell the other person as much as possible about your products/services.

- Compliment the other person on their talk, clothes, appearance, etc.

- Ask the other person lots of questions about themselves.

- Arrange to go for a drink together with each other's boss.

- Introduce the other person to someone you know before moving away.

B ◄)) CD1.3, 1.4 **Listen to two conversations between some conference delegates. Tick the strategies that you hear the speakers using. Which of them could you use as an ice-breaker? What other ice-breakers do you know?**

1 Introduce yourself.

2 Compliment someone.

3 Ask for an opinion.

4 Agree with someone.

5 Check the pronunciation of someone's name.

6 Swap business cards.

7 Refer to future contact.

8 Introduce someone to someone else.

C ◄)) CD1.3, 1.4 **Good networkers often ask open questions. Complete these questions. Which of them did you hear? Listen again if necessary.**

1 What............ ....the conference so far?

2 ....in your part of the world?

3 ....most about living in your city?

4 ....for asking, but how much do you earn, by the way?

5 ....of any good places to eat near here, do you?

6 ....asking where you are from?

7 I didn't enjoy the dinner very much last night............ ....?

8 I don't think you've met (*name of person*),............ ....?

D Work in pairs. Decide which questions from Exercise C you would use when networking. Think of five questions of your own. What kind of questions *shouldn't* you use when networking?

E ◄)) CD1.3 **Listen to Conversation 1 again, or look at the audio script on page 167. What do the people say to break the ice and keep the conversation going?**

F Look at the expressions in the Useful language box on the opposite page and answer these questions.

1 Which expressions did you hear in Conversation 2?

2 Which ones would you like to use next time you are networking?

3 What do you usually say to move away and start talking to someone else?

G Role play. Introduce yourself to another participant at an international conference.

Student A: Turn to page 149.
Student B: Turn to page 159.

Writing: formal and informal register

H Your local Chamber of Commerce has asked you to give a talk at an important business event on a subject of your choice. Complete each gap in this invitation using the most suitable words or expressions (a, b or c) below.

From:	Metropolitan Chamber of Commerce
Subject:	'Business Today' event

Dear …,

…………[1] you that the Metropolitan Chamber of Commerce is organising a special event from 17 to 20 November on the subject of 'Business Today'.

…………[2] if you could …………[3] and give a talk to the local business community on a topic of your choice. We expect local businesspeople and dignitaries to be present, including the Minister of Business and Innovation.

If you …………[4] participate in this prestigious event, …………[5] confirm your attendance and the subject of your talk no later than 31 August. …………[6] a speaker's proposal form. …………[7] whether you wish to come to the charity dinner that will be held on the last day of the conference? …………[8] any further details, please …………[9] to contact me.

…………[10] forward to hearing from you.

Kind regards

Gloria Patterson
Events Manager, Metropolitan Chamber of Commerce

	a)	b)	c)
1	I'm writing to tell	I am writing to inform	I'd like to tell
2	We'd be so happy	It would be great	We would be delighted
3	attend	come along	make it
4	want to	wish to	feel like
5	would you mind	can you please	I would be grateful if you could
6	Please find attached	I'm attaching	Here's
7	Please tell me	I'd also like to know	Could you also let me know
8	If you want	If you need	Should you require
9	just	do not hesitate	don't hesitate
10	Looking	I'm looking	I look

I Write a reply accepting the invitation, but requesting more information, e.g. ask about the event details. Use formal or semi-formal language.

➡ *Writing file* page 142

USEFUL LANGUAGE

ICE-BREAKERS

Excuse me, could you do me a favour and (pass the water)?

That's a great calling card, if you don't mind me saying.

Do you mind me asking where you're from?

And how's … in your part of the world?

I don't suppose you know of any good places to eat near here, do you?

INVOLVING OTHERS

I don't think you've met (*name*) from (*department, company, etc.*), have you?

You might like to meet (*name*). He's/She's in your field.

FINDING THINGS IN COMMON

I always enjoy her talks, don't you?

It's funny you should say that, I think my colleague might …

I was there not long ago, actually.

I thought your face looked familiar!

That's a coincidence! So am/have/do I.

I know what you mean. Neither am/have/do I.

KEEPING IN TOUCH

I'll write down my details for you.

(Do) give me a ring when you get back, won't you?

You must call me / look me up if you're ever in (*town/city*).

We should do lunch one day.

It'll be great to hear from you.

GETTING AWAY

(It's been) good talking to you.

Excuse me, but I've just seen a friend. I'll see you later, hopefully.

Excuse me a moment. I'm afraid I have to make a quick call.

Movers and shakers

An international aid organisation wants to raise its profile and build contacts with influential people who can help its work

Background

Logistaid is an international humanitarian aid organisation that provides emergency assistance in more than 50 countries. It transports food, clothing and medical supplies and gives logistical help to underprivileged areas all over the world, especially to those regions that have poor local infrastructure, have suffered natural disasters or that are in conflict.

Logistaid is currently trying to increase its donations from the public and attract well-known figures to take an interest in the organisation in order to raise its international profile.

A group of influential people has been invited to a charity dinner to increase public awareness of the organisation's work. The people invited to the dinner are 'movers and shakers' – successful businesspeople, sports personalities and politicians, as well as people who work in the media.

A planning meeting

Work in groups. You are employees at Logistaid. Hold a meeting to decide on the missing information in the formal invitation that has been prepared (see right) and discuss these questions concerning the charity event.

1   Which successful businesspeople and celebrities are you going to invite?

2   What else should you take into account when deciding on the ticket price?

3   Which members of Logistaid and/or guests should give a speech during the dinner?

4   What kind of entertainment will you provide at the event, if any?

5   What kind of follow-up are you going to have after the event?

Logistaid

12 September
Dear Sir/Madam

I am delighted to invite you to the event of the year, the **Movers and Shakers Gala Dinner**! This night to remember will take place at .... on Friday 14 October at .... Tickets are priced at €............ each and .... per cent of the proceeds will be donated to Logistaid.

   Please find enclosed an information pack about our logistical work in over 50 countries and news of our latest projects. These have included getting essential medical aid and food supplies to earthquake victims in South-East Asia, helping refugees to build new homes in Central Africa, and supplying teachers and educators to local schools in remote areas in Central America.

   Please note that the Movers and Shakers Gala Dinner is a black-tie event and we are pleased to inform you that .... and .... will also be attending. We would be very grateful if you could reply in writing at your earliest convenience.

   Should you require any further information about this special event, or wish to make a donation, do not hesitate to contact me.

Yours faithfully

Ed Kaminski

Ed Kaminski
Managing Director, Logistaid
Europe and US

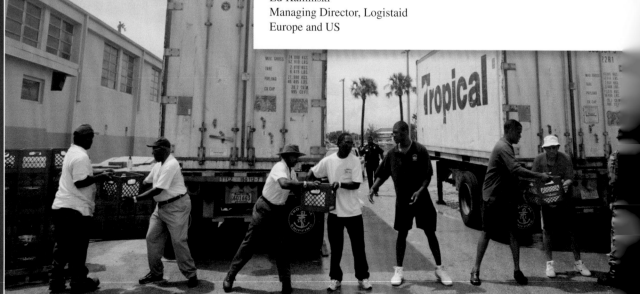

◀)) CD1.5 You are attending the charity dinner for Logistaid and are listening to the Managing Director, Ed Kaminski, giving a speech. When and why did he get involved with Logistaid? What doesn't he talk about in his speech? How effective do you think his speech is?

Task

Work in groups of six. You are networking with some of the influential people at Logistaid's charity event.

Student A: See below.
Student B: Turn to page 155.
Student C: Turn to page 163.
Student D: Turn to page 164.
Student E: Turn to page 158.
Student F: Turn to page 158.

Student A

You are a director of Logistaid. You need to raise the international profile of the organisation and increase public awareness of its work. You are also thinking of setting up a special educational programme dedicated to children living in remote areas in developing countries where there are few schools and those that exist have few teachers and little or no resources. However, Logistaid would need substantial funding to set up this kind of programme.

Network with as many people as possible and find someone who:

1   could finance Logistaid's educational programme;

2   would be able to help increase its public profile;

3   shares one of your personal interests, e.g. film, sport, food, travel, etc.

Once you find a useful contact, agree to a further meeting before moving on and talking to someone else.

What happens next?

You are staff from Logistaid. You meet the day after the gala dinner to discuss the success of the event and ideas for the next stage. Consider these questions.

1   Who will you choose to promote Logistaid's new educational programme and raise your profile?

2   What will be their role, e.g. visiting disaster areas in developing countries, filming promotional videos?

3   What kind of publicity campaign will you organise?

*Watch the Case study commentary on the **DVD-ROM.***

Writing

You are the Press Officer at Logistaid. Write a formal letter to your chosen public figure on behalf of the Managing Director. Include these points.

1   Thank them for attending the charity dinner. Mention how much money was raised.

2   Say you are very happy that they have been chosen to promote Logistaid's new educational programme.

3   Briefly describe any forthcoming event(s) you are organising and invite your chosen public figure to discuss more details about the campaign.

➡ *Writing file page 142*

'It's all to do with the training: you can do a lot if you're properly trained.'
Elizabeth II, British monarch

OVERVIEW

LISTENING AND DISCUSSION
Apprenticeships

A **Discuss these questions.**

1 What courses have you attended recently? Which have been the most rewarding?

2 Which format of training do you prefer – in groups, online or individual training with a coach? What are the pros and cons of each?

3 Have you ever done a work placement as part of a training programme? If so, how useful was it?

Dr Bernd Atenstaedt

B ◀)) CD1.6 **What do you think are the benefits of apprenticeships a) for the apprentice, and b) for the employer? Listen to the first part of an interview with Dr Bernd Atenstaedt, Chief Executive of German Industry-UK, and check your answers.**

C ◀)) CD1.7 **Listen to the second part of the interview and complete these sentences using no more than four words in each gap.**

1 About .... per cent of school leavers ....

2 The majority of apprentices like to work for .... , e.g. ....

3 Apprenticeship programmes in Germany usually last .... three and a half years, and apprentices .... at the start.

4 Apprentices tend to work .... and spend .... doing their vocational training.

5 Apprenticeships are well established in Germany: there even exists a .... including various .... for different kinds of professions.

6 Germany is proud of the two expressions .... and ....

7 They have been in talks with the .... to set up a similar .... in the UK.

*Watch the interview on the **DVD-ROM**.*

D **What are the training options for young people in your country?**

Brendan, Managing Director

Falak, Master Technician

Rachel, Product Manager

Marieke, graduate

E ◀)) **CD1.8, 1.9, 1.10, 1.11 Listen to four people (Brendan, Falak, Rachel and Marieke) talking about their training experience. Write B, F, R or M for each initial question and answer the second one.**

1 Who began as an apprentice? What type of apprenticeship was it?

2 Who has a university qualification? What in?

3 Whose parents weren't happy that he/she was leaving school at 16? Why?

4 Who was planning on going to university, but didn't? Why?

5 Who has worked in a variety of areas in their industry? Which ones?

6 Who has no work experience? Why?

7 Who worked abroad as part of his/her training? Where?

8 Who mentions the most rewarding thing about the job? What is it?

F **Who gives the best advice for embarking on a career? What is it? What advice would you give Marieke?**

G **Complete the categories with the missing words related to training.**

verb	noun	person
train	............[1]	.... / ....[2]
employ	............[3]	.... / ....[4]
	apprenticeship	............[5]
allow	............[6]	
............[7]	education	............[8]
intern	............[9]	intern
qualify	............[10]	
place	............[11]	
advise	............[12]	.... / ....[13]
............[14]	graduation	............[15]

H **Complete these paragraphs about two of the speakers in Exercise E, using the correct form of the words in brackets.**

Falak looks back on his ....[1] (*intern*) with a great sense of achievement. As a master ....[2] (*technique*), he is involved in research and ....[3] (*develop*). Falak had always had an interest in aviation, so he got in touch with his local careers ....[4] (*advice*). Falak has obtained several ....[5] (*qualify*) in aeronautical maintenance and repair. Although he'd completed his apprenticeship, he did further ....[6] (*train*).

Rachel says being an intern or doing a work ....[7] (*place*) is a good way of getting some insight into an ....[8] (*industrialist*), even if you don't always get a monthly ....[9] (*allow*)! After finishing university, Rachel went on a ....[10] (*graduation*) programme consisting of three different placements. At the end of the training, she was offered ....[11] (*employ*) as a sales analyst and now works as a product manager.

I **Discuss these questions.**

1 What advice would you give someone embarking on a career in your field of work or study?

2 In Germany, there are 340 recognised trades with apprenticeships. What kind of apprenticeships are the most popular in your country?

3 What can be done to encourage young people to take up vocational training?

READING AND LANGUAGE

A **Read the anecdote below about the Chinese fridge-maker Haier and answer these questions.**

1 What lesson did the new boss want his employees to learn?

2 How would you react if a manager at your organisation did something similar?

FT

Creative destruction

by Ben McLannahan

Call it the legend of the sledge-hammer. In 1985, the Qingdao Refrigerator Factory, a small enterprise in China's Shandong province, was in trouble: sales were slipping, customer complaints were high and rising.

The new boss, Zhang Ruimin, a 36-year-old economist dispatched from the municipal government, decided to take a stand. Lining up 76 fridges found to be defective, he demolished one with a sledgehammer, then ordered the shocked staff to destroy the rest.

The tale has probably been embellished in the telling, but it speaks volumes of Mr Zhang's determination. A quarter of a century on, the Chairman and CEO has transformed the biggest fridge-maker in Shandong into the biggest fridge-maker in the world. Along the way, he has broadened the portfolio: Haier sells more domestic appliances than any company in 19 product categories in China, and is the world's fourth-largest white-goods group by sales.

B **Read the article below about Haier and discuss these questions.**

1 What is Haier's approach to executive education?

2 What are the benefits of this approach?

FT

Training leaders to connect the dots

by Don Sull

Firms navigating through turbulent markets face many challenges. One of the most daunting, however, is how to develop their executives to manage effectively the range of diverse threats and opportunities that volatile markets generate. And how to provide this executive education in a way that offers good value for money and time.

The Chinese appliance maker Haier has risen from a nearly bankrupt collective enterprise 25 years ago to one of the most successful companies in China. Haier's leaders have done many things well, among them setting up a productive system of formal executive education designed to produce versatile general managers that Haier can deploy against a range of possible opportunities or threats.

When I visited Haier's headquarters in Qingdao a few years ago, I interviewed the faculty that ran their training centre, as well as many executives who participated in the company's programmes. Every Saturday morning, all Haier's senior executives based in China (totalling more than 70) attend a weekly training session. What training, you may

ask, could possibly justify half a day of Haier's 70 most senior leaders every week?

Executives bring current problems or opportunities to these sessions and work in teams of six to eight to discuss their individual challenges, explore possible solutions and discuss how best to implement proposed changes. Faculty mixes executives from different functions, business units and provinces to increase diversity of viewpoints and periodically rejigs the teams to keep them fresh. During the week, executives experiment with proposed solutions and report results back to their teammates in later sessions, discuss what worked and did not and explore ways to refine their actions.

This approach to executive education confers several benefits. First, it enables managers to understand interactions between various parts of the organisation and spot opportunities for productive collaboration. Second, ongoing exposure to the issues faced by different parts of the business helps executives to connect the dots to understand Haier's situation as a whole, rather than looking at the market through the window of their own silo. Third, this approach builds general management skills by helping executives hone the skills to recognise and deal with a range of challenges.

These courses are anything but 'academic', in the pejorative sense of 'divorced from practice'. Faculty coaches provide tools and functional training closely linked to the challenges and opportunities at hand. They also help the executives refine their action plan, devise practical ways to track progress and facilitate mid-course correction.

A downturn provides an ideal opportunity for companies to rethink how they can get the most value for their investment in executive development.

C Complete these summary sentences. Read the article again if necessary.

1 Haier's executive education involves training general managers to deal with …

2 The writer of the article interviewed …

3 More than 70 of Haier's senior managers take part …

4 Executives on the programme discuss possible solutions to problems and then …

5 Executive teams are mixed up regularly on the course to …

6 Two of the main outcomes are that managers can better understand …

7 Participants become more versatile as they learn to face different challenges …

8 The coaches think of ways to check progress; they provide correction and …

D Match these words or phrases in *italic* from the article (1–10) to the correct definition (a–j).

1 periodically *rejigs* the teams (lines 45–46)

2 *confers* several benefits (line 54)

3 *spot* opportunities (lines 57–58)

4 *ongoing exposure to* the issues (lines 59–60)

5 *connect the dots* (lines 61–62)

6 *looking … through the window of their own silo* (lines 63–65)

7 helping executives *hone* the skills (line 67)

8 in the *pejorative sense* (line 71)

9 *divorced from practice* (line 72)

10 *track* progress (line 78)

A) understanding something only from your own position and not that of others

B) record the development of something or someone over time

C) chance to experience new ideas and ways of looking at things

D) arranges in a different way

E) too theoretical

F) brings/offers

G) notice something, especially when it is difficult to see

H) with a negative meaning

I) improve/refine

J) realise that something is related to something else

E Discuss these questions.

1 How could you adapt Haier's approach to training to make it work in your organisation? What issues would you have to overcome?

2 How can colleagues learn from their team-mates rather than relying on a trainer?

F Why is the ability to emphasise important in business communication? Find examples in the article for each of these techniques.

1 Using lists of three

2 Using superlative forms

3 Using two contrasting ideas

4 Using interesting or extreme adjectives

5 Emphasising a negative statement

➡ *Language reference: Emphasising your point page 128*

G Your HR Manager has asked you to write for your organisation's intranet about a successful training course you have attended. Use some of the techniques from Exercise F to emphasise your points. Write 100–120 words and include the following:

• the outcome(s) of the training and why it has been successful;

• why you would recommend it for others;

• suggestions for any follow-up, e.g. further training.

BUSINESS SKILLS
Clarifying and confirming

A 🔊 CD1.12, 1.13 Listen to two telephone conversations about the staff induction day at Ashley Pharmaceuticals. What is the purpose of each call? Which conversation is more formal, and why?

B Look at the expressions in the Useful language box below. Which of the expressions would you probably use with someone a) you know well, and b) you don't know so well?

C 🔊 CD1.12 Listen to the first conversation again. What techniques does each speaker use to check or confirm the information they hear? Match each of the techniques (1–3) to the phrases (a–f).

1 Echoing/rephrasing what was said

2 Using questioning intonation to check information

3 Asking a direct question for confirmation

A) So, you didn't receive the programme we e-mailed you?

B) Can I just check that? Did you say half past nine?

C) And the room was ...?

D) So, that's B15, thanks.

E) And it doesn't matter if I haven't got a copy of the programme?

F) Sorry, could you give me your name again?

D 🔊 CD1.13 Listen to the second conversation again. How does the relationship between the speakers affect how they check, confirm and correct information?

E Role-play a phone call. Use appropriate techniques to check, confirm and correct information.

Student A: See below.   Student B: Turn to page 149.

Student A
You are Mel Van Der Horst, the Training Manager at Ashley Pharmaceuticals. You have planned a series of courses with a freelance trainer. You now want to finalise the details and make some changes. Look at your notes and phone the trainer. Check and confirm the details, including the fees.

Course title	No. of participants	Date
Organisational skills	26	15 May (half day, p.m.)
~~Leadership skills~~		~~17 May (full day)~~
Cancelled, not enough interest. Replace with Effective communication? Numbers and date to be confirmed.		
Assertiveness training	30	23 May (half day, p.m.)
Team building	21	30 May (full day)

Fee schedule		
	Half day (3 hours)	Full day (6 hours)
Up to 12 participants	$900	$1,600
Up to 20 participants	$1,500	$2,800
Up to 30 participants	$2,200	$4,300

USEFUL LANGUAGE

CLARIFYING PHRASES AND QUESTIONS

Would you mind repeating that / going over that again for me?

Sorry, could I ask you to give me those details again?

Could you explain/clarify what you meant by / when you said ... ?

And the date was ... ?

CONFIRMING PHRASES AND QUESTIONS

So that's nine o'clock on Thursday, then.

Let me see if / make sure I understood you correctly. You're saying ...

Is that right/correct?

Can I just check that?

I'd just like to confirm that.

CORRECTING MISUNDERSTANDINGS

No, I meant to say that / what I meant was ...

Not quite, it's ...

Well, actually, what I said/meant was ...

Not exactly, I said/meant that ...

Writing: effective e-mails

F Read these e-mail writing tips. Do you agree with them? What other tips would you add? What do you think are your own strengths and weaknesses when writing e-mails?

1 Make sure that the language is clear and concise.

2 Keep the sentences and paragraphs short, so your message is easy to read.

3 Maintain a polite tone. Even in the briefest messages include an opening greeting and a polite ending, e.g. *Best wishes*.

4 Use a subject header that relates to the content of the e-mail. Don't leave it blank.

5 Get to the point quickly. Emphasise key information and any action that is required.

6 Show consideration for the recipient and make requests politely, e.g. *I realise this is a busy time for you, but could you …*

7 Give all the relevant background information that the recipient will need.

8 Personalise your e-mail to establish a good rapport, even if you have never met the recipient in person.

9 Proofread your message. Check that your spelling and grammar are correct.

10 Think about the impression your writing style will give the recipient.

G To what extent does this e-mail follow the advice in Exercise F?

From:	Al Gardiner
Subject:	FYI Database training via teleconference

Dear Caroline and Markus,

I'm writing to confirm what we agreed during our discussion about the training earlier today. Markus is responsible for leading the first session and he will send the agenda to participants. The main task of the session is to determine what the staff already know about the database and decide how many days of training are required. Markus should briefly explain the course objectives. I have attached these here. He can then interview each participant, finding out what their individual needs are. The time and date of the second session need to be agreed with the participants. It is my understanding that Caroline will be responsible for preparing and leading the second session. BTW I suggest that Caroline also introduces herself in the first session.

I'd be very grateful if you could confirm that these details are all correct.

Best wishes,

Al

H Look at these two situations and write an e-mail in response to each one. Decide which e-mail needs to be more formal and which can be less formal. Use some expressions from Exercise G to help you.

1 You work for a company where everyone is on first-name terms. You've heard something about a Staff Development Day on 14 May; you might like to attend, but you don't have any details about the event (e.g. focus, activities, length, participants, trainer(s) and location). You also have a meeting scheduled for that morning. Write to Pat Fischer, the Human Resources Manager, asking for more information. Find out if you need to attend the whole day. Remember to include a subject line.

2 You manage a team of 10 staff. You are organising interviews for the annual staff appraisals to discuss employees' performance and professional development. Send an e-mail to the team about this topic and ask them to reply, giving you three options for dates and times (in order of preference) when they can attend a session of about 90 minutes next month. Attach a staff feedback form to complete and return to you within 14 days. Remember to include a subject line.

➡ *Writing file page 143*

2

Training at Carter & Randall

A large multinational is looking for a fast and efficient way of training its globally dispersed sales staff in the use of new technology

Background

Based in Cleveland, Ohio, US, and with operations in over 100 countries, Carter & Randall (C&R) is one of the world's leading consumer-goods companies. Its brand portfolio contains hundreds of household names.

The company's sales representatives play a crucial role in C&R's success. In this fiercely competitive market, they are the public face of the company with retailers, and need to provide excellent customer service. The company also relies on its sales force for timely market information about product sales, customer buying habits and competitor activity.

🔊 **CD1.14 – 1.17** Listen to some of the UK and Ireland sales team and take notes about their training needs. In what ways is C&R's training programme working well? If you were the Director of Sales, what would your priorities be for the coming year?

| Amy Cheng, graduate recruit | Charlie Turner, Sales Representative | Kamal Satinder, Regional Manager | Jessica Armstrong, Regional Manager |

Read this press release on C&R's intranet. What new challenge does the Director of Sales now face?

G10 mobile software for retail sales force

We have selected G10 Corporation's mobile technology solutions to maximize the productivity of our retail sales force.

The G10 mobile software runs on a PDA-style device, enabling our retail sales reps to manage and plan visits, execute in-store audits and analyze their performance. The software also allows us to electronically manage and distribute sales activities, and access results in real-time.

"C&R is always looking for solutions for its needs that will improve the company's products and services. The automated field solution will increase productivity, reduce costs, and ultimately benefit our customers," said Larry Bramson, C&R's Business Solutions Manager.

Implementation in the US, Western Europe, and Latin America will shortly be underway.

Task 1

Clarifying and confirming

Work in pairs. Read your information and prepare for a meeting to discuss how to implement training for the new G10 software. Remember to check and confirm what is said at the meeting.

Student A: You are the Director of Sales (UK and Ireland). Read your information below.

Student B: You are the IT Project Manager (UK and Ireland). Turn to page 149.

Student A: Director of Sales (UK and Ireland)

- How long and what form should the training take? Sales reps need to be out on the road as soon as possible, and they get easily bored sitting in a training room.

- How can over 200 sales reps all over the UK and Ireland be trained up in a short period of time?

- Who should provide support post-training, and what documentation should there be?

Task 2

Devising a training programme

Work in small groups. You are representatives from the Sales, IT and HR departments. Devise a training programme for the sales force in the UK and Ireland.

- What are your top three priorities?

- What are the goals and desired outcome of the training?

- Which training should be done by a) peers, b) line managers, c) the IT department, and d) external training companies?

- What training can be on a short, intensive basis? What extensive training is needed?

- Which training should be done a) face to face, b) online, and c) in a blended learning package? What are the pros and cons of these options?

- How will the training be evaluated?

Breaking news

It is two months later. Turn to page 149 and find out what has happened.

*Watch the Case study commentary on the **DVD-ROM**.*

Writing

You are the Director of Sales (UK and Ireland) for C&R. Write a covering e-mail to your colleagues thanking them for their input and summarising the main points you agreed in your meeting to devise a training programme. Say that you have attached a detailed training programme. Mention the goals, desired outcomes and evaluation of the training. Ask your colleagues to contact you if they have any queries or comments.

➡️ *Writing file page 145*

3 Energy

'Giving society cheap, abundant energy would be the equivalent of giving an idiot child a machine gun.' **Paul R. Ehrlich, US biologist and conservationist**

LISTENING AND DISCUSSION
Clean energy

A **Discuss these questions.**

1 Which energy sources are commonly used a) at home, and b) at places of work or study in your country?

2 Which sources of energy are considered to be a) the cleanest, and b) the dirtiest?

3 To what extent is solar energy used in the area where you live and work?

4 Would you be prepared to live in an area with wind turbines? Why? / Why not?

Angus McCrone

B ◀)) CD1.18 **Bloomberg New Energy Finance provides news, research and analysis on energy. Listen to its Chief Editor, Angus McCrone, and complete this summary about the company.**

Bloomberg New Energy Finance (NEF) provides news and in-depth analysis on clean energy. Clean energy includes ....[1] and solar, small-hydro, marine, geothermal and other ....-............[2] technologies and energy efficiency. They look at the markets and predict ....[3]. NEF also collates energy data from projects all over the world; for example, 155 billion dollars were invested worldwide in ....[4] in 2008. They study factors such as falls in gas prices and whether that prevents people from investing in ....[5] energy, and the possible affect on coal and nuclear energy.

C **Which alternative energy supply would you feel happiest about using in the future, and why?**

D ◀)) CD1.19 **Listen to the second part of the interview and say which of these points are mentioned.**

1 Currently the most mature clean energy is wind power.

2 People know where to locate wind turbines.

3 Energy supply and storage are the most important issues.

4 Solar power will become the most viable alternative energy.

5 New Energy Finance studies the price of carbon in the future.

6 When the technology falls in price, there will be a huge market for solar energy.

*Watch the interview on the **DVD-ROM**.*

E **Look at these word partnerships related to alternative energy. Which word in each group *cannot* form a partnership with the word in bold?**

1	wind / tidal / carbon / wave	**power**
2	alternative / consumption / renewable / clean	**energy**
3	reduction / carbon / gas / solar	**emissions**
4	**solar**	power / panels / turbine / energy
5	**wind**	turbine / power / renewable / farm
6	**fuel-cell**	technology / photovoltaic / energy / car

F ◀)) CD1.20 **Listen to some experts being asked about reductions in carbon emissions and clean energy. Choose the most accurate ending for each of these sentences.**

1 According to Speaker 1, the world's governments should …

   a) reduce carbon emissions worldwide by 2 per cent.

   b) prevent global temperatures from rising.

   c) replace gas and oil with renewable energy.

2 Speaker 2 thinks it is up to business to encourage …

   a) both industry and citizens to reduce their energy consumption.

   b) companies to use alternative gases in their manufacturing processes.

   c) companies to reduce CO_2 emissions by using alternative energy.

3 Speaker 3 says hydrogen-powered cars …

   a) are one example of fuel-cell technology.

   b) work much better than electric cars.

   c) can already be seen on the roads.

G ◀)) CD1.21 **Listen to the same speakers giving more opinions on energy and correct these sentences, according to what they say.**

1 Speaker 1 thinks airlines should make donations to offset their carbon emissions.

2 Speaker 2 says paying a carbon tax would only work in certain industries.

3 Speaker 3 insists that wealthier countries should stop aid to developing countries.

4 Speaker 3 says that many people in developing countries still don't have fossil fuels.

5 Speaker 2 wouldn't mind living near a wind farm because it would improve the surrounding countryside.

6 Speaker 3 says having wind turbines is better than living next to a chemical plant.

H **Discuss these questions.**

1 Is there a carbon tax in your country? Why would/wouldn't you introduce one?

2 What else can governments do to ensure businesses reduce their carbon emissions?

READING AND LANGUAGE

A **Discuss these statements about energy, deciding whether each one is True (T), False (F) or you don't know (DK). Give reasons for your answers.**

1 A carbon tax on industry could help to reduce greenhouse gas emissions.

2 Changing to a low-carbon world can be achieved quite quickly.

3 Rapid growth of the world's population will soon increase demand for energy.

4 Most forms of alternative energy are easier to transport, store and use than oil and gas.

5 Private companies need government support to make technological advances.

6 Oil and gas prices will increase in the future.

B **Read the article on the opposite page and, in pairs, compare your answers to Exercise A with Helge Lund's views.**

C **Find the words or phrases in the article that are similar to or mean the following.**

1 changing, especially in a way that improves a situation (paragraphs 1 and 4)

2 opposing change and refusing to accept new ideas (paragraph 2)

3 get involved in (paragraph 2)

4 controlling or limiting something in order to prevent it from having a harmful effect (paragraph 3)

5 gradually stopping someone from doing something they do habitually (paragraph 4)

6 ready to (paragraph 5)

7 organisation responsible for making sure that companies do not do anything illegal or harmful (paragraph 5)

8 say that something is not true (paragraph 7)

9 draws people's attention to something by making it easily visible (paragraph 7)

10 stop something from happening or developing (paragraph 7)

11 establishing (paragraph 8)

12 think of an idea, answer, etc. (paragraph 8)

D **Discuss these questions.**

1 In what ways are Helge Lund and Statoil both pioneers?

2 In what way does Helge Lund think government intervention in the energy industry is positive? In what way does he think it is negative? Do you agree?

3 In what ways can the pressure on global energy demand be curbed? Which do you favour?

4 Do you think energy companies should be in private or public hands? What are your reasons?

E **Look at the nouns and articles in bold in the article. Why do we use the indefinite, definite or zero article in each case? Look at pages** 129–130 **of the Language reference and compare your answers.**

➡ *Language reference: Articles; countable and uncountable nouns* page 129

FT

The danger of losing touch with reality

by Ed Crooks

Politicians often underestimate the massive challenge of cutting greenhouse gas emissions by moving away from **fossil fuels**, according to
5 Helge Lund, Chief Executive of StatoilHydro, Norway's national oil and gas company, who is **an** adviser to the United Nations Secretary-General on energy.
10   Mr Lund is far from **the stereotype of the** die-hard oilman. He believes it is important to engage with the debate over climate change, and is **the only** oil company repre-
15 sentative on the group advising the UN Secretary-General, on energy.
    Norway has **a good record** for curbing greenhouse gas emissions from its oil industry, having been **one**
20 **of the** first countries to impose a carbon tax, in 1991. Statoil is a pioneer of storing carbon dioxide underground, with projects in Norway and Algeria.
25   Mr Lund accepts that, in the future, his customers will use less of **the oil and gas** that his company produces. Yet even he is concerned that politicians are in danger of losing touch
30 with reality in their push for a low-carbon world. Weaning the world off **oil and gas**, he says, will be harder than many people realise. 'Governments are moving away from the
35 energy source that our entire civilisation is built on: hydrocarbons. That is not an easy task,' he says. 'It is very important that the debate is based on energy realities.'
40   The first of those realities is demography. By 2050, the world's population is set to grow to 9 billion, from about 6.8 billion today, while economic development lifts hun-
45 dreds of millions out of poverty, enabling them to buy cars and fridges and air conditioning. That creates massive upward pressure on global energy demand which, given 'busi-
50 ness as usual' policies, will rise by 45

per cent by 2030, according to **the** International Energy Agency, the rich countries' watchdog.
    The second is the effectiveness of
55 hydrocarbons – oil and gas – as energy sources that can be easily extracted, transported, stored and used. Few of today's alternatives offer anything like as attractive a
60 combination of characteristics. Mr Lund's conclusion: 'You can see that planning to move away quickly from hydrocarbons is unrealistic.'
    He does not deny the science of
65 climate change, and says there is an 'urgent' need to respond to it. But he does want to stop responses that he thinks will be counter-productive. 'The debate is sometimes too sim-
70 plistic, and overstates the opportunity for quickly changing to a low-carbon economy,' he says. 'If we start the discussion on an unrealistic basis, we are less likely to make any real prog-
75 ress.' The danger he highlights is of politically driven support for particular technologies, which he argues will stifle innovation.
    'Some people seem to believe that

80 technology can be decided politically: it cannot,' he says. 'Technology advances best when you have competitive companies working on concrete projects.' That means set-
85 ting a price for carbon, whether through a carbon tax or, as seems more politically feasible, an emissions trading scheme, and letting industry respond freely to that price
90 to come up with profitable solutions.
    'Oil and gas are finite resources, and we should expect that over time they will become more expensive, so we should use them more carefully,'
95 Mr Lund says. 'We are going to be telling our customers to use less of the products that we make.'
    If Mr Lund is right about the transition being slow, however, there
100 is still plenty of profit to be made from Statoil's traditional business. Its gas reserves in Norway and around the world can also play an important role as a 'transition fuel',
105 providing a lower-carbon alternative to coal-fired power generation while other forms of energy are built up.

BUSINESS SKILLS
Decision-making

'OK, all those in favour of
delegating decision-making,
shrug your shoulders.'

A How often do you attend decision-making meetings? How easy is it generally to reach decisions in meetings?

B Which of these statements best describes what happens in meetings you attend?

1 Decisions are already made by the managers beforehand. Most meetings are just informative.

2 Meetings are generally the best place to take important decisions.

3 Not everyone's opinion carries equal weight when we're deciding issues.

4 It takes a lot of convincing for me to change my mind during a meeting.

5 Arguing is a healthy part of trying to solve problems and reach decisions.

6 It's not always clear what decisions have been made, or who is responsible for carrying them out.

7 Humour is a good way to release tension during heated discussions at meetings.

8 Participants are sometimes reluctant to put forward proposals because they might be criticised.

C ◄)) CD1.22 Listen to an extract from a meeting between three managers at an oil company: Alain, Tony and Caroline. What has happened, and what do they decide to do?

D ◄)) CD1.22 Complete these expressions from the meeting. Then listen again if necessary. Match the expressions with the sections in the Useful language box below.

1 Would it .... to close the refinery for a while?

2 I'm not .... we want to disrupt production at this ....

3 So, we .... look into what's going on there urgently.

4 That said, I .... we should .... a decision until we have all the facts.

5 Here's a .... : .... an investigation team first.

6 I'm .... that another incident may not be so ....

E Why do you think Tony phrases his first proposal as a question? Why does Alain disagree indirectly?

F Work in groups of three. Look at your information and hold meetings in order to discuss your proposals and make decisions.

Student A: Look at your information on the opposite page.
Student B: Turn to page 150.
Student C: Turn to page 159.

USEFUL LANGUAGE

PUTTING FORWARD PROPOSALS

We could consider ...
One option would be to ...
The best course of action is to ...

DISAGREEING INDIRECTLY

I'm not so sure I agree with you there.
I see things a little differently from you.

Yes, but I'm not convinced that ...
Another way of looking at it is that ...

EMPHASISING A POINT

I *do* think it's important to act quickly.
We just can't afford to ...
I know I keep going on about this, but ...

AVOIDING MAKING DECISIONS

Let's not make any hasty decisions.
Let's keep our options open.
We should think this through a bit more.
I'm in two minds about it, really.

Student A

Meeting 1

You are the company CEO. Your company provides all its top management and sales staff with luxury cars. In order to cut costs, there is a proposal to replace these with smaller electric cars. You can see the argument for replacing the sales teams' cars, but you don't think this is a good idea for the morale of the management team. Meet the Sales Manager and the CFO to discuss your ideas and reach a decision. You chair the meeting.

Meeting 2

You are the Human Resources Manager. Your company is thinking about relocating to new, larger offices outside the city centre. You don't think this is a good idea because you live near the city offices, like many of your colleagues, and the transport links to the proposed location are very bad. Meet the Production Manager and the CEO to discuss your ideas and reach a decision.

Meeting 3

You are going to share a new office with your two colleagues. There is only one desk by the window and you think you should have it. Talk to your colleagues and try to reach a decision.

Writing: layout and structure of reports

G Complete the report-writing tips below with the words in the box.

| draft errors headings layout plan readers register rewrite |

Report-writing tips

Read a similar report first. Write a ....[1] or outline, and then your first ....[2]. Always write with your ....[3] in mind.

Edit your draft report for style and ....[4], e.g. formal language, passive or active forms.

Proofread your report for typical ....[5], e.g. subject–verb agreement, prepositions and punctuation.

Organise the ....[6] and structure. Use an appropriate title, ...[7] and sub-headings.

Revise and ....[8] your report in order to improve it if necessary.

Take a break for a few hours and re-read your report before finalising it.

H Discuss these questions. Then check your answers on pages 146–147.

1 What is the logical order of these headings in a report? In what order would you write these parts of a report? Why?

a) Recommendations

b) Conclusions

c) Executive summary

d) Introduction

e) Findings

2 What is the difference between an introduction and an executive summary?

3 What other sections might be found in a report?

I Work in pairs. Look at the plan and recommendation report on pages 152–153. Re-organise the report so that the information is in a logical order. What else would you do to the report to improve the layout and structure?

➡ *Writing file pages 146–147*

Energy saving at Tumalet Software

A leading software company is developing strategies to reduce energy bills and operating costs

Background

Tumalet is a large software company based in California's Silicon Valley. The company's headquarters spans four buildings and comprises over 90,000 square metres of office space.

Tumalet is committed to improving energy efficiency and reducing its CO_2 emissions as part of its sustainable business strategy. Over the past five years, the company has invested half a million dollars in energy projects, which have resulted in US $600,000 in savings, a total return on investment of 120 per cent.

A recent downturn in business and rapidly escalating electricity and gas prices are forcing the company to find new ways to reduce energy costs and minimise the impact of price increases on its operations.

Typical energy consumption in office buildings

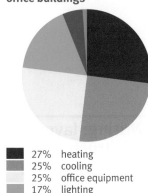

■	27%	heating
■	25%	cooling
■	25%	office equipment
■	17%	lighting
■	5%	ventilation
■	1%	cooking

Read this article. What initiatives have enabled Tumalet to reduce energy costs so far?

Green business makes sense

Commercial and residential buildings are a major source of energy consumption. According to the non-profit group, the US Green Business Council, they gobble up over one-third of the energy produced in the US, and account for 38 per cent of all carbon-dioxide emissions. Not just that, it's estimated that as much as 30 per cent of the energy consumed in office buildings is wasted. Companies once concerned about the affordability of sustainable business have found that green initiatives are good for the bottom line as well as the environment.

For the past five years, Tumalet has been improving energy efficiency at its Californian headquarters. Some of the retro-fits are surprisingly quick and simple. By switching to low-energy bulbs and dimming hallway lighting during the day, to make the most of natural light, the company made immediate savings on electricity bills. The company's low-cost policies of turning things off, turning things down, and keeping up with cleaning and maintenance has generated significant savings.

🔊 **CD1.23** Listen to part of a meeting between Tumalet's Sustainable Business Manager, Joanne Hopper, and the Energy Project Team. Make a list of action points for them to work on.

Look at this article. How does this news affect Tumalet?

California utility expands rebates

Pacific Gas & Electric is expanding a program that provides financial incentives for companies to cut their energy use. PG&E, which serves much of Northern and Central California including Silicon Valley, has set aside US$50 million to spend on a set of rebates and incentives over the next three years. Those rebates will go to customers who employ energy-saving technologies, such as high-efficiency power supplies.

That's up from the $7 million PG&E doled out last year, and the utility can increase the money available if enough customers are interested, said Mark Bramfitt, the Head of PG&E's customer energy-efficiency program.

Bramfitt sees rebate programs as beneficial for both utilities and their customers. Utilities can save money by avoiding construction costs for new power plants or buying electricity at higher rates during peak times from other utilities, while businesses get to offset the cost of installing energy-saving technologies that can reduce their electricity bills.

Task

Work in groups of three. You are members of the Energy Project Team at Tumalet. You have been asked to investigate and propose some energy-saving ideas.

1 Read your information and prepare to present it to your colleagues at the meeting.

Student A: Look at your information below.
Student B: Turn to page 150.
Student C: Turn to page 159.

Student A

- Enabling staff to work virtually from home reduces office occupancy and energy costs.

- Planting grass and other plants on the roof will act as natural insulation and reduce heating bills.

- By contributing money to carbon-offset projects – such as forest planting – the company can compensate for its CO_2 emissions.

2 Hold a meeting to devise an energy strategy for your company. Use the agenda below. Decide who will chair the meeting.

ENERGY PROJECT TEAM MEETING

Agenda

1 Ways to encourage staff involvement in energy efficiency
2 Options for reducing and offsetting CO_2 emissions
3 Feasible sources of renewable energy and benefits
4 Schedule for short-term and long-term measures to save energy
5 Other measures as part of its sustainable business strategy (e.g. waste management, product packaging, transportation, water conservation)
6 AOB

 Watch the Case study commentary on the DVD-ROM.

Writing

As a member of the Energy Project Team, write a report for Joanne Hopper outlining the options you considered and your recommendations for improving your company's energy efficiency.

 Writing file pages 146–147

1 International presentations

A Work in small groups. Look at these statements about presenting to an international audience. Do you agree or disagree with them? Why?

1 Humour is appreciated by audiences anywhere in the world.

2 In today's globalised business world, it's a waste of time to research your audience's cultural background.

3 A good presentation should be fast-paced and entertaining.

4 The speaker's appearance is an important aspect of the talk.

5 Greeting the audience by saying a few words in their language won't go down well.

6 The end of a presentation is the most important part.

7 The main problem for an international audience is the slang that presenters use.

8 The audience should never interrupt or ask questions during a presentation.

B Rewrite the statements in Exercise A, adding or changing any details you like, so that everyone in your group agrees with them.

C ◀)) CD1.24–1.26 Listen to three people talking about being an international presenter. What element of presentations do they talk about? What lesson(s) have they learned from their experiences?

D Complete the tips on the website below using the words in the box. Which tips are the most useful? What other non-verbal signals could a presenter look out for? Add a sentence to each section about your culture/country.

> Q&A sessions self-deprecating privacy
> unnerving thumbs up hand gestures
> non-verbal signals punch lines

○○○
◀ ▶ +   (Q▾)

Know your audience

Lost in translation

Humour about situations works best across cultures – not ridiculing certain groups of people or being ....[1]. Rarely tell jokes. Many jokes are culture-bound and will not have a clear meaning to the international part of the audience. Also, some ....[2] might have different meanings when taken literally by those for whom English is a second language.

Hands up all those who …

Comfort levels with an audience's active participation differ greatly from culture to culture. Interaction between a presenter and the audience is appreciated and expected in the US. Some audiences are more willing to participate in ....[3] than others. In some countries, such as Russia, it is normal for the audience to talk to each other during the presentation.

Gauging reactions

It is important to understand the ....[4] from your audience, such as smiling and nodding. These signals are different in different cultures. For instance, an Asian person who nods and says *Yes … yes … yes* is probably just telling you that they have understood you, but is not saying that they agree. It can be a little ....[5] if an audience gives relatively few signals, such as in Finland.

It's not just what you say

Some cultures are quite animated and will appreciate it when a presenter uses ....[6] and expresses emotion through the body. However, others are unimpressed with exaggerated hand gestures and may find them distracting. The ....[7] may mean 'good' in the USA and many parts of Europe, but it means something very different in Iran. Eye contact can also be a major intercultural difference. Some cultures consider strong eye contact a sign of sincerity; others find it rude and an invasion of ....[8].

E ◀)) CD1.27 Listen to Anneliese Guérin-LeTendre, an intercultural communications expert. What are the four components of her training course on international presentations? Write one to three words in each gap.

- Explore what is meant by '............¹' and '............²'.
- Look in detail at the ....³ of this ....⁴ and the ....⁵.
- Think about the use of ....⁶.
- Look at the ....⁷ of the client and how it needs to be ....⁸.

F ◀)) CD1.27 Listen again and answer these questions.

1 How does Anneliese Guérin-LeTendre define the 'culture iceberg'?
2 What might the audience want to know about the presenter?
3 What three types of communication might different audiences value?
4 How might an audience feel about the use of humour in a presentation?
5 What is 'context', and why is it an important consideration?

G Which of these aspects of culture would you put above the surface of the 'culture iceberg'? Which do you think are underlying and more difficult to notice? Why do you think so?

- dress code
- attitude to time
- age
- greeting styles
- body language
- humour
- emotion shown in public
- physical gestures
- attitude to authority
- directness of speech

Task 1

Work in pairs or small groups to prepare a five-minute presentation about what, in your experience, makes a good presentation in your profession, organisation, culture, country or a country you know well. Talk about some of these items:

- length of speech
- level of detail
- visual aids
- body language
- taboo subjects
- Q&A sessions
- use of humour and personal anecdotes
- audience interaction and reactions
- seating arrangements

Task 2

Use the Internet to find a presentation in English, or an excerpt from a presentation, about a topic that interests you. What did you like/dislike about the presenter's style? Present your findings to the class.

1 First impressions

VOCABULARY

Complete the article below about body language in presentations with the words in the box. You will not need all of them.

| contact | fidgeting | flick | gestures | leaning | mannerisms |
| nodding | posture | scanning | slouching | staring | upright | wander |

Body language is culture and context specific, and very few ....[1] are universally understood and interpreted. For instance, in most parts of the world, ...[2] your head is used to show agreement. However, in Bulgaria this gesture means 'no'. In the West, a high level of eye ....[3] is regarded as a sign of sincerity. Yet, in many Eastern cultures, it can be considered rude and aggressive.

Presenters need to be aware of their own gestures and ....[4], as well as those of the audience. Inexperienced speakers often show their nervousness by moving from one side to another, ...[5] at one part of the audience only rather than ....[6] the room, or ....[7] with a pen.

............[8] is another aspect of body language; standing ....[9] with your weight balanced on each foot makes you look confident and relaxed. Try to stand or sit up straight – ....[10] can suggest lack of interest or enthusiasm.

ADVERBS

Put the adverb in brackets in the correct position in each sentence to complete these presentation tips.

1 I would recommend that you rehearse your presentation several times. (*strongly*)

2 Don't rely on PowerPoint. People come to see you, not the slides. (*heavily*)

3 It's important that your own personality comes across in the presentation. (*hugely*)

4 Check that all the multimedia equipment is working beforehand. (*properly*)

5 Try to breathe – it'll help you to relax. (*deeply*)

6 It's impossible to give the perfect presentation, so don't put too much pressure on yourself. (*utterly*)

SKILLS

Complete this conversation between two people during the morning break at a conference.

Jessica: Excuse me, could you d............ me a f............[1] and pass me the orange juice?

Nazim: Certainly. Do you m............ m............[2] asking where you're from?

Jessica: Well, from London originally, but I live in Birmingham now. And you?

Nazim: I thought your face l............ f............[3]! You work at Cronwicks, right?

Jessica: That's right.

Nazim: So do I!

Jessica: Really? That's a c............[4]! Which department are you in?

Nazim: Well, I used to be in Finance, but I transferred to the Dublin office recently.

Jessica: Dublin, very nice. And how's b............[5] in your part of the world?

Nazim: Not bad, not bad. It's starting to pick up again after the recession.

Jessica: I know what you m............[6]. It's the same for us.

Nazim: Listen, it's been good talking to you, but would you e............ m............[7], I have to make a few phone calls.

2 Training

VOCABULARY

Complete the article below about training with the words in the box.

apprentices   developed   employees   employer   graduate   intern   internship
qualification   training

Apprenticeship programmes were first ....[1] in Germany. They are funded by the individual companies involved, and traditionally, ...[2] must find their own apprenticeships. The model enables school leavers to gain work experience, obtain a ....[3] without going to university, and start earning money. In order to ....[4], they need to pass an official exam run by the Chamber of Industry and Commerce.

Germans can also participate in other types of on-the-job ....[5] in specialised schools for healthcare professionals, hotel workers or civil servants.

The ....[6] model more common in the United States and Canada tends to be an isolated, short-term project as opposed to the three-year commitment of most German apprenticeship programmes. The benefit to the ....[7] is often negligible, although having an ....[8] pool does allow a company to pre-screen potential new ....[9] before hiring them permanently.

EMPHASISING YOUR POINT

Complete the second sentence in each pair so that it emphasises the point, using the word in brackets. Use one to four words in each gap.

1   The career's adviser wasn't very helpful.

The career's adviser .... helpful. (*anything*)

2   The exam was long and quite difficult.

.... the exam long, ... quite difficult. (*not*)

3   I didn't understand that last part of the lesson.

.... I didn't understand .... that last part of the lesson. (*what*)

4   Her excellent qualifications got her the job.

.... her excellent qualifications .... the job. (*was*)

5   Their language courses are very expensive.

Their language courses .... cheap. (*but*)

6   Trainees gain practical work experience, and attend classes once a week.

.... trainees gain work experience; .... attend classes once a week. (*do*)

WRITING

1   Complete this e-mail with a word or short phrase in each gap.

From:	Annabel Harper
Subject:	Invitation: Hosting Effective Webinars

Dear Carla,

I ....[1] invite you to ....[2] a training session on Hosting Effective Webinars. This session will be delivered online, so that you can join us from the comfort of your living room, office or hotel!

The main purpose of the session ....[3] provide you with the knowledge and skills required to effectively deliver professional training online using the Webex software.

Plese find ....[4] an outline of the training.

This session will be ....[5] on:

Wednesday September 1st   11.00–12.30 (EST)   16.00–17.30 (GMT)

If you would like to attend, ...[6] me know by return e-mail.

For those of you who wish to ....[7] this training, but are unable to at this date/time, please respond that you are interested and I will add your name to a session to be held later in the year (date TBC).

If you have ....[8] with regards to this training, ...[9] to contact me.

Look ....[10] to meeting you online.

Best regards,

Annabel

2 Write a reply to the e-mail in Exercise 1.

- Thank Annabel for the invitation.
- Explain briefly why you cannot do the training on that day.
- Request information about the later session.
- Ask what the technical requirements are in order to do the online training (e.g. a webcam).

3 Energy

VOCABULARY

Complete the sentences below about energy with the phrases in the box.

> carbon tax   energy efficiency   fossil-fuel   greenhouse gas emissions
> renewable-energy   solar panels   wind farms   wind turbines

1 The efficiency of .... on cloudy days can be boosted by simple reflectors – mirrors.

2 In many wealthy countries, ... have fallen in recent years as the global recession has taken hold.

3 Japan's top industries are opposed to a .... on them, as they say it would damage the economy.

4 Nine new offshore .... will create up to 70,000 permanent and temporary jobs in the UK.

5 According to the International Energy Agency (IEA), $557bn was spent by governments in 2008 to subsidise the .... industry.

6 A report by analyst Bloomberg New Energy Finance concluded that in 2009, governments provided subsidies worth between $43bn (£27bn) and $46bn to .... and biofuel industries.

7 Celebrity chef Jamie Oliver wants to make his new restaurant in Cornwall more eco-friendly by installing two .... on the roof.

8 New EU legislation will make it compulsory for .... ratings to be published in all UK homes for sale advertisements.

ARTICLES

Complete this text with *the*, *a* or *an*, or leave the gap blank if no article is necessary.

FT

A long way to go for electric mobility

by Peter Voserl

While we cannot predict the future, it is clear that mobility is ....[1] growth market. Between now and 2050, one billion new vehicles will come onto ....[2] world's roads, mostly in Asia, more than doubling today's total.

Today if you ask ....[3] 10-year-old child what will be his or her first car, the chances are ....[4] response will be '............[5] electric one'. Electric mobility is ....[6] talk of ....[7] global village. That is not surprising.

However, hybrids are likely to out-compete full electric cars for ....[8] some time to come. For one thing, ...[9] journey range of batteries – currently less than 160km (100 miles) on ....[10] single charge – needs to go up. In addition, making a big shift to electric vehicles would require ....[11] expansion in the world's capacity to mine and recycle lithium for the batteries.

Perhaps ....[12] most important thing is how we will generate the electricity itself. By themselves, ...[13] wind and solar will not be sufficient to power ....[14] large-scale electric mobility, at least not for ....[15] foreseeable future.

In ....[16] coming years, like it or not, most electric vehicles will rely to ....[17] large extent on conventional coal-fired power, which is responsible for ....[18] fastest growth in greenhouse gas emissions worldwide. If electric mobility is to fulfil ....[19] hopes of future customers, we will have to find ways to reduce emissions from ....[20] coal.

SKILLS

1 Correct the wrong word in each of these sentences heard in a meeting.

1 I know I keep going out about this, but it is important.

2 The best path of action is to call another meeting.

3 I'm not so clear I agree with you there.

4 Will it be an idea to issue a press release?

5 I'm in two heads about this proposal.

6 I don't think we should make any hurry decisions.

7 I see things a few differently from you.

8 Let's not run into a decision until we have all the facts.

2 Match each of the sentences in Exercise 1 to one of these functions.

a) Putting forward proposals

b) Disagreeing indirectly

c) Emphasising a point

d) Avoiding making a decision

Cultures 1: International presentations

Complete the sentences below with the words and phrases in the box. You will not need all of them.

delivery technique   dress code   establish credibility   get straight to the point
get the message across   go down well   interactive approach   personal touch
punch line   self-deprecating   take it for granted   underlying

1 The 'culture iceberg' is the difference between what you can see on the surface and what are more subtle .... cultural differences.

2 The presenter told some funny stories about mistakes he'd made, but some of the audience seemed uncomfortable with his .... humour.

3 In the US and Europe, politicians will stick to the standard .... of dark suit and tie when they make public appearances.

4 As a young, female executive, I sometimes find I have to work harder to .... with an audience, so I make sure to mention my expertise.

5 Don't .... that everyone will understand you. You need to slow down, speak more clearly and avoid slang and idioms.

6 Audiences in the UK and US go for concise, lively presentations which ...., whereas German and French audiences appreciate more technical detail.

7 Jokes don't always .... Some audiences can interpret humour as being quite frivolous, even cynical.

8 A good use of visual information helps to .... during a presentation.

9 My typical .... involves a lot of movement and hand gestures, but I try to adapt this with international audiences so I don't distract people.

10 Sharing real-life experiences with the audience adds a .... to a presentation.

E-mails

Objectives

Writing
Can write a detailed summary of work-related information.

Reading
Can distinguish between fact and opinion in complex formal contexts.

Lesson deliverable
To write e-mails dealing with sensitive or difficult issues.

Performance review
To review your own progress and performance against the lesson objectives at the end of the lesson.

A SPEAKING

1 In small groups, discuss these questions from a recent survey.

1 Is e-mail an effective tool?

2 What is the main problem with e-mail?

2 Look at this pie chart showing opinions about the effectiveness of e-mail. Are you surprised by the results?

Results of effectiveness questionnaire

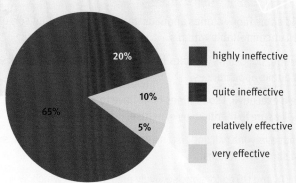

- highly ineffective
- quite ineffective
- relatively effective
- very effective

20%
10%
65%
5%

3 Here are some of the words used in answers to the survey. What do you think people said?

1 unnecessary	4 unclear	7 phone
2 polite	5 quickly	8 long
3 properly	6 weapon	9 mistakes

4 Turn to page vii. Read the survey results and try to complete the gaps. Check your ideas from Exercise A3.

B READING 1

Anita Sanjay works for WebPower, a brand and website design company in Bombay. Anita has sent an e-mail to Patrick Dupont of CafeVital, a company which wants to refresh its brand image and website. Read the e-mail and Patrick's reply. Answer the questions opposite.

Dear Patrick

It was great to finally put a face to the voice and meet today after all the conference call discussions over the last few months. I'm just going to run through the four points we discussed and agreed, as I think it best to document a few things as a kind of informal set of minutes.

1. Design concept
Having talked through everything in some detail, I believe we're in a position to agree that the final design specification which we submitted (10 August) can finally be said to be signed off, and will be the basis of the website build, which we will now commence asap. Admittedly, concerns have been expressed on your side on some of the specific graphics, but these shouldn't stand in the way of the build getting started. Speed is of the essence, as I believe you said on more than one occasion.

2. Costs
Costwise, the proposal which we submitted at the meeting was agreed with cost of build put at 8k, and an additional 2k, budgeted, but available on a need-to-use basis only.

3. Timelines
You need things done and dusted by end of next month, sixish weeks or so from now, to which we agreed. It is envisaged that migration of the website data may cause a few problems due to the need to reformat bits and pieces. But from the data supplied to us, it all looks pretty manageable.

4. Quality
We undertake to keep you informed at every point as to any quality issues which crop up, and likewise, expect to hear from you as and when. If we have any concerns, it was proposed to raise them in our planned weekly call.

I think that's it. If you can confirm these minutes before the weekend, it means we can hit the ground running on Monday morning.

Have a good weekend.

Anita

Dear Anita

This all looks fine to me and is in line with our meeting today. I agree that it's good to get started and am very much looking forward to seeing the first version of the website.

Best

Patrick

1 What does Anita refer to as a *set of minutes*, and why does she use the word *informal*?

2 What is *signed off* by this e-mail?

3 The e-mail refers to 2k of budget in addition to a main budget of 8k. Under which conditions is this additional budget available?

4 How does Anita suggest that future quality issues be managed?

D LISTENING

◀)) BSA1.1.1 **Listen to a meeting between Patrick and his IT manager, Bruno Lobo, and answer the questions.**

1 What is Patrick's response to Anita's e-mail, and in particular to the use of the extra budget?

2 What is Bruno's interpretation of Anita's e-mail?

3 What advice does Bruno give Patrick when writing back to Anita?

C READING 2

Turn to page vii. Read the text and answer the questions.

Task

E-mail 1

A team member is working on an international project. Recently this person told you they were struggling; the project leader is giving them too much work, a lot of which is administrative and uninteresting. They also find the project leader too directive and aggressive. You decide to write to the project leader about the issue.

1 In groups decide:

- the name of the project leader
- which problems and how much detail to include in your e-mail
- how to express the issues in a positive way
- which solutions you might propose to move the situation forward

2 Now work in pairs within your group and write the e-mail. Consider:

- how to start the e-mail and explain its objective
- how to get your message across in a clear and professional manner
- which solutions/suggestions to make to resolve the issue(s)
- how to end the e-mail

3 Pass your e-mail to another pair in the other group.

E-mail 2

1 Read the e-mail you received and write a reply. Decide how to:

- give your point of view (you feel your leadership has been effective; the team member has required 'pushing' in order to deliver; as their competence is not high, simple tasks have been given)
- respond to the specific details of the feedback given
- respond to the proposed solutions offered
- propose how to continue (or not) discussion of the issues raised

2 Pass your reply to the pair who sent the e-mail.

E PEER REVIEW

In small groups, evaluate the e-mails you received and wrote. Give both positive feedback and constructive criticism. Use the questions below to help your discussion.

- Were your e-mails effective in getting across difficult/sensitive messages positively and professionally?

- When reading e-mails, how effective were you at recognising fact, idea and opinion?

F SELF-ASSESSMENT

Look at the e-mails you sent and received in this lesson and refer back to the lesson objectives. Think about these questions:

- Which e-mail writing skills have you developed well in this lesson?

- Which skills need more practice?

G PROFESSIONAL DEVELOPMENT AND PERFORMANCE GOALS

Complete the following sentences to create an action plan for developing your e-mail skills, particularly when dealing with sensitive and/or complex issues.

- To ensure I read others' e-mails fairly and positively, it's important for me to …

- One thing I will do to improve my writing in sensitive/difficult e-mails is to …

- I will also try to …

Small talk

Objectives

Speaking

- Can bring a work-related discussion back to the main points when the participants have gone off topic.
- Can express opinions on topics, using linguistically complex language.

Listening

Can follow an animated conversation between two fluent speakers.

Lesson deliverable

To participate in an activity to practise small talk in a business context.

Performance review

To review your own progress and performance against the lesson objectives at the end of the lesson.

Ⓐ SPEAKING 1

1 Discuss the comments. How far do you agree with them?

- *It's not what you know but who you know.*

- *I'm terrified of networking events.*

- *Most people love talking about themselves.*

- *Be interesting but, even better, be interested!*

- *Small talk is just another way of saying 'unnecessary, mindless chatter'.*

2 Discuss the questions.

1 What strategies do you use when meeting people for the first time?

2 How important do you think first impressions are? Why? What factors contribute to a positive or negative first impression?

3 At international gatherings, how aware are you of non-verbal communication when you meet people? Why?

Ⓑ READING

Read the extract below and answer the questions.

1 Which tip do you find the most helpful?

2 Add two tips of your own to the list and compare ideas in pairs.

Ⓒ LISTENING

1 ◀)) BSA1.2.2 Listen to the first conversation and answer the questions.

1 Which people have already met?

2 How does Steve ask Ines what she does?

3 How does Hans feel about the seminar so far?

4 What did Steve and Ines both find useful?

5 What does Hans change his mind about?

6 What was Hans's motivation for attending the event?

2 ◀)) BSA1.2.3 Listen to the second conversation and answer the questions.

1 What does Henrik say to get Steve's attention?

2 What does Steve say when he realises that he and Henrik have met before?

3 How does Henrik exit the conversation?

Small talk is not as small as you might think

The *Longman Dictionary of Contemporary English* defines small talk as 'polite, friendly conversation about unimportant subjects' and yet 'small talk' is a vital part of effective communication. Building personal relationships could lead to future lucrative contracts or deals, and you will gain only a superficial knowledge of someone via business communication only.

To this end, countless websites and articles give advice on how to do it well. Here are some suggestions to help you prepare when meeting new business contacts at a networking event.

- research the people you want to meet beforehand and prepare insightful questions

- have a couple of ice-breakers up your sleeve to jump-start conversations

- discover the motivation behind others' decisions to attend the event

- pay compliments where you can – about their clothes, hairstyle, etc.

- be aware of others' sensitivities and deflect conversations that are uncomfortable for someone

- give the other person/people a chance to speak

3 🔊 **BSA1.2.4 Listen to the third conversation and answer the questions.**

1 Why do you think Steve says 'I think you're getting ahead of yourself, Julia'?

2 How does Julia deal with the rather long pause in the conversation?

3 How does Ilya react to Julia's statement about his children being in Russia?

4 How does Julia react to Ilya's question about her personal life?

D SPEAKING 2

Work in small groups of three or four. You are at a networking event. Participate in small talk and keep the conversation going as long as you can. You will each have a role card indicating two strategies which you must include in your conversation.

Student A: Turn to page viii.
Student B: Turn to page viii.
Student C: Turn to page viii.
Student D: Turn to page viii.

When you have finished your conversations, try to guess which strategies each student had to include.

Task

Pre-task: Discussion

What strategies do you use to keep the conversation flowing? Think of some suitable ice-breakers you can use to join or start a conversation. How do you feel when there are long pauses in a conversation?

Part 1: Preparation

1 Work in groups of three or four. Read the task.

Context: Your multinational company has organised a management training week for its staff from around the world. You are going to have a chance to chat to people at lunchtime.

Task: Have small talk conversations with as many people as you can in your groups and use as many of the expressions as you can from the conversations in Section C.

2 To prepare for your conversation, decide what kind of management position you have, how long you've been with the company, what your future plans are and anything else that may be appropriate as the conversation develops. Think about positive and negative comments to make about the training programme so far.

3 During the conversation you will have a card instructing you to use a behaviour that could cause problems. Decide who is going to take each role.

Student A: Turn to page viii.
Student B: Turn to page viii.
Student C: Turn to page viii.
Student D: Turn to page viii.

Part 2: Small talk conversations

Each group meets at lunchtime around a table and starts chatting. Your aim is to make as many contacts from other countries as possible. Try to keep the conversations flowing as much as you can and deal with any embarrassing situations as politely and as smoothly as you can. Remember you want to leave the lunch with some contact details.

Part 3: Reporting back

Report back to the class on how your conversations went. Did you manage to work out what each person's potential problem behaviour was? Discuss how you handled these situations.

E PEER REVIEW

Look again at the objectives at the beginning of the lesson and think about the conversations you had.

- Were you able to engage in extended conversation and keep it on track?

- Could you follow the conversations without any problems?

- How did your partner(s) perform?

- What observations can you make about your and your partners' body language?

- How did you and your partners deal with pauses in the conversation?

- What can you and your partners do to improve your skills?

F SELF-ASSESSMENT

Write 140–160 words to assess your performance in the small talk conversations. Think about these questions:

- How well did you achieve the objectives?

- What feedback did you receive from your partners?

- How did you keep conversations flowing and on track?

- How did body language affect the conversations?

- How do you feel you can improve your performance?

G PROFESSIONAL DEVELOPMENT AND PERFORMANCE GOALS

Think of opportunities you can use to practise and improve your small talk skills, both inside and outside the classroom.
Write a paragraph about ways of improving these skills.

'Marketing today is dramatically different. It's no longer just market share and how much you can sell. It's also owning the customer relationship.' **John Sculley, US businessman**

OVERVIEW

LISTENING AND DISCUSSION
Customer relationship management

READING AND LANGUAGE
Is the customer always right? Yes, she is.
What women really want!
Defining and non-defining clauses

BUSINESS SKILLS
Making an impact in presentations
Writing: presentation slides

CASE STUDY
Relaunching Home2u

LISTENING AND DISCUSSION
Customer relationship management

A **Which of these opinions about marketing methods do you agree or disagree with? Interview your partner about their views and give reasons for your answers.**

1   Cold-calling (randomly phoning prospective customers) can serve a useful purpose.

2   Mailshots (bulk advertising sent by post) should be banned.

3   Social media marketing (via YouTube, Facebook, etc.) will soon replace print and television marketing.

4   Text messaging is an acceptable way to market to customers.

5   I don't mind pop-up adverts on my favourite websites if it helps to keep them free.

6   Catalogues are a thing of the past. Most people want to consult websites now.

7   I'm happy to receive e-mails about special promotions.

8   Word-of-mouth referral is a powerful form of marketing.

Jonathan Reynolds

B ◀)) **CD1.28 Listen to the first part of an interview with Dr Jonathan Reynolds, Academic Director of the Oxford Institute of Retail Management and lecturer at the Saïd Business School. Complete this information with no more than three words in each gap.**

Customer relationship management, CRM for short, refers to the systems and processes that companies use to ....[1]. Some people associate CRM with the software used to manage interactions, such as e-mails and ....[2].

CRM is a way for organisations to create more ....[3] businesses where the customer experience is ....[4] of everything that the company thinks and feels about its market. Although CRM software seems systematic and mechanical, in a mass market it can help to record personal ....[5]. At the same time, it helps to manage interactions efficiently and provide a ....[6] to the customer.

C **Complete the extract below about customer-centric marketing with the expressions in the box.**

customer experience	customer loyalty	direct mail	multichannel relationship
long-term customers	market share	word-of-mouth referrals	intrusive marketing

CUSTOMER-CENTRIC MARKETING

Most retailers cling to product-focused and promotion-centric models. However, there is increased consumer resistance to ....[1], such as unsolicited e-mails and ....[2].

In response, some retailers are beginning to pay more attention to the ....[3] and have adjusted their marketing practices so that they are delivering fewer, more relevant messages that reflect the ....[4] they have with the customer, e.g. retail stores, website, and catalogs, or "brick, click, and flip".

Switching to a customer-centric marketing approach helps to increase ....[5] and as a result, customers will buy more from you over a longer period of time. Research by Bain and Harvard Business School shows that the longer a customer stays with you, the greater the annual profit generated from that customer. These increased profits come from a combination of increased purchases, cost savings in marketing, and ....[6].

The majority of multichannel retailers do not design their marketing programs around acquiring new customers that have the best potential to become ....[7] and rewarding existing high-value, loyal customers with special treatment in order to retain them. Instead, they wrongly focus on ....[8] as the key measure of success.

D **Discuss these questions.**

1 Do you think being more customer-centric leads to greater business success? Why? / Why not?

2 Which of the following do you think make a business more customer-centric? Are there any drawbacks to any of these?

• E-mailing customers with personalised special offers

• Using marketing intelligence to figure out the best time to phone customers

• Sending customers a discount voucher or gift as a gesture of goodwill when resolving a complaint

3 What other examples of customer-centric business do you know of that work well?

E ◀)) CD1.29 **Listen to the second part of the interview. What methods are retailers using to retain customers? Which does Jonathan Reynolds feel is the best, and which has the biggest drawbacks? Why?**

F ◀)) CD1.30 **Listen to the third part of the interview and answer these questions.**

*Watch the interview on the **DVD-ROM**.*

1 What exactly is 'the glass consumer'?

2 What does Jonathan Reynolds say about the different attitudes to privacy?

3 Which attitude best describes you?

G **Discuss these questions.**

1 To what extent do you think you are a 'glass consumer'? Which companies do you think probably have the most information about you?

2 Which channels do companies most often use to contact you? Which do you think are the most effective? Which are the most annoying?

3 What do retailers do in your country to retain customers? Do you have any shop loyalty cards? What advantages do they give you?

READING AND LANGUAGE

A Work in pairs. Student A, read Article 1, and Student B, read Article 2 on the opposite page. Then discuss these questions and compare your answers with the information from both articles.

1 What percentage of consumer spending would you say is controlled by women?

2 Do you think the difference in salaries between men and women will narrow or widen?

3 Which retail sectors would you consider traditionally 'male'?

4 Why might a business run by a woman be more/less risky than one run by a man?

5 Can you name two companies that have successfully marketed their products for women?

B Read the article you didn't read in Exercise A and complete these marketing

Article 1

1 c........... spending

2 make stores more a........... to women

3 l........... a range of home products

4 based on a market s...........

Article 2

5 women are less likely to be i........... by a...........

6 ways of communicating such as w...........-of-m........... marketing and v........... marketing

7 a marketing h........... to t........... women

8 accommodate the i........... r........... of each customer

expressions from both articles.

C Discuss these questions.

1 Who is in charge of consumer spending in a household you know well?

2 Do you think female consumers behave differently from male consumers? How?

3 How could you make stores appeal across genders, e.g. car showrooms?

D Identify four examples of defining and/or non-defining clauses in the articles. When do we use these kinds of clause?

➡ *Language reference: Defining and non-defining clauses* page 130

E What are the missing word(s) in these sentences from the articles? Why have they been left out?

1 *Women want more* is the latest title from Michael Silverstein, ... a senior partner at Boston Consulting Group. (Article 1, lines 1–3)

2 ... the number of women .... being educated grows at a faster rate than men. (Article 1, lines 11–13)

3 Silverstein and Sayre offer an ambitious and systematic view of the opportunities, ... based on a study of 12,000 women in 21 countries ... (Article 1, lines 38–42)

4 ... the book argues that consumer companies, ... still predominantly run by men, need to listen to female customers ... (Article 1, lines 55–58)

5 Harley-Davidson, ... long .... a symbol of male pride, has added a section on its website .... dedicated to women motorcyclists ... (Article 2, lines 34–37)

6 Women now buy 10 per cent of all Harleys .... sold ... (Article 2, lines 38–39)

7 What we do *not* do is provide specific financial products .... aimed at women only ... (Article 2, lines 58–60)

F Think of a friend who feels differently about shopping than you. What would their 'dream day' consist of? What would they (not) buy? How else would they spend their money in one day? Discuss your answers in small groups.

Article 1

Is the customer always right? Yes, she is.

by Jonathan Birchall

Women want more is the latest title from Michael Silverstein, a senior partner at Boston Consulting Group. According to Silverstein and his BCG co-author Kate Sayre, women control 72 per cent of purchasing and consumer spending in the US and about $20,000bn of consumer spending globally. And the earnings gap with men is expected to narrow further as the number of women being educated grows at a faster rate than men.

Many retailers and consumer-goods companies already theoretically acknowledge that women are in charge of shopping and households: executives at Wal-Mart, Tesco and Procter & Gamble talk about customers as 'she', rather than 'he'. But the top management ranks of the consumer industry remain predominantly male, even amid signs that some companies have worked out where the money is.

Ikea, the Swedish home furnishing retailer, provides a child-minding room. Best Buy, which is a seller of electronic toys for children, has been promoting more female staff and trying to make stores more appealing to women and girls. Home Depot, the US home improvement retailer, also seems to agree. As it strives to increase sales, the über-male DIY store has launched a range of home products by a woman designer.

Silverstein and Sayre offer an ambitious and systematic view of the opportunities, based on a market study of 12,000 women in 21 countries from the US and Sweden to Saudi Arabia via China, Mexico and India. The research also asked the open question of what a 'dream day' would comprise, delivering some insight into the needs of female consumers.

Some interesting statistics emerge. 'Demands on time' is the top challenge for 47 per cent of respondents; 72 per cent say their mother is the dominant person in their lives; 42 per cent are made extremely happy by pets but only 27 per cent by sex.

Overall, the book argues that consumer companies, still predominantly run by men, need to listen to female customers, and that politicians might be well served by listening too.

Article 2

What women really want!

by Robert Craven, Kiki Maurey and John Davis

It is time to design products and marketing campaigns that actually appeal to the buying needs and habits of women. Women do buy differently from men – they like to research more and are less likely to be influenced by ads. So, one lesson is that less direct/print/traditional advertising will be effective and subtler ways of communicating, such as word-of-mouth marketing and viral marketing, might work.

In the States, women are dramatically changing how products are designed and marketed. It is only a question of time before this theme reaches across the Atlantic. In 2001, 3.6% of all new products were specifically tailored to women. That number more than doubled to 7.9% by 2005, according to Datamonitor's Productscan Online. Some were just a marketing hook to target women, but others fare better.

In 2006, 80% of women planned on

doing some home-improvement project, and 75% of them did it themselves. Barbara K's 30-piece tool kit is designed to help. These tools are not only better looking but are also made for a woman's hand and strength, and weigh a little less than regular tools.

Harley-Davidson, long a symbol of male pride, has added a section on its website dedicated to women motorcyclists, with tips on how to ride a bike safely with the right gear. Women now buy 10% of all Harleys sold, which is a stark contrast to a mere 2% in 1985.

Barclays' market research suggests that the majority of women do not want woman-specific products. Female business owners have a continued desire to be treated as equals with their male contemporaries. Marketing Director at Barclays Local Business, John Davis, comments: 'We know that women small business customers are less risky and more profitable for us, so it makes business sense to attract women to buy from us. We do put effort into communicating specifically with women. Examples are sponsoring "Women In Business Awards" and running marketing seminars. What we do *not* do is provide specific financial products aimed at women only; our range of products has been designed to be flexible enough to accommodate the individual requirements of each customer.'

from Critical Eye

BUSINESS SKILLS
Making an impact in presentations

A How would you adapt your presentation style if you were a) giving a talk at a conference, and b) giving a presentation to a group of colleagues? Why?

B ◀)) CD1.31, 1.32 Listen to two speakers talking about marketing. Identify the presenter and the kind of presentation they are giving.

C ◀)) CD1.31, 1.32 Look at these sentences. Who says what at the start of their talk, Presenter 1 or 2? Listen again if necessary.

1 As you probably know, I'm ... , and today I'm going to be talking about ...

2 You know, a funny thing happened to me the other day.

3 What is *unseen* is the extensive market research and development of products, ...

4 Have you seen this coat?

5 But what is marketing?

6 According to marketing guru Philip Kotler, there are five key processes in marketing. First, ...

7 Anyway, I'm not here to tell you about ...

8 Did you know that China's fashion market will probably grow to around US$12.4 billion over the next two years?

9 I bet you didn't know that, did you?

10 Now, you're probably wondering, what's the significance of all of this?

D ◀)) CD1.33, 1.34 What do you think are the missing words in these expressions for staging and signposting? Listen to two more extracts and check your answers.

Presenter 1

1 So, to go back to .... earlier, ...

2 Right, ... to that slide.

3 So, to sum .... , ...

4 Sorry, folks, but .... time for today.

Presenter 2

5 Right then, let's .... those figures, shall we?

6 I'd like to .... a journalist from the *FT* here: ...

7 If there's just .... you all to remember, it's ...

8 And .... , ... reveal our new marketing strapline.

USEFUL LANGUAGE

REFERRING TO SURPRISING FACTS OR FIGURES

Marketing is too often confused with selling.

You'll see we're talking about over five billion euros.

QUOTING SOMEONE

I'd like to quote the words of ... here.

According to the marketing guru, ...

Kotler would argue ...

EMPHASISING KEY WORDS

What is *unseen* is the extensive market investigation ...

And that's what I'd like *you* to do for your next assignment.

CALLING FOR ACTION

And that's what I'd like you to do.

If there's just one thing I'd like you all to remember, it's ...

BUILDING RAPPORT WITH THE AUDIENCE

Houston, we have an innovation problem. (*using humour*)

Clearly, we've got to do something different here. (*involving the audience*)

You know, a funny thing happened to me the other day. (*telling an anecdote*)

That's a huge increase in growth, isn't it? (*inviting agreement*)

E Categorise the expressions in Exercise D (1–8) according to their function (a–d). Some can go under more than one function.

A) referring to visuals   B) changing topic   C) quoting someone   D) closing remarks

F Which of the techniques below did each presenter use?

Student A: Look at the audio scripts for Presenter 1 on page 171 (Tracks 31 and 33).
Student B: Look at the audio scripts for Presenter 2 on pages 171–172 (Tracks 32 and 34).

Techniques for making an impact

1 Use of repetition

2 Referring to a surprising fact or figure

3 Asking 'real' or rhetorical questions

4 Quoting someone

5 Emphasising key words or figures

6 Building rapport with the audience, e.g. telling an anecdote, referring to a news story, using humour, etc.

7 Listing points in threes or fives

8 Calling for action, e.g. asking the audience to reflect on or do something

---

G Which of the expressions in the Useful language box on the previous page would you use for a) a formal presentation at a conference, and b) an in-house talk?

Writing: presentation slides

H Consider the visual impact of these slides. If you were giving a presentation, which of the slides would/wouldn't you use? Why?

A)
What are the marketing trends for the future???
marketing report

B)
M M
Companies think that marketing exists to support manufacturing, to get rid of the company's products. The truth is the reverse: manufacturing exists to support marketing. (*US marketing guru*)

Marketing Talk

C)
Looks like an Armani, feels like an Armani. Costs a fraction of the price

D)
I've come to the conclusion this is how most of you see the marketing department: thick-skinned, short-sighted and charging all the time

E)
The key to successfull presentations is 95% preparation and 10% being yourself.

PRESENTING STYLES

I Match the errors in the slides in Exercise H to these tips.

Tips for writing presentation slides

1 Don't use too much text. Avoid using type sizes, colours and fonts that are hard to read.

2 Check spelling and punctuation.

3 Use bullet points or lists of three or five.

4 Make an impact with your first and final slides.

J What other tips do you have for using visuals in presentations?

K Give a brief presentation to your partner on the topic of *Tips for successful presentations*. Use anecdotes of presentations you have seen or given. Think of a way to start that will create an impact, and end on a high note.

Relaunching Home2u

A chain of home-improvement stores needs a new marketing campaign to attract young Hispanic customers

Background

Home2u is the largest home-improvement retailer in the United States. It has more than 2,000 stores in the US, Puerto Rico, Mexico and Canada. It sells home products that include easy-to-assemble fittings and furnishings, DIY tools and equipment, paint and flooring, as well as garden furniture.

The Hispanic community comprises 15 per cent of the US's population and is the nation's largest ethnic minority. Market research shows that young Hispanic customers are an important target group. It is estimated that the Hispanic population of the US will reach 102.6m by 2050, by which time Hispanics will constitute 24 per cent of the total population.

Home2u recently introduced a cultural marketing campaign specifically designed to appeal to the Hispanic market, with an emphasis on family, watching soccer and salsa music. However, the campaign was seen as too stereotypical and didn't appeal to younger US Hispanics. According to market research, many of them have high aspirations and are interested in new social media and pop culture. Interestingly, many prefer information to be in Spanish or bilingual (English and Spanish). Home2u has decided to relaunch its campaign. The marketing department needs to come up with a new campaign that's edgy and appealing, not patronising to young Hispanics.

Customer survey

Look at this extract from the recent online customer satisfaction survey for Hispanic customers. What are the key findings?

Hispanic customer survey

Comments: *Although the new marketing campaign has had some favourable feedback, many Hispanic customers found it a turn-off.*

		Yes	No
1	I think the latest Home2u marketing campaign is edgy and cool.	4%	91%
2	I prefer reading assembly instructions in Spanish.	60%	33%
3	I think store signs should be bilingual in English and Spanish.	58%	39%
4	I like hearing salsa music being played in the store.	42%	44%
5	Home2u staff are helpful and not patronising.	13%	74%
6	I'd recommend Home2u to my family, co-workers and friends.	24%	54%

Task 1

Brainstorming meeting

You are members of the marketing team at Home2u. You hold a meeting to re-launch the campaign. Look at these suggestions for making your stores and products more appealing to Hispanic customers. Discuss the ideas and brainstorm some of your own.

- Make your home-improvement products more appealing to Hispanic customers
- Improve store layout and make information bilingual
- Install bilingual computers around the store to help customers find products
- Hire more US-Hispanic staff (7 per cent at present)
- Target younger Hispanic customers
- Come up with a Spanish-sounding name for the new marketing campaign

Task 2

Decision-making meeting

You have decided to find a celebrity to endorse the new campaign. Read the four profiles. What are the strengths and weaknesses of each celebrity? Decide who you would choose to endorse the re-launch and why, then present your favourite to the group.

Eddie Velázquez

Cuban-born rapper Eddie is very popular with Hispanics between the ages of 25 and 39. He has had cameo parts in a couple of Hollywood films and has recently presented a music programme on Mexican TV, where he has something of a cult following. He is divorced with three children.

Leona Pedraza

A Mexican golf player, Leona is a young professional who's on the up and has already been approached by a sportswear brand to endorse their products. At 24, she might be a little young for Home2u's existing market, which currently consists of 30- to 40-somethings. She has a 'girl-next-door' kind of image.

Elvira Olivas

Glamorous, successful, Colombian-born actress Elvira has appeared in several action movies as a super-heroine. Popular with teenagers and 20-somethings, she might not appeal to the older market segments. Like many celebrities, Elvira prefers to do advertising and promotional work in markets overseas, where she has featured in an extensive advertising campaign for a low-fat breakfast cereal.

Vanessa Flores

Mexican pop singer with international appeal, Vanessa is extremely popular with younger Hispanic women and teenagers. She was recently on the point of signing a sponsorship deal with a mobile company, but it fell through because of her high fees. Famous for her on-off relationship with US musician Kurt Holmes, the couple have reunited again and there is talk of wedding bells.

🔊 **CD1.35** Listen to Jodie, the Marketing Director, talking to Emilio, a recruitment agent, about the availability of celebrities for Home2u's TV commercial. What new information comes to light? Who do they finally choose, and why?

🔊 **CD1.36** Listen to the filming of the TV commercial. Do you think it will be successful? Why? / Why not? Discuss if you still want to go with the same choice.

Task 3

Presentation

Work in pairs or small groups. You are members of the marketing team. Jodie, the Marketing Director, is now on maternity leave. She has asked you to prepare a presentation of your final choice for the product endorsement to management at Home2u. Think of an original way to make an impact at the start and a marketing strapline to end on a high note, then give your presentation. Consider these questions:

- Which media will you use for the marketing campaign, e.g. TV, radio, press, billboards, viral marketing (including social media), online banners and videos, concerts/interviews streamed live on the Internet, etc.?

- What promotional events will you organise, bearing in mind the target market?

- What kind of accompanying publicity and promotional material will you prepare?

*Watch the Case study commentary on the **DVD-ROM**.*

Writing

Write a press release for the product endorsement. Outline the marketing campaign and the media you have chosen.

 Writing file page 148

'Job security is gone. The driving force of a career must come from the individual.'
Dr Homa Bahrami, Senior Lecturer at the Haas School of Business, California

LISTENING AND DISCUSSION
The future of work

A 🔊 CD2.1–2.8 **Listen to eight speakers and decide which of the work patterns below (a–h) each person is talking about. What are the advantages and disadvantages of each for a) employers, and b) employees?**

a) seasonal work   b) teleworking   c) casual labour   d) migrant work

e) self-employment   f) shift work   g) fixed-term/temporary contract   h) part-time work

B **Discuss these questions.**

1 What are the employment trends in your region/country in terms of:

- length of working week
- types of contract
- self-employment
- unemployment?

2 Do you think there is an acceptable work–life balance in your country, or is there a corporate 'work-all-hours' culture?

3 What are the arguments for and against employment legislation to regulate working hours and practices?

Ian Brinkley

C 🔊 CD2.9 **Listen to Ian Brinkley, Director of the Knowledge Economy programme for the Work Foundation, talking about employment trends in the UK. Write a summary of what he says in 50–60 words.**

D Relate each of these jobs to one of the five high-value service industries Ian Brinkley mentioned in Exercise C.

> accountant   architect   biochemist   financial analyst   games designer
> journalist   lawyer   lecturer   radiologist   software developer
> technician   telecommunications engineer

E ◀)) CD2.10 **What do you think Ian Brinkley will say about the impact of technology on work? Listen to the next part of the interview and make a list of the points he mentions.**

F What are the most important ways in which technology has changed the way you work or study? How do you think it might change the way you work in the future?

G ◀)) CD2.11 **Listen to the final part of the interview about job skills and correct the five factual errors in this summary.**

When starting out on a career, it's important to get the most specialist set of skills and experiences possible. Nowadays, most employers are not looking for specialist staff; they want people who can perform a wide variety of tasks within the company. Employers especially want people who have good organisational skills, who can manage other people, and who can work independently, as well as people with some intercultural competence.

Watch the interview on the DVD-ROM.

H Read this blog and complete the gaps with the words in brackets in the correct form.

Skills for 21ˢᵗ-century jobs

Just what skills are needed to capture and retain the high-value jobs of tomorrow? While ....¹ (*know*) and strong analytical skills will be necessary, they may not be sufficient to keep these jobs. Those employees who hope to make themselves ....² (*dispensable*) must have much more. They must be capable of coming up with unique, breakthrough ideas and express these ideas in a way that will be ....³ (*compel*) and elicit the desired response from others. Easy to say, but very tough to do.

And how will we begin teaching another trait that may prove to be even more important in ensuring lifetime career ....⁴ (*succeed*) in an increasingly volatile, ...⁵ (*predict*) world? How will we teach the type of ....⁶ (*adapt*) that will be required to ....⁷ (*continue*) reinvent oneself to meet the demands of conditions we cannot even imagine, or jobs that we cannot yet define?

Although schools, family, peers and employers must all play some role in teaching these ....⁸ (*increase*) critical skills, there is no escaping the uncomfortable truth. Every individual must assume greater ....⁹ (*responsible*) for defining their own skills ....¹⁰ (*require*) and for ensuring that they develop these skills.

I Discuss these questions.

1 To what extent do you agree with the writer of the blog in Exercise H?

2 What skills are essential for your job, or the job you would like to do in the future?

3 Would you like to work in the same field or profession for the rest of your life?

4 Do you know of anyone who has successfully changed career?

READING AND LANGUAGE

A How many people do you know that have a 'job for life'? How many do you know who do different jobs at the same time?

B Look at the photo in the article. What do you think *giganomics* might be? Read the first two paragraphs of the article to check your ideas.

C Discuss these questions.

1 In which fields or sectors would you tend to find portfolio workers?

2 What are the benefits and disadvantages of being a portfolio worker? Discuss with a partner and report to the group.

D Read the complete article and check your answers.

Giganomics: And what don't you do for a living? by Judith Woods

If you ever meet John Lees at a party, he might talk about being a career coach, mention that he writes books on business or drop in the fact that
5 he's also a part-time Anglican priest. 'I've got a classic portfolio career,' says Lees, 50. 'The advantage is that by working for a variety of employers, no one has complete power over
10 you to switch work on or off. The drawback is that I have an immensely complicated diary.'

These days, many of us are juggling one-off projects, short-term
15 contracts and assorted consultancies in a bid to survive. Job security used to be a given. But growing numbers of professionals are reinventing themselves by setting up as portfolio
20 workers in a new employment phenomenon dubbed giganomics. Instead of jobs for life, they rely on a series of 'gigs'.

Former *Vanity Fair* and *New*
25 *Yorker* editor Tina Brown, who coined the term, writes: 'No one I know has a job any more. They've got gigs: a bunch of free-floating projects, consultancies and bits and
30 pieces.'

Tina Brown paints a bleak picture of freelancers' lives, burdened with all the 'anxieties, uncertainties and indignities of gig work', grafting
35 three times as hard for the same money as a salaried employee, without any of the benefits, such as sick and holiday pay or a pension.

Nick, 37, a graphic designer based
40 in London, can attest to the stress felt by portfolio workers. 'I was made redundant two years ago and went freelance,' he says. 'I hated it, because I am terrible at selling
45 myself and I'm not laid-back enough to live with the insecurity of not

knowing where I'll be in six months. I managed OK, and I earned as much as I had done previously, but there
50 was a price to pay in terms of sleepless nights.'

Suzy Walton, a former senior civil servant and mother of four, with a background in central government,
55 including the Ministry of Defence, has taken up a series of non-executive directorships. A portfolio career has proved a lucrative alternative to corporate life.

60 'I sit on the boards of a military organisation Combat Stress, which looks after veterans with post-traumatic stress disorder, the Internet Watch Foundation and Birmingham
65 Children's Hospital, and a few others,' says Walton, 45.

Walton admits that none of these roles generates a substantive salary on its own – a FTSE 250 company
70 might pay about £30,000 a year to a non-executive board member – but when combined, her directorships provide a good income. Just as importantly, she enjoys the chal-
75 lenges. 'It's hard to keep up to speed with the issues in each, but I enjoy doing that. A portfolio career isn't for the fainthearted; there's a zero-

tolerance attitude to being late or
80 missing a commitment. But it's a fantastic lifestyle.'

Anyone with this pick-and-mix approach to work needs to be excellent at time management. The upside
85 is the freedom to pick and choose work, and to do it at a time that suits. Cary Cooper, Professor of Organisational Psychology and Health at Lancaster University, says it's a clas-
90 sic swings-and-roundabouts scenario. 'The good news is that you're supposed to have control over what work you do. The bad news is that you feel you can't say no to
95 anything,' he says. 'You should also be able to have a better work–life balance. But the people who employ you expect you to be on call whenever they want you.'

100 The creative industries such as advertising, graphic design and the media already rely heavily on freelancers, as does IT. Many more companies will need portfolio work-
105 ers in future. 'There's going to be much more multiple part-time working,' says Professor Cooper. 'Organisations are getting rid of staff, but they will buy back some of
110 them on a portfolio basis.'

from the *Daily Telegraph*

E **What do the words and expressions in *italic* mean? Correct the definitions, according to the context in the article.**

1 'These days many of us are juggling *one-off* projects …' (lines 13–14)

happening or done several times, not as part of a regular series

2 '… consultancies and *bits and pieces*.' (lines 29–30)

various kinds of big things

3 '… *paints a bleak picture* of freelancers' lives …' (lines 31–32)

gives the impression that something is or will be good

4 'It's hard to *keep up to speed* with the issues …' (lines 75–76)

continue to learn about a subject so that you know all the historical facts, etc.

5 'A portfolio career *isn't for the fainthearted* …' (lines 77–78)

used humorously to say something is easy and doesn't need a lot of effort

6 '… it's a classic *swings-and-roundabouts* scenario.' (lines 89–91)

when two choices have more gains than losses so that there's little difference

F **Choose the correct meaning of these words as they are used in the article.**

1 drop in (line 4)
a) mention something casually in conversation
b) visit someone without arranging a particular time

2 juggling (line 13)
a) changing things or arranging them in the way that you want
b) trying to fit two or more jobs or activities into your life, especially with difficulty

3 bid (line 16)
a) an attempt to achieve or obtain something
b) an offer to do work or provide services for a specific price

4 setting up (line 19)
a) starting your own business
b) preparing the equipment that will be needed for something

5 gig (line 23)
a) a job, especially one that does not last a long time (*AmE*)
b) a performance by some musicians or a comedian

6 coin (line 26)
a) make pieces of money from metal
b) invent a new word or expression

7 grafting (line 34)
a) working very hard (*informal*)
b) getting money by the dishonest use of influence (*AmE*)

8 commitment (line 80)
a) hard work and loyalty that you give to a company
b) something you have promised you will do, or have to do

G **Work in pairs. How would you feel about being a portfolio worker? Use information from the article and expressions like these.**

I am pretty good at selling myself, so I …   I think there's a price to pay in terms of …

I enjoy having the freedom to pick and choose, so I …   I'm a laid-back sort of person, so I …

H **How many examples of the *-ing* form or the infinitive (with or without *to*) can you find in the article? Which forms do we use in these cases?**

1 after a preposition

2 after a modal verb

3 as a noun

4 after *It* + *is* + adjective

5 to express purpose

6 when we want to avoid repeating the subject + a relative + verb

7 with certain verbs, e.g. *decide, expect, be able, afford*, etc.

8 after certain expressions, e.g. *in a bid, be* + adj. + *enough, be supposed* …

➡ *Language reference: -ing forms and infinitives* page **132**

BUSINESS SKILLS
Resolving conflict

A **Do you agree or disagree with these statements? Discuss your answers.**

1 Conflict isn't necessarily a bad thing.

2 When there's a conflict, it's best to keep things rational rather than show your emotions.

3 The most common kind of workplace conflict is between colleagues of the same grade.

B **Look at this checklist of techniques used to deal with conflict. Which do you most often use? Which get the best/worst results? What other techniques have you used or seen used?**

1	Ignore the problem – it'll sort itself out. ☐
2	Try to put yourself in the other person's shoes. ☐
3	Use humour to defuse a tense situation. ☐
4	Say loudly and clearly exactly what's on your mind. ☐
5	Remain calm and don't get emotional. ☐
6	Ask lots of open questions. ☐
7	Speak more than you listen. ☐
8	Try to reach a compromise. ☐
9	Accept you're in the wrong – anything for a quiet life. ☐
10	Summarise what the other person says in your own words. ☐

C **Do you consider yourself to be a good listener? How do you show other people you're listening to them? Read this description of communication problems. To what extent does it reflect your experience?**

According to Roger Fisher and William Ury in their book *Getting to Yes*, there are three major problems in communication. Firstly, people may not be talking to each other. Frequently, each side has given up on the other and is no longer attempting any serious communication. Secondly, people don't pay enough attention to what other people say. Then there are misunderstandings which are compounded when people speak different languages.

The solution they propose is to listen actively; acknowledge what is being said and question your assumptions. Understanding is not agreeing, but unless you can show that you grasp how the other person sees things, you may be unable to explain your point of view to them. You therefore maximise the chance of having a constructive dialogue.

D 🔊 CD2.12 **Listen to a conversation between two work colleagues. What techniques does Carl use to show he's listening actively to Yolanda? How would you resolve the situation?**

E **Which of these expressions are used to a) paraphrase and summarise, b) show understanding, and c) encourage someone to keep talking?**

1 So, your point is that the office is too noisy. Is that it?

2 Tell me more about what you were just saying.

3 You sound as if you're disappointed.

4 I sense you're feeling anxious about the meeting.

5 So, what you're saying is you have too much work.

6 If I understand you correctly, you're saying the plan isn't viable.

7 I'm not sure I understand. Could you explain what you mean?

8 I'm listening. Please go on.

9 OK, from your point of view, we should scrap this idea. Correct?

10 It sounds like you're not convinced by that argument.

11 I appreciate how you feel.

12 So, you're telling me that this is the wrong document. Is that right?

13 I can see why you feel that way.

14 What exactly do you mean when you say it can't be done?

F **Work in pairs. Read this information and try to resolve the conflict with your partner.**

You are both sales reps for a direct-banking organisation. The company rule is that if you get a first contact, then the client is yours and no other banker can approach that client. However, in this highly competitive environment, it's common practice for bankers to go after clients they know their colleagues are also following up. What's more, the company does nothing to stop this happening.

Student A: Turn to page 151.
Student B: Turn to page 159.

Writing: avoiding conflict in e-mails

G **Does your company or organisation have a training programme on 'e-mail netiquette'? What would such a course deal with? Do you think it would be useful? Why? / Why not?**

H 🔊 CD2.13 **How would you answer these questions? Listen to Rob Giardina, an intercultural communications consultant. Does he mention the same points as you?**

1 Why are there sometimes problems and misunderstandings when people write e-mails to each other?

2 What can you do to avoid these misunderstandings?

3 What can you do to solve the problem when there's obviously a conflict?

Rob Giardina

I **Work in pairs to rewrite these e-mails so that they sound more polite and neutral in tone. Student A, rewrite e-mails 1–3; Student B, rewrite e-mails 4–6. Then exchange your e-mails and write your replies.**

1

> Hello everyone. I must have an update on all your projects for a departmental report ASAP.

2

> Hi guys, Samira wants a meeting on Tuesday morning at 10.00. Plan on being there. This meeting is very important!

3

> CAN YOU SEND ME THE MONTHLY FIGURES ASAP??? OR EVEN SOONER ;-)

4

> I'm extremely busy and I just don't have time to deal with this right now!!!!!

5

> Hi, guys. What the *$#@ is happening with that %*@& product presentation?

6

> You don't understand. I was simply asking you to follow up with them and report back to me.

➡️ *Writing file* page 143

Delaney
Call–centre absenteeism

A call centre wants to find ways to reduce absenteeism and retain staff

Background

Delaney is a Dublin-based call centre working for a major European car-hire company. Delaney employs 260 full-time and part-time agents. Most agents are European women in their mid- to late 20s, many of them fluent in English, Spanish, Italian, French or German. The car-hire company has outsourced most of its booking operations to Delaney.

In common with many call centres, Delaney has problems with absenteeism and high levels of staff turnover. The average length of service is only three years. This means high costs in terms of recruiting, selecting and training call-centre agents. Added to that cost is the fact that new agents are not as productive as experienced agents. There is also concern about the competitiveness of the Irish call-centre industry.

Report on absenteeism

Read the report. What possible reasons could there be for the high levels of absenteeism in Delaney? How could the company try to reduce it?

Report on absenteeism

Executive summary

The Human Resources Department monitored absenteeism over a 12-month period.

The findings show that there are high levels of absenteeism in the company. The average is seven days taken in sickness per agent each year. The most common causes of absenteeism are reported as headaches and migraine, colds and flu, back problems and stress.

This level of absence may be causing delays in answering calls and is placing extra work and stress on colleagues. In addition, there is the cost of finding replacement staff to cover absences and the uncertainty that absences can cause in planning services.

Ultimately, our callers and clients may become dissatisfied with the level of customer service. The imperative, therefore, is for the company to find ways to reduce absenteeism and to deal with it effectively when it occurs.

Task 1 — Meeting

Student A, you are a team leader at Delaney. Student B, you are a call-centre agent at Delaney and Student A is your manager. Read your information and meet to discuss Student B's sickness record.

Student A: Turn to page 151.
Student B: Turn to page 159.

The consultant's findings

◀》 CD2.14–2.19 Delaney recently hired a consultant to run a series of stress-management workshops. Listen and summarise the main problems based on comments that the call-centre staff made to her. How would you try to deal with the problems?

Task 2

Decision-making meeting

Work in groups. You are the management team at Delaney. You have heard rumours that your main client, a major European car-hire company, is investigating an alternative supplier, possibly in Eastern Europe, where staff and operating costs are more competitive than in Ireland. The CEO and Chief Financial Officer of the car-hire company are coming to visit you next week.

Hold an emergency meeting. Prioritise the issues to deal with. Then discuss and decide how best to resolve them.

- Decide a company policy to manage and reduce absenteeism rates.

- Define good practice for the use of call recording and monitoring.

- Review staff performance targets and the bonus scheme.

- Decide the company's internal e-mail policy.

- Devise a strategy to reduce staff attrition rates.

- Decide how best to persuade our main client not to change suppliers.

Watch the Case study commentary on the **DVD-ROM**.

Writing

Look at this draft e-mail and decide how to improve it before you click on SEND.

 Writing file page 143

Subject: Monthly performance

Tricia

For the second consecutive month, you have failed to reach your target. This is simply NOT ACCEPTABLE. As I have told you in the past, all agents are expected to deal with a customer's booking in no more than five minutes. The average time you spend with a client is 6.2 minutes.

As for absences, you were off sick three days this month, and arrived late for work on four occasions. Try to do better next month.

Regards

Bernadette

'On the whole, human beings want to be good, but not too good, and not quite all the time.' *George Bernard Shaw (1856–1950), Irish playwright*

OVERVIEW

LISTENING AND DISCUSSION

Trust me: corporate responsibility

READING AND LANGUAGE

The corporate conscience: Sherron Watkins, Enron whistleblower

Drug whistleblower collects $24m

Modal perfect

BUSINESS SKILLS

Ethical problem-solving

Writing: meetings and action points

CASE STUDY

Dilemmas at Daybreak

LISTENING AND DISCUSSION

Trust me: corporate responsibility

A Look at the opening quote above and these quotes. Which one is closest to your views on business ethics? How relevant are they to the business world today?

1 'Greed is good. Greed is right. Greed works.'
Gordon Gekko, in the movie *Wall Street*

2 'A business that makes nothing but money is a poor kind of business.'
Henry Ford (1863–1947), US industrialist

3 '*Corporation*, n., an ingenious device for making profit without individual responsibility.'
Ambrose Bierce (1842–1914), US columnist and writer

4 'The one and only social responsibility of business is to make profits.'
Milton Friedman (1912–2006), US economist

B ◀)) Name some companies or industries that have had bad press over one of these issues. Was anything done to rectify the problems as a result?

employment practices   environmental concerns   financial irregularities mislabelling of products   product pricing   supply chains

C ◀)) CD2.20 Listen to Philippa Foster Back OBE, Director of the Institute of Business Ethics, talking about attitudes to corporate responsibility. Read the summaries on the opposite page and choose the most accurate one.

Philippa Foster Back

1 Philippa Foster Back explains there was a significant change in attitudes to corporate responsibility about 15 years ago with the growth of 24/7 media and the Internet. It's almost impossible now for a company to hide what it's doing. The public is much more sensitive to environmental issues, long supply chains, how work is outsourced and the use of child labour.

2 Philippa Foster Back explains there was a major change in attitudes to corporate responsibility about 20 years ago, primarily concerning the energy industry. That, plus the growth of the Internet, has increased public awareness to the extent that it has become difficult for companies to hide any unethical activities. We are now more aware of the effects of outsourcing processes, supply chains and environmental issues.

3 Philippa Foster Back explains that 15–20 years ago, there was a slight change in attitudes to corporate responsibility when the public first took an interest in manufacturing industries and their adverse affects on local communities. Then came the growth of 24/7 media, which meant it became impossible for a company to hide activities concerning the environment and financial irregularities.

D ◀)) CD2.21 **Listen to the second part of the interview, about how attitudes to accountability have changed. What are the first three models mentioned?**

E ◀)) CD2.22 **Listen to the final part of the interview and complete this summary about the other two models. Use no more than three words per gap.**

Watch the interview on the DVD-ROM.

The ethical language that was being used changed around 2000: people who had an interest in how a company was run started talking about ....[1]. They asked companies to ....[2] those outside the organisation how they were doing business.

In addition to annual report accounts, some companies began to produce ....[3], also known as ....[4]. Companies were being asked to show how they conduct their business not only to their customers but also to their ....[5]: their shareholders, employees and suppliers.

The latest stage is the '............[6]' model. This is when a democratic society considers that companies are ....[7] and, therefore, they encourage their governments to ....[8] to make them behave.

F **Which model do you think is used by a) your company or organisation, and b) most companies in your country today?**

G **Complete these statements using words related to business ethics.**

1 Most businesses are still quite p............ and follow the 'trust me' model.

2 With the 24/7 media world, more companies are being brought to ac............ for how they do their business, especially those involved in any corporate sc............ .

3 Although sustainability r............ are standard practice nowadays, a business can always find ways to hide illegal activities such as financial ir............ .

4 Long s............ chains that involve a great deal of outsourcing are particularly difficult to manage both logistically and ethically.

5 If we banned child l............ altogether, or boycotted products made by children, it would only cause more poverty.

6 Sustainability is the responsibility of all st............ – not just the shareholders.

7 Companies should be wary of using celebrities to endorse their brands because they may behave inappropriately and damage the brand's re............ .

8 The majority of multinationals are guilty of un............ behaviour at some time or other.

H **Mark the statements in Exercise G with these symbols. Then compare and discuss your answers.**

A+ = agree strongly   ? = don't know   D = don't agree in most cases

A = agree in most cases   D+ = disagree strongly

READING AND LANGUAGE

A What do you think a whistleblower is? Read either of the articles on the opposite page quickly and choose the correct definition (a, b or c).

A) someone who behaves illegally or immorally in order to get promotion

B) someone who sells company secrets and commercial information to rival organisations

C) someone who reveals dishonest or illegal practices at the place where they work

B Student A, read Article 1. Student B, read Article 2. Answer these questions, then tell each other about your answers.

1 What type of company did the whistleblower work for?

2 What type of wrongdoing did the whistleblower expose, and how?

3 Did the person blow the whistle internally or externally?

4 Do we know if the whistleblower gained financially from the situation?

5 What, if anything, do the two whistleblowers have in common?

C Read both articles and find the words or expressions which have a similar meaning to the following.

Article 1

1 stuck in a bad situation and unable to get out or make progress (paragraph 1)

2 discovered something by chance and unexpectedly (paragraph 4)

3 find the courage (paragraph 4)

4 started being in charge of something such as a business or organisation (paragraph 5)

5 refused to consider someone's idea, opinion, etc. because you think it is not serious, true or important (paragraph 5)

6 dishonestly changes official records and figures in order to steal money or give people false information (paragraph 7)

7 finally tell the truth about something you have been hiding (paragraph 7)

Article 2

8 to state in a court of law that you are responsible for a crime (paragraph 1)

9 to end an argument or solve a disagreement (paragraph 1)

10 officially gave information to someone in authority (paragraph 1)

11 a very large amount of money paid to a professional person for their work (paragraph 2)

12 repayment of money to someone when their money has been spent (paragraph 4)

13 gave a document to a court of law so that it could be officially recorded and dealt with (paragraph 5)

14 when someone obeys a law, rule, agreement or demand (paragraph 7)

D Read this extract from a discussion between two people, commenting on Article 1. If you had been in Sherron Watkins's position, would you have done anything differently?

A: Don't you think Sherron Watkins should have done something sooner? She herself says she should've seen the warning signs.

B: Maybe it was a case of too little, too late. She could've gone outside the company. But with the benefit of hindsight, it's easy to criticise.

A: Yes, I would've gone to the company's auditors.

B: I doubt that would've helped. The auditors were taken to court after Enron collapsed and went out of business too.

E What language is used in Exercise D to hypothesise about and comment on the past, to criticise past actions and to express regret?

➡ *Language reference: modal perfect page 134*

The corporate conscience: Sherron Watkins, Enron whistleblower by Lesley Curwen

from *The Guardian*

Sherron Watkins, one of the world's best-known whistleblowers, made global headlines in 2001 for telling her boss, Ken Lay, that Enron was
5 mired in accounting fraud.

Back in 1996, Watkins was working with Andrew Fastow, the Chief Financial Officer later convicted of fraud, when she began to witness
10 aggressive accounting. 'I was starting to see Andy Fastow cross the line,' she says, claiming he asked her to lie to one of Enron's partners about an investment. 'It should have been a
15 huge warning flag,' she admits. It merely prompted her to move to a different part of the empire, Enron International, where she later became a vice-president.
20 All this time, Harvard graduate Jeffrey Skilling had been growing in influence at Enron, reinventing what it did for a living to include power trading, selling retail electricity and
25 even the provision of broadband internet services. In 2001, he became Chief Executive Officer.

By mid-2001, Watkins was working for Fastow again. This time, she
30 stumbled across evidence of massive accounting fraud. 'I thought, I have got to get out of here. I can't work for a company that is doing this. I'm gonna work up the guts, if I can, to
35 confront Jeffrey Skilling on my last day.' But soon after, Skilling resigned unexpectedly, for what he said were personal reasons.

So Watkins sent an anonymous
40 memo to the man who'd taken the helm, the founder and Chairman, Kenneth Lay. Later, she met Lay to convey her fears face to face. Enron began an inquiry, but it failed to use
45 independent investigators, and her claims were largely dismissed.

Shortly after, Enron, the world's biggest energy trader and once the seventh-biggest company in America,
50 filed one of the biggest US bankruptcy cases to date. Thousands of workers lost their jobs and their pensions invested in its shares, and other investors lost billions
55 of dollars.

Watkins never took her concerns outside the company, to the financial regulator or a third party. Why not? 'When a company cooks the books,
60 it rarely has a chance of surviving, but to do that, it has to come clean itself, to admit its problems and re-state its financials. I felt here was Enron's chance to come clean.'
65 Watkins now gives lectures about corporate ethics.

Article 2

Drug whistleblower collects $24m
by Lloyd de Vries

from *CBS News*

Pfizer, the world's biggest pharmaceutical company, has agreed to plead guilty and pay $430 million in fines to settle criminal charges. The settle-
5 ment includes a $24.6 million payment for whistleblower David Franklin, the scientist who first uncovered wrongdoing of one of its subsidiaries and reported the market-
10 ing abuses to authorities.

The company acknowledged spending hundreds of thousands of dollars to promote non-approved uses for the drug Neurontin, in part by
15 paying doctors hefty speakers' fees and flying them to lavish resorts as 'educational' trips.

"This illegal and fraudulent promotion scheme corrupted the information
20 process relied upon by doctors in their medical decision-making, thereby putting patients at risk," said U.S. Attorney Michael Sullivan.

"We believe we have exposed an
25 illegal practice in the pharmaceutical industry that caused the Medicaid program—funded jointly by the states and the federal government—to pay tens of millions of dollars for off-
30 label prescriptions that were not eligible for reimbursement under the Medicaid program," said Franklin's attorney, Thomas Greene.

The case began in 1996, when
35 Franklin filed a whistleblower lawsuit against Parke-Davis and its parent company Warner-Lambert, alleging it used an illegal marketing plan to drive up sales of the drug Neurontin
40 in the 1990s. Pfizer bought Warner-Lambert in 2000.

The lawsuit alleged that while Neurontin was approved only as an epilepsy drug, the company promoted
45 it for relieving pain, headaches, bipolar disorder and other psychiatric illnesses. While doctors can prescribe drugs for any use, the promotion of drugs for these so-called "off-label
50 uses" is prohibited by the Food, Drug and Cosmetic Act.

Pfizer said the activity alleged in Franklin's lawsuit and charged by prosecutors occurred years before it
55 bought Warner-Lambert. "Pfizer is committed to compliance with all healthcare laws and to high ethical standards in all aspects of its business practices," the company said in a
60 statement.

The whistleblower lawsuit alleged that the company's publicity plan for Neurontin included paying doctors to put their names on ghost-
65 written articles about Neurontin and to fly them to lavish resorts. One doctor received almost $308,000 to speak at conferences about the drug.

F Discuss these questions.

1 Sherron Watkins said, 'It should have been a huge warning flag' when she first spotted unethical practices. Why is it sometimes easier to ignore warning signs?

2 Is it a good idea to pay whistleblowers? Why? / Why not?

3 Is anything gained by the actions of whistleblowers in companies?

4 What unethical business practices have you heard about in your country?

BUSINESS SKILLS
Ethical problem-solving

A Look at these personal dilemmas from an agony column and discuss how you would respond to the situations.

Friends in business
Feb 7, 43 comments

I need to choose between two rival suppliers for a large order of staff uniforms. Both offer products of a similar quality, but one of the suppliers is slightly more expensive than the other. My dilemma is that this supplier is an old college friend and we often meet socially. If I order the uniforms from the other supplier, my friend will be offended. But if I order the uniforms from my friend, I will have to justify to my boss that their uniforms are better than the others. To make matters worse, my friend is assuming he will win the contract and has already invited me to dinner at an expensive restaurant to 'celebrate'. What should I do? Should I choose my friend's company at the risk of damaging my reputation at work? Or should I choose the other supplier at the risk of losing a close friend?

Male manager, 36

Spoilt for choice
Feb 2, 39 comments

I have recently received three job offers, but don't know which one to take. Having attended my university's recruitment fair, I went for an interview with a tobacco company and was offered a well-paid job in the finance department with excellent benefits and opportunities for promotion. I used to smoke, but gave up last year.

However, I've also been offered a position at my uncle's company. We get on really well, although he hasn't given me a formal job interview yet. And I have some concerns about what my future colleagues might say about my uncle giving an inexperienced graduate a managerial post. On the other hand, if I say no, I may upset my family.

The third job offer is as a junior accountant for a fair-trade company, where the salary is pretty low, but there's a good office atmosphere, and the company has a decent ethical record. My reservation is that if I accept, there will be little scope for moving up. Which job should I take?

Female graduate, 22

B ◀)) CD2.23, 2.24 Listen to two podcasts by the agony aunt about the situations in Exercise A. Did you come to the same conclusions? What do you think of her response?

C Complete each of these extracts from the podcasts with between three and six words in each gap.

Friends in business

1 Of course, it's not always easy ....

2 Whether one of the suppliers is a friend or not is ....

3 .... , I'd want to go for the best price.

4 On the other hand, your friend should understand that ....

5 .... to speak to your boss.

Spoilt for choice

6 Most readers seem to think ....

7 You have to .... and cons ...

8 Do you really want to .... by working for an unethical company?

9 .... , I doubt if you'll be happy at the fair-trade company for long.

10 What you finally decide ....

11 .... , is your first job won't be your last.

D Look at the expressions in the Useful language box below. Which ones are more diplomatic or neutral? Which ones sound more forceful and direct?

E Think about a typical dilemma you might have at work. Student A, explain the dilemma to your partner. Student B, give your partner some advice. Decide how direct you are going to be. When you have finished, swap roles.

USEFUL LANGUAGE

GIVING ADVICE

Another thing you could do is ...

You might like to ...

The important thing is to ...

Oh dear, that's a tricky one.

If it were up to me, I'd ...

You have to weigh up the pros and cons.

On the other hand, ...

On balance, I think ...

What I *would* say, though, is ...

I wouldn't do that if ....

Are you sure you *really* want to ...?

**Writing:
meetings and
action points**

F Look at these tips for meetings. Do you agree with the advice? Add another tip of your own.

> **Tips for effective meetings: PARTAKE**
>
> 1 **PART**icipants: no more than 12; make sure all participants can contribute and choose a variety of good decision-makers, problem-solvers and troubleshooters.
>
> 2 **A**genda: check all aims have been covered; set a date and time for the next meeting.
>
> 3 **K**ey points and actions: summarise the who/what/when. Minutes or action points should be short and concise and sent out within 24 hours.
>
> 4 **E**nd by allocating 5–10 minutes to review how you performed as a team: what were the positive/negative points, e.g. time-wasting, misunderstandings or conflicts?

G CD2.25 Listen to an extract from a meeting discussing procedures for making staff redundant. How effective was the meeting? How much conflict was there? How well did Becky lead the meeting?

H You are the management team at Maynard Electronics. Hold a meeting to discuss ways of monitoring employees and surveillance measures. Decide who is going to lead the meeting; however, all participants should take notes. Look at the agenda and your information before you start.

Student A: Turn to page 151. Student C: Turn to page 160.
Student B: Turn to page 160 Student D: Turn to page 163.

> ▶ *Maynard Electronics*
>
> **Agenda: Security and workplace surveillance**
>
> 1 Installation of security cameras – where?
> 2 Monitoring of e-mail and Internet usage
> 3 Background checks when recruiting new staff, e.g. criminal records
> 4 Communicate new measures to staff, e.g. circulate a written policy

I Using your notes from the meeting in Exercise H, write up the action points of what was decided.

➡ *Writing file page 144*

Dilemmas at Daybreak

A food company has to improve the way it labels its products

Background

Daybreak is a UK-based company that sells breakfast cereals and snack bars. It has recently received bad publicity due to mislabelling of its products, including its popular range of children's breakfast cereals, Ready-to-go.

An ex-employee, an expert nutritionist, has alleged that Ready-to-go cereals are high in sugar, salt and carbohydrates and therefore unsuitable for children, despite marketing claims that the cereals are healthy.

The day the news broke, the company website froze and its customer services department was overwhelmed with calls from outraged parents and nutritionists claiming the cereals were 50-per-cent sugar. Furthermore, the nutritional information on the side of the packet only gives details per 30g, a typical serving, and not per 100g. The nutritional content also lists sodium and salt as separate items, which is misleading.

Daybreak says it will review the nutritional content and be more consistent in its labelling. However, despite protests, Daybreak hasn't yet issued a public apology. The company now recognises the need to rethink not only its food labels but also its business ethics.

Breaking news

🔊 **CD2.26** Listen to the TV report and take notes on the key points. What could be the consequences for Daybreak?

Task 1

Discussing recommendations

You are the management team at Daybreak. Hold a meeting to discuss how you could have prevented this kind of scandal from happening. Discuss these recommendations, amend them and add some of your own ideas.

- *Be transparent*: Label correct nutritional content, both per 30g and per 100g, in all markets; give the recommended intake of nutrients for children, not adults, on children's breakfast cereals.

- *Act faster:* Daybreak only became concerned when the press published the real nutritional content of its cereals.

- *Own up:* The current crisis wouldn't have escalated if Daybreak had owned up and apologised sooner; an immediate public apology is required.

- *Don't blame the press or the experts:* Empathise with customers and parents instead.

- *Develop a sustainable policy for the future:* Lower the content of sugar, sodium and carbohydrates; the sugar content in Ready-to-go children's cereals is higher than in adult cereals.

Task 2

Meeting

Hold another meeting to discuss how to move forward from the present crisis and communicate any new developments to the press. Your main concern is how to improve food labelling and regain consumer confidence. Look at your information, add some of your own ideas and make some preparatory notes before you start.

Student A: Turn to page 151.
Student B: Turn to page 154.
Student C: Turn to page 160.

Six months later

🔊 **CD2.27** Listen to another TV report six months later. What action(s) did Daybreak take to improve their business ethics? Was it successful? What else could they have done?

*Watch the Case study commentary on the **DVD-ROM**.*

Writing

Write a press release summarising the outcome of the meeting. Include these points:

- admit mistakes were made in the past;

- empathise with parents, children and nutritionists;

- say you are committed to reducing sugar/salt in children's cereals;

- explain what further steps you will take to improve Daybreak's business ethics.

➡ *Writing file page 148*

2 Ethical international business

A Work in pairs. Say whether you agree or disagree with these ideas with respect to your country's culture.

1 Business leaders in my country are generally honest and trustworthy.

2 Our manufacturing industries always respect the environment.

3 The ethics of an international business should override any national or local culture.

4 Socially responsible companies are more prosperous.

B ◀)) CD2.28 Listen to an ethics expert talking about accountability in business. Correct the five factual errors in this summary.

All companies worldwide are now more accountable for their ethical conduct. Businesses are checking their activities using internal and national standards of accountability. These frameworks are flawed, however, because they are too industry-specific. The expert believes that companies should address the same set of ethical issues regardless of their sector. A responsible business may also be listed on a sustainable index, such as the FTSE4Good index in the USA.

C ◀)) CD2.29 Listen to the second part of the interview and answer these questions.

1 How might trust be lost in business ethics?

2 What can companies do to regain public trust?

3 What kind of attitude to ethics did the defence and aerospace industry previously have?

4 What exactly was the Woolf Committee?

5 Which international code(s) of conduct for defence and aerospace companies are mentioned?

D Look at these statements about business ethics at work and say which ones are true for your culture (NT = not true, GT = generally true, AT = always true). Compare your answers in pairs.

1 You don't get anywhere in life by following the rules.

2 Choosing the right suppliers largely depends on whether you like them or not.

3 It always helps if you went to the same school or university as the person who's hiring you.

4 If you become a trade-union representative, you'll never get promoted.

5 In a job interview, it's usual to ask a woman if she's planning to have a family.

6 Disagreeing with your boss might cost you your job.

7 It is acceptable to criticise management and work colleagues on a personal blog.

8 There is a significant black economy, and tax avoidance at all levels is very common.

E Work in two groups. What would you do or say in each of the situations? Try to reach consensus. When you have finished, present your situations and conclusions.

Group A: See below.   Group B: Turn to page 157.

Group A
BRIBING PUBLIC OFFICIALS

Your company has been waiting for planning permission for a long time now in order to renovate its head offices, which are in a protected building in a historic part of the city. If the future project goes ahead, you would be put in charge of supervising the work. In a meeting with the city's Mayor, she insinuates she could push for the local council to approve the project with a little 'financial support' from your company in the coming election. An added complication is that the Mayor is an old friend from university days – but you have been trying to keep this quiet. The Mayor leaves the room momentarily and your boss asks for advice. Bearing in mind bribery is common practice in certain business sectors, what do you say?

DISASTER STRIKES

There has been a major oil spill off the coast in your country. A week has gone by, and oil continues to spill into the sea, ruining the coastline, destroying marine life and affecting tourism. Engineers, marine biologists, conservationists and volunteers are all working around the clock. You are the CEO of the oil company, and anything you say seems to make matters worse. One option is to resign quickly in return for a pay off. You are due to give another press conference tomorrow, but the engineers are nowhere near solving the problem. It has transpired that the security alarms were switched off at the time of the disaster so that workers on night duty could get some sleep. What are you going to say? How can the company regain the public's trust?

Task

You are members of an internal ethics committee for Wright International, a multinational. The committee is investigating wrong-doing in the organisation around the world. Consider these four points that have been brought to the committee's attention.

- The hospitality expense claims of various sales departments are very high.
- Bribing government officials is common in some areas, e.g. one director has regularly given generous donations from company funds to the ruling political party.
- Members of the same family are working together in one of the branches.

- There is an ongoing legal dispute in one subsidiary concerning a temporary employee who fell off the roof during routine maintenance and was badly injured. The company has paid out minimum compensation, but the former employee is going to appeal to the courts.

In groups of four or five, hold a meeting using the agenda below to decide which situations need to be dealt with most urgently and what should be done in each case. Then compare your decisions with another group and see if you agree on the best course of action.

Wright International
Corporate Governance Agenda: Better ethics; better business results

1 Anti-corruption programme:
    1.1 Gifts and hospitality
    1.2 Political donations and contributions
    1.3 Nepotism and abuse of personal contacts
    1.4 Health and safety
2 Internal audit programme, e.g. accounting and expense claims, government funding, etc.
3 AOB

4 Marketing

Complete the article below with the words and phrases in the box.

| attract customised loyalty scheme marketers marketing tool online |
| personalise privacy concerns reductions social networks special offers store |

FT

Best Buy taps promotions into smartphones

by Don Sull

Best Buy, the electronics retailer, has become the first leading US retailer to start sending ....[1] and deals to customers' smartphones when they walk into one of its stores. Best Buy stores have deployed a location-based ....[2] developed by Shopkick.

Customers who activate the Shopkick application on their phones will automatically receive 'kickbucks' credits just for entering the ....[3] that can be traded for benefits, including gift cards or music downloads. Best Buy will also use the system to send participants in its ....[4] promotional offers that can be ....[5] to reflect customers' shopping history and interests.

Best Buy said that combining location technology and rewards in order to ....[6] shopping was at the heart of their business strategy. Price ....[7] are then automatically deducted from the bill at the store's checkouts. The Shopkick application responds to an audio signal that is transmitted in the store. It is far more accurate than GPS-based alternatives, which can be off by a few hundred metres, and which

raise ....[8] because they are automatically activated.

Recent years have seen the emergence of a number of location-based systems with marketing applications for ....[9]. They allow ....[10] to offer credits or local promotions to phone users who 'check in' to locations such as coffee shops. Mobile shopping applications are likely to become increasingly important to retailers as they seek to ....[11] shoppers with smartphones that can compare prices ....[12] at rival stores.

Complete this blog with the six missing relative pronouns.

Q: What's the difference between a brand and a reputation?

Expert 1: Brands certainly contribute to a company's reputation, but they are not always synonymous. You can have a great, powerful brand in a company reputation has been damaged. Conversely, you can have some companies enjoy a great reputation, but don't own any world-class brands.

There are aspects of the company's reputation will affect their brands. We're seeing increasing evidence that a company's corporate social responsibility policies can have a very strong impact on how people feel about their brands. As more consumers worry about obesity, leading fast-food brands have altered their menus to provide healthier choices, has led to significant growth as a result.

Expert 2: Interesting question, because a strong brand might have co-existed in the past with a weak reputation for ethical manufacturing. I think a brand is a product or a service, while a reputation is something attached to the parent company. When both have the same name, it can be difficult to untangle the two. The people go out and buy the product are not always the same ones notice corporate reputations. The danger is when a bad corporate reputation starts to tarnish a brand.

SKILLS

1 Match the halves of these extracts from a presentation on social CRM.

1 Today we're looking at social CRM: what is it,

2 As you know, social CRM emerged via the Internet,

3 It has led to organisations losing control of the customer relationship.

4 So, if you're a large retailer, you're probably

5 Let's break down the meaning of *social*, shall we? And here

6 According to Kolsky, whereas social media is about tools and short-term tactics,

7 If there's one thing I'd like you to remember, it's that CRM is not hype. It's about

a) *Customers* are now more in control and have more freedom to talk amongst themselves.

b) and is it a source of real business value?

c) I'd like to refer to the definitions of CRM expert, Esteban Kolsky.

d) reinventing your organisation to collaborate with employees, partners and customers.

e) social CRM is about setting long-term goals for working better with your customers.

f) getting back into the conversations controlled by your customers.

g) social networks and online communities.

2 Match the extracts in Exercise 1 (1–7) to these techniques for making an impact (a–f). Some of the extracts use more than one technique.

a) Quoting someone

b) Asking rhetorical questions

c) Emphasising key words or phrases

d) Listing things in threes

e) Building rapport, e.g. including the audience

f) Calling for action

-*ING* FORMS AND INFINITIVES

5 Employment trends

1 Complete these sentences with the verbs in brackets in the correct form. The verbs are not given in the correct order.

1 He thinks .... self-employed might .... more rewarding than .... for someone else. (*work / be / be*)

2 It's virtually impossible .... a job for life nowadays. The worst thing about .... a freelancer is the insecurity of .... what you'll be doing in six months' time. (*be / not know / find*)

3 Scandinavian companies can often .... flexible working hours, the chance .... from home, and are more likely .... extended maternity or paternity leave. (*give / work / offer*)

4 She enjoys .... several part-time jobs, although .... track of her diary and .... different projects is hard work. (*juggle / keep / have*)

5 The downside of .... as a hotel manager is the shift work and .... to give up your weekends. The upside is the freedom .... on holiday out of season. (*go / work / have*)

6 .... talented staff is only one part of an HR department's many functions: .... and .... them are the others. (*train / retain / recruit*)

7 If we're supposed .... staff attrition rates and absenteeism, we seriously need .... how .... stress in our call centre. (*manage / look at / reduce*)

8 We really must .... the way we think about work and retirement. People who wan to carry on .... after the age of 65 should be able .... so. (*change / do / work*)

2 Complete the article below with the verbs in the box in the correct form.

be	be	devise	fix	include	listen	meet	range
set up	take over	think	work				

FT

Your company on the couch

by Charles Wallace

Larry Gould is a psychoanalyst on Manhattan's Upper West Side. His consultations are based on the teachings of Wilfred Bion, a British psychiatrist who pioneered the study of group behaviour. Bion helped ....[1] ways to select officers in the British army in the Second World War.

Mr Gould spends about half his time ....[2] executives who have hired him ....[3] apparently intractable company problems, ...[4] from labour disputes to low morale. He cites one example of ....[5] with an international airline. It had experienced difficult labour relations between the pilots and managers for five years.

After ....[6] to the pilots, he realised they all felt like orphans. 'Over a long period of time, pilots went from ....[7] heroes to ....[8] interchangeable commodities that no longer have status,' he says. The pilots were very anxious because of the upheavals in the airline industry that led to a succession of management teams ....[9] in a short space of time.

Mr Gould proposed ....[10] a committee of senior management and pilots, who would meet ....[11] about how to present these issues and see if some headway could be made. The committee met regularly with two facilitators, and the company reported that the two sides were finally dealing with the underlying issues, ...[12] the pilots' status.

WRITING

Rewrite this e-mail so that it sounds more polite and neutral in tone.

To:	All staff
cc:	Managing Director
Re:	Sick joke

Hi everyone

Whoever was responsible for 'borrowing' one of the projectors, can you pls return it ASAP!!! I was really annoyed this morning when I'd previously booked PRO-5 but ended up spending half an hour looking for it just before I was supposed to be presenting this quarter's office expenses. You are all perfectly aware that such equipment is COMPANY PROPERTY and should only be used ON THE COMPANY PREMISES by IT technicians and managers, like yours truly.

If no one owns up by the end of the week, we have ways of finding out ...
You know who you are!!

Office Manager

---

6 Ethics

MODAL PERFECT

Think of a meeting you attended recently that didn't go to plan or wasn't as effective as it could have been. What should have been done or said? Write five sentences.

EXAMPLE: *We should have started and finished on time.*

VOCABULARY

Complete this article with words related to business ethics and working conditions. The first few letters of each word have been given.

FT

Ethics: Islands of best practice

by Jane Bird

Unilever is proud of the medical care, schooling, clean water and re...........¹ energy it provides for the 20,000 workers on its tea plantation in Kenya. The site sets sta...........² the company aims to replicate worldwide.

Unilever produces about 12 per cent of the world's black tea and has started implementing Rainforest Alliance certification for sus...........³ farming. Organisations such as the Rainforest Alliance and Ethical Trading Initiative (ETI) include working con...........⁴ in their certification standards. But even a company as big as Unilever struggles to meet these.

Unilever was recently rep...........⁵ for the high proportion of temporary workers at its tea factory in Pakistan. Hundreds of its employees were employed on lo...........-p...........⁶ temporary contracts. Unilever has agreed to 200 permanent contracts.

Factors such as the 'casualisation' of the workforce are among the biggest problems. M...........⁷ workers often work very long hours harvesting seasonal crops such as grapes and producing turkeys at Christmas says the ETI.

Improvements are being made, partly because supermarkets need to identify their sou...........⁸, and partly because of awa...........⁹

heightened by incidents such as the deaths of Chinese workers at Morecambe Bay, England, in 2004.

The food industry is under pressure to ta...........¹⁰ responsibility for supply chains, says Rainforest Alliance. 'Consumers increasingly expect their food to be from farms where people are treated with re...........¹¹. Companies didn't use to know where their products came from, but there is now an effort to understand this and get workers' rights included in their social and environmental res...........¹²'.

SKILLS

Correct the wrong word in each of these sentences.

1 What you finally decide is completely round to you.

2 Oh dear, that's a sticky one. Decisions, decisions …

3 You have to weigh up the mods and cons.

4 I shouldn't do that right now if I were you. If it were up to me, I'd wait a bit.

5 On balance, I think you should say yes. On the other arm, you might want to say 'maybe'.

6 What I would say, although, is don't do anything unless you're absolutely sure.

Cultures 2: Ethical international business

Complete the extract below with the words in the box.

alarmed criticised cut back fault food-makers irresponsibly obesity processed put pressure responsibility

When food companies were ....¹ for producing too much junk food, confectionery and snack ....² claimed the obesity epidemic was not their ....³. Lack of exercise, not diets, was the problem they said. But early attempts to avoid ....⁴ backfired as the extent of the problem became clear. Adult ....⁵ is now the third biggest cause of premature death in the affluent world. ....⁶ at how fast obesity rates were rising, governments ....⁷ on food companies to ....⁸ on fats, salts and sugars. But critics say food-makers are still continuing to promote their products ....⁹, such as offering three for the price of two, as well as introducing ....¹⁰ foods into emerging markets where people have traditionally had a healthier diet.

Presentations

Objectives

Speaking
Can compare the advantages and disadvantages of possible approaches and solutions to an issue or problem.

Listening
- Can evaluate the strength of a speaker's argument in a linguistically complex presentation or discussion.

- Can recognise the use of persuasive language in a linguistically complex presentation or lecture.

Lesson deliverable
To plan, prepare and give a presentation about the pros and cons of a workplace issue.

Performance review
To review your own progress and performance against the lesson objectives at the end of the lesson.

A SPEAKING 1

Choose one of these opinions. Work in pairs and list two points in agreement and two not in agreement.

> **Recycling is a waste of time.**

> **Some companies create but most just copy.**

> **Only boring people work in offices.**

> You can never spend too much money on advertising.

> People should be allowed to bring their pets to work.

B LISTENING 1

1 Norway was the first country to introduce 40% quotas for women in the boardroom. Does a similar quota exist in your country?

2 Discuss some of the pros and cons of quotas for women on company boards. What is your opinion?

3 ◀)) BSA2.1.5 Listen to a presentation at an international conference about quotas for women. Is the speaker in favour of quotas or against them? What is her main message?

4 ◀)) BSA2.1.5 Listen again and note down the pros and cons of quotas she mentions.

Pros	Cons

5 Which arguments do you think are the strongest and the weakest? Work in pairs and agree on the three best.

C LISTENING 2

1 ◀)) BSA2.1.6 Listen to six extracts from the presentation. Decide which rhetorical technique the presenter uses each time, in order to sound more persuasive.

Rhetorical techniques	Extracts
a extreme adjectives and adverbs	
b metaphor	
c superlative forms	
d repetition of a word or phrase	
e a controversial statement	
f inversion	

2 Look at audio script BSA2.1.5. Find more examples of the rhetorical techniques mentioned in Exercise 1

3 Turn to page viii. Listen to the extracts and practise the pronunciation.

D SPEAKING 2

1 Work in two groups.

Group A: Brainstorm the pros and cons of a workplace dress code.

Group B: Brainstorm the pros and cons of using social media in business.

2 Choose two pros and two cons of the issue you discussed and choose one or two rhetorical techniques from Section C. Prepare and give a short presentation to a student from the other group.

Task

Pre-task: Discussion

Look at an extract from the programme for the Smarter Working conference. What issues do you think will be mentioned in these two presentations?

Smarter Working

Hot-desking: a permanent desk is history.

Going paperless: is it possible?

Part 1: Preparation

You are presenters at the Smarter Working conference. Work in small groups. Half of the groups are Team A, half are Team B. Prepare a short presentation (3–5 minutes).

Team A: The title of your presentation is *Hot-desking: a permanent desk is history*.

Team B: The title of your presentation is *Going paperless: is it possible?*

Brainstorm ideas and make notes about the pros and cons of the two workplace issues. (There are extra ideas in the texts on page ix.)

Prepare your presentation. Think about:

Structure
- Agree on your main message. Make this clear at the beginning and end of your presentation.
- Choose strong pros and cons to include in your presentation.

Techniques and language
- Include at least three different rhetorical techniques in order to sound persuasive.
- Look at audio script BSA2.1.5 on page ii again. Identify at least one linguistically complex phrase/sentence you could incorporate into your presentation.

Part 2: Presentations

Presenters: Use the guidance in Part 1. Give your presentation.

Audience: Note down the pros and cons. Identify any persuasive rhetorical techniques you noticed.

E PEER REVIEW

Decide which arguments used by the other teams were the strongest, and why. Which persuasive language was most effective? Give feedback and make suggestions.

F SELF-ASSESSMENT

Look back at the lesson objectives. What linguistically complex language did you use to suggest the pros and cons of a topic? What did you do well? What would you change next time?

G PROFESSIONAL DEVELOPMENT AND PERFORMANCE GOALS

Write three sentences about ways you will present pros and cons in your presentations in future.

Meetings

Objectives

Speaking

- Can develop an argument with appropriate highlighting of significant points and relevant supporting detail.

- Can participate in extended, detailed professional discussions and meetings with confidence.

Lesson deliverable

- To plan, prepare and participate in a crisis meeting by the end of the lesson.

- To write a short business report.

Performance review

To review your own progress and performance against the lesson objectives at the end of the lesson.

A SPEAKING 1

In pairs, discuss the following points. Make a list of ideas and then share it with the rest of the class.

1   How can you use your voice to best effect when expressing an opinion or giving important information? Think about speed and pausing, for example.

2   What other techniques can you use to get your point across effectively?

B LISTENING

1   ◀)) BSA2.2.7–BSA2.2.8 Listen to version A of the first part of a meeting. Then listen to version B. In pairs, decide which version is more effective and why. Then share your thoughts with the group.

2   ◀)) BSA2.2.8 Listen to version B again. Write down the four sentences between 'Let's get this meeting underway' and 'I'm afraid it's going to be quite a long day!'

3   Check your answers to Exercise B2 using the audio script on page iii. In pairs, underline any structures in the four sentences which add emphasis.

C PRONUNCIATION

Look at the four sentences you wrote down in Exercise B2. In pairs, practise delivering the introduction effectively.

D SPEAKING 2

1 You are going to participate in a crisis meeting. Using the agenda below and the notes opposite, work in pairs and write the dialogue between the meeting leader and a participant. Mark intonation and pauses.

Agenda

Aim: Crisis Meeting

1   35% drop in sales turnover

2   50% rise in customer complaints

3   20% employee turnover

4   40% increase in absenteeism rate

2 Use the meeting leader's opening statement provided. Practise delivering the dialogue as effectively as possible.

Meeting leader: *Right, so let's start with the first item on the agenda.*

Meeting leader	Participant
• large drop in turnover / 1st time witnessed / this company	• not surprised / lots of mistakes made
• only one other downturn / company 20 year history	• CRM system upgraded 2 years ago / product upgrade better
• how dropped / by 35%?	• should have followed competitors' example
	• would not have dropped from 2nd to 5th position in market

3 🔊 BSA2.2.9 Listen to a model answer and compare it with your dialogue.

Task

Pre-task: Preparation

In groups of four or five, plan a meeting to discuss a difficult situation. Use either the agenda provided in Section D above or change the issues to suit your company or organisation.

- If you change the topics, make a fresh agenda.
- Decide on roles. You will need a Meeting Leader, a Human Resources Manager, a Marketing Manager, a Finance Manager and at least one Observer.
- Turn to page x for your role cards. (These may need to be adapted if you set your own agenda.)
- Prepare some effective arguments before the meeting.

Part 1: Meeting

Hold your meeting, using the emphatic language practised in Section B, and agree on a set of actions to be taken.

- Audio or video record the meeting if possible, or perform it to the class.
- Refer to language for emphasising your point in Exercise B3 and language for the modal perfect on page 134.
- Use the role cards on page x to role-play your meeting.

Part 2: Report writing

Work in pairs. Write a short report outlining a set of actions arising from the meeting.

◎ **Extra practice: DVD clip and Worksheet 18**

E PEER REVIEW

Allow the observers to give feedback on your performance. Review the audio/video recording if you have one.

- What worked well?
- What examples of emphatic language did you hear?

F SELF-ASSESSMENT

Write a 150-word report to assess your performance in the meeting. Think about these questions:

- How successfully have you achieved the business skills objectives?
- What improvements do you need to make?
- How are you going to make them?

G PROFESSIONAL DEVELOPMENT AND PERFORMANCE GOALS

Identify two or three work or study situations in which you will be able to continue to practise or further develop the skills set out in the lesson objectives.

LISTENING AND DISCUSSION
Sustainable banking

A **Discuss these questions.**

1 Would you describe yourself as a spender, a saver or an investor? What is the difference between a saver and an investor?

2 Look at these savers' and investors' comments. Which statements are closest to your own attitude?

> I'll leave my money in a savings account. It's low interest, but safe.

> I'd go for a high rate of return, regardless of the risks.

> I'll always opt for less return, but with a trade-off of less risk.

> Transparency in how my money is invested is important to me.

> I'd never invest in anything I didn't fully understand.

> It's essential that my money goes into ethical investments.

> I'd be happy to buy shares in the company I work for.

B ◀)) CD2.30 **Listen to the first part of an interview with Charles Middleton, UK Managing Director of Triodos Bank. Complete this summary using a maximum of three words in each gap.**

Triodos Bank invests in projects that have a positive ....[1] and ....[2] impact. The bank's business model involves working with the ....[3]. Triodos depositors are mostly ....[4] rather than ....[5]. Triodos funds projects that are ....[6], and the bank has ....[7] in these sectors. The return on investment is a combination of three factors: financial, social and environmental. This is known as the '............'.[8]

Charles Middleton

Watch the interview on the **DVD-ROM**.

C ◀)) CD2.31 **Listen to the second part of the interview. Correct the six errors in this information about the projects that Triodos invests in.**

> Triodos invests in over 9,500 projects. They cover a very limited range of activities. One such activity is nuclear energy. The bank is lending to some of the major providers in the EU. It is also financing some of the big providers of social networks, such as Mencap*. And it is involved in training activity, for instance with organisations like Café Direct, a major wholesale provider of hot drinks. The bank provides these organisations with debt funding, so the return is just the interest on the loan.

* A UK charity for people with learning disabilities and their families

D **What changes to the banking system would you like to see? Why?**

E ◀)) CD2.32 **Listen to the third part of the interview. Which two changes would Charles Middleton like to see, and why?**

F **Which of the words in each group does** *not* **form a word partnership with the noun in bold? Think of another word partnership for each noun.**

1	sustainable / investment / customer / commercial	**bank**
2	bad / national / loan / external	**debt**
3	money / debt / public / crisis	**funding**
4	interest-free / savings / short-term / bridging	**loan**
5	booming / black / real / deposit	**economy**
6	down / fair / free /overseas	**trade**

G **Complete each group of sentences below with the correct form of one of the words in the box.**

> deposit   expose   invest   lend

1   a) .... in property is no longer as safe as it used to be.

  b) Foreign .... are showing considerable interest in the venture.

  c) Buying shares in blue-chip companies is always a sound ....

2   a) A lot of banks are unwilling to .... money to new businesses.

  b) House prices depend on the level of mortgage ....

  c) They were unable to keep up with their .... repayments.

3   a) The money will be .... into your account on the 25th of the month.

  b) We've put down a 10 per cent .... on the flat.

  c) The government has agreed to cover all savers' .... at the troubled bank.

4   a) The global crisis has clearly left many bank customers financially ....

  b) The bank was concerned that employees' e-mail transactions might .... sensitive data.

  c) Oman's top banks said they had a total .... of $77 million to the troubled conglomerate.

H **Would you open an account with a sustainable bank as a a) retail client, or b) business client? Why? / Why not?**

A Which of these professions are paid high salaries or large bonuses in your country? Why do you think they receive such high awards?

accountants	air-traffic controllers	CEOs of multinationals	dentists
estate agents	government ministers	investment bankers	school teachers
social workers	top football managers	TV presenters	

B Which of these best summarises the headline of the article? Read the article quickly and check your answer.

a) How large bonuses led to the fall of investment banks

b) The end of incompetent banking as we know it

c) The collapse of the financial world because bankers couldn't count

FT

Day of reckoning for innumerate bankers

by Martin Taylor

The late Eddie George (a former governor of the Bank of England) was very fond of a little joke that went as follows: 'There are three types of bankers: those that can count and those that can't.' Sometimes jokes capture profound truths. In all the **fuss** about bank bonuses, we have heard about labour market 'realities' (from the bankers) and moral and political philosophy (from everybody else). We need to think more about simple arithmetic.

All businesspeople know that you can carry on for a while if you make no profits, but that if you run out of cash, you **are toast**. Bankers, as providers of cash to others, understand this well. They just do not believe it applies to their own business.

In general, banks have no measures of cashflow that work for banking. They do think about **liquidity** – can you borrow from other market participants, can you get money from the central bank? Being turned down in the market **means curtains** – it happened to Northern Rock in 2007 and Midland Bank a quarter of a century before, and forced its sale to HSBC.

That means banks are not conscious of making cash decisions of the sort that other businesses face daily. But, of course, they frequently make decisions with cash consequences, and in the mid-noughties, they began to splash out. The recipients were employees, in the form of bonuses, and, to a lesser but still significant extent, shareholders, in the form of **dividends**.

The existence of bonuses reflected

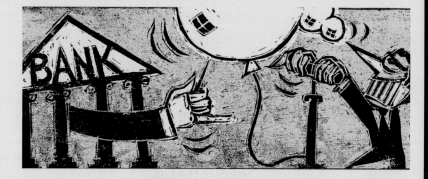

the nature of financial businesses, where labour always represented a major cost, while revenues were unpredictable. It therefore became essential to make labour costs variable, as banks couldn't always guarantee high profits, and bonuses were the mechanism used to do this.

People in **the City** have always been paid well relative to others, but megabonuses are quite new. From my own experience, in the mid-nineties, no more than four or five employees of Barclays' then investment bank were paid more than £1m, and no one got near £2m. Around the turn of the millennium, things began to take off and accelerated rapidly – after a pause in 2001–03 – so that exceptionally high remuneration was paid out between 2004 and 2007.

Observers of financial services saw unbelievable prosperity and apparently immense value added. Yet two years later, the whole industry was bankrupt. A simple reason underlies this: any industry that pays out in cash **colossal** accounting profits that are largely imaginary will **go bust** quickly. Not only has the indus-

try – and by extension societies that depend on it – been spending money that is no longer there, it has been giving away money that it only imagined it had in the first place. Worse, it seems to want to do it all again.

How could they pay this imaginary wealth out in cash to their employees? Because they had no measure of cashflow to tell them they were idiots, and because everyone else was doing it. Paying out 50 per cent of revenues to staff had become the rule, even when the 'revenues' did not actually consist of money.

How did the shareholders let them get away with this? They were **sitting on the gravy train** too, enjoying the views from the observation car. How did the directors let it happen? Innumeracy and inability to understand accounts. How depressing the **shame** and **folly** of it all is, when one considers that the system was brought down not because risk management was deficient (though it was), nor because greed was **rampant** (though it was), but because bankers could not count.

C   **The article was written by a former Chief Executive of Barclays Bank. Read it again and say which of these ideas are those of the writer. Which of the statements do you agree with?**

1   As everyone knows, if a business runs out of money, it eventually goes bankrupt.

2   Despite banks being concerned about liquidity and borrowing money, they have no systems in place for managing their own cashflow.

3   The financial crisis arose not because consumer spending was out of control, nor because the banks were out of control, but because the government was spending too much money.

4   The fact that some investment bankers received more than £2m in bonuses in the 1990s is not only unacceptable but also incomprehensible.

5   Professionals in banking and financial services deserve to be paid 50 per cent of revenues.

6   It is shameful to think that neither shareholders nor bank directors were able to prevent the financial crisis of 2008–09.

D   **Match these definitions to the words and expressions in bold in the article.**

1   are in trouble because of something you have done

2   an action that is very stupid and likely to have serious results

3   part of a company's profits divided between people with shares in the company

4   when there is a lot of something bad, such as crime or disease, and it is very difficult to control

5   when a business or person has money or goods that can be sold to pay debts

6   extremely big

7   area in the centre of London with many banks and financial institutions

8   being part of an activity from which people can make money without much effort

9   attention or excitement that is usually unnecessary or unwelcome

10 used to say that something will end (*informal*)

11 go bankrupt

12 feeling of being publicly embarrassed because of something wrong you did

E   **What do these multiword verbs mean in the article? What other meanings do you know for *turn down*, *take off*, *give away*, *get away (with)* and *bring down*?**

1 carry on (line 15)	4 splash out (line 38)	7 give away (line 77)
2 run out of (line 16)	5 take off (line 61)	8 get away with (line 91)
3 turn down (line 27)	6 pay out (line 64)	9 bring down (line 99)

F   **Which of the multiword verbs in Exercise E *don't* take an object? With verbs that do take an object, when does the order of the particle and object change? Use examples from the article and your own examples.**

➡ *Language reference: multiword verbs page 135*

G   **Discuss these questions.**

1   Which well-known banks or financial institutions have gone bankrupt or have run into financial difficulties in recent years? What happened?

2   How good is your organisation at managing its spending or cashflow?

3   How much money would you need to feel happy and prosperous?

BUSINESS SKILLS
Managing questions

A In what situations might you ask or be asked difficult questions?

B Where or when might you hear the questions below? Match the questions (1–6) to these situations (a–f).

a) a company audit
b) a meeting with a venture-capitalist firm
c) a job interview
d) a TV interview
e) a talk on banking bonuses
f) a political press conference

1 Yes, I have a question. What would you say about the fact that there are still many in the sector who are being paid an amount that is beyond the dreams of most people?

2 So, with all due respect, Mrs Collins, what you're really saying is you don't think the country's economy will improve until more jobs are created?

3 Do you think you could sum up your business idea in one minute? I mean, do you know exactly what kind of service you will be offering?

4 Perhaps I'm not making myself clear. Have you any idea what these expense claims are for?

5 I wonder if you could tell us where you imagine yourself to be in five years' time?

6 I'll rephrase the question, if I may. Our viewers would like to know at what point you realised that two million pounds had disappeared from the company's pension fund.

C ◀)) CD2.33–2.36 Listen to four speakers in situations from Exercise B, dealing with probing questions. Match the strategies they use (a–g) to the speakers (1–4). Some strategies are used more than once.

Speaker 1   a)   paraphrasing the question to check understanding and/or play for time

Speaker 2   b)   dealing with an interruption in order to continue speaking

Speaker 3   c)   avoiding the question by referring to a higher authority

Speaker 4   d)   admitting it's not the speaker's area of expertise/interest

           e)   referring to a knowledgeable colleague or source

           f)   building rapport, e.g. asking the questioner to identify him/herself, referring to the questioner by name, etc.

           g)   answering the question the speaker wants to answer and not the question asked

D Look at these presentation tips. Would you use any of these techniques for dealing with the question-and-answer session at the end of a presentation? Why? / Why not? What other strategies do you know of? Compare your ideas with a partner.

> **Presentation tips: Q&A**
>
> • Anticipate any tricky questions.
>
> • Paraphrase the question to check you've understood.
>
> • Don't leave questions until the end – it looks like you're avoiding them.
>
> • Invite questions after each slide or main point.
>
> • If someone asks more than one question, answer them separately.
>
> • If you don't know, refer the person to someone else, or say you'll follow up.
>
> • Approach the questioner and address the person by name if possible.
>
> • Make eye contact with the questioner, smile and open out your hands to show you are willing to answer the question.

E ◀)) CD2.37 **You are going to listen to a financier at a private equity firm giving a magazine interview called *Any Questions?*. What kinds of question do you think the interviewer will ask? Listen and check your answers. How were the interviewer's questions phrased differently from yours?**

F ◀)) CD2.37 **Listen again and tick the expressions in the Useful language box below that the interviewer used. When do we use more indirect question forms?**

G ◀)) CD2.37 **Listen again and complete some of the financier's answers using no more than three words in each gap.**

1 I.............and assess their management teams.

2 No. I've............a great deal richer than I ever imagined. When I was a young lad, I............what I wanted to do and someone advised me............private equity. Things just............there, really.

3 ...., without a doubt. He............out of nothing.

4 .... I hate doing it, but sometimes it's.............

5 It would have to be............ – I don't do it very often and then I.............

6 As a loving husband and father who lived life.............

H **Practise asking and answering five of the interview questions, or similar questions, with a partner. You can use these ideas.**

- Your job in 10 words
- Your worst job ever
- Your biggest influence
- A time you lied
- What you would have done if ...
- A 'guilty pleasure'
- A celebrity you'd like to invite to a meeting
- How you'd like to be remembered

I **Practise doing probing interviews in pairs. Choose one of these scenarios.**

- an interview with the Minister of Finance for a business news programme
- an internal company audit investigating expense claims
- a job interview with a bank
- a press conference with the Financial Director of a multinational, who is suspected of corruption

Student A: Turn to page 154.
Student B: Turn to page 160.

USEFUL LANGUAGE

ASKING QUESTIONS
Do you think you could ...?
Would you mind telling me ...?
I was wondering if/whether you ...
What would you say was/were ...?
Have you any idea ...?
I'd be interested to hear ...
I'd like to know/ask ...
I'm sure we'd all like to hear why ...

INSISTING ON THE QUESTION OR PROBING
Let me put it another way.
I'll rephrase the question.
Perhaps I'm not making myself clear.
Yes, but what I'd like to know is ...
With all due respect, you haven't answered my question.
Are you denying that ...?
Surely you're not saying ...?

PARAPHRASING THE QUESTION
So your question is, ...
I'm not sure (if) I entirely understand your question. Do you mean ...?
If I understand you correctly, ...
Are you asking/saying ...?

DEALING WITH INTERRUPTIONS
If I could just finish what I was saying, ...
If you'd just let me finish, ...
Hang on a minute. (*informal*)

DRAGONS & ANGELS

Angel investors quiz entrepreneurs to find the best new ventures to support

Background

Dragons & Angels (D&A) is a small syndicate of angel investors based in Edinburgh that provides companies and entrepreneurs with capital and expertise. Being part of a syndicate allows investors to make larger and more frequent investments. Some are successful entrepreneurs themselves.

D&A is prepared to back start-ups or established companies that are seeking to expand. The typical investment is from £50,000 to £500,000. The investors often attend face-to-face 'speed-funding' events, where they interview entrepreneurs in five minutes.

Angel investment is a risky business, but as one of D&A's senior partners puts it, 'Companies which might otherwise have financed growth plans through bank loans have had to consider equity, while investors who might traditionally have invested in the stock market or property are looking to diversify their portfolios to spread the risk.'

Research shows that business angels stand to make a significant profit by investing in start-up companies, with an average rate of return of 22 per cent over four years.

Task 1

Evaluating business ventures

You are investors from D&A and are planning to attend the next speed-funding event in Edinburgh. You can invest up to £500,000 in total and you may invest in more than one venture. Read the three profiles on the opposite page and evaluate the different entrepreneurs according to how successful and profitable you think their ventures will be. Then discuss these questions.

1 Which of the ventures sounds the most interesting and promising? Do any of the products have a distinct advantage in the marketplace?

2 How much money are you prepared to invest or lose?

3 Which business do you think will give you the best return on your investment?

4 What kind of stake would you be interested in as an investor, e.g. 30–40 per cent ownership?

5 What will your role be? Are you interested in being a 'sleeping' partner or taking an active role in the business?

Angel Investors Association

THIS WEEK'S ENTREPRENEURS

1 **Evan Griffiths, founder of E-sellers and maker of an e-reader**

Investment required: £400,000–£500,000, mainly product development for designing a smaller and smarter e-reader

Return on capital: 25%–30% over four years

'I'm the founder of E-sellers, an e-book publisher and online bookstore. We already have an 18 per cent share of the e-book market. I've now developed my own e-reader. I'm not worried by the competition from bigger companies. Their e-readers are over-priced or don't fit easily in a pocket or handbag like ours do. E-books and physical books will co-exist for many years. Whenever I buy a book, I usually buy two: one to have on the shelf and another to read on my e-reader.'

2 **Agnes and Morag McQueen, cheese makers and co-directors of McQueen's, an Edinburgh-based family business**

Investment required: £100,000–£125,000 for investing in renewable energy, expanding the current premises and taking on more staff

Return on capital: 20% over four years

'I'm joint director of McQueen's. We make quality Scottish goat's cheese, which I'm passionate about. Our customers value our environmental standards, quality and years of experience. We pride ourselves on organic farming and using resources more sparingly. We're trying to become a carbon-neutral company. That means we would also need to invest in alternative energy, which would reduce our greenhouse gas emissions even more. I think that would give us an edge over our competitors.'

3 **Danish adventurer Troels McClintock, Soul-air**

Investment required: £45–£55 million to build a solar-powered aircraft

Return on capital: 40%–45% over four years

Soul-air – the sky's the limit!
'My dream is to fly around the world in a solar plane. I want to demonstrate the potential of renewable energy. Airplane manufacturers are sceptical such a plane can be built, but I have always believed in thinking creatively and outside the box. Currently, we have a society based on oil dependency. The result is car manufacturers are going bankrupt. It's a typical example of people who did not make the turnaround early enough. Join me on this adventure of a lifetime – you won't regret it!'

🔊 **CD2.38 – 2.40** Listen to three investors at the speed-funding event asking the entrepreneurs questions and take notes. Which entrepreneur(s) dealt best with the questions? What other questions would you ask at this stage?

Task 2

Decision-making meeting

Work in groups. After the speed-funding event, compare notes as investors. Discuss these questions.

1 Which venture(s) will you invest in, and why? Does the product have a large and fast-growing market?

2 How much money will you invest collectively as a syndicate?

3 What will be your role in the business(es); for example, a mentor, a management advisor or a partner with a stake in the firm? How much control would you like?

4 What quality contacts could you pass on to the entrepreneur? Which of your family, friends or associates could be interested in the product(s) as potential customers?

Watch the Case study commentary on the DVD-ROM.

Writing

You are one of the investors at Dragons & Angels. Write an e-mail to a colleague who missed the presentations, proposing the business idea you would like to invest in. Include these points.

- Say why you want to invest in this particular venture.

- Mention the background and expertise of the entrepreneur or management team.

- Say how much money you have decided to invest and what kind of return on investment you expect (a minimum of 20 per cent at this stage).

- Briefly describe D&A's role in the venture.

➡ *Writing file page 145*

UNIT 8 | Consultants

'My greatest strength as a consultant is to be ignorant and ask a few questions.'
Peter F. Drucker (1909–2005), US management consultant and author

OVERVIEW

LISTENING AND DISCUSSION
Operations consulting

READING AND LANGUAGE
Day in the life of a management consultant
Ellipsis

BUSINESS SKILLS
Negotiating
Writing: summarising terms and conditions

CASE STUDY
New market opportunities

LISTENING AND DISCUSSION
Operations consulting

A **Discuss these questions.**

1 What sort of services do management consultancies provide?

2 Why do you think companies might hire management consultants?

3 What are the implied criticisms made about consultants in the comments below?

4 If these are the consultants' answers, what questions did the companies originally ask?

Top five things you'll never hear from your consultant

1 I don't know enough to speak intelligently about that.

2 How about paying us based on the success of the project?

3 Implementation? I only care about writing long reports.

4 Actually, the only difference is that we charge more than they do.

5 Everything looks OK to me. You really don't need me.

B **Complete the extract below about consultants using words and phrases in the box.**

best practices   brief   deliverable   implementation   operational
performance   scope   specialised expertise   tangible   techniques and methods

Management consultants can help organisations to improve their............[1]. They can provide external, objective advice and............[2] which companies do not have in-house. Because consultants work with multiple clients, they are also aware of industry............[3].

Companies typically hire consultants to help with financial management, human resources services, IT............[4], change management, strategy development and improving............[5] efficiency.

Consultants generally use their own ....[6] in order to identify problems, and recommend more effective and efficient ways of working. In the past, a consultancy's main ....[7] on a project was generally the report. Nowadays, clients want more............[8] and practical approaches to helping them stay in business. Critical, therefore, to the success of a project is agreeing the objectives and............[9] of the work, together with the benefits to be expected and how they will be measured. Clients need to provide as clear a ....[10] as possible, which identifies the value that the project will bring.

Peter Sirman

C ◀))) CD2.41 **Listen to the first part of an interview with Peter Sirman, Head of Operations Consulting at the PA Consulting Group, and complete each gap with between two and four words.**

Peter Sirman uses the phrase '............'[1] to explain what *operations* refers to. The first step in the consultation process is to find out what the company............[2] to its customers and to see how well they're actually doing that.

Operations is essentially about............[3], so it's important to understand what the customers want to ensure that the company is providing a............[4], a product that they like, and that this is happening every time to the right............[5]. Therefore, the consultants begin by talking to customers. These are quite detailed conversations about the............[6] that the customers value. This information can be used later to............[7] the company is delivering services and products.

D ◀))) CD2.42 **Listen to the next part of the interview and decide if these statements are true or false. Correct the false ones.**

1 The technique mentioned is called Value Stream Planning.

2 It is used to analyse all processes needed to deliver the goods or services.

3 The technique looks at the amount of money spent on each stage of the process.

4 It helps to identify where problems arise and any duplication of processes.

E ◀))) CD2.43 **Listen to the third part of the interview and answer these questions.**

1 What is the second phase of the consultants' work?

2 What type of advice might the consultants give a company at this stage?

3 What term is used for the time period between the beginning and end of a process?

4 What information is used to set targets?

5 What is identified in the second step?

F ◀))) CD2.44 **Listen to the final part of the interview and make a note of the three options that Peter Sirman mentions for improved performance.**

Watch the interview on the DVD-ROM.

G ◀))) CD2.44 **Listen to the last part of the interview again. How do Peter and his team try to win support for their recommendations?**

H **Discuss these questions.**

1 Why might the client staff be resistant to some of the ideas presented by operations consultants?

2 How can a company overcome this resistance?

3 How can consultants go about building trust when advising a company?

READING AND LANGUAGE

THE CONSULTANTS HANDBOOK PART 4:
A GOOD DOCUMENTATION IS ESSENTIAL FOR THE SUCCESS OF YOUR PROJECT

geek and poke

A Would you make a good management consultant? Do this quick quiz and find out. Then turn to page 150 to check your answers.

1 As a successful consultant, you should be familiar with management thinking, mostly so that you can impress people with how well-read you are. So which of these is NOT a management guru?

a) C.K. Prahalad b) Henry Mintzberg
c) James Dyson d) Tom Peters e) Rosabeth M. Kanter

2 Do you like the idea of getting paid for telling others what to do?

3 As part of the recruitment process, consultancy firms often give candidates logic puzzles. How would you answer this question: *Why are manhole covers typically round?* Do you enjoy this sort of task?

B Read the extract on the opposite page from a blog about a day in the life of a management consultant, then answer these questions.

1 What type of project is the consultant working on?

2 Why do you think a client might choose a consultant for this type of project?

3 How many formal and informal meetings does the consultant attend?

4 What impression does the blog give of the consultant and his attitude to the work?

5 What evidence is there to suggest the client is happy with some aspects of the project and less happy with others?

6 What setbacks and surprises were there during the day?

C Match the words and expressions in bold in the blog with these definitions and synonyms.

1 finishes a job, meeting, etc.

2 puts things into bags, etc. ready to finish work at the end of the day

3 read, look at or explain something quickly

4 decide on an agreement, contract, etc. after a lot of discussion and disagreement

5 read or discuss something in order to make sure it is correct

6 discussion about a job just done in order to gather information

7 follow up with certain people at a later point in time

8 spending time finding out what has been happening while you have been away

9 a trivial detail

10 filled with a large quantity of something

11 stop being worried or frightened about something

12 didn't include someone or something

D The consultant has often omitted certain words from the blog. This is typical of informal language use. Find five examples of this. What types of word have been omitted? Why do you think the writer does this?

➡ *Language reference: ellipsis* page 136

E What do you think you would enjoy most/least about this consultant's job? In what ways is it similar to your own daily life?

Day in the life of a management consultant

 **BLOG**

Background – I am on a four-member team (manager and three associates). We are on an operations turnaround project with a focus on personnel (read: reward the best employees, train the average ones, and develop systems to remove or improve the underperformers).

7:30 a.m. – Hotel alarm wakes me. I automatically reach for the BlackBerry. The Production team has e-mailed me with PowerPoint slides I sent them the data for last night. **Breathe sigh of relief**, as this means I won't have to spend two hours this morning getting my client presentation slides ready.

7:45 a.m. – BlackBerry buzzes. Manager says he'll be 15 minutes late this morning. The team usually meets in the hotel lobby to share a taxi to the client (client is particularly cost-conscious on this project). I contemplate going back to sleep until I look at my work shirts. All are wrinkled. No extra sleep for me.

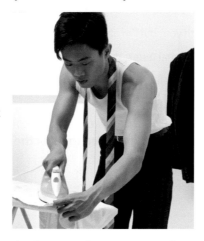

8:45 a.m. – Arrive at client headquarters. The CEO's secretary has just confirmed the CEO's attendance at today's monthly progress meeting. I do a quick scan of my e-mails and open the attachment from the Production team. Thankfully most look good – there are the usual typos, missing footnotes and weird alignment issues to fix, but could have been much worse.

10:30 a.m. – I've fixed all the minor issues with my part of the presentation or "the deck". I can now focus on cleaning out my inbox. It's **piled up** with e-mails from ex-teammates asking me questions about work I did on past projects, surveys and questionnaires, random forwards from friends and other analysts.

12 noon – Team meeting starts. The main partner on our team is dialling in from Toronto today.

12:30 p.m. – It's my turn to present. I carefully **run** them **through** the slides—partner has **a small nit** on the source for a particular chart. I realize I **left out** the footnote. Damn!

1 p.m. – Team meeting ends. Partner **wraps up** by mentioning that the senior client had some questions recently about scope being too narrow (i.e. we're not doing enough), and has scheduled a late-afternoon call with the broader team (read: more partners) to **hammer out** this issue. I wonder if this means workload will increase.

1:30 p.m. – We're at lunch, and have invited some of the four-member client team. Through the last eight weeks, we've built strong working relationships with them–and through forced socializing have gotten to know them.

2 p.m. – Client meeting starts.

2:10 p.m. – CEO enters room. She smiles, shakes each of our hands—I briefly wonder if she'll ask me how old I am as she shakes mine. But no—they're too professional for that.

2:45 p.m. – Manager is leading CEO through one of my slides. The CEO points at a graph and says, "Wow, is this really the improvement you've been seeing?" Everyone rotates their heads toward me. My time to shine. I quickly share facts and figures that by now I've memorized. Manager flashes a relieved smile, and the CEO nods in silence.

3 p.m. – Meeting over! CEO seems happy with our findings. Mentions to partner on phone (with whom she's worked several times before) that once again, he found an excellent team. CEO says she looks forward to seeing where we'll be by project end (in four weeks' time). Our team heads back to our room for a post-meeting **debrief**.

4 p.m. – Scope issue discussion call with three partners begins. Manager spends next hour in increasing frustration as partners cannot agree on anything. Two of the partners have to leave for another meeting. Finally, the lead partner tells us that he'll **circle back** with the other two partners to try and reach consensus. We return to our laptops.

5:30 p.m. – Receive large e-mail attachment from client team. It's new employee performance data gathered from this quarter. I **go through** the data—it's a mess. This is going to take hours to clean up.

6:15 p.m. – Manager **packs up** and suggests we pack up early. Tomorrow, we have a busy schedule packed with client interviews. We all jump into a taxi back to the hotel. Manager is **having a catch-up** call with our partner. I plan out my night—which will include the gym, room-service dinner, and several hours spent cleaning and incorporating the new data in time for tomorrow.

BUSINESS SKILLS
Negotiating

A **Discuss these questions.**

1 What kind of things do you negotiate in your daily life?

2 How effective are these negotiating styles?

   A) Playing the 'tough guy'; being persistent in stating your demands and negotiating as long and hard as possible until the other person finally gives in

   B) Being flexible; being prepared to make concessions when appropriate and achieving a win–win situation, although you may not get everything you want

   C) Staying 'silent'; pausing between sentences, listening more and talking less so that the other person trusts you and is more vulnerable

B **Match these negotiating techniques (1–4) with what the negotiators actually say (a–h). What other negotiating techniques do you know?**

1 Explaining the value of a concession

2 Testing the situation

3 Responding to an unacceptable concession

4 Checking with a higher authority

A) What if I take 4,000 units? How much would that cost me?

B) Yes, and your sales also increased because of that, right?

C) Let me run this by my boss and I'll get back to you, OK?

D) I see … (*silence*)

E) What would you say if we were to extend the deadline by a fortnight or so?

F) I'd like to do business with you, but I'm afraid we're simply too far apart.

G) We'll pay for the delivery. In real terms, that's a saving of about €500.

H) Here she is! Well, if you don't mind, our Purchasing Manager will take over from here.

C **Complete a sales manager's notes below on making concessions with the words and phrases in the box. What do you think of the advice?**

| understands its full value   'take-it-or-leave-it'   big concession   walk away |
| some sort of compensation   willing to make concessions   get a concession |
| ill-will   one by one |

Sales negotiations: making concessions

1 Don't give the first ....

2 Don't assume you have to match your customers' concessions ....

3 Don't give a concession away without ....

4 Never give away a concession unless the customer ....

5 The best time to .... is when you're offering one.

6 Whatever you do, don't advertise you're ....

7 The .... offer is unacceptable – it only creates ....

8 If the customer isn't planning to buy, you need to ....

D 🔊 **CD2.45, 2.46 Listen to two negotiations and answer these questions.**

1 How effective were the negotiators?

2 Which techniques did they use?

3 How would you describe their relationships?

E Which of these expressions did you hear the supplier (S) and the buyer (B) use in Exercise D? Which expressions sound more tentative or polite (T)?

Negotiation 1

I was wondering if you could deliver a bit sooner.

Maybe we could talk a little about terms of payment at this point?

We could deliver sooner, provided you paid in cash.

I suppose I could look into it.

I'd have to check with my supervisor first.

He'd have to confirm the payment terms, you see.

What if we delivered one week earlier and you gave us ...?

I think that should be do-able.

Leave it with me. I'll see what I can do.

I'll wait to hear from you, then.

Negotiation 2

Actually, it seems a couple of the products aren't doing that well.

It might do better if it wasn't in a 500g container.

So, we were wondering whether you'd be able to ...

Our usual price is ... But for *you*, we're offering it at ...

That's a 5% saving.

What would you say to a 10% discount?

So, do we agree on €9 per bottle, then?

It's always good doing business with you.

You'll put it all in writing, won't you?

Consider it a deal.

F Work in pairs to negotiate situations. Use different negotiating techniques and expressions from Exercises B and E. When you have finished, discuss how successful the outcomes were.

Student A: Turn to page 155.
Student B: Turn to page 161.

Writing: summarising terms and conditions

G Look at the writing expressions in the Useful language box below. Would you use them with someone you a) know quite well, or b) don't know very well? Why? Can you think of any alternative expressions that are more formal?

H Write an e-mail summarising what was agreed in one of your negotiations in Exercise F. Then check your partner's summary. Did you describe the same terms and conditions?

➡ *Writing file* page 145

USEFUL LANGUAGE

OPENING REMARKS

I'm writing to confirm what we discussed in our meeting / phone call this morning.

I'm sending you a copy of our agreement as we discussed on ...

CONFIRMING

We're pleased / We'd like to offer you ...

As we discussed in our meeting/call, our usual terms are ...

As for payment and delivery, ...

When it comes to / Re delivery charges, I'd (just) like to point out ...

WHEN THINGS GO WRONG

If (*this happens*), please remember / don't forget that ...

In case ..., please remember ...

MAKING A REQUEST

Could/Can you please confirm your order by e-mail as soon as possible?

Could/Can you confirm ..., please? Thanks.

CLOSING REMARKS

If you need any more information / have any questions, just phone/e-mail me.

Please let me know if ...

Looking forward to doing business with you (again).

New market opportunities

A consulting firm is asked to study the mobile phone market in South Africa for a new client

Background

Heitinga T-com Consulting is a consultancy based in Johannesburg, South Africa. The latest dossier lying on the senior partners' desks is from Bajaj-tel, one of India's largest mobile operators, which sees market opportunities in South Africa's fast-growing telecom market.

Bajaj-tel has ambitious plans to buy African networks and become a global operator focused on emerging markets. Bajaj-tel would like Heitinga T-com to help with this huge project. One of the advantages of Bajaj-tel is its low-cost model, which it has pioneered in India.

However, Bajaj-tel must contend with competition from other foreign operators in the African market. The valuation of the South African network is US $24bn, but a deal could be rejected on the grounds of regulatory objections from the government, which regards South African SANphone as a national champion.

South Africa's public investment in past sports tournaments has significantly improved its infrastructure and productivity. Together with Brazil and India, South Africa forms the G3 group of developing economies. Although it has a population of under 50 million and its economy is the smallest of the three countries, South Africa's influence in Africa makes it an attractive business partner.

Task 1

Preliminary meeting

Work in groups of two pairs.

You are in a meeting to discuss telecom opportunities in the South African market. Annabel Kuper, a junior consultant from Heitinga T-com, has already presented the preliminary feasibility report – item 1 on the agenda. You now have a 20-minute break in which you can consult your respective partners. Look at the meeting agenda and your information before you start the meeting.

Students A and B: You are consultants at Heitinga T-com.   Turn to page 155.
Students C and D: You are representatives of Bajaj-tel.   Turn to page 161.

🔊 **CD2.47** Listen to a meeting between one of the consultancy's senior partners, Jeff Carstens, Annabel Kuper and Sunil Sukkawala, Chief of Finance at Bajaj-tel. Make a note of the opportunities and challenges you foresee in working with the new Indian client.

Heitinga T-com Consulting

Meeting with Bajaj-tel

1   Presentation of the preliminary feasibility study: the Bajaj-tel project in South Africa ✓

2   Immediate deliverables required of the consultancy, e.g. an in-depth research study? Discussion of estimated schedule and cost

3   Long-term deliverables required by the client, e.g. implementation and follow-up

4   The project management team – in case of implementation

5   Confirmation of Heitinga T-com's fees, e.g. preliminary feasibility study, meetings, etc.

6   AOB

Task 2

Negotiation

Work in groups of two pairs. It's the same day, but the Bajaj-tel negotiating team changes because their CEO has now arrived at the consultancy. Study your information and prepare your strategy before you negotiate with your client. You will need to double-check anything that was agreed in the first meeting. Be prepared for possible interruptions.

Students A and B: You are consultants at Heitinga T-com. Turn to page 154.

Students C and D: You are Bajaj-tel directors. Turn to page 162.

Writing

You are one of the consultants. Write a formal e-mail to your client summarising the main points of the negotiation. Include these points.

- Confirm the deliverables of the project, e.g. reports, role as advisors, implementation, etc.

- Mention any important milestones – remember, your client is keen to set up the network in 12 months' time.

- Confirm the consultancy fees to date.

- Add any other fees or terms and conditions negotiated.

→ *Writing file* page 145

 Watch the Case study commentary on the DVD-ROM.

UNIT 9 Strategy

'However beautiful the strategy, you should occasionally look at the results.'
Winston Churchill (1874–1965), British Prime Minister

OVERVIEW

LISTENING AND DISCUSSION
Strategy, goals and values

READING AND LANGUAGE
Living strategy and death of the five-year plan
Rhetorical questions

BUSINESS SKILLS
Brainstorming and creativity
Writing: mission statements

CASE STUDY
Stella International Airways: strategy for the skies

LISTENING AND DISCUSSION
Strategy, goals and values

A Look at the statements below about company goals and strategy. To what extent do you agree? Justify your ideas to your partner by giving examples.

PA = partially agree   PD = partially disagree
CA = completely agree   CD = completely disagree

1   Any organisation should only have to communicate its business strategy to management, shareholders and investors.

2   A successful business should make a positive contribution to society.

3   A good company should mainly focus on competitive pricing and good profits.

4   The greatest companies can make an impact on the way consumers shop, think and behave.

Marjorie Scardino

Watch the interview on the DVD-ROM.

B ◀))) CD3.1 **Listen to the first part of an interview with Marjorie Scardino, CEO of Pearson, the international media group, and improve the summary by adding five or six more details. Use one to five words per detail.**

Pearson has always been devoted to content, so, for example, a child can use interactive tools. Pearson starts with the premise that the company has to communicate what it is. Chief Executive Marjorie Scardino believes organisations have a strong company culture. Whenever necessary, she personally writes to all staff in Pearson. Management also makes an effort to communicate in a transparent way so that every one of the company's employees understands.

C ◀))) CD3.2 **Listen to the second part of the interview. How does Pearson communicate its goals? Write a summary.**

D Discuss how you would communicate the goals and values of your place of study/work.

E Read this letter from Marjorie Scardino to investors. Imagine you are a manager talking to a group of staff at Pearson. How would you communicate the strategy in your own words?

> **Our strategy**
>
> 1 Long-term investment in content
> 2 Digital and services businesses
> 3 International expansion
> 4 Investment through efficiency gains
>
> **Reasons to be confident**
>
> • We're in a strong financial position (having unfashionably resisted the idea that we should take on a lot of cheap debt during the credit bubble).
>
> • We're now a global rather than a largely US or UK company, so our geographic diversity gives us wider markets and less exposure to two challenged economies.
>
> • We're in a very strong position relative to our competitors, in industries that face both cyclical challenges and structural change.
>
> • We make real products and essential services that meet two genuine consumer needs: the need to understand this fast-moving and interconnected world and the need to be educated to make the most of its opportunities.

F Choose the correct word to make a partnership related to strategy with each word in bold. All the word partnerships appear in the letter in Exercise E.

1	**digital**	businesses / bubble	5	**wider**	competitors / markets
2	**international**	expansion / world	6	**challenged**	economies / profits
3	**financial**	debt / position	7	**strong**	position / change
4	**geographic**	industries / diversity	8	**fast-moving**	diversity / world

G ◀)) CD3.3–3.6 Listen to four people talking about companies they admire. How has each company been successful, according to the speakers?

H Look at this advice on business strategy. Which strategies are mentioned by the speakers in Exercise G? Discuss which ones you think are the most valuable.

1 It is best not to run before you can walk.
2 Holding on to talented staff is one of the biggest challenges.
3 Innovation is key.
4 Hold back from launching new products or entering new markets and you'll lose out.
5 A retailer can differentiate itself through pricing and an affinity with the customer.
6 Business leaders must be able to deploy specialist knowledge.
7 The goal of a company should be to produce perfect products.
8 Big companies must foster the entrepreneurialism that exists in smaller ones.

I Consider the strategy of two companies you admire. What do you think they set out to achieve, and how have they been successful?

READING AND LANGUAGE

'Long-term planning is essential for any company. It plots where a company wants to go, and how it's going to get there.'

'Strategic planning is a complete waste of time. In this day and age, you simply cannot foresee exactly how markets will evolve.'

P&G

A Look at the two views about planning on the left. Which do you agree with, and why? Work with a partner to produce a statement about planning that you both agree with.

B In what ways do you think the four companies on the left below have developed good strategies? Read the article on the opposite page quickly and compare your answers.

C Read the article again and complete this summary, using between one and three words in each gap.

According to the article, old-style strategic planning is a thing of the past. However, beyond trying to survive, companies do need a strategy for ....[1], even in periods of ....[2], in order to ensure healthy ....[3] and competitive advantage.

In a paper on strategic development, experts at Boston Consulting Group talk about the concept of ....[4]. They argue good companies act in five key ways: they respond to ....[5] very fast; they try to work with ....[6]; they perceive changes in ....[7]; they trial their goods and services effectively; and they work with the best ....[8]. Strategy has changed, and companies need to be more ....[9].

D Discuss these questions.

1 Who do you think is the intended audience of the article?

2 What is the writer's purpose? Is there more than one, e.g. to explain/persuade?

3 Are there any quotations used in the article? For what purpose are the quotations used?

4 What emphatic techniques are used? Are any repeated?

➡ *Language reference: rhetorical questions page 137*

E Match the words and expressions from the article (1–8) to their definitions and synonyms (a–h).

1 downturns (lines 23–24)

2 deductive (line 48)

3 oversee (line 71)

4 hidebound (line 77)

5 awareness (line 106)

6 resilience (line 107)

7 building in some slack (lines 107–108)

8 endure (line 114)

a) creating some free time when you're not busy

b) periods when business activity is reduced and conditions become worse

c) ability to become strong and successful again after a difficult situation or event

d) using the knowledge and information you have in order to form an opinion about something

e) continue to exist for a long time

f) knowledge or understanding of a particular subject or situation

g) be in charge of a group of workers and check that the work is done satisfactorily

h) having old-fashioned attitudes and ideas

F Replace the words in *italic* in these sentences with the words or phrases from the article in the box.

| are alive to   free-flowing   hardly   sharp   thriving |

1 The new shopping mall is *very successful*, but the local shops are closing down.

2 Their legal team is *able to think and understand things very quickly*.

3 Everyone was relaxed at the meal, and the conversation was *continuous and uninterrupted*.

4 This is *not* the best time to make radical changes to our strategy.

5 The shoe manufacturers *know about the importance of* the threat posed by foreign imports.

FT

Living strategy and death of the five-year plan

by Stefan Stern

Is strategy dead? Chief strategy officers will deny it. Some strategy consultants may reject the idea, too. But markets are unpredictable. The economic outlook is uncertain. The world has changed. If old-style strategy formulation is not exactly dead, then it is hardly in the best of health.

During periods of recession, many leadership teams have only one strategic goal in mind: survival. Grander visions are filed away or forgotten. In a recent paper, 'Thriving under adversity', senior Boston Consulting Group partners Martin Reeves and Michael Deimler argue that, in recessions, simply cutting costs has not been enough to ensure a healthy recovery. 'If survival buys time, it does not guarantee sustainable competitive advantage,' they write. The winners in downturns have pursued, and achieved, increased sales.

So companies need a strategy for growth. But I began by arguing that the traditional approach to developing strategy – long, internal debate leading to the announcement of three- or five-year plans – seems to belong to another era. So what does smart, 21st-century strategy development look like?

Unsurprisingly, some sharp minds in the strategy consultancies have been giving this question some thought. At BCG, the same double act of Reeves and Deimler has produced another paper, 'New bases of competitive advantage', that looks at something they call 'adaptive advantage'. This is strategy, too, but not as we know it.

'Organisations with adaptive advantage recognise the unpredictability of today's environment and the limits of deductive analysis,' they write. New problems are constantly emerging. Well-run businesses respond effectively to them.

How? First, they process relevant data – 'signals' – quickly, and react to them. Google is an obvious master of this, getting closer than anyone else to understanding how online advertising works. Second, they see clearly how their business fits into a wider context. Amazon has made sure its Kindle e-book reader is supported by a network of valuable partners. Third, they are alive to social change and shifting customer preferences. Toyota managed this with its hybrid Prius car. Fourth, they experiment effectively, as Procter & Gamble does when trialling products. Lastly, they draw on the talents of the best people they can find – whether they employ them or not. Software companies such as Red Hat and TopCoder oversee large networks of programmers, using the best people with great flexibility. Their permanent staff is relatively small. But they have access to many more.

This vision of a far more free-flowing, less hidebound corporation, ready to change strategic direction fast, is shared by Lowell Bryan, a director at McKinsey. He may be a 30-year veteran of the firm, but he discusses these ideas with the enthusiasm of a new hire.

'You have to give up the pretence that you can predict the future,' he says. 'This is about managing much more dynamically. It is a complex, adaptive world, and leaders have to navigate their way through it. How can you say today what the economy will be like even six months from now?'

Leaders need to show a bit more humility, while living with all this uncertainty. 'Strategy is really an evolving idea which develops over a long period, on a long and winding road,' he says. 'And this new world calls for just-in-time decision-making.'

Adapt to survive. The danger for successful companies, Mr Bryan says, is that over time they lose the very abilities or qualities that earned them their market-leading position in the first place. They no longer have the same flexibility, awareness and resilience they once did. Building in some slack – unscheduled meeting time, for instance – might create the space where some resilience can be re-established, Mr Bryan adds.

Strategy has changed. While the eternal truths – about market position, scale and capabilities – endure, a more dynamic and adaptive approach is now needed. Leaders need to be ready to make necessary adjustments and bigger changes.

G How have businesses you are familiar with adapted to change? You could choose from one of these sectors. Talk about the challenges they faced and how they responded.

- a bank • a supermarket • a mobile phone company • an Internet service provider
- a car manufacturer • a gym chain • a clothes brand • an airline

BUSINESS SKILLS
Brainstorming and creativity

Linus Pauling

A **Discuss these questions.**

1 What do these quotes on creativity mean? Which do you like best?

> 'The way to get good ideas is to get lots of ideas and throw the bad ones away.'
>
> **Linus Pauling, chemist and Nobel prize winner**

> 'Creativity comes from trust. Trust your instincts.'
>
> Rita Mae Brown, writer

> 'Decision by democratic majority vote is a fine form of government, but it's a stinking way to create.'
>
> **Lillian Hellman, playwright**

2 When are you at your most creative? First thing in the morning? Late at night? Working with a group of people or on your own?

3 Which of these statements do you agree with most/least? Why?

- The management in an organisation should be responsible for coming up with any new ideas.
- The typical work environment is not conducive to being creative.
- Whenever we have brainstorming meetings, any interesting ideas are usually dismissed by some of the more cynical team members.
- A brainstorming session should represent our customer base. If half our customers are women, then 50 per cent of participants should be women, too.

B ◀)) CD3.7 **Listen to a trainer discussing brainstorming techniques with some clients. Complete these tips with between one and four words in each gap. Do you know of any other techniques?**

> **Tips for brainstorming**
>
> - Clearly define the ....^{1}.
> - There shouldn't be more than ....^{2}.
> - Think of as many ....^{3} as possible.
> - ....^{4} all ideas, however wild.
> - Don't spend too long ....^{5}.
> - Be enthusiastic and ....^{6} of other people's ....^{7}.
> - ....^{8} ideas after the session.

C ◀)) CD3.8 **Listen to the next part of the training session and note down the seven principles of Koinonia.**

D **Look at the expressions in the Useful language box below and decide which ones you would use for a) leading the session, b) contributing and building on ideas, and c) responding to ideas.**

USEFUL LANGUAGE

EXPRESSIONS FOR BRAINSTORMING

So, who'd like to get the ball rolling?

I've got one! What if we ...? / How about ...?

Let's just get the ideas down at this stage.

That's a great/wacky/cool/unusual idea!

Yes, and here's what I'd add to your suggestion ...

I'm thinking (more) along the lines of ...

You've taken the words right out of my mouth.

Does anyone have any more ideas?

The rule is there are no bad ideas.

I was just going to say that!

Try and suspend judgement until later.

I'd like to expand on that.

Let's go around the table once and then open the discussion up.

Here's another thought ...

Yes, I like that.

E ◀») CD3.9 **Read this information about high-street retailer Ross & Franks. Then listen to a management meeting between the CEO, the Director of Marketing and the Head of Corporate Communications to discuss the brand's future and take notes.**

For over 50 years, Ross & Franks (R&F) has been a well-known high-street retailer in the UK serving a wide range of customer needs from food to furniture, clothes to car insurance. R&F is best known for its womenswear, an intensely competitive market of which it has a 10% share. However, in the past two years, sales have taken a nose-dive. It seems the public has fallen out of love with R&F. On a mission to rejuvenate the brand, R&F's management team is now reviewing the company's marketing strategy.

F **Hold a meeting to brainstorm a new marketing strategy for R&F.**

Writing: mission statements

G **Look at parts of some mission statements (a–f) and match them to the organisations (1–6). Which ones do you think are the best and most creative?**

1 Avis
2 Google
3 Procter & Gamble
4 Microsoft
5 International Committee of the Red Cross
6 The World Bank

a) To fight poverty with passion and professionalism for lasting results

b) We will ensure a stress-free car-rental experience by providing superior services that cater to our customers' individual needs.

c) To protect the lives and dignity of victims of armed conflict and other situations of violence and to provide them with assistance

d) To organise the world's information and make it universally accessible and useful

e) We will provide branded products and services of superior quality and value that improve the lives of the world's consumers.

f) To help people and businesses throughout the world realise their full potential

H **Identify four criteria for writing mission statements based on this extract.**

How to develop a mission statement

Mission: *Why you do what you do; the organisation's reason for being, its purpose. Says what, in the end, you want to be remembered for.*

Changing the mission – or creating an organisation's first mission statement – is a process of gathering ideas and suggestions for the mission and honing them into a short, sharply focused phrase that meets specific criteria. Peter Drucker says the mission should 'fit on a T-shirt', yet a mission statement is not a slogan. It is a precise statement of purpose. Words should be chosen for their meaning rather than beauty, for clarity over cleverness. The best mission statements are in plain speech with no technical jargon and no adornments. Like the mission statement of Google – *To organise the world's information and make it universally accessible and useful* – they come right out and say something. In their brevity and simplicity is power.

I **You are developing the mission statement for your organisation. Set your criteria (see Exercise H) and brainstorm some ideas. Write the first draft.**

Stella International Airways:
strategy for the skies

An airline needs to make strategic changes in order to secure its long-term future

Background

Stella International Airways is a Dutch company with over 250 aircraft. It is one of Europe's leading scheduled carriers, operating both short-haul and long-haul routes. In recent years, structural shifts in the European aviation business have become apparent, with the trend of passengers trading down to low-cost carriers (LCCs).

Stella, like other established carriers, has been badly battered by the success of low-cost airlines, losing market share on many short-haul routes. In addition, the rise in oil prices has mirrored the fall in Stella's shares over the past year.

The company has managed to offset much of the rising cost through fuel surcharges passed on to customers, but this has also led to further falls in passenger numbers, and a shift away from first- and business-class to economy travel has become evident. The company is expected to report a second consecutive annual loss this year.

Given this outlook, the airline's CEO has to devise a strategy to secure the long-term future of the business.

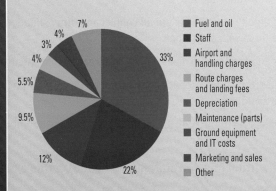

Stella International Airways' operating cost breakdown, last quarter

Fuel and oil — 33%
Staff — 22%
Airport and handling charges — 12%
Route charges and landing fees — 9.5%
Depreciation — 5.5%
Maintenance (parts) — 4%
Ground equipment and IT costs — 3%
Marketing and sales — 4%
Other — 7%

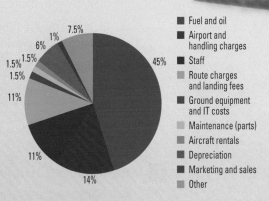

Rival LCC's operating cost breakdown, last quarter

Fuel and oil — 45%
Airport and handling charges — 14%
Staff — 11%
Route charges and landing fees — 11%
Ground equipment and IT costs — 1.5%
Maintenance (parts) — 1.5%
Aircraft rentals — 1.5%
Depreciation — 6%
Marketing and sales — 1%
Other — 7.5%

Stella passenger numbers down

Stella's first-class and business passenger numbers fell last month by five per cent. First-class and business passengers are vital to Stella, generating 28 per cent of the airline's revenues, but representing only 14 per cent of capacity. It's evident that a large number of business passengers have chosen price over service, especially on short-haul routes.

Not a stellar quarter

After announcing worse-than-expected results for the first quarter this year, Stella International Airways' CEO, Ted Verhagen, has signalled major change. Although he didn't give details of the plan, it seems certain to include cost reductions.

An alliance with another airline is inevitably one option on the table. Another possibility would be to use a lower-cost vehicle for European operations, such as a subsidiary LCC. But meanwhile, the airline is heavily focused on first-class and business travel, and on the long-haul routes where the airline has a significant market share in the US.

From:	tired traveller
Subject:	budget versus business class

I long ago transferred my loyalty back to the scheduled airlines on European routes, but recently had to fly on a budget airline to get to a meeting. It was a crazy experience, the flight attendants were saying, 'buy this and buy that'. I didn't get a minute's peace, and the seat was so cramped that there was no room to stretch my legs or work on my laptop. It's definitely 'no frills', but I'm always willing to pay a premium for business class, so long as it isn't exorbitant.

The CEO asked the management team at Stella to report on the airline's strengths and weaknesses. Listen to these comments and take notes.

🔊 **CD3.10–3.12 Managers**   🔊 **CD3.13–3.15 Staff**

Task 1

SWOT analysis

You are the management team at Stella responsible for devising a new strategic plan for the company. Use a SWOT analysis and brainstorm ideas to help you prepare your new strategic vision for the company.

How can you seek to capitalise on the strengths, eliminate the weaknesses, seize the best opportunities and counter the threats?

Strengths (internal) *safety record*	Weaknesses (internal) *losses over two consecutive years*
Opportunities (internal and external) *reducing operating expenses, esp. staff costs*	Threats (internal and external) *competition from LCCs*

Task 2

Brainstorming

Brainstorm a marketing campaign for this alliance based on the new strategy.

Stella International Airways has agreed the terms of a strategic alliance with the Australian carrier Victoria Jets. 'The deal will create a strong group capable of competing more effectively,' Ted Verhagen, Stella's CEO, said. 'Both airlines will achieve significant advantages as a combined force.' The airlines have yet to decide a name for the new alliance. Shares in both companies rose at the announcement of the deal.

Watch the Case study commentary on the DVD-ROM.

Writing

Prepare a summary of your proposals to present to the company's board of directors.

 Writing file pages 146–147

3 Socialising

A Think of a misunderstanding that you experienced when socialising with people from different cultures. What happened? Was anyone offended? How could the misunderstanding have been avoided? Consider these topics:

- greeting people you've never met before
- avoiding certain conversation topics
- paying a compliment • using humour
- socialising with someone in authority
- turning down an invitation

B Look at these statements about relationship-building and say whether they are true or not in your culture. Which cultures might agree with some of the statements you disagreed with? Compare your answers in small groups.

1 You should never turn down an offer or invitation from your host.

2 It is not unusual to be invited to your manager's home on a social occasion.

3 Telling jokes or pulling someone's leg is just part of relationship-building in the workplace.

4 You should never talk about politics, religion, illness or death when making small talk.

5 If you are socialising with a female work colleague, it is best if she is accompanied by a male escort.

6 Socialising is more important in some professions than others.

C Discuss these questions.

1 What could you say when greeting an international delegation of work colleagues?

2 Is it usual in your culture to pay someone a compliment as a way of breaking the ice? What could you say if you wanted to pay a compliment to a work colleague?

3 What would you say if your manager invited you to go out with the team after work, but you didn't want to go?

D 🔊 CD3.16–3.18 Listen to three situations at a UK company that has organised an annual strategy meeting with overseas partners. Say what each situation is, and what you think the misunderstandings might be.

E 🔊 CD3.19–21 Listen to Elvira and Nathan explaining what the problem was from their point of view. Were you right? What could have been said or done to avoid these cultural misunderstandings?

F Work in pairs. How could you improve the last conversation at dinner (track 3.18)? Role-play the situations. Talk about suitable topics of conversation and be careful not to offend your partner.

G Which of these phrases would be acceptable when socialising with an overseas business contact? How would you change the other sentences so that they sounded more socially acceptable?

1 Those are great shoes. Where did you get them?

2 No, I don't want to try one of those. Frankly, they look disgusting!

3 Yes, I know Marcello. Let's put it this way, he's the last person on earth I'd want to work with!

4 They look delicious, but I'm fine for now, thanks.

5 Actually, I think you're wrong there – I think she's a brilliant head of state.

6 So, how many children do you have?

7 Do you mind explaining why people pray so often during the day in your culture?

8 That's really kind of you, but I'm afraid I'm busy this evening. Maybe some other time?

9 Why is it that people are so quiet in restaurants here? It's like going to a funeral!

10 The thing is, we're not used to going out so late here. Could we make dinner a bit earlier?

H Some of these comments may sound indirect or ambiguous. Match the comments (1–10) to the correct responses (a–j).

1   Is that the time?
2   That's a very stylish gadget.
3   I'm not too keen on strong cheese.
4   The thing is, I'm new around here.
5   It's just that we don't do breakfast meetings.
6   Actually, I have an urgent report to finish tonight.
7   Sailing isn't really my sort of thing, I'm afraid.
8   You're looking fantastic!
9   It must have been a lot of work for you.
10 It's a bit stuffy in here, isn't it?

a) OK, shall we make it a bit later, then?
b) OK, would you prefer a sightseeing tour instead?
c) Oh, it was nothing really.
d) Yes, shall we get the bill?
e) Sorry, do you want the air-con on?
f) So sorry, let me introduce you to the rest of the team.
g) Do you like it? It was on sale at the airport.
h) Not to worry. Maybe tomorrow, then?
i) Would you like to try something else?
j) Thanks. I've lost about five kilos, you know.

I What would you say in these situations?

1   A partner on a joint project pays you a compliment and you want to return the compliment without sounding insincere.

2   A work colleague starts talking about the details of his/her past illness and you want to change the topic without sounding impolite.

3   A male client invites you out for a business lunch. You are female and you want to accept the invitation as long as another colleague of yours comes along too.

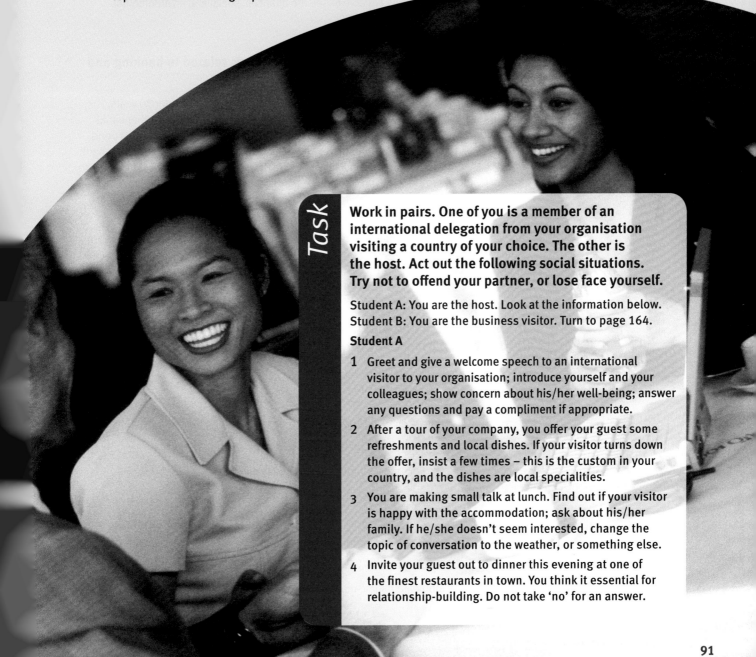

Task

Work in pairs. One of you is a member of an international delegation from your organisation visiting a country of your choice. The other is the host. Act out the following social situations. Try not to offend your partner, or lose face yourself.

Student A: You are the host. Look at the information below.
Student B: You are the business visitor. Turn to page 164.

Student A

1   Greet and give a welcome speech to an international visitor to your organisation; introduce yourself and your colleagues; show concern about his/her well-being; answer any questions and pay a compliment if appropriate.

2   After a tour of your company, you offer your guest some refreshments and local dishes. If your visitor turns down the offer, insist a few times – this is the custom in your country, and the dishes are local specialities.

3   You are making small talk at lunch. Find out if your visitor is happy with the accommodation; ask about his/her family. If he/she doesn't seem interested, change the topic of conversation to the weather, or something else.

4   Invite your guest out to dinner this evening at one of the finest restaurants in town. You think it essential for relationship-building. Do not take 'no' for an answer.

7 Finance

1 Choose the correct options to complete this information about Triodos Bank.

The business model of Triodos Bank is based on working with the real economy, which means it funds itself with deposits from real individuals and physical businesses, and then it *lends / invests*[1] that money to real projects. The real economy is concerned with using resources to produce goods and services that satisfy people's needs, as opposed to the purely *financial / economy*[2] side of things. As a provider of *public / debt*[3] funding, the return for Triodos Bank is merely the *interest / investment*[4] that it is paid on the loan.

Charles Middleton from Triodos says the triple bottom line is a reflection of the recognition that banking is not just about *finance / interest*[5]. In terms of *making / taking*[6] a loan to a project, there should be a social and environmental *return / earning*[7], too. He says people who place their money with Triodos by way of *mortgages / savings*[8] are looking for something more. In addition to getting interest on their savings, they also expect Triodos to show *debtors / savers*[9] everything that the bank does. This kind of *transparency / exposure*[10] means customers are able to see the financial, social and environmental returns very clearly.

2 Complete the missing letters in the key words related to banking and finance.

Triodos, the Dutch group that has been a flagship of _ t h _ c _l[1] banking for 30 years, thinks its seven-per-cent ROE (return on equity) is the kind of f _ g _ r _[2] that other banks should aim for – 'Our pension-f _ _ _[3] investors are quite happy with that, it's like a bond with a little bit of upside,' says Peter Blom, Chief Executive. Mr Blom's thinking is that bank p r _ _ _ _ s[4] should basically grow in line with GDP. 'The world has been expecting banks to grow far faster than the _ c _ n _ m _ _ s[5] they are designed to support. That is what is not s _ s t _ _ _ _ b l _[6].'

B _ _ _ _ _ s s _ n g _ l s[7], also called informal investors, may be individuals or private companies that provide capital for a new business or _ t _ _ t - _ p[8]. An increasing number of these private investors organise themselves into networks to share research and pool their _ _ _ _ s t m _ _ t c _ _ _ t _ l[9]. They typically invest using their own funds, unlike _ _ n t _ r _ c _ p _ _ _ l _ _ s[10], who manage the money of others.

3 Complete each line with the correct multiword verb in the box which can form word partnerships with all the words and phrases in that line.

bring down   carry on   get away with   give away
pay out   run out of   take out   turn down

1 to .... murder / charging high interest / it

2 to .... a huge amount of money / discounts / a secret

3 to .... massive bonuses / interest on a loan / dividends to shareholders

4 to .... as usual / funding the project / overspending

5 to .... cash / ideas / time

6 to .... an invitation / an opportunity / a job offer

7 to .... a government / VAT / interest rates

8 to .... a mortgage / some money / an insurance policy

SKILLS

Put the words in the correct order to make questions that an investor might ask an entrepreneur.

1 Do / in one sentence / business idea / describe / you could / your / you think / ?

2 Would you / the projected sales / me / for year one / mind telling / what / are / ?

3 Who / target market / would / say / you / was / your / ?

4 What / people / think / buy / your products / are going to / makes you / ?

5 I / before / you had / was wondering / ever done / like this / whether / anything / .

6 I'd / return on investment / we are / like / what / looking at / sort of / to know / .

VOCABULARY

8 Consultants

Match the words related to consulting (1–7) to the definitions (a–g).

1 brief

2 scope

3 expertise

4 tangible

5 deliverable

6 order to cash

7 value stream planning

a) skills or knowledge in a particular subject that you learn by experience or training

b) official description that explains what a job or project involves and what the consultant's duties are

c) a tool designed to analyse and streamline the process of delivering a service or product in order to identify its maximum benefit and reduce waste

d) the range of things that a project or activity deals with

e) clear or definite enough to be easily seen or noticed

f) something that a consultancy has promised to have ready for a client, e.g. computer systems

g) a company's normal activities related to providing services or producing goods, from the time an order is placed until it is delivered to the customer and paid for

ELLIPSIS

Add the words which have been left out of this e-mail. Would you include them if you were writing the e-mail? Why? / Why not?

To:	Martin Blake
cc:	Sylvia Carlyle
Re:	Employee performance data

Martin

No need to thank me for doing the slides. Thanks for the corrections. Great that you picked up on my typos!

Was wondering if there's any chance of you cleaning up the employee performance data by Friday? Really busy this week – in Vienna. Sorry. Richard's been asking for it. Owe you one …

Looking forward to catching up with you guys Monday morning. Any idea what time and where?

Speak soon

BW

Sylvia

SKILLS

Match the sentence halves.

1 Actually, we were wondering if   a) you placing the order and we got paid in cash?

2 Maybe we could talk about our   b) so that's a significant saving of €300.

3 We normally charge €90 per pack, but   c) you could deliver a few days earlier.

4 Let me run this by my Sales Manager   d) agreement terms at this stage?

5 What if we delivered within 10 days of   e) I'm offering it to you at half the price.

6 We'll pay for all transportation costs,   f) and she'll get back to you, OK?

WRITING

Find and add the 11 missing words in this e-mail.

> Dear Eugeneia
>
> I'm writing to confirm what discussed in our meeting. Thanks again for taking the time to see me at such short notice.
>
> We're pleased offer you our Moroccan Mist body spray at €9.50 per 30ml. I've also made a note that you may be interested stocking the complete Spa Gift pack in Dionysius department stores in the future – subject to confirmation.
>
> As discussed, our usual payment terms are 30 days from date of invoice. As delivery, I'd like to point that it is completely free on your first order. But we do charge for deliveries of fewer than 50 items on any subsequent orders.
>
> Please find a copy of our terms of agreement, including details of our sale-or-return policy. In the unlikely event that you, or your customers, are not fully satisfied with our products, please let me know soon as possible.
>
> Finally, I'd be grateful if could confirm your first order in writing by Thursday in order to ensure prompt delivery next month. In case you need any more information our product range or promotional offers, please don't hesitate to contact.
>
> Looking forward doing business with you.
>
> Regards
>
> Sebastian

9 Strategy

VOCABULARY

Complete these two extracts with the correct form of the words in brackets.

> *Blue Ocean Strategy* was written by W. Chan Kim and Renée Mauborgne from INSEAD and covers 150 successful ....^{1} (*strategy*) moves over 120 years of business history and across 30 industries. The authors argue organisations can generate high ....^{2} (*grow*) and profits by ....^{3} (*create*) new demand in an uncontested market space, what they call a 'blue ocean', whereas 'red oceans' are known marketplaces where companies ....^{4} (*competitor*) in an ....^{5} (*exist*) industry.

> Don Sull at London Business School says Reckitt Benckiser is one company that is ....^{6} (*thrive*) and showing the necessary agility to ....^{7} (*endurance*) in a new, more turbulent world. The consumer-goods group communicates its core ....^{8} (*valuable*) simply and clearly, links rewards to ambitious ....^{9} (*perform*) targets and hires only candidates who are the best fit with its ....^{10} (*corporation*) culture.

RHETORICAL QUESTIONS

Complete these dialogues with the rhetorical questions in the box.

> Are you serious?   How do they get away with it?   How long is a piece of string?
> Is it just me?   So, what else is new?   What's the point?

1 A: What is it about consultants? They're always charging us for something we already knew.

   B: ....

2 A: How long is the client brief?

   B: ....

3 A: .... Or are we all running out of ideas?

   B: Sorry, it's getting a bit late for brainstorming.

4 A: I don't believe those SAP consultants installed an entire system without an anti-virus!

   B: .... Worse things have happened …

5 A: You might want to proofread your business plan …

   B: .... No one ever reads beyond the executive summary.

6 A: I think we should walk away from the negotiations.

   B: Break off the negotiations? ....

SKILLS

Complete the words in the expressions for brainstorming. The first letter of each one is given.

1 Let's g............ around the table once and then o............ the discussion up.

2 So, who'd l............ to g............ the ball r............? Anyone?

3 Let's just g............ the ideas d............ at this stage, shall we?

4 You've t............ the words r............ out of my m............. Great minds think alike!

5 The rule is t............ are no b............ i............. We'll analyse them afterwards.

6 Try and suspend j............ until l............. Keep the ideas flowing.

Cultures 3: Socialising

1 Complete the missing phrases in these sentences, according to the social function. Use three to five words in each gap.

1 .... designer suit, Dominique. Where did you get it? (*paying a compliment*)

2 The roasted grasshoppers look wonderful, but............. (*turning down food*)

3 A: ....! You know my friend Jason! (*finding common ground*)

   B: Jason? He's, er, quite a character, isn't he?

4 A: Actually, ... wrong there … (*contradicting someone*)

   B: Wrong? No, I'm sure the rate of growth slowed down to 1.5 per cent in the last quarter.

5 A: So then I asked the Minister what she thought of fulfilling her promises …

   B: Er, excuse me, I think I'll just go and .... (*getting away*)

6 A: Well, if you're not free to go bungee-jumping on Saturday, what about Sunday?

   B: ...., but I'm playing tennis this Sunday. Maybe some other time? (*turning someone down*)

2 Choose the real intention of the speaker, a) or b), for each of these statements.

1 Is that the time?
   a) I didn't know that was the time.
   b) I want to get away now.

2 Opera isn't really my sort of thing, I'm afraid.
   a) I can't stand going to the opera.
   b) I don't mind going to the opera sometimes.

3 Actually, I'm not very keen on spicy food.
   a) Spicy food disagrees with me.
   b) I quite like spicy food actually.

4 It's just that we don't normally have dinner here at 11 p.m.
   a) We occasionally have dinner here at 11 p.m.
   b) We never have dinner here at 11 p.m.

5 Oh, it was nothing really.
   a) Yes, it was a lot of work.
   b) No, it wasn't much work at all.

Negotiations

Objectives

Speaking

- Can explain main points of a negotiation position with precision.

- Can propose a range of different options in a complex negotiation.

- Can present a negotiating proposal in detail.

Lesson deliverable

To have participated in a complex negotiation, practising language to propose multiple options, test the situation and propose resolution to conflicts.

Performance review

To review your own progress and performance against the lesson objectives at the end of the lesson.

A SPEAKING

Which towns and cities in your country are 'invaded' by tourists? Is it a good thing? What is the down side?

B LISTENING 1

🔊 **BSA3.1.10** Listen to the news report about sustainable tourism in a busy international port, in which members of a committee are being interviewed on the impact of tourism on their city. What are the main issues identified by the speakers?

1 Mayor of the city:

....

2 Minister of Tourism:

....

3 Chair of the Business Association:

....

4 President of the Neighbourhood Association:

....
....

C VOCABULARY

1 **Match the negotiating techniques (1–3) to the definitions (a–c).**

1 testing the situation

2 bluffing

3 walking away

a) abandoning a negotiation because your aims are too far apart from the other parties'

b) checking people's reaction to a plan or proposal before you decide to use it

c) pretending something, especially in order to achieve what you want in a difficult or dangerous situation

2 **Work in pairs. Discuss the use of these negotiating techniques. In which situations would you use them?**

walking away   testing the situation   paraphrasing
explaining the value/benefits of something
checking with a higher authority   bluffing
dealing with conflict   playing for time   insisting
avoiding giving a straight answer

D LISTENING 2

1 🔊 **BSA3.1.11** The City Council has invited key figures from the community to negotiate a sustainable tourism policy for the city's port and city centre. Listen to four extracts from the negotiation between members of the Committee for Sustainable Tourism. Which of the techniques from Section C do they use? Give examples.

1 Minister of Tourism:

....

2 Mayor of the city:

....

3 Chair of the Business Association:

....

4 Mayor of the city:

....

2 **What is difficult about chairing a negotiation like this? How do you think the negotiation might end? What possible outcomes could there be?**

E LISTENING 3

1 ◀)) **BSA3.1.12 Listen and match expressions (1–12) to the correct categories (a–h) below. Some categories are used more than once.**

a) testing the situation

b) asking indirect questions

c) insisting

d) explaining value or benefits

e) hypothesising about the past

f) checking with a higher authority

g) walking away

h) dealing with conflict

2 ◀)) **BSA3.1.12 Look at the audio script on page iv. Listen again and practise the intonation.**

Task

Pre-task: Discussion

Context: You are members of the Committee for Sustainable Tourism in your city, which is an international port. You need to put forward proposals and negotiate an agreement which will make tourism more sustainable for local residents and also benefit the local economy.

Discuss these questions in groups:
- What could happen to the city and its residents if tourism continues to develop in an unsustainable way?
- What would happen to the city and local businesses if tourism development was strictly controlled?

Part 1: Preparation

Work individually. Read your role card and prepare for the negotiation.

Student A: Turn to page xi.

Student B: Turn to pages xi–xii.

Student C: Turn to page xii.

Student D: Turn to page xiii.

Part 2: Planning

Work in pairs with another student with the same role and brainstorm your proposals and negotiation position to make tourism sustainable while benefiting the local economy.

Part 3: Negotiation

Regroup in groups of four (A, B, C and D). Hold the main body of the negotiation. You need to agree on a five-point plan for sustainable tourism in your city. The Mayor should start chairing the meeting, but rotate the role of the chairperson. If the meeting becomes conflictive, the chairperson should mediate. Make sure everyone has presented their proposal before you take any decisions.

Look again at the Useful language box in Managing questions on page 71 and the negotiating expressions in Exercise E on page 79.

Part 4: Rethinking positions

There have been some web leaks about the participants in the meeting. Look at the information on page xiii. Your reputation and careers are at stake.

Rethink your negotiation positions according to this new information and then conclude your negotiation. You now need to come up with a five-point plan for sustainable tourism and improve your public image. The Mayor should conclude the meeting.

Part 5: Press release

There is a press conference directly after your negotiation. Together, write a short press release summarising your proposal for sustainable tourism and present it to the rest of the class. Be prepared to answer any questions.

◎ **Extra practice: DVD clip and Worksheets 19 & 20**

F PEER REVIEW

Work in pairs and be prepared to give feedback to your colleagues at the end of the task. Think about these questions:

- What outcome did you achieve? Was it difficult to achieve a successful outcome in this kind of negotiation? Why?
- How did you resolve conflict in the negotiation? Who mediated?
- How could you improve your performance if you were going to negotiate again with the committee?

G SELF-ASSESSMENT

Look again at the lesson objectives at the start of the lesson and reflect on the feedback from your teacher and colleagues. Think about these questions:

- Which learning objectives did you achieve?
- Which expressions did you use from the listenings and the language on pages 71 and 79?
- What do you still need to improve when negotiating an antagonistic situation?

H PROFESSIONAL DEVELOPMENT AND PERFORMANCE GOALS

Think of a time when someone got angry with you or your organisation. Was there someone who mediated? How did you resolve the conflict? What would you have done differently? Work in pairs outside class and record part(s) of your answer. Listen to it before your next class.

Objectives

Speaking

Can participate in extended, detailed professional discussions and meetings with confidence.

Speaking

Can infer attitude and mood in discussions by using contextual and lexical cues.

Lesson deliverable

To prepare and participate in an interview in a persuasive and professional manner.

Performance review

To review your own progress and performance against the lesson objectives at the end of the lesson.

A SPEAKING 1

1 Work in pairs. Why do people find job interviews difficult?

2 What advice would you give to someone who is going for a job interview?

B READING

1 Look at the covering letter an applicant has sent to a potential employer. Choose the more formal options to complete the letter.

Dear Mr McPherson,

Please ¹*take / accept* this letter and enclosed CV in application for the Executive Assistant ²*position / job* in Brown Services. My interest in this post ³*comes / stems* from my commitment to ⁴*giving / providing* highly organised and efficient ⁵*support / help* to management teams.

You will ⁶*see / note* in my CV that I have over six years' experience in a similar role and have successfully ⁷*done / managed* a ⁸*variety / load* of tasks simultaneously, through strong organisational skills and team co-ordination. My computer skills, information management abilities and people-oriented approach have ⁹*enabled / helped* me to perform my role with confidence.

If given the opportunity to work with your organisation, you would find me a friendly and resourceful ¹⁰*extra / addition* to your team.

I look forward to the opportunity of meeting you to discuss how my skills and experience could ¹¹*help / benefit* Brown Services.

Thank you for your time and consideration.

Sincerely,
Kate Jordan

2 Do you think this is a good covering letter? Why? / Why not?

C LISTENING

1 What do you think is the hardest question to answer in an interview?

2 ◀)) BSA3.2.13 Listen to Tim, a recruitment expert, giving advice on interviews. Does he agree with your answer to Exercise C1?

3 ◀)) BSA3.2.13 Listen again. What suggestion does Tim make for rephrasing negative facts in a more positive way?

4 ◀)) BSA3.2.14 Now listen to three people answering the question 'What's your biggest weakness?' Take notes on how they phrase controversial statements in a more positive way. Who doesn't follow Tim's advice?

5 What would be your answer to the question?

D SPEAKING 2

Work in pairs. Practise answering some difficult interview questions. Give extended, detailed answers to the questions you are asked.

Student A: Turn to page xiv.

Student B: Turn to page xvi.

Task

Pre-task: Brainstorm

1 You are going to hold job interviews. Identify a job you would be suitable for. Think about the type of company, the position and the candidate profile.

2 Turn to page xiv and complete the covering letter for the job you have chosen.

Part 1: Preparation

1 Work in pairs or small groups and prepare for the interview(s). Decide how you are going to work together. Allocate roles for the first interview.
   - Who will be the interviewer?
   - Do you want more than one interviewer?
   - Who will be the candidate?

2 Think about the following points.

Candidate:
   - highlighting your strengths
   - dealing with questions about weaknesses

Interviewer:
   - the qualities you need in the candidate
   - the questions you need to ask

Part 2: The interview

1 Hold your first interview. At the end, make notes in the table in E below.

2 Swap roles in your pair/group and repeat until everyone has been interviewed for their chosen job. Make notes at the end of each interview.

E PEER REVIEW

Use your notes from Part 2 of the Task and give feedback to your colleagues.

	Good points	One thing to change
The candidate's ability to maintain extended, detailed discussion		
The candidate's ability to deal with controversial facts, such as weaknesses		
The candidate's choice of appropriate register during the interview		

F SELF-ASSESSMENT

Write a 150-word report assessing your performance in the interview. Think about these questions:

- How successfully have you achieved the lesson objectives?
- How did you feel about feedback on your performance?
- What do you need to improve?
- How are you going to achieve a better result in future?

G PROFESSIONAL DEVELOPMENT AND PERFORMANCE GOALS

Think about the job you would like to do next.

1 What job would you like to apply for in the future?

2 How could you discuss your / your company's weaknesses in a positive light?

'What we do know now is that the "e" in e-commerce doesn't stand for "easy".'
John Hagel, US author and consultant

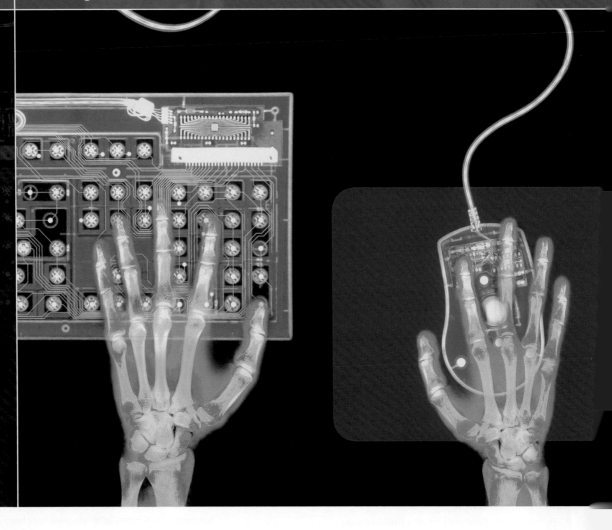

LISTENING AND DISCUSSION
Developments in online business

A **How much do you know about the history of the Internet and e-commerce? Complete the gaps.**

1990 ....[1] creates the first web browser, the World Wide Web.

1995 Jeff Bezos launches online bookseller............[2] and sets the standard for customer-oriented e-commerce. The online auction site............[3] is founded, enabling Internet users to trade with each other.

1997 The PC maker............[4] announces a single-day sales record of a million dollars on its website.

1998 The search engine............[5] arrives. It pioneers a ranking system that uses links to assess a website's popularity.

1999 The peer-to-peer file-sharing software............[6] is launched. Internet users can swap music files stored on their computers.

2000 The dotcom crash

2003 ....[7] has its first full year of profit in online sales.

2004 Mark Zuckerberg launches............[8] at Harvard University. By 2009, the site boasts over 200 million active users.

2005 ....[9] launches, enabling people to easily publish videos online.

2006 ....[10] is created. Unlike online blogs, messages are limited to 140 characters.

B **Look at the chart on the right and discuss these questions.**

1 Which goods and services do you buy online? Which would you never buy online?

2 Which websites do you spend most money on?

3 Which websites do you spend most time on?

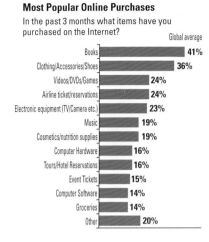

Most Popular Online Purchases

In the past 3 months what items have you purchased on the Internet?

Global average

Books	41%
Clothing/Accessories/Shoes	36%
Videos/DVDs/Games	24%
Airline ticket/reservations	24%
Electronic equipment (TV/Camera etc.)	23%
Music	19%
Cosmetics/nutrition supplies	19%
Computer Hardware	16%
Tours/Hotel Reservations	16%
Event Tickets	15%
Computer Software	14%
Groceries	14%
Other	20%

C ◀)) CD3.22 **What sort of companies have been the main winners in terms of doing business online? Listen and compare your ideas with David Bowen, a senior consultant for Bowen Craggs & Co., a website consultancy group.**

David Bowen

D ◀)) CD3.23 **Listen to the second part of the interview and complete these notes, using one or two words in each gap.**

Key features of a global website

A truly global company website is ....[1] in its nature. It has to serve many people who are often ....[2] and also different types of audiences, e.g. customers, ...[3], ...[4], governments and so on. Therefore the ....[5], the navigation and the ....[6] of the website are very important. Another issue is ....[7], which means that the company's image and website must be much more ....[8] than in the past.

E ◀)) CD3.24 **Listen to the third part of the interview about the impact of social media on e-business, then correct the six factual errors in this summary.**

Through the use of social media, businesses can get their messages across in a different way from the method they use in more traditional media. They can have more engaging, two-way conversations with customers. Companies can also use social media for other purposes, such as using Facebook to contact young people to investigate market trends.

On the other hand, social media present a big financial risk. A story can spread very fast, so companies have to react much faster to counter the risk. One example is a story that was going around that Ford had tried to buy out a very small dealership's website. Ford's Social Media Manager sent out e-mails to find out Ford's side of the story and he was able to take legal action against social media sites and successfully deal with the problem.

Watch the interview on the DVD-ROM.

F ◀)) CD3.25 **Listen to David Bowen's views on where e-business is heading. What three developments does he mention?**

G **Discuss these predictions about trends in e-business. Which do you think are most likely to happen? What other developments do you see happening?**

1 E-commerce and online shopping will become more related to blogging and social media.

2 User-generated content will be king – for instance, people will increasingly expect to see customer reviews as a standard feature.

3 As companies spend more on advertising on the Internet, many newspapers will run out of advertising revenue and go bankrupt.

4 Online video will become the most important medium online.

5 The Google search monopoly will become even more apparent in more countries.

6 Retailers will start monetising (*making money from*) their web pages by linking to other sites offering products and services that suit their target market.

READING AND LANGUAGE

A Are you a keen blogger? Under what circumstances do you or would you a) read a blog, b) contribute to a blog, or c) create your own blog?

B Read the article about social media and business on the opposite page and answer these questions.

1 How many different titles can you find for the new social media job?

2 In how many different ways is Dell interacting with customers online?

3 What impact has customer feedback had on Dell's business?

4 What are some of the financial benefits of engaging with social networks?

5 What are some of the PR benefits for companies?

C Find words or phrases in the article that are similar to or mean the following.

1 when you become involved with someone or something in order to understand them (paragraph 1)

2 major change in the way people think about something or in the way something is done (paragraph 2)

3 It doesn't happen any more. (paragraph 2)

4 appeared, often unexpectedly (paragraph 2)

5 be or become familiar with the way someone thinks or behaves so that you can react to them in a suitable way (paragraph 3)

6 searching through a lot of documents, lists, etc. in order to find out information (paragraph 4)

7 to do something to show you are sorry for hurting or upsetting someone, especially something that makes it better for them (paragraph 4)

8 sending out a message or programme, especially by radio, TV or the Internet (paragraph 6)

9 achieved (paragraph 7)

10 extinguish fires by pouring water on them (*figurative*) (paragraph 8)

11 improve a difficult or dangerous situation, for example by making people less angry or by dealing with the cause(s) of a problem (paragraph 8)

12 a potentially bad or unpleasant situation (paragraph 8)

D Metaphors are often used in business and business journalism. What types of metaphors are used to refer to crises in the headline and paragraph 8 of the article?

➡ *Language reference: rhetorical devices page 138*

E These are three techniques that are often used in order to emphasise a point. Match the techniques (1–3) and the examples (a–c).

1 **anaphora:** the deliberate repetition of a word or phrase at the start of successive clauses, phrases or sentences

2 **hyperbole:** a conscious exaggeration of a statement which is not meant to be taken literally

3 **paradox:** a statement that seems contradictory on the surface but often expresses a deeper truth

a) The Internet has made life easier, harder and more complex all at once.

b) This is it. This is exactly what I want from a summer movie. This is fun, fun, fun.

c) This new e-reader will save the publishing industry from certain death.

F Find examples of each technique from Exercise E in the article.

The new corporate firefighters

by David Gelles

A growing number of companies, including Ford Motor, PepsiCo, Wells Fargo and Dell, are creating new high-level jobs to ready them-
5 selves for engagement with social media, with titles such as Director of Social Media, Vice-President of Experiential Marketing, and Digi- tal Communications Manager.
10 The role of these new executives is to monitor and influence what is being said about their companies on the Internet.

These new jobs represent a broad
15 shift in media relations strategy at large companies. 'Corporate com- munications have radically changed,' says Andy Sernovitz, Chief Execu- tive of the Blog Council, an
20 organisation for heads of social media at big companies. 'It's no longer just companies talking to the press, and customer service talking to customers. All these other people
25 showed up in the middle. They may not be press and they may not be customers, but suddenly their collective voice is bigger than the traditional channels.'
30 Jeanette Gibson, Director of New Media for Cisco Systems, says there is now a mandate at Cisco that all staff be attuned to what is being said about Cisco online. 'It has definitely
35 shifted how we've done communica- tions,' she says. 'Our executives are video-blogging every day. Every- body's job is now social media.'

Dell, the computer maker, has one
40 of the most robust corporate social media programmes. Bob Pearson, former Senior Vice-President of Corporate Communications, became Vice-President of Communities and
45 Conversation for Dell in 2007. He now has 45 people working for him. The core team works on 'blog resolution' – trawling the web for dissatisfied customers, then
50 attempting to contact them to make amends. Others on Dell's social

media team manage the company's 80 Twitter accounts and 20 Face- book pages. Still others manage
55 IdeaStorm, Dell's forum for cus- tomer feedback.

Dell is taking its customer feedback seriously. When the company launched the Latitude
60 laptop last summer, six of the fea- tures, including backlit keyboard and fingerprint reader, were ideas that came from IdeaStorm. 'It's always worth talking directly with your
65 customers. It's always worth listening to them,' says Mr Pearson. 'It's the wisdom of crowds.'

Peter Shankman, a social media expert, says many companies are
70 still reluctant to get involved: 'Companies are slow to adapt because they're still not 100 per cent sure they can make money with social media,' he says. Yet Dell, for
75 one, has made a business of it. By broadcasting discount alerts on Twitter, it says, it has generated more than $1m in sales. And in the US, 59 of the 100 leading retailers,
80 including Best Buy and Wal-Mart, now have a fan page on Facebook, according to Rosetta, an interactive marketing agency.

Other savings can be realised
85 through the Web's ability to reach many people at once. 'If you solve someone's problem on the phone, nobody knows,' says Mr Sernovitz. 'If you solve that same problem in
90 writing on a blog, it costs you no more, but thousands of people are satisfied. And then, if 100 people never call because they found the answer, you very, very quickly get to
95 multimillion-dollar savings.'

Other companies are using Twitter to put out public-relations fires before they erupt or to defuse a brew- ing crisis. In October, Comcast cable
100 customers turned on their TVs to watch a playoff between the Boston Red Sox and the Tampa Bay Rays. Instead, they found an old sitcom. On Twitter, furious viewers
105 began complaining about the problem. Frank Eliason, Comcast's Director of Digital Care, saw the 'tweets' and soon informed users that the problem was a power outage.
110 'Twitter allows for an immediate response,' he says.

'Social media is much more than getting out there and having conver- sations,' says Mr Pearson of Dell.
115 'It transforms a business if you use it correctly.'

G **Discuss these questions.**

1 In what ways would a social media team be useful for your organisation?

2 Which do you think is the best department in a company to set up and run a social media team? Why?

3 What sort of skills would you expect the head and members of such a team to have?

4 What do you think would make being a social media director rewarding/difficult?

BUSINESS SKILLS
Presentations: thinking on your feet

A   What would you say or do in these situations?

1   You are just about to start your presentation when you realise that the projector is not working. The audience of 50 people is looking at you expectantly.

2   You are finishing a formal dinner with some important clients from abroad. Your boss suddenly asks you to give an after-dinner speech, thanking your hosts on behalf of your organisation.

3   You are in an interview for your ideal job. The interviewer asks you, 'What can you do for us that other candidates can't?'

4   Your manager tells you some auditors are coming and you need to give them a tour of your place of work. You should start with a five-minute presentation, giving a brief overview of your company. You have only 20 minutes' notice.

5   You are responding to questions at the end of a presentation, and the same member of the audience keeps asking you difficult questions. There are still 10 minutes left.

Sophie Rawlings

B   ◀)) CD3.26 Sophie Rawlings is Head of Information Management in a UK government department. Listen to her giving a talk about creating web pages for small businesses. How does she deal with each of the questions? What other strategies could you use for dealing with questions?

C   ◀)) CD3.26 Complete the gaps with expressions the speakers use to introduce their questions. Listen again and check your answers. When do you use these kinds of question?

- ....[1] were the main differences between government websites and those in the private business sector?

- ....[2] how a company can improve its online sales through web-page design.

- ....[3] about copywriting. ....[4] what kind of language you think works well on websites?

- ....[5] there was any kind of language that you would *avoid* using?

D   Look at the strategies for dealing with questions in the Useful language box on the opposite page. When might you use each of these strategies? Can you think of any other similar expressions?

E **Look at what a speaker is thinking. What would he actually say? Compare your answers with a partner.**

1 I wish you hadn't asked me that question.

2 As I've already told you all before, ...

3 I don't really want to talk about that right now.

4 I really haven't got a clue what you're talking about.

5 That's not what this talk is about.

6 I don't know the answer, but I'll make a guess so that I don't appear stupid.

7 We really don't have time to go into that kind of detail now.

8 At last! Someone who thinks like me! But the rest of the audience looks bored ...

F **Look at these tips for giving a five-minute presentation. Which ones do you find the most/least useful? Compare your ideas with a partner.**

The five-minute presentation

How can I get anything across in a five-minute presentation?

It is not as daunting as it seems. Advertisers can get a story across in less than 30 seconds, so five minutes should be fine. The structure could be as follows:

- Introduce yourself.
- Start with an 'attention grabber', e.g. a surprising fact or figure, or a funny story.
- Make one main point in the presentation and use a few slides and examples to illustrate it.
- Break this point down into three main concepts.
- End on a high point, e.g. a pertinent quote, a memorable image or a call for action. Experts say this makes a psychological impact and will be what people remember most, along with the start.

G **Work in groups of two pairs. Each pair is going to give a five-minute joint presentation. Before you give your presentation, anticipate any challenging questions you may be asked.**

Students A and B: Turn to page 166
Students C and D: Turn to page 162.

USEFUL LANGUAGE

PLAYING FOR TIME

Funnily enough, I'm often asked that question.

That's an interesting question.

Sorry, could you just repeat the question because I don't think everyone heard.

What I usually say is ...

I'm pleased you raised that point.

REPEATING IDEAS

As I've already said, ...

As my colleague pointed out, ...

Well, it's really what I was talking about at the start of my talk.

SAYING YOU DON'T KNOW

I'm afraid I don't have that information at hand, but ...

I'm sorry, but that's not really my field / area of research.

I'm afraid I don't have the answer to that one.

Can I get back to you on that one?

DELAYING AN ANSWER

Do you mind if we deal with that later?

Actually, I'll be coming to that point later in my talk.

I don't want to go into too much detail at this stage, as ...

Could I come back to you about that later?

I'd be happy to discuss this with you after my talk.

The fashion screen

An online tailored-clothing retailer wants to improve its business and brand reputation

Background

Zayna Meerza set up her tailoring business 10 years ago in Paris and she is now regarded as one of the leading figures in new tailoring. Meerza Tailoring Fashions has built a high-profile client base, mainly by word of mouth, and she recently won an award for Best Female Entrepreneur in France. Most of her long-term clients are senior executives, both men and women. A typical Meerza suit sells for around €750, which is not expensive by Parisian standards.

Zayna says her business relies on constant innovation and she has made a successful transition from having a 'bricks and mortar' studio to growing her online business. Clients' measurements are saved, so returning customers can easily order new suits online or update their own measurements after an initial face-to-face measuring session. Zayna also employs staff in London, Frankfurt and Brussels to facilitate fabrication and delivery. She is now offering men's tailored shirts online – clients just need to enter their measurements.

However, cut-price online fashion sites are a threat. Competitors are taking advantage of viral marketing, including blogging and social networking, in place of more conventional marketing.

Task 1

Prioritising complaints

Look at the home page of Meerza Tailoring Fashions below and the entries on a discussion blog on the opposite page. Would you buy a Meerza suit or shirt online? Why? / Why not? What kind of complaints have they received? Which issues are the most urgent? How should they deal with them?

Meerza Tailoring Fashions

Handmade in Paris

ABOUT US   MEERZA TAILORING FASHIONS   CONTACT US   FAQS

Suit designs

Create your original suit

Shirt designs

Create your shirt

Customer reviews:

'Top quality, original and an excellent fit – my third suit was just as good as the first two.'
Dean, *Media Sales Executive, UK*

'Seriously impressed with these shirts – great gift idea for your husband, father, etc.'
Natalie, *France*

'Shop-bought shirts are too big around the neck or the sleeves too long. My Meerza shirts are a perfect fit.'
Karol, *MBA student, Paris*

fashion blog

Comments

What can I buy my boyfriend for Valentine's Day? I'd like to get him something original and personalised. Can't afford a suit. Any (serious) ideas?
Lidia, Belgium

Dear all
We offer quality, fitted shirts at competitive prices. See our smart designs at our website. The site allows you to mix and match fabrics using computer-generated tailoring for the right fit. Why buy off the peg when you can wear garments that are made to measure?
Meerza Tailoring Fashions, France (www.meerzatailoringfashions.fr)

Thanks for the tip! BTW, it'd be good if the pics on the site were high resolution because it's tricky to see all the details.
Lidia, Belgium

I'd like to know if Meerza Tailoring Fashions are against sweatshop labour. If you are, please sign our petition at <u>dontsweatshop.com</u> and make a stand against under-paid labour in the fashion industry.
Bombay Chique-chick

Great petition, guys. I had an 'original' MTF suit made but then saw it was an exact copy of one worn by the singer Françoise. If I'd wanted a standard suit, I wouldn't have bothered paying €789!!!
One unhappy customer

I needed a new shirt for some job interviews, so I got a Meerza shirt online. The self-measuring guide wasn't at all easy to follow. The shirt looked OK, but was too tight around the neck and baggy in the waist, so I sent it back. Still waiting for my refund.
Shirtless Stevie, London

Meerza's website says shirts are 'made in Paris', but mine was made in Frankfurt! The shirt's a good fit, but I think you should call a spade a spade.
Aaron, Antwerp

Thanks to everyone who's signed our anti-sweatshop petition. Meerza Tailoring Fashions and your ill-fitting shirts – are you out there? 'Made in Paris', or is it Timbuktu? Made in some sweatshop, no doubt. Shame on you, Zayna! Boycott MTF!
Bombay Chique-chick

🔊 **CD3.27** Listen to an online interview with Zayna at a fashion event.
How does she cope with the interview? How would you have answered the questions?

Task 2

Social media presentation

Work in pairs or in groups of four. Zayna is considering taking on a social media manager to improve the customer online experience and manage the company's brand reputation. She asks two technology consultants to present their ideas on the way she could use social media in her business. Look at your information and prepare for the presentations.

Student A (consultant): Turn to page 156.
Student B (consultant): Turn to page 165.
Students C and D (company directors): Turn to page 162.

*Watch the Case study commentary on the **DVD-ROM.***

Writing

Write a summary of your discussion for improving the online experience and sales at Meerza Tailoring Fashions, saying which proposals were chosen and why.

➡ *Writing file page 145*

UNIT 11 New business

'To open a shop is easy, to keep it open is an art.'
Chinese proverb

LISTENING AND DISCUSSION

Advice for start-ups

A In pairs, answer the questions on this website aimed at potential entrepreneurs. Would your partner make a good entrepreneur? Check your scores on page 154. If you wanted to start a business, which areas would you need to work on?

New Business

| My business | What's new? | FAQs | Directories |

Are you ready to start up? Have you got what it takes?

Starting up a business requires a considerable investment of time, funds and energy. Before you begin, you need to assess whether you really have what it takes, and how well you might handle the risks involved.

- Are you prepared for the personal demands of setting up a new business?

- Do you handle uncertainty well? Are you prepared to gamble on your ideas?

- Do you have the key qualities of an entrepreneur, e.g. self-confidence, determination and initiative?

- Can you bounce back from setbacks?

- Are you able to delegate?

- Do you have core business skills, e.g. financial and people management, sales and marketing skills?

- Are you prepared to spend time carrying out in-depth market research?

- Do you have sufficient funds to set up a new business?

- Are you willing to draw on expert help when you need it?

B Match the business skills (1–5) to the definitions (a–e). What other core business skills do you think a successful entrepreneur might need? Which of these skills do you have, or would like to develop?

1 Financial management

2 Product development

3 People management

4 Supplier relationship

5 Sales

a) Identifying reliable partners, negotiating successfully with them and managing the relationship

b) Identifying potential customers and their individual needs, explaining your goods and services effectively and converting potential customers into clients

c) Making long-term plans for your products or services and identifying the people, materials and processes required to achieve them; knowing your competition and your customers' needs

d) Managing recruitment, resolving disputes, motivating staff and managing training; helping employees to work together as a team

e) Having a good grasp of cashflow planning, credit management and maintaining good relationships with your bank and accountant

C Research has shown that there are key qualities commonly found among successful entrepreneurs. How would you define these personal characteristics? Compare your answers with the ones on page 156.

1 Self-confidence

2 Self-determination

3 Being a self-starter

4 Judgement

5 Commitment

6 Perseverance

Mike Southon

D ◀)) CD3.28 Listen to the first part of an interview with Mike Southon, an expert on starting new businesses. What types of start-up does he talk about?

E ◀)) CD3.29 Listen to the second part of the interview, where Mike Southon talks about the classic mistakes that first-time entrepreneurs make. Tick the ones that he mentions.

1 Being over-optimistic

2 Spending too much time developing products/services

3 Not having a good team

4 Giving up when the going gets tough

5 Not having a good sales pitch

6 Not finding customers

7 Spending too much time on market research

8 Not having enough seed capital

F ◀)) CD3.30 Listen to the third part of the interview and answer these questions.

1 Who can become a mentor, and why does Mike Southon recommend getting one?

2 What key elements should a good elevator pitch include?

3 How does Mike define the two purposes of a business?

*Watch the interview on the **DVD-ROM**.*

G Discuss these questions.

1 If you started a new business, would you do it on your own or with a partner? Why?

2 What kind of setbacks would you foresee in the first year of setting up a company?

3 How important are these factors when starting a new business?

• discovering a niche market • timing • knowing potential customers
• analysing costs • market research • differentiation
• employing a skilled workforce • the competition

A If you were going to start a product-based business, what kind of product would it be? What could be the disadvantages of selling only one product rather than a range?

B Read the article below and answer these questions.

1 What do you understand by the expression *a one-trick pony*?

2 What is probably the most challenging task for product-based start-ups? And for more established businesses?

3 Why is the Anywayup Cup unique? How successful has it been?

4 How did Mandy Haberman get her first orders? To what extent does she owe her success to luck?

5 What is her selling tip for product-based businesses?

Article 1

FT

Go the distance with a one-trick pony

by Jonathan Moules

If you are trying to launch a new product-based business, your most difficult task is likely to be finding a buyer. If you already have an estab-
5 lished business, it's probably getting paid by customers. Mandy Haberman managed to solve both these problems at a stroke. She came up with a clever design for a non-spill
10 child's drinking vessel, called the Anywayup Cup.

She hawked a prototype cup around 18 companies, from pharmacy chain Boots to baby-bottle
15 manufacturer Avent. However, no one wanted to buy from a company with a single product. 'I walked around with my prototype in my bag for about a year,' she says.
20 The solution came about by accident. A couple of entrepreneurs suggested that she try to market her idea at a baby-products trade show. 'We went with the intention of just
25 gauging interest, but took £10,000 of advance orders,' Haberman explains.

The positive reaction to her product was all the more remarkable given that the choice of show had
30 actually been a mistake. Haberman had been advised to attend a show called The Nursery Fair, but booked one called Nursery World, which was aimed at childcare providers and
35 nursery managers. 'I made a complete cock-up,' she admits.

However, the error proved to be the making of her business because it put Haberman into contact with
40 people eager to buy her product in significant volumes. 'We were mobbed,' she recalls. The order money gave her the seed capital she needed to start manufacturing.
45 The Anywayup Cup is now sold worldwide, generating annual sales of about £40m. Haberman licenses the product to five companies, netting her up to about £1m a year.
50 Now that the Anywayup Cup is a 'mature' product, Haberman only expects to make between £250,000 and £500,000 this year. However, she is putting this money into
55 developing a new range of products.

Haberman's selling tip for product-based businesses is to try and find something that will grab someone's attention. It is notoriously
60 hard to get a meeting with buyers at large retailers – and even harder to achieve a deal. Haberman's tactic was to send one of her Anywayup Cups filled with Ribena* in the post,
65 with a message to the recipient that if the item arrived still full, then the product had worked. This tactic worked on Tesco's** buyer, Haberman says.
70 At a meeting with another buyer, she decided to grab his attention by throwing her Ribena-filled Anywayup Cup on his desk. The fact that the cup did not burst
75 open all over his in-tray did not turn into any orders. 'It wasn't that he wasn't interested. It was just that he didn't talk a number that was acceptable,' Haberman says.

* Ribena: a blackcurrant-flavoured drink
** Tesco: a multinational supermarket chain

C   **What do the words or phrases in *italic* mean? Choose the correct meaning (a or b) according to the context in the article.**

1   '... both these problems *at a stroke*.' (lines 7–8)

   a) at a certain exact time

   b) with a single, sudden action

2   'She *came up with* a clever design ...' (lines 8–9)

   a) thought of an idea or answer

   b) produced an amount of money

3   'She *hawked* a prototype cup around ...' (lines 12–13)

   a) tried to sell goods by going from place to place and persuading people to buy them

   b) offered goods for sale in the street, especially in an aggressive way

4   '... with the intention of just *gauging* interest ...' (lines 24–25)

   a) measuring or calculating something using a particular instrument or method

   b) judging how people feel about something or what they are likely to do

5   '... the error *proved to be the making of* her business ...' (lines 37–38)

   a) led to the success of someone or something

   b) had the necessary qualities or skills to do a particular job well

6   '... *netting* her up to about £1m a year.' (line 49)

   a) earning a particular amount of money as a profit after tax (*informal*)

   b) succeeding in getting something, especially by using your skills

D   **What lessons can be learned from Mandy Haberman's experience of starting a business?**

E   **What do you understand by the term *olderpreneurs*? Read the article on page 166 and check your answers.**

F   **Complete the gaps in these sentences. What kind of sentences are they, and why do you think the writers used them?**

1   '............ .... he wasn't interested............. .... just............ he didn't talk a number that was acceptable.' (Article 1, lines 76–79)

2   '............ I find interesting – and............ could change the face of business –............ that they may prefer to do that working for themselves.' (Article 2, lines 11–14)

3   .... then............ she realised she had to find something that would grab someone's attention.

4   .... Mandy............ next............ to go to see the buyer of a larger retailer.

5   .... the motto 'If at first you don't succeed, try, try again'............ has a particular resonance for many entrepreneurs.

6   .... Billy Wilder, the Hollywood director,............ said, 'Trust your own instinct. Your mistakes might as well be your own, instead of someone else's.'

➡ *Language reference: cleft sentences page 139*

G   **Discuss these questions.**

1   Do you know of any 'olderpreneurs'? What do they do?

2   What is more essential to success: youth and enthusiasm or age and experience?

3   What do you imagine yourself doing after the age of 65?

BUSINESS SKILLS
Chasing payment

A ◄)) CD3.31 Dunbarry Jewellers is a new business. Listen to this phone call with a major customer, Carswell Department Stores. What is the call about?

B Work in pairs. Decide how to complete these tips for new business owners. Then turn to page 158 and compare your answers. What other tips would you add?

> **Tips for new business owners**
>
> *Dealing with customers and suppliers on the phone*
> - Always give your name and use the other person's …………[1]. It helps to establish a good working …………[2].
> - Quote any relevant account/customer/invoice/reference …………[3] and have the …………[4] to hand.
> - Listen actively and …………[5] that you are listening. Connect with the …………[6] by apologising or empathising as appropriate.
> - Check that you have …………[7] what's been said by restating the …………[8] you are given.
> - Confirm any follow-up …………[9] that you and/or the other speaker have agreed to.
> - Make sure you agree on dates or set a …………[10] for follow-up action.

C ◄)) CD3.31 Listen again to the call in Exercise A. Is there any room for improvement in Val and Max's telephone skills?

D Read these tips for chasing payment. What other strategies can a growing business use to avoid or reduce late payment?

> # Managing cashflow guides
>
> ## 7 Chasing payments
>
> *Many growing businesses suffer the problem of late payments. So, what can you do about it?*
>
> 1 If the invoice is large, call the customer before the payment due date to make sure it has been received and there is no query; this is good customer service.
>
> 2 Make immediate contact when payment has not arrived; be polite but firm about what you expect and when you expect it, and make the consequences of non-payment clear.
>
> 3 Be persistent – follow up promises to make sure they're met.
>
> 4 If the client is withholding payment owing to a problem with your goods or service, try to rectify the situation as soon as possible.
>
> 5 If a customer persistently pays you late or makes excuses, consider whether you're prepared to continue supplying on credit terms.

E ◄)) CD3.32 Listen to another phone call in which Dunbarry Jewellers is chasing Carswell Department Stores for payment. What follow-up action does each speaker agree to?

F ◄)) CD3.32 Listen again. Tick the expressions you hear in the Useful language box on the opposite page and add any other useful expressions they use.

G Role-play this situation in pairs. Look at your information and make the phone call about the late payments.

Student A: See below.
Student B: Turn to page 165.

Student A

> You are Val Bailey from the accounts office at Dunbarry Jewellers, a company set up less than two years ago. You have to chase up late payments at Carswell Department Stores every month. Your company has a good working relationship with Carswell, a major customer which places big orders, but they are notoriously late payers.
>
> • It's late July, and payment is now outstanding on three invoices: BJ1712 dated 8 June; BJ1728 dated 13 June; and BJ1735 dated 22 June.
>
> • You want immediate payment of the invoice dated 8 June, and may allow up to 15 days for the other two.
>
> • Decide your best course of action and phone Max Bryson at Carswell.

H You work in the accounts office at Dunbarry Jewellers. Use these prompts to write an e-mail reminder to Max Bryson at Carswell.

Date:	30 July
Subject:	Final payment reminder

Dear Mr Bryson

writing / inform / despite earlier requests / payment, invoices no. BJ1728 / €2,915 / 13 June / and BJ1735 / €2,670 / 22 June / unpaid. Please / attached copies / invoices / information. / you know, / agreed payment terms / 30 days / date of invoice.

In view / good commercial relationship / past, / like / resolve / matter amicably. We ask / settle / account within five working days. In / event / you / already paid / invoices, / ignore / reminder.

If there / problem / goods which has caused / withhold payment, / contact / immediately / telephone number below, / that we can resolve / issue.

Should / fail / pay this invoice / stated date, then / may have / no alternative / review / account / us, which means / that we will / longer / able / supply / company / jewellery.

Best regards,

➡ *Writing file page 143*

USEFUL LANGUAGE

CHASING PAYMENT

I'm phoning about the outstanding payment(s) on ...

I/We (also) sent you an e-mail reminder on ...

When can you make payment for ...?

As you know, our credit terms are 30 days.

Payment is now (well/way) overdue.

REACHING AGREEMENT

Would that be acceptable?

I think we can work with that.

Yes, that seems reasonable/do-able.

CONFIRMING FOLLOW-UP ACTION

Can you confirm that you'll ....

I'll get back to you when/if/at/on ...

(As I say), I'll need to ...

Can/Could you tell me when that will be?

When will you call me back?

BEING FIRM BUT POLITE

I'm sorry, (but) we'd like/expect/want ...

(Under the circumstances), we're considering ...

(Given the situation), we'll have to consider ...

(You see), we may have no alternative but to ...

As I mentioned earlier, ...

Healthy growth for OTC Tech

A start-up company making diagnostic test kits is looking for ways to grow its business

Background

OTC Tech

Home | About us | Products | Research | Tests

About us

OTC Tech sells over-the-counter diagnosis products. The company was set up four years ago in Copenhagen, Denmark, by Anders Larsen, an engineer with a passion for the 'mechanics' of the human body, and Ulla Hofmann, a research chemist with many years' experience in the pharmaceutical industry.

OTC Tech was born out of a personal experience. The need for a routine test entailed a week-long wait to see the family doctor, followed by a trip to the hospital for the test, and finally the results were received over the telephone. The whole

process took three weeks. In the end, it just seemed that life would be easier for all concerned if patients had easier access to such tests.

The use of home pregnancy tests is now very common, so why shouldn't other easy-to-use diagnostic test kits for a wide range of conditions be available for home use?

There are many good reasons for people to take control of their own health, and OTC Tech can help by providing you with home-test kits. Our range of products includes a cholesterol test, diabetes tests and allergy testing.

What problems do you think this new business might have selling its products?

Reviewing current performance

Growth at OTC Tech has been consistent over the first couple of years, but a little slow. The company directors recently hired a consultant to help them decide how to develop the business.

🔊 **CD3.33 Listen to their conversation and make notes on these points.**

1 **How effectively is OTC Tech matching its goods and services to customer needs?**

2 **What improvements are suggested?**

3 **Does the company have the right management team in place for growth?**

Task 1

Assessing options

You are the directors of OTC Tech. Read the report below outlining the options for growth, and hold a meeting to consider the pros and cons of each. Which ones are low risk and which are high risk? Choose the two options you think are best for the company.

Ways we can achieve growth at OTC

1   Try to increase sales of existing products to our existing customer base. How can we increase the frequency of purchase and maintain customer loyalty?

2   Diversify and start to sell new, related products that potential customers currently buy from our competitors, e.g. home pregnancy tests.

3   Move into other areas of the industry, e.g. low-tech items, like blood-pressure monitors, or high-tech monitoring equipment.

4   Increase spending on R&D in order to develop and market new products. We could work on joint projects with a university or hospital research centre.

5   Find new distribution channels. Our products could be sold via new or emerging channels which might boost sales, e.g. e-commerce.

6   Consider overseas expansion. Which markets would provide most opportunities? For instance, the US is the world's largest market for medical products.

7   Outsource manufacturing to a country with lower labour and production costs, and focus the business on R&D, marketing and sales.

8   Form strategic partnerships, e.g. with a company selling dietary products or herbal remedies.

A radio report

🔊 **CD3.34** **Listen to a radio programme and meet again to decide how you want to change any parts of your growth strategy.**

Task 2

Negotiation

A major chain of pharmacy stores in the UK wants to negotiate a retail distribution agreement with OTC Tech. Work in pairs and role-play the negotiation.

Student A: Read your information below.
Student B: Turn to page 156.

Student A

You represent OTC Tech. This distribution agreement could bring substantially enhanced sales for you. You want to:

- negotiate a two-year agreement – either company can give 60 days' notice of termination to end the agreement;

- receive payment within 60 days of the date of invoice;

- be able to give 30 days' notice of price rises in order to be able to pass on cost increases such as currency fluctuation and inflation;

- split the cost of marketing in the UK 50/50 – you'd like that to include TV ads;

- ensure that your distributor is not selling or developing rival products to compete with yours.

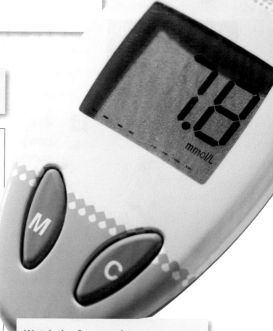

Watch the Case study commentary on the **DVD-ROM.**

Writing

Write an e-mail to your business consultant, summarising your growth strategy for your company. Outline your plans for new products, sales growth, marketing initiatives and distribution plans.

➡ *Writing file page 145*

'*The six phases of every project: 1 Enthusiasm; 2 Disillusionment; 3 Panic; 4 A search for the guilty; 5 The punishment of the innocent; 6 Praise and honour for the non-participants.*' **Anonymous**

OVERVIEW

LISTENING AND DISCUSSION
Issues in project management

READING AND LANGUAGE
Fine-tune your project schedule
Instructive texts

BUSINESS SKILLS
Teleconferencing

CASE STUDY
Creating a world-class port

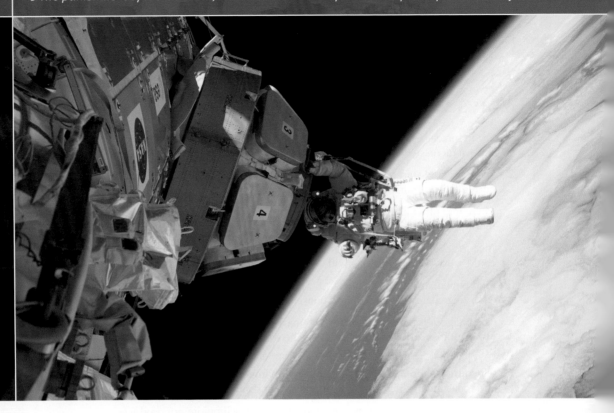

LISTENING AND DISCUSSION
Issues in project management

A **Discuss these questions.**

1 What types of project do you work on in collaboration with other people?

2 What are some of the challenges involved when planning a large project?

B ◀)) **CD3.35 What do you think makes a good project manager (PM)? Listen to two project managers talking about the qualities of a PM and complete this summary using between one and four words in each gap.**

A project manager essentially needs good interpersonal skills. He/She should clarify people's ....[1], but avoid ....[2] and include all members of the team in the ....[3]. A successful PM also knows how to ....[4] tasks to different people, is excellent at ....[5], is detail-focused, but is also able to stand back and see the ....[6]. Organisational skills and ....[7] the team are key, as is the ability to ensure everyone fully understands the ....[8].

C **Match the elements of a project plan in the box to the descriptions below and on the opposite page. Two are given.**

Aim of the project	Dependencies	Management structure	~~Milestones~~	Outputs
Quality criteria	~~Resources~~	Risks	Scheduling	Tolerances

1 .... : What do you want to do or produce (e.g. upgrade the IT structure in a department)?

2 .... : What do you need to deliver in order to achieve your aim (e.g. a new software system or a new building)?

3 .... : The level of quality needs to be defined, together with the stakeholders.

4 *Resources:* These include staff, particular knowledge or skills, money and time. Some tasks can't be hurried along by throwing more money at the problem, e.g. delivery times or the time needed for concrete to set on a building project.

5 ....: How are you going to manage the work? Who will be the decision-makers for different types of work? How will you share progress on the project? How will the project manager report to the project sponsor(s)?

6 Milestones: It makes sense to break up any project into discrete chunks, with a sensible deadline for each main task. On an IT project, this may include gathering requirements, tender writing, project tendering, contract negotiation, deployment and testing.

7 ....: In terms of finance, these may be +/−5 per cent; in terms of time, +/−10 per cent, or in terms of quality, to what extent are you prepared to accept changes in quality?

8 ....: What needs to happen before something else? These can sometimes be internal (under the project manager's control) or external (beyond the project manager's control).

9 ....: What could go wrong? What could damage your ability to deliver? Is there anything you can do to avoid these?

10 ....: This is the Gantt-style chart that many people visualise when a project plan is mentioned. In this way, you can describe what you can expect to happen when. It will provide a general overview of the project. But you cannot make a perfect one.

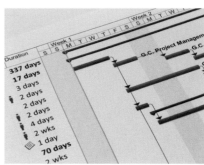

Tom Taylor

D ◀)) CD3.36 **Tom Taylor is an experienced project manager and a vice-president of the Association for Project Management. Listen to him talking about successful projects and answer these questions.**

1 How does Tom Taylor define a successful project?

2 What two examples of projects does he give?

3 What could be the possible criteria for the success of these projects?

E ◀)) CD3.37 **What do you think are the main challenges for project managers today? Listen to the second part of the interview and tick the six issues that Tom Taylor mentions.**

a) choosing the right project team

b) associates not delivering on time

c) keeping within the budget

d) adapting to change

e) delivering on time throughout the project

f) environmental concerns

g) changing demands of the client

h) knowing how to manage people

i) understanding value for money

j) making the most of technology

*Watch the interview on the **DVD-ROM**.*

F **Discuss these questions in pairs.**

1 What kind of project manager would you prefer to work with – someone who leaves you to get on with your own work, someone who involves you in the decision-making process or someone who tells you what to do?

2 Think of a successful project you have worked on, either at work or outside work – for example, a sports/charity/music event or theatre production. What were the aims, milestones, resources and schedule?

3 Why was it successful? What were the additional factors that made it particularly challenging, enjoyable or fulfilling for the different team members involved?

4 Think of a project you know, either at work or outside work, that wasn't so successful. What went wrong? Look at the issues in Exercise E to help you.

5 If you had been the project manager, or had had the chance to work on the project again, what would you have done differently?

READING AND LANGUAGE

A How important is it for managers to know how to delegate work? What advice would you give to someone with a heavy workload?

B Work with a partner. Do you agree with these statements related to project planning? Why? / Why not?

1 One minor aspect of project planning is knowing which tasks are dependent on other ones.

2 Project managers often set their expectations too high, and clients complain that timelines are unrealistic.

3 Periods of non-productivity or inactivity are unacceptable at any time during a project.

4 All the team should devote as many hours as necessary to complete critical tasks.

5 One way of speeding up a project is getting more than one person to work on a critical task at the same time.

6 By focusing on key tasks, a project manager can ensure the project is delivered on time or is finished ahead of schedule.

7 The project manager's aim should be to complete the project as soon as possible without compromising the original schedule.

C Read the article on the opposite page and rewrite the statements in Exercise B if necessary, according to the writer's ideas.

D Match the words or expressions in bold in the article to these definitions.

1 making very small changes to something so that it works as well as possible

2 range that an activity, subject, etc. deals with

3 used to give an example of someone or something

4 it is likely

5 completely stupid and without any purpose

6 makes a subject or problem more difficult to understand, especially by introducing unnecessary ideas or items

7 say that something is not allowed by the rules, especially in sports

8 resources, such as money, space, people or time, that are not being used fully

9 cry or complain about something bitterly

10 giving someone too much work or too much responsibility for a particular job

11 not working, or doing something without any specific purpose, intent or effort

E Which of the words and expressions in Exercise D are a) formal or literary, b) informal, and c) 'neutral'? Why do you think the writer mixes styles?

F Look at the article again and find two examples for each of these techniques. What effect does the writer's style have on you or might have on other readers?

1 Gives definitions

2 Illustrates points with examples

3 Uses imperative forms

4 Exaggerates for dramatic or humorous effect

5 Repeats certain words and grammatical forms to make the text easier to follow
   e.g. *Doing the right things and doing them right are two important ingredients to successful project planning.* (-*ing* forms; *doing right*)

➡️ *Language reference: instructive texts* page 140

Fine-tune your project schedule

Do you have a staff member sitting **idly** *in the midst of the other busy ones? If so, your project schedule might need fine-tuning.*

5　One of the most common problems that project managers **weep** about is 'unrealistic timelines', a common consequence of clients having set their expectations too high.
10　Ironically, there are times in a project when a staff member is waiting for a colleague to finish so he can start his own task. Does the project manager **shout foul** and blame other people?
15　**Chances are**, the project schedule needs a second look.

The basic foundation of managing a project is creating an efficient and realistic project schedule. During
20　project planning, the project manager is given the chance to give it some **fine-tuning**. Given that most projects do not have the luxury of time, the project manager's objective
25　is to create the shortest schedule possible without sacrificing its **scope** and quality.

THE CRITICAL PATH

If you want to deliver on time, or
30　shorten the project duration, focus your attention on the critical path. When the critical path is shortened, the project is finished early. When the critical path is maintained, the
35　project is finished on time. When the critical path is extended, the project is delayed. It cannot be overemphasised here that if there are any tasks in the schedule that a manager should
40　pay close attention to, it is always those in the critical path.

It is quite funny to note that some managers simply stretch the bars in the Gantt chart so that all tasks
45　finish in parallel; doing so simply **clouds** the entire project schedule. Doing the right things and doing them right are two important ingredients to successful project planning.
50　Here are some right things done right:
• Estimate the tasks individually. Make a list of tasks first. Do not put them directly into the
55　Gantt chart, because doing so may influence the estimates and the timeline.

60　• Identify the task dependencies. Some tasks cannot start until prior tasks are finished. Obviously, you can't install a roof over a house with no walls.
65　• Create your Gantt chart. Make sure you use the original estimates and adjust the task based on dependencies. Don't try to schedule putting on the roof and building
70　walls in parallel.
• Identify your critical path(s). Find the longest path of tasks in the Gantt chart. Take note that you may have more than one critical
75　path in your schedule; and not all tasks are part of the critical path.

SLACK TIME

Slack time, as the name implies, is the time when one can relax, delay
80　a task but still finish the project on time. Managers tend to remove it from the schedule to impress their bosses or clients. While this may look good on the surface,
85　there are consequences when it is not done properly.

For starters, accept the fact that slack times are a normal phenomenon in project schedules. The role of
90　a manager is to identify and mini-

mise them. Once there is acceptance, start thinking of ways to reduce slack times and improve productivity.

CRASHING

95　Crashing is the process of shortening delivery time. It is used when stakeholders ask for a faster delivery without reducing the scope of work. **For one**, do not crash tasks that are
100　strictly interdependent on one another, such as applying a second coat of paint. Note that crashing works only on tasks in the critical path because reducing time on non-
105　critical tasks will not affect the project delivery time.

You can put two people to work in parallel and have the task completed in half the time. Or you can assign a
110　more productive resource who can finish the work earlier. In any case, make sure you assess the risks. Also, make sure you are not **over-assigning** critical tasks to your best team
115　member. It is **mindless** to assume that your best resource can work 16 hours a day for three weeks.

G　Work in pairs. Give a short presentation to another pair, explaining how (not) to do something. Choose a topic from this list, or think of something you know how to do well.

• How to appear busy at work
• How (not) to build a good team
• How (not) to cook dinner for 12 guests
• How (not) to form a rock band

BUSINESS SKILLS
Teleconferencing

A In what ways is the etiquette for leading and participating in a teleconference different from that of a face-to-face meeting? When might a teleconference not be ideal for a meeting?

B ◀) CD3.38–3.41 **Listen to four short extracts and answer these questions.**

1 What are the problems in each of these conference calls?

2 Which of these problems could also occur in a face-to-face meeting?

3 Which problems are unique to or heightened by teleconferences?

C **Complete the gaps in the advice below for leading a successful teleconference using the phrases in the box. Then match the sentence halves. What other tips would you add?**

> the agenda   basic rules   an eye on   get feedback   go over what was discussed
> keep track of   take a roll call

1 Always .... at the beginning

2 Then outline ....

3 Quickly go over the .... and guidelines

4 Remember to keep .... the clock

5 Don't forget to .... who

6 Then pause periodically to ....

7 Before ending the teleconference, briefly .... and

a) and the objectives of the meeting.

b) to make sure the telecon doesn't overrun.

c) and take questions from the other participants.

d) is contributing to the discussion and who is not.

e) clarify any action the participants need to take.

f) for the call, such as speaking time limits.

g) so that everyone knows who is involved and listening.

D 🔊 CD3.42 **The product development team for a food manufacturer is discussing a new project. How effective is the host of the teleconference?**

E 🔊 CD3.42 **Listen again and complete the expressions in this box with one or two words in each gap.**

TELECONFERENCING

INTRODUCTIONS

Let's start by taking the .... [1].

Hi, all. .... [2] Dong Chen in Hong Kong .... [3].

Esther Holmes from Marketing in Singapore here.

Daniel Matthews from R&D has just .... [4].

[name] will be with us shortly.

MOVING THINGS ALONG

Rachel here. Let's look at .... [5] for discussion today.

We only have 45 minutes, so let's make .... [6] . Esther?

OK, moving on to the next item.

SIGNPOSTING

Daniel again. I have a .... [7].

This is [name]. I have a question for [name].

[name] here. May I ask a question?

[name] again. I'd like to add to what [name] has just said.

TURN-TAKING

Can we hear first from [name], then from [name]?

Sorry, Daniel, ... [8].

No, please, ... [9].

OK, Dong Chen, what were you .... [10] say?

[name] here. Can I comment on that?

CLARIFYING DECISIONS AND ACTION POINTS

Let's summarise what we've said so far.

Can I just check who's doing what, and by when?

Let's go over the action points before we finish.

F **Which expressions in the box above are most useful for leading a teleconference?**

G **Work in groups of three or four. Look at the main objective of each meeting and your notes for each teleconference.**

Objective of meetings

Meeting 1:
Plan an international advertising campaign for your new unisex perfume and give it a suitable name.

Meeting 2:
Your company has decided that 10 per cent savings have to be made across the board in all departments and countries. Decide how best to make cutbacks.

Student A: Turn to page 157.
Student B: Turn to page 161.
Student C: Turn to page 158.
Student D: Turn to page 158.

Creating a world-class port

An international consortium is developing a major port in India, but the project has hit troubled waters

Background

A bottleneck on the road to growth

India stands poised for unprecedented economic growth. However, inadequate port and transport infrastructure pose a critical bottleneck to its trade potential and growth plans. Roads are frequently gridlocked, and ports are close to capacity.

Infrastructure is an important priority for the country. Major projects include the $50bn Delhi–Mumbai industrial corridor, high-speed rail links between main cities, improved cargo handling at ports and new airport facilities.

India is trying to attract more private investment and project management expertise from abroad to help with infrastructure development.

Blake Ports Management

Press Release

The Blake–Martins consortium has won a bid for the $1 billion Raghavan Port in Gujarat, western India. The private consortium is led by Blake Ports Management, based in Australia, and the civil-engineering firm Martins, from Denmark.

The new deepwater cargo-handling port will be built in three phases over a 48-month period as traffic grows. Much of the 600 acres for the development will be on land reclaimed from the sea.

The Gujarati Ports Authority and the Gujarati State Government each have a 15 per cent share, with the consortium holding the remaining 70 per cent stake in the venture. The consortium will have tenure of the port for 30 years.

What problems and delays do you anticipate a project of this scope might encounter?

Report findings

In less than a year, the first phase of the project is already six months behind schedule and 20 per cent over budget. Read this report about the problems. Which ones are under the project manager's control? How could the project manager solve the problems?

Delays to the first phase of Raghavan Port
Summary of findings

Change of scope
The developer had to revise the scope substantially without extending the opening date of the port. This came about because a new study projected a larger increase in port traffic than originally planned for.

Road conditions
Congestion and crumbling roads are causing difficulty in accessing the site. The State Investment Board is planning the construction of a four-lane road and dedicated rail link connecting the port to the national rail grid if it can get the help of a public–private partnership.

Procurement
The delivery of structural steel had to be delayed. Indeed, on-time delivery of the steel would have caused a storage problem. The knock-on effect has been an increase in the cost of steel.

Water and power supplies
The site does not have a fresh-water supply and there are frequent power cuts.

Weather conditions
Building work was planned on 18 hours a day. However, summer monsoons caused havoc with the schedule, sometimes causing delays for several days at a time.

Sydney	Delhi	Copenhagen
16:00h	11:30h	08:00h
18:00h	13:30h	10:00h
20:00h	15:30h	12:00h

Feedback from the team

There are also issues with the relationships between the developer and the multinational, multi-disciplinary team. The project manager has held a number of confidential meetings with the team.

Listen and make a note of the problems mentioned.

◀)) **CD3.43** The project developer   ◀)) **CD3.45** The civil engineer

◀)) **CD3.44** The lead contractor

Task 1

Meeting

Work in pairs. You are the project manager and the project sponsor. Hold a meeting to discuss the problems and devise a strategy to rescue the project.

1 What lessons can be learned from the first phase of the Raghavan Port project, which should be applied to the second and third phases?

2 What can be done to improve the information exchange and coordination of tasks?

3 What needs to be done to improve communication, team morale and working practices?

4 How can you create a safe atmosphere in the project so that team members will talk about problems and risks?

Task 2

Teleconference

Work in groups of three or four. The project manager holds a teleconference with key members of the team to discuss the issues and agree the way forward.

Student A: Turn to page 157.
Student B: Turn to page 163.
Student C: Turn to page 164.
Student D: Turn to page 165.

*Watch the Case study commentary on the **DVD-ROM**.*

Writing

Write a short report of your main findings and a list of action items for the project sponsor, the project manager and other team members. Include the following information.

• Background to the project
• Reasons for this review
• Key findings
• Recommendations
• Immediate action plans

 Writing file pages 146–147

4 Managing an international team

A Read the first part of a management trainer's story. Why do you think this project team ran into problems?

The client rang me out of the blue. Could I fly to Munich and solve a major crisis? I agreed, but after hearing a brief account of what had happened, I wasn't optimistic I could provide a solution. I was concerned that anything I could do would now be too little, too late.

Eighteen months earlier, two famous international companies – one Japanese, the other German – had signed a joint-venture agreement to develop, produce and launch a product that had the potential to capture a whole new market. The joint venture would combine the marketing skills of one company with the technology and design skills of the other (my client).

To the board members of both companies, it must have seemed the perfect business marriage. Within weeks of the deal being signed, a group of Japanese design engineers was sent to work alongside a German team of similar size and expertise at the German company's plant in Bavaria. The energy and enthusiasm surrounding the deal was infectious.

B ◀)) CD3.46 Listen to the next part of the story. What cultural misunderstandings arose between the two teams? Take notes under these headings.

- Participation in meetings
- Communication style
- Attitudes to time

C ◀)) CD3.47 What do you think should have been done to avoid the failure of this project? Listen to the management trainer's final comments and compare your answers.

Carlos Ghosn, CEO of Renault-Nissan

"When you have a very diverse team – people of different backgrounds, different culture, different gender, different age – you are going to get a more creative team."

D Complete the tips below with the correct form of the words in the box.

> behave   decide   effect   lose   patient
> punctual   share

Tips for managing an international team

- The first step is to be aware of your own ....¹, values, ways of working and preferences. Remember, what's 'normal' for you isn't necessarily normal for everyone.
- Have ....². Try to learn as much as you can about the working practices, customs and nuances of the culture(s) that you're working with, but at the same time, recognise that you're never going to know everything.
- Pay particular attention to your own attitudes and those of others in terms of:
  - relationships (e.g. how you relate to older or senior staff);
  - meetings (e.g. do you expect to be involved in ....³-making?);
  - time (e.g. are ....⁴ and sticking to deadlines highly valued?);
  - communication (e.g. are people frank and direct / is there a culture of ....⁵ information?);
  - social values (e.g. attitudes to risk, ...⁶ of face, sense of individuality, etc.).
- Know what positive and negative perceptions people from other cultures have about you and your culture.
- Adapt your communication style to work ....⁷ with people from other cultures.

E ◀)) CD3.48 Listen to an expert talking about an example of a successful international project and answer these questions.

1 What is the purpose of a 'kick-off' meeting?
2 What did Renault decide to do early on in its alliance with Nissan? Why?
3 How has the alliance adapted its working practices?

F Discuss these aspects of business culture. How do they vary from what you would consider to be 'normal' in your culture?

- Titles are important. Older and senior staff are addressed in a highly respectful way.
- Social activities after work are very important in business relationships.
- It is common for meetings to be cancelled or changed at the last minute.
- Meetings are frequently interrupted, with other people wandering in and out.
- Punctuality is highly valued.
- Deadlines are often viewed as fluid, rather than firm commitments.
- It's important to avoid saying no to any proposal. You risk causing offence, so always be indirect.
- There is a strong tendency to avoid giving bad news.
- Personal dignity is very important, and people work hard to save face and to avoid others losing face.
- Strong individuality is generally tolerated.

G Rewrite the statements in Exercise F, adding or changing any details you like, so that everyone in the group agrees with them.

H What extra challenges do you think a virtual team would face, and how could a team leader ensure the success of the team?

Task

Managing an international project team

You work for an international sports federation. You have been put in charge of a new multinational, multi-disciplinary project team responsible for promoting the federation. The team will work mostly face to face.

1 Work in pairs. Draw up a list of 10 questions you would like to ask your new team members about their culture and ways of working at a kick-off meeting. Compare your list with another pair and choose the best 10 questions. How would you answer these questions about your culture?

2 In pairs, brainstorm the standard operating procedures (SOPs) for your new team (e.g. response time to e-mails, working hours, frequency and purpose of meetings).

3 At the kick-off meeting, you plan to dedicate some time to getting-to-know-you activities, team building and discussion of cultural similarities and differences. Brainstorm possible activities, then discuss their suitability for the event.

4 Present your ideas for the SOPs and kick-off activities to the whole group. Discuss and agree a final list.

10 Online business

VOCABULARY

Complete the article below with the words and phrases in the box. You will not need all of them.

> advertising revenues   auction   customer reviews   digital media   dotcom
> e-commerce   online   personalised   retailers   search engine   sites
> social networking   user-generated   Web

FT

Back to the future

by Tim Bradshaw

Ten years after the first ....[1] boom, digital-media investors are once again turning their attention to ....[2]. Venture capitalist Fred Destin predicts the rise of 'super-niche, high-quality ....[3]' that sell a much greater range of products or services in their chosen niches than the high street could offer. In addition, 'the ....[4] gives people the ability to deliver a much more ....[5] experience,' says Saul

Klein, partner at Index Ventures.

Investors are interested in companies that sell goods or services, rather than those that hope to make money from ....[6]. Even the mighty ....[7] Google is still working out how to extract the most value from its $1.65bn (£1bn) acquisition of YouTube. Investors are also less confident when it comes to selling ....[8] such as music and movies online.

Popular second-generation e-commerce sites include Moo.com, which prints individually customised business and greeting cards, and Glasses Direct, which is exploiting the untapped market for ....[9] spectacle sales. Video games are another popular investment. Online video-gaming services such as Playfish are offering their games (and selling products related to them) on ....[10] sites such as Facebook.

RHETORICAL QUESTIONS

Complete the missing letters in the metaphors in these sentences.

1   The size of the car company's losses after the product recall is helping to f u _ _ a growing debate about whether a corporate reputation can be insured.

2   In the modern digital world, reputational crises can e r _ _ _ and spread quickly, but if combatted well, can burn out just as fast.

3   The government put forward measures to limit salaries and bonuses in financial services in order to d e f _ _ _ the crisis.

4   The news led to a f l _ _ _ of traffic to celebrity news websites and social media sites such as Twitter.

5   The US rescue plan is a priority in the fight to p _ _ o _ _ the financial f i _ _ engulfing the banking system.

6   Trouble is b r _ _ _ _ _ for the beer industry in Russia, where the government plans to increase excise duty on beer by 200 per cent.

7   Every marketer's dream is to have a g r a _ _ - r _ _ _ _ campaign, with consumers talking about the brand on social networking sites.

SKILLS

Complete these expressions for dealing with questions in presentations.

1 I'm afraid, I don't have that information a............h............. .

2 I'm pleased you r............that p............ .

3 I don't want to go i............too much detail at this s............ .

4 Actually, I'll be c............t...........that point later in my talk.

5 Funnily e............, I'm often asked that question.

6 As my colleague p............o............earlier, it's a matter of cost.

7 I'm sorry, but that's not really my a............of research.

8 I'm a............I don't have the answer to that o............ .

11 New business

VOCABULARY

1 Match the verbs (1–5) to the nouns (a–e).

1	set up	a)	expert help
2	draw on	b)	an idea
3	pitch	c)	a business
4	bounce back from	d)	uncertainty
5	handle	e)	setbacks

2 Complete these sentences with the correct verb–noun combination from Exercise 1.

1 Successful entrepreneurs are not discouraged by failure. They know how to............and learn from experience.

2 Very few entrepreneurs are strong in all of the areas required to run a successful business, so be willing to............when you need it.

3 An entrepreneur must be able to............, such as the lack of job security, well.

4 When you............, it's essential to have anticipated the questions you will be asked, and to have prepared your answers.

5 When you............, you do not have set working hours, but you do work a lot of hours.

CLEFT SENTENCES

Complete the second sentence in each pair so that it emphasises the point. Use two to five words in each gap.

1 We need our first big customer now.

What............our first big customer.

2 My father encouraged me to start my own business.

My father was............encouraged me to start my own business.

3 The start-up failed because consumers didn't want the product.

The reason............because consumers didn't want the product.

4 An entrepreneur should identify where there are needs not being met in the marketplace.

What............where there are needs not being met in the marketplace.

5 I learned that a good mentor can really help you to develop your business.

What............a good mentor can really help you to develop your business.

6 She loves the freedom of being her own boss.

The freedom of being her own boss............ .

7 Martin started his first business when he was at university.

It............at university that Martin started his first business.

SKILLS

Find and correct the 12 wrong words in this e-mail.

Dear Mrs Boyle

We are writing to advice you that, despite our previous requests, payment remains overstanding on invoice no. AU10-0093911 for €358. Our records also indicate that payment is now debited on invoice no. AU10-0096745 for €260. Please find adjoined copies of both invoices for your information.

We would like to recall you that our agreed payment terms are 60 days from date of invoice. Therefore, we would be grateful if you could give this thing your urgent attention and fix your account within the next five working days. Unless payment is received by this date, we may have to consider eradicating your credit terms.

If there is a problem with our goods which is causing you to evade payment, please contact us immediately in order to solve this issue.

In the circumstances that you have already paid these invoices, please accept our apologies and regard this message.

Best wishes

Olga Antipova

WRITING

Write an e-mail to Olga Antipova. Include these points.

- Introduce yourself and explain that you are now doing Mrs Boyle's job.
- Say you have paid invoice AU10-0093911 today by bank transfer.
- Apologise for the delayed payment and give a reason.
- Mention that you have not yet received the goods in the second invoice.
- Ask when you can expect to receive the goods.
- Request they cancel the second invoice and issue a new one when the goods are delivered.

12 Project management

VOCABULARY

1 Match these words associated with project management (1–6) to their definitions (a–f).

1	dependency	a)	person who monitors, funds and has ultimate authority over the project
2	milestone		
3	sponsor	b)	planning the completion of a project within a certain time and with designated resources
4	tolerance	c)	desired result from a project
5	output	d)	relationship in which a task relies on other tasks to be performed (completely or partially) before it can be performed
6	scheduling	e)	level of deviation from the formal plan (in terms of time, budget or quality) which is permitted
		f)	significant event in the project, usually completion of a major task

2 Replace the phrases in *italic* with the correct form of the verbs in the box.

assess   assign   crash   delegate   fine-tune   multi-task   report   schedule

1 Good project managers know how to *give tasks to other members of the team* rather than do all the work themselves.

2 Constantly *making small changes to* the plan is an essential part of the project manager's job.

3 A project manager *is managed by and responsible* to a project sponsor or executive sponsor.

4 It is important to *plan* a kick-off meeting for all project team members to participate in.

5 Fast-tracking and *getting the work done more quickly* could get this project back on schedule.

6 Women are said to be better than men at *doing several things at the same time*.

7 Project managers sometimes *give* tasks to members of the project team without considering their availability or other work commitments.

8 The project team should identify and *make a judgement about* potential risks. Then think of risk management strategies.

SKILLS

Complete these extracts from a teleconference conversation.

DM: Hello, everybody. David Markov h............¹. I'd like to start by taking the r............ c............².

LG: Hi, Leticia González from Mexico DF s............³.

JK: T............⁴ is Jeff Knight in London. My colleague, Angela Bennett, will be j............⁵ us shortly.

DM: Thank you all. Let's m............⁶ a start.

DM: OK, m............ o............⁷ to the next i............⁸ on the a............⁹ – Delays in software development.

LG: Leticia a............¹⁰. I have a question, David. When will the new developers be able to start work?

JK: Can I c............ o............¹¹ that?

DM: Sure, g............ a............¹², Jeff.

DM: What do you think of the revised schedule? Can we h............ f............¹³ Leticia first?

LG: Well, these seem like very tight deadlines for my team.

JK: Jeff here. I'd like to a............ t............¹⁴ what Leticia has just said – my guys in London will also find it a challenge.

DM: OK, let's g............ o............¹⁵ the action points before we finish.

Cultures 4: Managing an international team

1 Complete the questions below with the words and phrases in the box.

communication style   deadlines   decision-making   group-oriented   hierarchical
highly valued   less direct   perceptions   respectful   working relationship

1 What positive and negative............ do you think people from other cultures have about your culture?

2 To what extent is the............ direct and explicit in a business context?

3 When is it necessary to be............, and why?

4 How can others build a good............ with people from your culture?

5 Would you describe your culture as individualistic or............?

6 Is punctuality............, and when is it acceptable to be late or miss............?

7 Is the management style strictly............ and............ of seniority, or more informal?

8 Who is expected to contribute to............ and discussion in meetings?

2 Prepare a short presentation designed to inform some international colleagues about working with people from your culture, profession or organisation. Include some of the points mentioned in Exercise 1.

Presentations

Objectives

Speaking
Can express attitudes using linguistically complex language.

Listening
- Can infer opinions in a linguistically complex presentation or lecture.
- Can follow presentations on abstract and complex topics outside their field of interest.

Lesson deliverable
To plan, prepare and give a 'How not to ...' presentation expressing opinion and attitude.

Performance review
To review your own progress and performance against the lesson objectives at the end of the lesson.

A SPEAKING 1

1 Look at these famous sayings. What do they mean? Do you agree? Discuss your opinions.

One man's meat is another man's poison.

A stitch in time saves nine.

Where there's a will, there's a way.

When in Rome,
do as the Romans do.

No man is an island.

The squeaky wheel gets the grease.

B LISTENING

1 Discuss these statements about consumer choice. Include any anecdotes of your own to support your point.

1 More choice for consumers is always better.

2 Sometimes making a purchasing decision feels overwhelming.

3 The more choices you have, the more likely you are to make the best choice.

4 Continuous innovation and new products is what consumers want.

2 Have you heard of 'the paradox of choice'? What do you understand by this term?

3 ◀)) BSA4.1.15 Listen to a marketing expert talking about a book called *The Paradox of Choice*. Check your answer to Exercise B2.

4 ◀)) BSA4.1.16 Listen to the whole presentation. What is the presenter's opinion of 'the paradox of choice'? Tick (✓) all that apply.

a She believes that shoppers spend more money if they have more choices available.

b She agrees that lots of choice is good in theory but less satisfying in practice.

c She understands why some companies have had more success by offering fewer products.

d She agrees that customer behaviour isn't predictable.

e She thinks that choice overload is not a problem for sales and marketing generally.

f Her own experience tells her that the research is probably true.

5 Do you think the presenter is objective or biased in her presentation? Why?

6 The presenter uses these techniques to support her opinion. Make notes about what she says under each heading.

a Tell a relevant personal anecdote.

b Refer to research.

c Mention experts or literature in the field.

d Give some real business examples.

e Refer to recent industry news.

TEAM BUILDING
- Company Trip
- Sports

7 🔊 **BSA4.1.17 Listen to six extracts from the presentation. Underline the word that indicates the presenter's attitude.**

1 Seemingly, abundant choice is more attractive in theory than in practice.

2 Remarkably, this has had unintended consequences.

3 Arguably, we want some choice, but don't give us too much of it.

4 His comments will inevitably send shockwaves through an industry.

5 Naturally, that made it so much easier for us to choose.

6 Let's face it, sometimes less is undoubtedly more.

C SPEAKING 2

1 Complete each of these statements with an adverb from Exercise B7 to indicate your attitude. Then, in small groups, take turns to choose a statement and discuss your views.

- Businesses .... shape, rather than merely reflect, consumer choices.

- The paradox of choice is .... a myth: less is definitely more.

- Most product advertising is .... banal and boring.

- The food industry will .... nudge consumers to make healthier eating choices.

- Online consumer reviews and ratings are .... contradictory, making it hard to choose.

Task

Pre-task: Brainstorm

Work in small groups. Take two or three minutes to brainstorm how NOT to organise an office party.

Part 1: Preparation

Task: Prepare a presentation (3–5 minutes) in the *How not to …* series of workshops. Choose one of the titles below or invent your own *How not to …* title.

- How not to retain customers
- How not to manage staff
- How not to …

1 Work together and brainstorm your ideas for the presentation. If necessary, go online to research your topic or for ideas turn to page xv.

2 Prepare your presentation. Decide who will speak in each section and think about the following points.

Structure:
- Select and organise your best three or four ideas from the brainstorm.
- Think of one or two relevant personal anecdotes to connect with your audience.

Techniques and language:
- Use techniques to support your opinions, e.g. real-world examples, references to research, recent news, or expert advice.
- Include adverbs to demonstrate attitude.

Part 2: Presentation

Presenters: Use the guidance in Part 1. Give your presentation.

Audience: Make notes as you listen. How does the presenter indicate their opinion?

D PEER REVIEW

Make notes about ways in which another team's presentation expressed their opinions on the topic. On a scale of 1 to 5, how strongly did the presenter indicate their attitude? Give feedback and make suggestions.

E SELF-ASSESSMENT

Look back at the lesson objectives. Think about these questions:

- What techniques and language did you use to express your opinions and attitudes on the topic?

- What do you think you did well?

- What would you like to do better next time?

F PROFESSIONAL DEVELOPMENT AND PERFORMANCE GOALS

Write three sentences about ways you will improve your linguistic complexity in presentations in future.

Teleconferences

Objectives

Speaking

- Can manage participants in a teleconference using appropriate language.

- Can manage discussions during teleconferences, helping participants stay on topic.

Listening

Can follow a work-related discussion between fluent speakers.

Lesson deliverable

To plan, prepare and participate in and lead a teleconference in a business context.

Performance review

To review your own progress and performance against the lesson objectives at the end of the lesson.

A SPEAKING 1

Work in pairs or small groups. Discuss your understanding of the following quotation.

'Communication – the human connection – is the key to personal and career success.'

Paul J. Meyer

1 How does your interpretation of the quotation change depending on the form in which the communication takes place?

2 How has technology changed the way we conduct meetings?

3 What are the challenges of effective communication in the following situations?

- Meeting face to face

- Making a telephone call

- Holding a teleconference

B LISTENING

1 **You are going to listen to an extract from a teleconference between colleagues in of an international company. The company manufactures machines for the ceramic tile industry. Before the teleconference, the participants received an invitation e-mail with an agenda detailing the points to be covered in the meeting.**

🔊 **BSA4.2.18 Listen to the teleconference. What difficulties do the participants experience?**

2 **Complete the agenda.**

From: Rosalba Mancini

To: Giancarlo Rossi, Martina Moretti, Daniel Schwarz, Jim Dawson, Elena González

Subject: Teleconference Thursday

Start time: 10.00 a.m. Central European time

Agenda:

1 ....

2 ....

3 ....

3 🔊 **BSA4.2.19 Listen to the rest of the call. How did the participants overcome and manage any problems**

4 **Work in pairs or small groups. Draw up a list of tips for holding an effective teleconference and dealing with problems.**

C SPEAKING 2

1 Work with your partner. Refer to audio scripts BSA4.2.18–4.2.19 on page vi and complete the table. Add any other appropriate phrases you know?

Identifying yourself and the other participants	
Getting the meeting started and explaining the agenda	
Keeping the meeting on track	
Dealing with interruptions and managing turn-taking	
Inviting contributions or asking to contribute	
Ending the meeting – summarising decisions and action points	

2 Work in groups of four or five. Role-play the main points from the teleconference you listened to.

Task

Part 1: Preparation

Context: You work for a language school, providing language courses to young adult learners and business professionals from across the region. The school wants to expand and appeal to learners globally, attracting more international business. The management team believes that one way to achieve this would be to improve their online presence and image. You are going to have a teleconference to discuss the company's website.

Work in small groups to plan the teleconference. Follow these steps:
- Turn to page xvi and look at the role-cards.
- Decide who is going to play each role.
- Think about your role and what you will be most interested in pursuing in the meeting.
- Discuss and identify the features of a good website for a private language school that you think would appeal to an international audience to attract new business.

- Write an invitation e-mail with an agenda to help you in your planning. You will take turns to lead the meeting, so you need as many points on the agenda as there are people in your group.

Part 2: Teleconference
Role-play the meeting, discussing the points you identified in Part 1. Your teacher will give you an object that identifies who the leader is. After you have discussed the first point on the agenda, hand the object to the person who is going to lead the discussion of the second point. The person who is the leader of the last point on the agenda must also summarise the points discussed, any agreement reached and what action points have been decided.

When leading: Make sure the other participants keep to the point. Manage any interruptions and make sure everyone gets a chance to speak.

When participating: Make sure you take turns and give your opinion. Include the problem specified at the end of your role-card.

◎ EXTRA PRACTICE: DVD CLIP AND WORKSHEET 21

D PEER REVIEW

Give feedback to the people in your group. Think about the lesson objectives and these questions.

1 How well did they lead their section of the meeting? Think about handling interruptions, dealing with people going off the topic and making sure everyone contributed.

2 What did each person do well?

3 What could they have done better?

E SELF-ASSESSMENT

Write 120–140 words about your performance. Think about these questions:
- the feedback from the other participants
- the lesson objectives
- what you feel you did well / could have done better
- whether you felt happier leading or participating.

F PROFESSIONAL DEVELOPMENT AND PERFORMANCE GOALS

Now think about the next time you participate in, or lead, a teleconference at work. Complete these sentences.

Before the teleconference, I will …

During the teleconference, I will …

If there are communication difficulties, I will …

After the teleconference, I will …

Language reference

Position of adverbs

The position of an adverb in a sentence depends on its meaning and the word or words it is modifying. There are three main positions for adverbs in a sentence:

1   Front position (before the subject)
2   Mid position (between the subject and the verb or immediately after *be* as a main verb)
3   Final position (at the end of the clause)

Different types of adverbs tend to be in certain positions, although there are sometimes exceptions to the general rule.

Front position

We often use adverbs in this position to link or contrast with information in a previous sentence. Linking adverbs, which join a clause to what was said before, come here.

> She prepared a speech for the occasion. **However**, she didn't need to use it.

Comment adverbs (e.g. *fortunately, luckily, understandably*) can also come here.

> **Frankly,** I find this confusing.

Adverbs of time can come here when we want to emphasise the time, although it is more common to see the time adverb in the final position.

> **Yesterday** I worked 12 hours.

Mid position

The most common use of adverbs is to modify adjectives. The adverb comes before the adjective it is modifying. The exception is *enough*, which comes after the adjective or adverb that it modifies.

> a **mutually** successful outcome
>
> a **highly** damaging report
>
> I don't feel confident **enough** to attend a networking event.

Adverbs of indefinite frequency (e.g. *almost always, often, occasionally, seldom, hardly ever*), adverbs of degree and certainty (e.g. *probably, possibly, certainly*), one-word adverbs of time (e.g. *already, just, now, soon*) and focusing adverbs (e.g. *just, even*) are usually in this position.

When auxiliary verbs are used, the adverb normally goes between the auxiliary verb and the main verb, or after the first auxiliary verb if there is more than one.

> We've **just** been discussing this issue.

Final position

The most frequent position for adverbs in English is the end of the sentence.

We usually put adverbs of manner (when we want to focus on how something is done, e.g. *quickly, badly, fast, well*), adverbs of definite time (e.g. *last week, every year*) and

adverbs of place (e.g. *in the city, by the door*) in the final position.

When more than one of this type of adverb is used, the order in which they come is usually: manner, place, time.

> They worked **hard in the training session all day**.

US English

In US English, mid-position adverbs are often put before auxiliary verbs and the verb *be*, even when the verb is not emphasised.

> She **probably** has left by now. (AmE)
>
> She has **probably** left by now. (BrE)

North Americans might use an adjective form or *real* + adjective instead of an adverb in casual speech.

> She drives **slow** in that old car of hers. (AmE)
>
> She drives **slowly** in that old car of hers. (BrE)
>
> His head hurt **real bad**. (AmE)
>
> His head hurt **really badly**. (BrE)

Adverbs and adjectives

Some adjectives and adverbs have the same form.

> There are **daily** flights to Madrid.
> Flights go to Madrid **daily**.
>
> We have an **early** meeting tomorrow.
> We are meeting **early** tomorrow.
>
> The team are **hard** workers.
> The team work **hard**.

Some adjectives and adverbs have the same form but different meanings.

> He's very **well** today.
> She can speak English very **well**.
>
> The design was very **pretty**.
> That was a **pretty** interesting discussion.

1   **Look at this e-mail and correct the errors in the position of the adverbs. There are 10 errors in total.**

> Hi Susan
>
> I'm terribly sorry, but I won't probably be able to make the meeting tomorrow. I completely had forgotten about it until I got this morning your reminder. I haven't unfortunately quite finished the programme for the Madrid conference. There always are last-minute changes to be made, as you know, and I have just to get it to the printers asap. Maybe
> I can send my assistant instead. She knows certainly my feelings on the subject and can talk on my behalf.
>
> By the way, I liked very much your report and definitely I'll try to send you later in the week more detailed feedback.
>
> All the best
> Julia

2 Certain adverbs form word partnerships with verbs and adjectives, and are used as intensifiers. Decide which adverb in the box would go with each group of sentences.

deeply   heavily   hugely   properly   strictly
strongly   terribly   utterly

1 You are............recommended to keep copies of all documents.

Many people are............opposed to the expected tax on energy sources.

We............believe in the need to reform employment laws.

2 It's been raining............all day.

The firm invested............in new technologies

Their marketing campaign will rely............on digital social media.

3 The event was............successful.

He was a............popular candidate.

The location of the new factory is a............important signal.

4 Without their help, it would have been............ impossible to arrange the conference.

Their proposal was............ridiculous.

The bank has............failed in its mission to help the developing world.

5 We're............sorry about the misunderstanding.

It was............difficult to hear what was being said.

Something went............wrong during the negotiations.

6 This computer isn't working..............

It's vital that staff be............trained to do their jobs.

It proved difficult to manage the department.............

7 Try to relax and breathe..............

We were............grateful to everyone for their help.

She was............disappointed not to get the job.

8 The ban on smoking is............enforced in the company.

............speaking, it's not mandatory to comply with the approved standard.

It's not............necessary to complete this now.

3 Look at the comments below and replace the phrases in brackets with an adverb in the box.

apparently   actually   by the way   fortunately
frankly   honestly   obviously   understandably

1 (This is evident I know, but) we'll have to pay someone to translate this into French.

2 (This is something I've heard, but it may not be true:) the CEO is retiring this year.

3 (This is my opinion, although it might be shocking:) I never thought she was right for the job.

4 (I'm pleased about this:) everything went very well at the presentation.

5 (What I'm going to say is not related to our conversation:) have you seen his new car?

6 (You can sympathise with this:) I was upset when I was told to redo the work.

7 (This is the situation:) I don't think you need me at this meeting.

8 (What I'm saying is true:) they didn't hear that rumour from me.

4 Some adjectives have two corresponding adverbs. Choose the correct form to complete each sentence.

1 deep/deeply

a) The firms sank............into debt during the recession.

b) He was............disappointed with the results.

c) Crews are working............underground to build the tunnel.

2 fair/fairly

a) The instructions seem............straightforward.

b) In international trade, very few countries play ....

C) We have a............good relationship with the supplier.

3 high/highly

a) The car industry is............competitive.

b) My boss always encourages me to aim..............

c) They contracted a............paid expert.

4 late/lately

a) Can you work............tonight?

b) What have you been doing............?

c) All the stores in the mall are open............for the sales.

5 near/nearly

a) It took............two hours to get there.

b) We haven't saved............enough money.

c) The job wasn't anywhere............finished.

6 sharp/sharply

a) We're meeting at one-thirty..............

b) London share prices fell............yesterday.

c) Opinion is............divided in the local community.

7 short/shortly

a) Excuse me, I will be back..............

b) The company's profits fell............of expectations.

c) Her boss cut her............in the middle of her presentation.

8 wrong/wrongly

a) Something's gone............with the format of this document.

b) He was............accused of illegal file sharing.

c) This isn't the place. We must have got the room number..............

2 Emphasising your point

We often want to emphasise an important point when writing an article, a report, an important e-mail, when speaking in a meeting (e.g. giving an opinion), making a proposal or when giving a presentation or speech.

We can emphasise our point in a variety of ways, e.g. listing points in threes, using superlative forms, contrasting two ideas, using more interesting adjectives, emphasising negative statements with grammatical forms such as cleft sentences and inversion, or using emphatic expressions.

Using lists of three

This is a very useful technique because it creates impact and makes the statement more memorable. With longer points or examples, we can use linkers such as *First(ly)*, *Second(ly)* and *Third(ly)* and/or *Finally*.

> *This product is well designed, it's reliable and cheap.*
>
> *The training programme was a great success. Firstly, it was practical; secondly, it was effective; and thirdly – and most importantly – it gave us the best value for our money.*
>
> *A man touched down on the Moon, a wall came down in Berlin, a world was connected by our own science and imagination.* (Barack Obama)

Using superlative forms

The most…, *the best…*, etc. are often used with expressions such as *(one of the) … in the world, in the country*, or with *ever*.

> *It is **one of the best** white-goods manufacturers **in the world**.*
>
> *It was **the most** innovative training session I'd **ever** attended.*

Using two contrasting ideas

The contrast of two different or opposite ideas using balanced or parallel words or the same grammatical forms can make an impact. It is a technique that is often used by public speakers and politicians.

> *We should look at **what we do well** and **what we need to improve**.*
>
> *Plato believed **rhetoric was to truth** as **cookery was to medicine**.*

(See also Unit 12, Parallelism, page 141)

Using interesting or extreme adjectives

If you want to emphasise your point when writing or speaking, it is much more engaging for the reader/listener if you use a variety of adjectives and extreme adjectives, rather than more ordinary ones like *good*, *bad*, *nice*, *difficult*, etc.

> ***turbulent/volatile*** *markets* (changeable)
>
> ***versatile*** *general managers* (flexible)
>
> *in the **pejorative** sense of the word* (negative)
>
> *a **challenging** problem* (difficult)

(See also Unit 1, Adverbs, page 126)

Emphasising a negative statement

- We can use an expression like *anything but* + an adjective that expresses the exact opposite of what we want to say.
- We can use expressions like *whatsoever/at all*.
- We can also use a negative statement and contrast it with a positive one using *It isn't/wasn't …*

> *This course is **anything but challenging**.* (It's too easy.)
>
> *The student didn't do any homework **whatsoever/at all**.*
>
> ***It isn't*** *what you know, it's who you know.*

Cleft sentences

Cleft means 'divided'. In a cleft sentence, information is divided into two clauses or parts, each with its own verb. A cleft sentence emphasises what you are saying.

> *I'd like to talk about our latest training programme.* →
>
> ***What I'd like to talk about is*** *our latest training programme.*
>
> *They make cheap products. They don't produce good-quality products.* →
>
> *They make cheap products. **What they don't do is** produce good-quality ones.*
>
> *Company A bought Company B.* →
>
> ***It was*** *Company A that bought Company B.*

(See also Unit 11, Cleft sentences, page 139)

Inversion

One form of cleft sentences involves inversion, or changing the position of the (auxiliary) verb and the subject. We do this with emphatic expressions such as *Not only … (but) also …*

> *He is extremely successful. He's also a nice guy.* →
>
> *Not only **is he** extremely successful, (but) he is also a nice guy.*
>
> *They won the contract. They got government funding too.* →
>
> *Not only **did they** win the contract, (but) they also got government funding.*

Other emphatic expressions

We often use adverbial expressions such as *above all, indeed, actually, in fact, to say the least,* etc. to emphasise what we are saying.

> *The company wasn't doing well, **to say the least**.* (The company was doing very badly.)
>
> ***In fact**, that brings me to my next point.*
>
> *Their development programme was, **above all**, highly practical.*

(See also Unit 4, Making an impact in presentations, pages 40–41; Unit 9, Rhetorical questions, page 137; Unit 10, Rhetorical devices, page 138)

1 Identify the expressions in these sentences for emphasising your point. Some sentences have more than one.

1 This course is anything but theoretical. In fact, it's incredibly practical.

2 Our coaches are some of the most experienced, qualified and effective trainers in the country.

3 Not only do our employees have weekly training sessions, but they also attend them at weekends.

4 One of our most daunting challenges, above all, is knowing how to ensure a return on investment on training.

5 You may ask, how can we get the most out of our staff? How can we produce the most versatile managers?

6 Now, as then, lifelong learning is vital.

7 Not only did the English programme improve our communication skills, it also helped us with our creative skills.

8 An MBA course is anything but cheap.

9 'You are your greatest asset. Put your time, effort and money into training, grooming and encouraging your greatest asset.' (Tom Hopkins, American sales trainer)

10 'Sixty years ago, I knew everything; now I know nothing; education is a progressive discovery of our own ignorance.' (Will Durant (1885–1981), US historian and philosopher)

2 Complete these sentences about the fridge-maker Haier using the expressions and structures in the box.

as then   crucial   extremely   indeed
not only…also   the biggest (x2)
the world's biggest (x2)   to say the least
what it does not have   whatever   wherever

1 The company was in trouble, …………: sales were slipping, customer complaints were high and rising.

2 …………you're buying from us – a fridge, an air-con unit, a TV set – you don't have to worry about it.

3 …………are their fridges economic, they are ………… rodent-free!

4 Haier's Chairman and CEO has transformed ………… fridge-maker in Shandong into …………fridge-maker in the world.

5 Now, …………, quality control is paramount. Attention to detail is ………….

6 …………you go, you'll find a Haier outlet.

7 When the new boss destroyed the fridge, it was an ………… useful lesson …………in quality control.

8 China has…………bank by market capitalisation, and …………mobile phone company.…………is a global consumer products brand of any real note.

3 Complete the second sentence in each pair using two to four words without changing the meaning of the first sentence. Contractions count as one word.

1 This training manual is too complicated.
This training manual is anything………….

2 He was a very good basketball coach. He also inspired us.
Our basketball coach was not only brilliant………… inspirational.

3 Don't press the red button!
…………do, don't press the red button!

4 My work placement was really good compared to previous ones.
I can honestly say it was the…………work placement …………done.

5 Their apprenticeship programmes are varied, well paid and really practical.
Their apprenticeship programmes are varied, well paid and…………practical.

6 Just focus on what you can do.
Don't focus on…………. Instead, focus on what you can do.

3 Articles

We use *a/an* in these ways:

- before unspecified singular countable nouns.
  *Norway has **a** good record.*

- with the names of professions and roles.
  *He is **an** advisor to the UN.*

- before a noun to mean all examples of the same type.
  *It's **a** tax on industry's CO$_2$ emissions.*

- in expressions of measurement.

*Petrol now costs €1.20 **a** litre.*

We use *the*:

- when it is clear what particular thing or place is meant.
  ***the** oil that his company produces*

- before a noun that we have mentioned before.
  ***The** meeting was held in Copenhagen.*

- when two nouns are joined with *of*.
  *He's not the stereotype **of the** die-hard oilman.*

- before adjectives to specify a category.
  ***the** Japanese, **the** rich, **the** poor*

- when someone or something is unique.
  ***the** world's first hybrid electric vehicle*

We do not use an article before:

- uncountable nouns used in a general sense.
  Weaning the world off oil and gas will be hard.

- unspecified plural nouns.
  fossil fuels, governments, companies

- the names of people and places.
  Helge Lund, Norway, Tokyo

Countable and uncountable nouns

- Countable nouns include:

  - individual things, people and places.
    a carbon tax, a project, an advisor, a country

  - units of measurement.
    a litre, a kilo, a euro, a dollar

- Uncountable nouns include:

  - substances.
    oil, gas, water, petrol, carbon

  - many abstract ideas.
    progress, poverty, health, wealth, happiness, safety

  - verbal nouns
    training, brainstorming, job-sharing, restructuring

- You can make some uncountable nouns into countable expressions by:

  - adding a phrase.
    a piece of news/advice/information/equipment/ furniture

  - adding a word.
    a training course, a research project, a traffic jam

  - using another expression.
    I'm looking for accommodation (a place to stay)/ work (a job)

- Some words have both countable and uncountable forms with a difference in meaning.
  innovation/innovations
  *There have been many **innovations** in alternative energy, but some say that the lack of competition could stifle future **innovation**.*

1 **Look at the first part of this news item about energy use in Japan and add the indefinite and definite articles (*a* x3, *an* x3, *the* x8).**

Japan: Land of Green Gizmos

by Mark Litke

Environmentally friendly bio-gasoline went on sale at 50 gas stations in Tokyo on Friday. The Japanese plan to offer fuel at another 50 stations over the next year and to expand to whole nation after that. It's experiment that might not work in many countries, but in Japan, green is definitely in fashion.

The new fuel costs more to make, but Japanese government and the oil industry are picking up extra cost, so the bio-fuel costs same as gasoline at the pump. That's more than $5 gallon, but the Japanese have been paying that for years without complaint.

The Japanese have embraced green technology – in their cars and in their homes. Maeda family in Tokyo have equipped their home with latest energy-efficient air-conditioning units and lowest-wattage electrical appliances, including energy-conscious refrigerator that emits signal if you don't close the door properly. For the Maedas and, in fact, most Japanese, energy conservation is about more than saving money – they see it as responsibility.

from ABC News

2 **There are 10 extra indefinite and definite articles (*a/an/the*) in this second part of the news item *Japan: Land of Green Gizmos*. Find and delete them.**

The Japanese have one of the world's most switched-on societies when it comes to managing and conserving energy, partly out of an insecurity.

In the 1970s, the Japanese economy was crippled by the Middle East oil embargo. The nation vowed it would never be an energy victim again.

Japan began setting a global standards for the energy conservation by dramatically raising the fuel-efficiency of its cars and by introducing the world's first hybrid and an electric vehicle.

Japan also turned to a nuclear power, which now provides a third of the nation's electricity. The nuclear energy produces no carbon, but some environmentalists consider it a bad bargain since it produces a dangerous radioactive waste.

All environmentalists, though, are the fans of solar power, and Japan has promoted solar panels so effectively that power companies now buy excess electricity from some consumers.

Jeff Kingston, Director of Asian studies at Japan's Temple University, said in Japan, the conservation has become a state of mind. 'It's normal here,' he said. 'It's part of how you should be, how you should live.'

And Japanese companies ignore that at their peril. The appliances in Japan now have prominent stickers with fuel-efficiency ratings. A two-star rating may cost a little less, but it's the five stars that most Japanese want.

from ABC News

3 **Decide whether the nouns in bold are countable (C) or uncountable (U).**

1 Have you heard the **news** about the new carbon tax?

2 How's **business** going these days?

3 That was a strange **business** about the auditor's visit.

4 This is my first **experience** of working abroad.

5 He has 20 years' **experience** in the energy business.

6 Your **responsibilities** include taking the minutes of meetings.

7 Our department has **responsibility** for waste reduction.

8 There was general **agreement** on storing CO_2 underground.

4 | Relative clauses: defining and non-defining

- Relative clauses are subordinate clauses with relative pronouns, such as *that, which, who, whose* or *where*.
  We use *that* or *which* as relative pronouns to identify things. We use *that* or *who* to identify people.
  *B&Q is a kind of store **which/that** specialises in tools and DIY.*

  *Dr Reynolds, **who**'s a lecturer at Saïd Business School,* *is an expert on CRM.*

***Whose** presentation did you like best?*

*I've had several job interviews, including one **where/when** I was told I'm a bit of a perfectionist, **which** surprised me.*

- In defining relative clauses where the main clause and the relative clause have different subjects, we can leave out *that* or *who/which* (but not if it is the object of a relative clause).

*That's the woman **(who/that)** they took on as the new Marketing Manager.* (object relative pronoun)

*That's the woman **who/that** was taken on as the new Marketing Manager.* (subject relative pronoun)

- We often use non-defining relative clauses in writing and formal speech. We sometimes shorten a non-defining relative clause by omitting the relative pronoun and (auxiliary) verb. This avoids repetition.

*Philip Kotler, **(who is)** the American marketing guru, says there are five key processes in marketing.*

*Harley-Davidson, **(which is)** the well-known motorcycle brand, has a website **(that is)** dedicated to female motorcyclists.*

*The campaigns **(which/that were)** targeted at women consumers have done well.*

- In informal speech and writing, we often prefer shorter ways of defining or adding information.

***People who work in marketing** need to be good at communication skills.* (relative clause)

***Marketing people** need to be good at communication skills.* (adjective)

***People in marketing** need to be good at communication skills.* (prepositional phrase)

- We use commas to separate the extra information in a non-defining relative clause.

Paul, who's a typical kind of guy, loves going shopping.

In defining relative clauses, there is no pause or comma between the main clause and the relative clause.

CRM is often associated with the software that companies use to manage their interactions with customers.

In non-defining relative clauses, there is a short pause after the main clause, or between the two parts of the main clause.

Retailers often promote loyalty cards, for example Tesco, which has invested a lot of money in its club-card scheme.

Bristol, where I was born, is a great place to live.

- We can use prepositions with relative pronouns. The position depends on formality.

*There are 91 million Visa cards in the UK, **of which** more than 70 per cent are debit cards.* (formal)

*The people **to whom** the presentation was addressed were mainly experts in the field.* (formal)

*The people **(that)** the presentation was addressed **to** were mainly experts in the field.* (less formal)

*Have you seen the case **(that)** I keep my laptop **in**?* (informal)

We can also use *where* to replace *in which* when we want to sound less formal.

*Have you seen the case **in which / where** I keep my laptop?* (formal/informal)

- *What* and *that* are sometimes confused. *What* as a relative pronoun means *the thing that.*

***What** is unseen in marketing is all the extensive market research.*

*I'd like to have **what** she's having.*

1 Complete these sentences using a suitable relative pronoun, if necessary, and adding commas. Why are some of the relative pronouns not necessary?

1 I first met Larry .... later became my father-in-law .... I started working for his PR company.

2 A 'glass consumer' is one .... a company can see through and knows exactly how she will think and behave.

3 Is this the marketing study .... you were looking for?

4 In an economic downturn, for some companies led by marketing managers .... are truly aggressive and .... dare to attack rather than defend, the worst of times will prove the best of times.

5 *Sex and the City* .... the popular US TV series .... based in New York .... starred Sarah Jessica Parker was an extremely successful example of how to market consumer goods to women.

6 Customer relationship management .... CRM for short is the collection of systems and processes .... companies use to interact with customers.

2 Rewrite these pairs of sentences as one sentence without changing the meaning. Reduce the relative clause, omitting the relative pronoun and verb where possible.

1 Young customers visit our stores. They are usually in the 25–34 age bracket.

2 Procter & Gamble is a manufacturer of household products. It has created various women-specific products.

3 Many large companies are cutting their marketing budgets. They are switching to viral marketing.

4 They need to re-launch the marketing campaign. It flopped with younger consumers.

5 Retailers need to take into account the spending power of women. Women are responsible for most household purchases.

6 Their last advertising campaign was mainly focused on baby boomers. It was a huge success.

3 **Complete this article using relative pronouns only where necessary.**

Right or wrong, the customer always matters

by Michael Skapinker

It was Henry Gordon Selfridge, …………[1] founder of London's Selfridges store, …………[2] said, 'The customer is always right'. Selfridge's quote has become a business truism. But is the
5 customer always right?

There are business leaders …………[3] don't agree. In his memoirs, Gordon Bethune, one-time Chief Executive of Continental Airlines of the US, had a section …………[4]
10 headed 'The customer is not always right'. Whilst Michael O'Leary, …………[5] boss of Ryanair, the Irish low-cost airline, recently went further, telling the *Financial Times*: 'The customer's usually wrong.'

15 You would think their customers would have abandoned them, but they did not. Mr Bethune and Mr O'Leary are two of the most successful chief executives of their generation. Mr Bethune, …………[6] book was called *From Worst to*
20 *First*, rescued Continental from a terminal dive. Whilst Mr O'Leary leads a successful airline.

It was not that Mr Bethune did not understand the importance of happy customers. It was that he knew only those staff …………[7] were committed
25 would provide the service that would keep the customers happy.

Mr O'Leary seems to go out of his way to antagonise customers. But Mr O'Leary is offering his customers one thing: cheap flights. That the
30 service is often quite cheerful then seems a bonus.

You need to know …………[8] your customers are and…………[9] you are offering them. Customers may not always be right, but they certainly matter. Unless you can give them …………[10] your competitors
35 cannot, you have no business.

5   *-ing* forms and infinitives

-ing forms

- We can use the *-ing* form of a verb in the same way that we use a noun – as the subject, object or complement of a verb. We often refer to the *-ing* form used in this way as a *gerund*.

  Advertising *is a creative industry.*

  Meeting *lots of people is one benefit of juggling different jobs.*

- We can also use the *-ing* form when a verb is used as an adjective.

  *Working for yourself can be hard but very **rewarding**.*

  *The **changing** face of employment means we need to change our attitude to work.*

- We use the *-ing* form after some prepositions.

  By working *for a range of employers, no one has complete power over you.*

  *Sam is talking **about becoming** a career coach.*

- We use the *-ing* form when we want to avoid repeating the subject + a relative + auxiliary verb (ellipsis).

  *It's a PR company **specialising** in advertising.* (that specialises)

- We can use the *-ing* form as the past participle, meaning 'after doing something'.

  Having *finished her degree, she went on to work as an intern.*

- The *-ing* form is also used with certain verbs e.g. *like, love, enjoy, hate, prefer, suggest, recommend,* etc.

  *She **hated working** nine to five.*

  *The careers advisor **suggested reinventing** myself.*

  *I **recommend setting** up your own consultancy.*

to + infinitive

- Infinitives with *to* can be the subject, object or complement of a verb. We make a negative with *not* + infinitive.

  To be *or **not to be**.* (Hamlet, William Shakespeare)

  *Not everyone loves **to work**.*

  *I try **not to look** at the clock all the time when I'm working.*

- We use *to* + infinitive after *It is* + adjective.

  It's hard to keep up *to speed with all the developments in the industry.*

  It's usual *in my country for employees **to have** a job for life.*

- We use *to* + infinitive to express purpose or give a reason for doing something (also called the infinitive of purpose).

  *I'm going **to check** their website to see if they've got any job vacancies.*

- We use *to* + infinitive after certain expressions.

  *There is **a price to pay** for being your own boss.*

  *The company made staff redundant in **a bid to survive**.*

  *When you're young, you have **the freedom to pick and choose** any career you want. You're not **supposed to change** jobs too often – it looks bad on your CV.*

- Certain verbs are followed by *to* + infinitive, e.g. *decide, want, need, hope, expect, be able, afford, seem, appear,* etc.

  *You **need to have** a degree to apply for this post.*

  *My parents **seemed to have** it easier than us when they were young.*

Infinitive without *to*

We use the infinitive without *to* after a modal verb.

>He **might change** jobs in the near future.

>When you work as a freelance, you **can't say** 'no' to anything.

Change in meaning

- Some verbs can take either the *-ing* form or *to* + infinitive, e.g. *start* and *begin*, with no change in meaning. But others have a subtle change in meaning.

  >I **love/like/enjoy working** in a team. (general statement)

  >I **love/like/enjoy to work** in a team when we're given specific goals. (something that is advisable, or that I like to do at certain times or in special circumstances)

- Compare these sentences.

  >I **started working** for the company when I was 23.

  >I've **started to send** my CV on spec to prospective employers.

  >**Stop doing** that whilst I'm working! It's annoying me.

  >Why don't we **stop** now **to have** a break?

  >I **remember working** as a waitress when I was at college.

  >**Remember to switch off** the computer before you leave.

  >**Try changing** the way you begin your letter.

  >**Try to make** an impact when you begin your letter.

1 Complete the rest of the article on giganomics by putting the words in brackets in the correct form.

A recent report by Friends Provident into the ....[1] (*change*) face of the British workforce revealed that where once the average worker might have had a handful of jobs ....[2] (*centre*) round the same career, some 13 million of us plan ....[3] (*change*) our occupation at least twice in our working lives.

A gift for ....[4] (*combine*) roles is at the core of giganomics, which is why women, with their innate ability ....[5] (*multi-task*), are particularly unfazed by the prospect of ....[6] (*take*) on a raft of responsibilities. Antonia Chitty trained as an optometrist, but now writes books on ....[7] (*be*) a parent and businesswoman, runs a PR company ....[8] (*specialise*) in baby and child goods and services, and does research for health organisations, ...[9] (*include*) the College of Optometrists. She also has three young children.

Chitty says, 'I decided ....[10] (*work*) for myself because the alternative just wasn't viable, and this is the only way I can see school plays without colleagues ....[11] (*frown*) at me for ....[12] (*have*) yet another afternoon off. I don't have a boss, I have a number of clients, and I plan my days in a way that suits me. ....[13] (*have*) worked this way, I can't imagine ever ....[14] (*go back*) to an office again.'

from the *Telegraph*

2 Complete the article below on the future of work using the verbs in the box in the correct form.

attend	boss	call	do	do	experiment
have	hire	maintain	run	spend	tell
use	work	work			

FT

The shape of workplaces to come

by Stefan Stern

In his book *The Future of Management*, Gary Hamel described three companies that were pointing the way to a more enlightened way of ....[1] things.

WL Gore

5 The high-tech manufacturer is a privately owned company that claims ....[2] virtually no hierarchy whatsoever. Job titles hardly exist, and no one is supposed ....[3] anybody else about. 'Management' is not a concept the company likes 10 ....[4] and never make the mistake of ....[5] their associates 'employees'. Teams work together based on consensus. 'If you call a meeting and people show up, you're a leader,' one Gore associate told Hamel. Another said: 'If you 15 tell anybody what ....[6] here, they'll never ....[7] for you again.'

Whole Foods Market

The fashionable US food retailer has an 'open book' policy, which means that most salaries are 20 known. Indeed, there is a highly unfashionable policy of ....[8] a relatively small gap between what the highest- and lowest-paid employees receive. Teams agree collectively on whom they want ....[9] and how they want 25 ....[10] their part of the store.

Google

When Eric Schmidt, now Chief Executive, first went to Google HQ ....[11] a meeting, he says he could not ....[12] who were the senior 30 colleagues and who were the interns. This is a business that feels like graduate school. Workers are encouraged ....[13] some of their time ....[14] and developing their own new ideas. Their approach seems ....[15] for them.

6 Modal perfect

- The modal perfect is formed using modal verb + *have* + past participle.
- We use the modal perfect to speculate about events in the past. The past modal we use will depend on how certain we are about our speculation.

completely certain	less certain	certain something is impossible
must have	may have may not have might have might not have could have	can't have couldn't have mustn't have

*He **must have been terrified** when the lift got stuck. He's claustrophobic.*

*I'm surprised he hasn't replied to your e-mail yet. He **might not have seen** it.*

*She didn't eat much, so she **can't have been** very hungry.*

- We also use *could have* and *might have* to imagine different events from the reality.

*Why did you drive so far without stopping for a rest? You **could have had** an accident.*

- *Could have* and *might have* can also express annoyance or irritation at someone's failure to do something.

*You **might have told** me that they needed this report urgently.*

- Missed opportunities are also expressed using *could have* and *might have*.

*She **could have gone** outside the company to report the wrongdoing.*

- We use *would have* and *wouldn't have* to make hypotheses about the past.

*I **would have gone** to the auditors (if I'd been her).*

*It **wouldn't have made** any difference. The auditors were covering up the problem.*

- We use *should have*, *ought to have* and *shouldn't have* to comment on, criticise or express regret about past events.

*I **ought to have seen** the warning signs.*

*You **shouldn't have included** private calls on your expenses claim.*

- We use *needn't have* to comment on an action that was unnecessary.

*We **needn't have gone** to the meeting. It was a complete waste of time.*

*You **needn't have bought** me such an expensive gift. That's very generous of you.*

1 Which modal verbs are possible in each sentence? More than one answer is possible in each one.

1 You .... have bothered to make me a copy. I already have one.

   a) needn't   b) shouldn't   c) mustn't

2 It's not like Harry to miss a meeting. He .... have known about it.

   a) mustn't   b) shouldn't   c) mightn't

3 She .... have stolen the money. She wasn't in the office at the time.

   a) needn't   b) can't   c) couldn't

4 If you'd gone into banking, you .... have been rich by now.

   a) might   b) could   c) would

5 He doesn't look too happy. It .... have been a tough negotiation.

   a) may   b) could   c) might

6 I'm annoyed. She .... have sent me these figures yesterday.

   a) could   b) should   c) would

7 We .... have come by plane, but it's so expensive these days.

   a) would   b) must   c) should

8 We were waiting in Room 2. You .... have told us about the change of venue.

   a) could   b) might   c) ought to

2 Read these findings of an investigation into an oil-rig accident. What do you think the investigators said to a) the company officials, and b) the federal government?

EXAMPLE: 1 *You shouldn't have put time and economic considerations above safety.*

Oil-rig accident: What went wrong?

1 Drilling and well completion was considerably behind schedule. Time and economic pressures were intense. Therefore decisions were designed to save time and money at the expense of safety.

2 The federal government failed to properly oversee the project.

3 The risks were underestimated.

4 The federal government didn't require the company to create a response plan for a worst-case scenario.

5 Deep-water drilling procedures are really procedures designed for shallow water.

6 Managers gave engineers permission to use equipment that did not meet industry standards.

7 Federal regulators allowed the company to delay mandatory safety testing.

8 The company skipped a quality test on cement, despite concerns raised by engineers.

9 More than five weeks before the explosion, the rig experienced 'kicks' – sudden pulsations of gas. Despite this, regulators did not demand a halt to the operation.

3 Read these brainteasers and speculate about what happened. The answers are on page 151.

1 Acting on a tip-off, the police raided a house to arrest a man suspected of fraud. They didn't know what he looked like, but they knew his name was John and that he was inside the house. The police burst in on a banker, a lawyer, a doctor, a politician and a businessman, all playing poker. Without hesitation or communication of any kind, they immediately arrested the businessman. How could they have known they'd caught the suspect?

2 Antony and Cleopatra are lying dead on the floor of a villa in Egypt. Nearby there is some broken glass and a pool of water. There is no mark on either of their bodies and they were not poisoned. The only other thing noticeable in the room is that the window is wide open and the curtains are flapping. How could they have died?

3 A man walks into a chemist looking a little embarrassed. He whispers something into the chemist's ear. The chemist then pulls out his gun and points it at the man. The man smiles, thanks the chemist and walks away. What did the man say to the chemist?

4 Professor Bumble, who is getting on in years, is growing absent-minded. On the way to a lecture one day, he went through a red light and turned down a one-way street in the wrong direction. A police officer observed the entire scene but did nothing about it. How could the professor have got away with such behaviour?

7 Multiword verbs

- Multiword verbs are formed when a verb is followed by one or more particles. Particles can be prepositions or adverbs. The meaning of a multiword verb is sometimes very different from the meanings of the two words taken separately. In addition, some multiword verbs have different meanings.

  You can **carry on** for a while if you make no profits.

  They've **run out of** cash.

  Here *carry on* is not the same as *carry*, and *run out of* is very different in meaning from *run*.

- Compare with:

  High remuneration was **paid out**.

  Here, the literal meaning of *pay* stays the same.

- There are two different types of multiword verbs:
  - intransitive (without an object)

    The plane has just **taken off**.

    Their business idea really **took off** in the third year.

  - transitive (with an object)

    She **set up** her own company.

    Can you **pay** us **back**?

- Some can have two particles.

  I'm **looking forward to** getting a high return.

  How did they **get away with** it?

- Some multiword verbs can be used in a transitive or intransitive way.

  The bank robbers **got away**. (intransitive)

  How did they **get away with** it? (transitive)

  A: *Any T-shirts left?*

  B: *Sorry, we've just **run out**.* (intransitive)

  I'm afraid we've **run out of** time. (transitive)

  The intransitive uses are very similar to the transitive ones, except that the object been left out.

- Multiword verbs can be separable or inseparable. An adverb particle can come before or after the object if the object is a noun.

  We've **put by** some money.

  We've **put** some money **by**.

- But you cannot put a pronoun after the particle with separable verbs.

  She **added up** the figures.

  She **added** the figures **up**.

  She **added** them **up**.

  NOT ~~She added up them~~.

- If the object is a long phrase, you usually put it at the end, after the phrasal verb.

  They've **called** the strike **off**.

  They've **called off** the strike that was planned for next week.

- If the particle is a preposition, the verb and particle are inseparable.

  We've **run out of** money. (NOT We've run ~~money out of.~~)

  She **splashed out on** a new car. (NOT She splashed ~~a new car out on.~~)

- We do not normally separate multiword verbs with two particles. However, there are some transitive three-word combinations that do.

  She **puts** her success **down to** luck and perseverance.

  Multinationals can **play** individual markets **off against** each other.

  I'll **take** you **up on** that.

- A good dictionary like the *Longman Dictionary of Contemporary English* will show which verbs are transitive or intransitive, and which are separable and which aren't.

1 Complete these sentences using the correct particle for each multiword verb.

1 How did the world's bankers get *out of / on with / away with* spending all that money that didn't exist?

2 Do you remember that rogue trader who brought *out / down / up* an entire multinational bank, losing them millions?

3 Deborah has set up a financial services company and she's already got lots of customers – it has really taken *to / off / over*.

4 Leon applied for equity finance from a business angel, but got turned *up / over / down*. The figures on his business plan didn't add up.

5 It would be sheer folly to increase our spending. We need to it bring it right *down / up / out* – we can't carry *over / on / out* spending like this.

6 Some years ago, banks and building societies were giving *away / to / over* mortgages like sweets – now it's impossible to get a penny out of them.

7 I came into some money recently from a lucrative investment, so I splashed *around / out / in* on a new home cinema.

8 Regulators should close down a bank when its capital runs *out / out of / off*.

2 Correct these multiword verbs. There is one error per item.

1 Could you add up it again? I think you've made a mistake.

2 If a business can't manage its cashflow, it'll go under it.

3 We took a bank loan out to buy a car. We're paying back it in monthly instalments.

4 How are we going to get this legal technicality round?

5 He had to give up on his business idea when he ran seed capital out of.

6 They need to come up a better business plan with.

7 The business has really taken it off, so we'll be taking new staff on soon.

8 She bought some shares when she came a colossal amount of money into from her aunt.

8 Ellipsis

Ellipsis – omitting words from a sentence or clauses – occurs in different positions.

Front or initial ellipsis

- We can omit words at or near the beginning of the sentence or clause which have a low information value. Typically these are subject pronouns (subject ellipsis) and auxiliary verbs (*be, have, do*).

  See the match on Saturday?

  The auxiliary verb and the subject *Did you* … are missing.

  Going to the meeting this afternoon?

  The auxiliary verb and the subject *Are you* … are missing.

- Initial ellipses occur more frequently than final or middle position ones.

Final or middle ellipsis

- Ellipsis can also occur in the final and middle positions of a sentence.

  A: *Going to the meeting this afternoon?*

  B: *Yes, I sure am.*

  The second speaker does not need to complete the sentence with *going to the meeting this afternoon*.

Use of ellipsis

- Ellipsis occurs most frequently in everyday speech between people who have a close relationship. As the conversation takes place within a shared context and in real time, it is not necessary to use a lot of words which would slow down the pace. It is essential that, when we omit words, it does not make the meaning of the sentence or clause difficult to understand or completely different.

- Ellipsis, especially subject ellipsis, is also common in informal written English, such as e-mails and text messages. We typically use elliptic expressions when signing off in both formal and informal correspondence.

  (I'm) Looking forward to seeing you soon.

  (I'll) See you soon.

- Ellipsis gives writing a punchy style – short but very clear and effective – and is particularly associated with diary and personal blog writing.

  Tues. 3 Jan., 9 a.m. Ugh! Cannot face thought of going to work.

- In more formal speech and writing, we usually omit words in order to avoid repetition. This contributes to clarity and emphasis, and focuses attention on important information.

  We're as keen to complete this project as you are (keen to complete it).

  Unless you particularly want to (write a long report), there's no need to write a long report.

1 Look at the following informal conversations. Decide which words can be omitted without making the meaning of the sentence or clause difficult to understand or completely different.

1 **A:** Would you like some coffee?

  B: Yes, please. I'd love some coffee.

  A: I won't be a minute. I just have to find a clean cup.

  B: Is there anything I can do to help?

  A: No, thanks. You just sit there and relax.

2 **A:** It's lunchtime. Are you ready to go?

  B: No, I'm not ready yet. I just want to send this e-mail.

  A: Hey, can you guess who I just saw?

  B: Who did you just see?

  A: Dave Bingham.

  B: Did you really? I thought he'd left the company.

  A: I know you did. So did I.

3 **A:** Hello, Adrian. I haven't seen you for a long time.

  B: I know. It's been ages, hasn't it?

  A: What are you doing these days?

  B: I'm still teaching at the university. And what are you doing?

  A: Well, it's nothing special. I just started my own business.

  B: Wow! What do you mean nothing special? That's great news.

2 **Look at this e-mail from a consultant to a colleague. Rewrite it to make it sound less formal and to avoid repetition.**

> Hi Sylvia
>
> I'm sorry I haven't replied to you sooner, but I've been very busy focusing on this client presentation for the last few days. I am writing to thank you for preparing those slides for me. I went through them this morning, and everything looks fine to me. There were just a few typos and a missing footnote, but I've fixed those minor points in the slides. I also left out a couple of the slides with more detailed figures. You can see the attached slides.
>
> We'll also need to clean up the employee performance data for last quarter. Can I leave it with you to clean up the data? There's no need to do it immediately, unless you particularly want to do it immediately. You can just send it to me and Richard by Friday so I can wrap things up for the presentation. I'm sure he's as interested to see the data as I am interested to see it.
>
> By the way, I'm meeting him on Monday morning for a catch-up. Would you like to join us? It could be useful.
>
> I'll speak to you soon.
>
> Best wishes
>
> Martin

3 **Write your own short blog for a day in your life. Use ellipsis where appropriate to give the blog a punchy style.**

9 Rhetorical questions

- We can use rhetorical questions to provoke, emphasise, argue or for humorous effect. We ask without expecting a reply. Sometimes, we ask a rhetorical question only as a thought-provoking gesture or a way to stimulate discussion.

  How can you say today what the economy will be like even six months from now?

  There is no concrete or measurable answer to this – it is opinion-based.

- Often the reply to a rhetorical question is so obvious that an answer is not required.

  Bankers' bonuses are huge again. Do the banks really want to trigger another financial crisis?
  He's taking terrible risks with his company. Does he really want to run it into the ground?

- Another type of rhetorical question is one in which a speaker raises a question and then immediately answers it.

  How? First, they process relevant data.

  This technique, like a conventional rhetorical question, enables a speaker to control a discussion and shape the terms of an argument. For this reason, rhetorical questions are commonly used in presentations for effect and to keep the audience's attention.

How, you may ask, can we plan for the future? Well, …

1 **Many rhetorical questions have become informal figures of speech. Complete these sentences by replacing the phrase in *italic* with a rhetorical question from the box.**

> Am I right or am I right?
> Do I look like I'm made of money?
> How long is a piece of string?
> Is it just me or are there …?
> So, what else is new?
> Well, what do you know?
> What are you like?
> What's the use?

1 **A:** I'd like a new laptop for my birthday.
  B: *It's too expensive. Can't afford that.*
2 **A:** I'm from Chicago.
  B: So am I.
  A: *That's a coincidence!*
3 **A:** I don't know what's wrong with me today. I can't remember where I parked the car.
  B: *That was silly of you.*
4 **A:** That 'Reach for the Stars' is a good series.
  B: Yes, and Mel Turner is one of the best actresses around. *I know I'm right.*
5 **A:** I think you should ask for a rise.
  B: *It's not likely to be successful so there's no point.* We all know there's a pay freeze this year.
6 **A:** My neighbour is a life coach.
  B: Really? So is my brother-in-law.
  A: *I think there are* a lot of life coaches around these days.
7 **A:** I see the price of petrol has gone up again.
  B: Yeah, that's the second time this month. *This unsatisfactory situation is always happening.*
8 **A:** How long will it take you to find out what the problem is with the software?
  B: *The length of time (or size) is unknown, infinite or variable?*

2 Complete the gaps in this extract from a presentation using these rhetorical questions (a–f). There is one item you don't need.

a) How, you're probably asking yourself, can businesses survive this threat?

b) What, you may be wondering, is commoditisation?

c) What exactly happens in the deterioration trap?

d) What conclusions can we draw?

e) So, what are these commodity traps?

f) How do you avoid deterioration?

Today I'm going to be talking about the threat of commoditisation and how companies can try to avoid it............[1] Basically, as a product becomes more similar to others like it, consumers care less about who they buy from and buy on price alone. So, the product becomes a commodity.

...........[2] Professor Richard D'Aveni in his book says survival requires smarter and subtler strategies. He describes three types of commodity trap............[3] First, there is deterioration, where low-end businesses enter with 'lower cost, lower benefit' options that attract the mass market. In the deterioration trap, prices go down, and the benefits for customers go down, too.

...........[4] Diesel, the fashion business, has done this by establishing expertise in denim products, D'Aveni says. Another alternative is the side-step strategy: 'Move away from the pull of the market power of low-end rivals.' Armani and Dolce & Gabbana preview part of their collections in private showings to avoid early copying.

The second type is proliferation. Here, either cheaper or more expensive alternatives with 'unique benefits' attack different parts of an incumbent's market – as Japanese and American motorcycle makers did to Harley-Davidson. Prices and benefits for customers may go up or down.

Third, there is escalation. Here, players offer more benefits for the same or lower price, squeezing everyone's margins, as Apple has done with iPods. Prices go down and benefits for customers go up.

...........[5] To move on, D'Aveni says companies must be resourceful and 'change the industry's structure', 'redefine price' or 'define new segments'. As he says: 'Commoditisation doesn't just happen to commodities.'

10 Rhetorical devices

Metaphor

- A metaphor is a figure of speech used to make an implied comparison between two different things. The words used in a metaphor are symbolic, not literal.

  Can you throw some light on the issue?

- Metaphors represent an important feature of business and business journalism. Typical metaphors include:

  – **Health and medicine**
  Common words used: *symptom, casualty, health, cure, remedy*
  Some forecasters see a fast economic **recovery**.
  The Chief Executive is battling to get the bank **back to health**.

  – **War and fighting**
  Common words used: *battle, fire-fighting, bombarded, wiped out, offensive*
  The public have been **bombarded** *with statistics about the bleak state of the public finances.*

  – **Natural phenomena, water and disasters**
  Common words used: *meltdown, flood, sink, shore up, dry up, freeze, pour*
  The stock market crash might lead to financial **meltdown**.
  They're **pouring** *money into social media.*

  – **Sport**
  Common phrases used: *hedge (your) bets, throw in the towel, score*
  Some borrowers are **hedging their bets** *by opting for a combination of fixed and variable rates.*
  Banks appear to be **scoring** *an early victory against the new rules.*

Repetition of words and phrases

- *Anaphora* is the deliberate repetition of a word or phrase at the start of successive clauses, phrases or sentences for emphasis. *Epiphora* is the repetition of a word or phrase at the end of successive clauses.

- Both techniques have the effect of emphasising an important point and help to tie the theme together and create clarity for the listener.

  'If the euro fails, then Europe fails.' (Angela Merkel)

Hyperbole

- Hyperbole is deliberate exaggeration for a desired effect. It is used to emphasise a point by provoking a strong reaction or creating a strong impression, but is not meant to be taken literally. Hyperbole is often used for humorous effect.

- The advertising industry typically uses hyperbole to promote products and services. The media and film industries also use the power of hyperbole to promote the latest releases.

  Gillette: the best a man can get

  The world's favourite airline

- The word *hype* has derived from *hyperbole* to describe the excessive promotion of something.

  Don't believe all the media hype!

Paradox

- Paradox is a statement that seems contradictory on the surface but often expresses a deeper truth.

  The less you have, the freer you are. (Mother Teresa of Calcutta)

1 Match these words (a–f) to the pairs of literal and more metaphorical meanings (1–6).

a) blow   d) grass roots

b) flood   e) offensive

c) fuel   f) track

1
- planned military attack
- planned set of actions in opposition to something

2
- part of grass that grows under the ground
- ordinary people in society or an organisation

3
- large amount of water that covers an area that is usually dry
- very large number

4
- a hard hit
- action or event that causes a bad effect for someone

5
- substance that can be burned to produce heat or energy
- make something bad, increase or become stronger

6
- two metal lines along which trains travel
- the direction in which an idea has developed or might develop

2 Complete the article below about social media with the correct word or phrase in the box.

> battle   blow   counter-offensive   flood
> fuelled   grass-roots   put out the fire   twin tracks

FT

Criticism that spread like a rash

by Jonathan Birchall

A new version of a leading brand of nappies has been beset in the US by online critics since its launch at the start of this year. As part of the promotion campaign, samples of the new, lighter product –
5 known as diapers in the US – were sent out to bloggers in order to build ....[1] enthusiasm.

Almost immediately, complaints appeared in online reviews, claiming the nappies worked poorly and caused nappy rash. Then, in a
10 surprise ....[2], the Consumer Product Safety Commission decided to look into parents' complaints, launching a ....[3] of mainstream media coverage.

The company immediately launched a full-
15 scale ....[4] and put out a strongly worded statement against what it called 'growing, but completely false, rumours ....[5] by social media'. 'When I first read their press release,' says one blogger, 'it did not help ....[6] or make
20 people feel their voices were being heard.'

The ....[7] is far from over. The brand is still scoring below competitors on consumer product-review sites. So, according to the company, it is pursuing ....[8]: vigorously repudiating
25 claims that the diapers are harmful, while also trying to 'communicate all that we're doing to listen and act to help moms and dads'.

3 Replace each less emphatic phrase in *italic* with an example of hyperbole from the box.

> a million times   a ton   an arm and a leg   forever
> hopping mad   horse   overnight   scared to death

1 He was *not very happy* when he saw that Facebook site.

2 It took *a fairly long time* to book the tickets online.

3 He won't go by plane. He's *a bit frightened* of flying.

4 I've told you *on more than one occasion* not to exaggerate.

5 This briefcase weighs *quite a lot*. What have you got in here?

6 I'm so hungry I could eat a *rather big meal* right now.

7 Their website became profitable *surprisingly quickly*.

8 Setting up an online shopping page will cost us *a very high price*.

11 Cleft sentences

- In cleft sentences, information which could be given in one clause is divided into two parts, each with its own verb. This device is used to emphasise new information, or to give explanations, or to contrast ideas.

  What a good entrepreneur does is focus on what he or she is good at.

  (A good entrepreneur focuses on what he or she is good at.)

- *It* cleft sentences are used to emphasise the subject or object, or an adverbial or prepositional phrase using the structure:

  It + a form of (*not*) *be* + emphasised phrase + *that/ which/who* clause.

  It was the best investment (that) I ever made.

  It is not just retailers such as Amazon or eBay that have built successful online businesses.

- *Wh-* cleft sentences highlight the action in a sentence using the structure:

  Wh- clause + a form of *be* + emphasised word or phrase.

  What we're offering is a free trial.

  What's done is done.

  What we provided was a highly professional accountancy service.

- It is possible to reverse the parts in *wh-* cleft sentences.

  It's amazing what they've achieved. / What they've achieved is amazing.

  A late-night decision was what saved the business. / What saved the business was a late-night decision.

- *Wh-* clefts are used with *who, where, when* and *why* to highlight a person, place, time or reason.

  The day (when) I called was last Thursday.

  The hotel where we stayed was near the company offices.

  The person (who's) responsible for accounts is on holiday.

  The reason (why) we've called this meeting is to discuss our quarterly sales.

- *The (only/last) thing* or *All* can be used instead of *what* to emphasise a noun or verb phrase using the structure:

  The thing / All + that/which/who clause + a form of *be* + emphasised word or phrase.

  The thing that / What made him successful was his adoption of a mentor.

  All (that) we need to do is improve our method of chasing payment.

1 Rewrite these sentences as cleft sentences as similar as possible in meaning to the original, starting with the words given.

1 Mandy Haberman invented the Anywayup cup.

   It was …

2 He then made his smartest business move to date.

   It was …

3 Investing in a passionate entrepreneur is often more important than the actual business idea.

   What is …

4 Understanding your strengths and weaknesses, as well as knowing which roles will be undertaken by other people, is crucial.

   What is …

5 Your business plan should say how you are going to develop your business, when you are going to do it, and how you will manage the finances.

   What your …

6 The business didn't work because it wasn't viable to send vans all over the country from one city.

   The reason …

7 The Swedish entrepreneur Ruben Rausing invented the triangle-sided Tetra Pak container.

   The Swedish …

8 The Nokia 2110 softened the angles of typical mobile phones and was a milestone in the mobile's transition to affordable consumer item.

   It was …

2 There are eight errors in this news article. Find and correct them.

FT

A pivotal moment in the life of a start-up

by Jonathan Moules

The ability to pivot is one of the key characteristics of a successful entrepreneur, according to Mark Suster, partner at an LA-based venture capital firm. That Suster describes as a pivot is when a business owner notices fundamental
5 changes in a market and adjusts to them 'on a dime'.

A recent example of this was Facebook, which made big changes to its business model inspired by the stream of messages seen on rival social
10 networking website Twitter. 'Facebook saw that Twitter was getting massive adoption and realised which people really cared about is the stream. What they did were obliterate their home page and in a single day refocused the entire orienta-
15 tion of the company.'

What is why Facebook founder Mark Zuckerberg has been so successful, Suster claims. Twitter itself is a triumph of pivoting. It started life as the offshoot of a website called Odeo. Odeo
20 didn't take off, but that its founders saw was that a lot of people were using the Twitter element. The rest is history.

When making investments, Suster judges entrepreneurs on how they pivot. He also may
25 not invest in individuals until they are on their third or fourth business idea. What is their ability to do this it shows Suster they have the potential to pivot.

12 Instructive texts

- In instructive or didactic texts, we often use a variety of devices and expressions for giving instructions or advice and explanations. We might also give definitions when explaining key concepts or difficult terminology.

  Slack time, as the name implies, is the time when …

  The role of a manager is to identify and minimise them.

  Fast-tracking is the process of rescheduling tasks …

- We might illustrate main points using certain expressions for giving examples and describing clear and memorable examples.

  Given that most projects do not have the luxury of time …

  For starters, accept the fact that slack times are a normal phenomenon.

  For one, do not fast-track tasks that are strictly interdependent on one another, such as applying a second coat of paint.

- We may use imperative forms for clarity and brevity, although this can seem too pedantic if over-used.

  Make a list first.

  Don't try to schedule putting on the roof and building walls in parallel.

  Start thinking of ways to reduce slack times.

  Make sure you assess the risks.

  Note that crashing works only on tasks in the critical path.

- Occasionally, we might use dramatic techniques such as exaggerating for dramatic, humorous or ironic effect.

  Most projects do not have the luxury of time.

  It cannot be overemphasised here ...

  It is mindless to assume that your best resource can work 16 hours a day for three weeks.

Parallelism

- When writing, we usually try to avoid repetition, although a useful way of making a text easier to follow and more memorable is to repeat similar words or grammatical forms. Parallelism involves repeating the same verb tense, word order or a grammatical form two or even three times.

  When the critical path is shortened, the project is finished early. When the critical path is maintained, the project is finished on time. When the critical path is extended, the project is delayed.
  (use of zero conditional sentences, passive forms and *when*)

- We try to avoid sudden changes in grammar, as this can make a text more difficult to understand.

  We'd like it to be safe. We'd like it to have minimum environmental impact. It's important it lasts. We'd like it to last for 50 years.

  Doing the right things and to do doing them right are two important ingredients.

- We can also repeat an unusual grammatical pattern for dramatic or humorous effect, and use inversion for greater effect. However, we usually use this technique in literary writing, speeches or jokes.

  Management is doing things right. Leadership is doing the right things.
  (Peter W. Drucker)

  Ask not what your country can do for you – ask what you can do for your country.
  (J.F. Kennedy)

  As the old joke goes, a recession is when my neighbour loses his job, but a depression is when I lose mine.

1 Choose the correct options to complete this article on project plans.

Project plans: 10 essential elements

Many people think only of a Gantt chart when they think of a project plan. *For instance, / By that I mean*[1] a project schedule, in that it shows when we expect the various stages of the project to happen.

What we *want to / must*[2] have in our project plan is: project aim, outputs, quality criteria, resources, management structure, milestones, tolerances, dependencies, risks and schedule. *Look / Let's have a look*[3] at these in turn.

The aim of the project can be linked to the main business case. *Such as / For example,*[4] your business case may have been written for high-level approval in your organisation. But now you *might want to / needn't*[5] put it in terms the project executive expects.

Taken / Given[6] the aim of the project, what will your completed project consist of? These outputs *could / need to*[7] be clearly defined. If your project's aim is to upgrade the IT infrastructure, your final outputs may be a computer network, a new computer on every desk, with appropriate software installed.

Now we have / Considering[8] the outputs, we need to understand what quality they need to be of. *In the example above / In the aforementioned example*[9], we have an output of a computer network. *However / The thing is*[10], we need to know that the network can cope with the amount of traffic going over it.

What this means / This means[11] we need the completed output to be of a certain quality, and we need to define what that quality is. The way to do this is to remember the principles of SMART: are they **specific**, are they **measurable**, are they **attainable**, **relevant** and **time-based**?

Finally, *make sure / be sure to*[12] produce this list with the stakeholders. But be careful not to promise everything without considering the costs.

2 Identify the parallel grammatical forms, repeated key words and use of other devices in these quotes.

1 'A man is not idle because he is absorbed in thought. There is visible labour and there is invisible labour.' (Victor Hugo)

2 'Organisations fail more often because of what they have not done than because of what they have done.' (Russ Ackoff)

3 'First, you have to get their interest. Second, you have to get their money.' (Doug Richards)

4 'It takes 20 years to build a reputation and five minutes to ruin it.' (Warren Buffet)

5 'Military justice is to justice what military music is to music.' (Groucho Marx)

6 'A good leader inspires people to have confidence in the leader, a great leader inspires people to have confidence in themselves.' (Eleanor Roosevelt)

Writing file

Formal letters

Tips

Remember to REWRITE!

- Read a text that's similar in style before writing.
- Edit your work for typical errors and confusable words.
- Write using clear layout with titles and headings.
- Remember to do a spell-check.
- Ideas work best when there is only one per sentence.
- Take a break before writing your final draft.
- Edit again and ask a teacher or colleague for feedback.

The style of this letter is similar to a formal e-mail. The ending can be *Yours sincerely* in a letter, but *Best wishes* or *Best regards* is more usual in e-mails.

This is a British English form of date. American English always puts the month first, i.e. May 6 or 5/6/2012

If known, include the name, title, position, organisation and address of the person you are writing to, and a reference number or heading where appropriate.

Salutations/Greetings

Dear Sirs
if you are writing to a company or organisation
Dear Sir/Madam
if you don't know the person's name.
Dear [name]
if you know the person's name.

Common titles

Mr for men
Mrs for married women
Ms for women if you don't know, or prefer not to specify, marital status
Note: in the US, *Mr, Mrs* and *Ms* require a full stop (period), e.g. *Ms. Howes.*

Endings

Yours sincerely, if you know the person's name.

Yours faithfully, if you don't know the person's name.

Yours truly, American English

The style of this letter is similar to a formal e-mail, although these endings are not used in e-mails. (*Best*) *regards* or *Best wishes* is more usual as an ending in e-mails.

Sign your name, then print your name and position under the signature.

Monroe Training Solutions
42, Preston Court
Norfolk PE27 5MR
Tel: 01485 597342
Email: jmonroe@gmail.com
Skype: MTS Joanna Monroe
www.monroetraining.com

6 May 2012

Victoria Howes Phd
Department of Economics
Vancouver Business School
2373 Canadian Walk
Vancouver
BC Canada V5P 9S8

Dear Ms Victoria Howes

With reference to your letter of 30 April, I would like to thank you for inviting me to speak as a keynote speaker at the Business Solutions conference organised by the Vancouver Business School this November.

It will be my pleasure to attend and I am planning on giving a talk on the following topic: Creative Innovation for Business Managers. Please find enclosed a copy of my latest book for your interest.

I would be interested in asking you a few questions about the event. Perhaps we could arrange a call at your earliest convenience to discuss further details.

Finally, I would like to confirm that I have sent my proposal and speaker form via e-mail to the administrator as requested.

I look forward to hearing from you.

Yours sincerely,

J. Monroe

Joanna Monroe
Training Consultant

Encl. copy of *Creative Innovation*

Common abbreviations

encl.	*document(s) are enclosed with the letter (also encs.)*
cc.	*(carbon) copies: the names of the people who receive a copy are included in the letter*
p.p.	*when you sign the letter for another person (per pro = on behalf of)*
Re.	*regarding*

E-mails

Making requests

Always use a strong subject line.

When writing to several people, you can use *Dear all* or *Hello everyone*.

In semi-formal e-mails, *Hello* and *Hi* are common greetings.

Your most important statements should appear in the first paragraph.

Limit sentence length and keep paragraphs short for easy reading.

Other less formal requests:
Can/Could you (please) …
More formal requests:
I/We would be grateful if you would …
I would appreciate it if you would/could …

Best wishes | Best regards | Regards | Kind regards are all suitable endings for an e-mail.

To:	Helen Dupont
From:	Martina Schulz
Subject:	Work with Ranson Training Services

▶ 🖉   1 Attachment, 35.0KB (Save ▼) (Quick Look)

Dear Helen

My name is Martina Schulz and I am the Human Resources Manager at Ranson Training Services. I am writing to you because we have received a copy of your CV and we would like to know if you are still interested in collaborating with us.

We are currently in need of a freelance business trainer. If you think you might be interested, please fill out the attached document (Trainer Profile) and return it to me as soon as possible. You can move from space to space with the tab key and save it with your name as the title of the document.

We will contact you shortly for an interview. In the meantime, if you have any questions, please feel free to contact me at this e-mail address.

Best wishes,

Martina P. Schulz
Human Resources Manager

Alternatively:
If you have any (further) queries (regarding this e-mail), please contact me/us.

Breaking bad news

Referring to previous communication. Alternatively:
With reference to …
Regarding …

Be clear and firm when giving the bad news, but also be brief, positive and low key about it. Give as much information as you can about the who, what, when, where and why.

Outline a specific plan of action that you and your company will take. Assume ownership for the customer's situation until it is resolved to their satisfaction.

To:	Silva Zoldick
From:	Aida Martínez
Subject:	Delivery of your order

Dear Ms Zoldick,

Re: your enquiry today about delivery of your order, I can confirm that it will be ready on Wednesday this week. However, we cannot confirm the delivery date because a transport strike has begun this week. We are hopeful the strike will not continue for too long, and that we can ship the order to you as soon as possible. We will keep you informed about the situation and let you know the new shipment date as soon as possible.

I am very sorry for any inconvenience caused. I appreciate that you wanted this order within 10 days.

Thank you in advance for your understanding in this matter.

Best regards,

Aida Martínez

Account Manager

Alternatively: *Please accept my apologies for* …

Apologise and show empathy for your customer's situation.

Action points/minutes

Minutes of meeting on our commitment to corporate responsibility

Date	8 February
Venue	North Building
Present	Lex van Wijk, Yulia Azarenka, Keith Clarke, Teresa Bueno

	Action	By

1 Overseas visits: Stitch Wear manufacturers

There is a summary of the discussion for each item on the agenda.

Following recent complaints of varying standards in our factories overseas, we agree that more frequent visits are essential for standardisation and quality assurance. Keith suggested drawing up a series of guidelines for these visits.   KC/YA   8 March

2 Supplier screening policy

The Purchasing Department will review the current supplier screening policy and send a report before the next meeting.   TB   15 Feb.

3 CSR programme

Various ideas were discussed, the most popular being sponsorship of a local project involving young people. Marketing will look into the proposal. To be discussed further at the next meeting.   LvW   22 Feb.

The initials of the person responsible for carrying out any action required are given in the margin, along with any deadline.

4 New position of CSR Officer

It was agreed that Lex van Wijk will take on the new role of Corporate Social Responsibility Officer and will coordinate any subsequent actions of the CSR team. Decision on Lex's request for a full-time assistant is pending. It was stressed all managers need to assume responsibility for their respective areas. Various ideas were discussed, the most popular being sponsorship of a local project involving young people. Marketing will look into the proposal. To be discussed further at the next meeting.   LvW   22 Feb.

The date, time and place of the next meeting are given.

Next meeting:	22 February, 10.00 a.m.
Venue:	Teleconference room in North Building
Aim of meeting:	Marketing and communication of CSR programme

Teleconference details to be confirmed.   YA   17 Feb.

Semi-formal e-mails

Summarising

As with action points, an effective summary should ensure key decisions or points discussed in a meeting are understood by all parties. Writing a summary involves:
- selecting the main ideas from a text, meeting, phone conversation, etc.;
- rewriting those ideas in a concise form, using your own language.

This style of e-mail is similar to a standard business letter. This kind of summary should be (semi-) formal and brief, particularly if further details or a contract agreement are attached.

This e-mail sets out the standard terms and conditions of the provision of services where a consultant is supplying business or management consultancy services to a client.

Use a positive opening to establish rapport. Refer to the company by name.

Referring to previous contact

Alternative expressions:

Following our meeting ...

With reference to ...

With regard to ...

Name the parties, companies or individuals involved.

Terms and conditions will differ depending on the products/ services offered and the relationship between the client and supplier.

To:	Sadhu Singh, Singh Catering
From:	Ed Taylor, TBC
Date:	2 March 2012
Subject:	Terms and conditions of our consultation

Dear Sadhu Singh

We are very pleased to offer Singh Catering our consultancy services. I'm writing to confirm what we discussed in our call on 1 March regarding our terms and conditions:

1 **Specification of service agreed**: Taylor Business Consulting (TBC) will provide Singh Catering with the following services:

   1.1 **Consultation:** Recommendations for improving turnaround times in the catering industry, innovation in advertising and marketing, and ways of recruiting and retaining catering staff.

   2.2 **Period of consultancy:** A two-day meeting, held at your premises; a written report will be delivered to you within seven days from the date of the consultation.

2 **Duties and responsibilities:** Prior to our next meeting, Singh Catering will provide TBC with a written brief as agreed in our last conversation. After consultation, TBC will provide Singh Catering with a written report of approximately 20 pages. This will include a description of the business's current strengths and weaknesses with regard to the competition and provide recommendations for improving your catering business.

3 **Payment:** A two-day consultation will be charged at €1,050.00 per day. Payment will be via bank transfer, and fees are to be paid on delivery of the work.

4 **Confidentiality agreement:** TBC will not disclose any confidential client information to other clients, competitors or other parties – please see the attached agreement.

5 **Intellectual property rights, termination and liability:** please refer to the attached document for details.

6 **Cancellation:** Should you decide to cancel our consultancy services with less than 48 hours' notice, TBC reserves the right to charge a cancellation fee of €250.

Finally, I'd like to point out we have agreed to meet the week of 15 March, but this is subject to your availability and confirmation. If you have any queries, please let me know.

Looking forward to doing business with you in the near future.

Regards,

Ed Taylor

Senior Business Consultant

Taylor Business Consulting

Main points in the summary could be numbered or listed. Further details and documents may need to be attached to avoid making the e-mail too long.

Referring to future contact and ending

Alternative formal expressions:

Should you require further information, please do not hesitate to contact me.

I look forward to hearing from you (soon).

Asking for confirmation

Alternative formal expressions:

Could you please confirm your availability?

I'd be grateful if you could confirm by the end of the week.

Reports

E-MAIL POLICY REPORT

Executive summary

E-mail is essential to our business. It is a highly cost- and time-effective method of communicating with clients, customers and colleagues. However, incorrect use of e-mail can reduce staff productivity and cause problems for our e-mail and other office systems.

Currently, the company has no written rules governing e-mail usage. I have been asked by the Human Resources Manager to investigate the need for a company e-mail policy. My research shows that there is a need for a formal policy, which I have outlined in this report.

Introduction

This report will look at:

- the issues associated with current usage of the e-mail system;
- the reasons why an e-mail policy is needed;
- the recommended content of our e-mail policy.

Findings

1 Incorrect e-mail usage

In interviews and meetings with managers and staff throughout the company, a number of issues have been raised:

a) Firstly, staff in many departments complain about the amount of time they spend reading unnecessary e-mails that have been copied to everyone.

b) Several people mentioned that chain messages are regularly circulated around the company.

c) Some employees spend time on personal e-mails, non-work-related websites and social networking sites during working hours. Managers find it difficult to tackle this issue with their staff, as there is no e-mail policy to refer to at present.

2 Security issues

a) Access to the e-mail system is password protected. However, some staff have their passwords written on yellow Post-it Notes which are left on the computer screen, which defeats the purpose of having a password.

b) The IT team would like to make it a requirement for everyone to have a password change every 30 to 60 days.

c) Furthermore, the IT team believes that staff need to be shown how to create secure passwords for themselves.

d) In some cases, unauthorised software has been downloaded onto our computer system.

e) The IT staff expressed concern about the risk of software viruses from unauthorised software and e-mail attachments that could corrupt our e-mail system and, indeed, other office systems.

f) The computer system is often slowed down by the circulation of large attachments.

g) Staff do not clear out their in-boxes regularly.

3 Legal considerations

a) Most employees who are using the company's e-mail system inappropriately are not doing it intentionally. They generally do not understand that e-mails are not private documents, and that inappropriate use of the system can open both the company and the individual to embarrassment and loss of reputation.

b) Moreover, e-mail has the same standing in law as any other document. Therefore sending discriminatory, harassing, offensive or other illegal or improper e-mails can potentially leave the company and/or the individual employee open to legal action.

The **conclusion** is what you think about the facts and how you interpret them.

Recommendations are practical suggestions to deal with the situation and ideas for making sure future activities are carried out more successfully.

Modal auxiliaries are used for emphasis in the recommendations of a report, e.g. *should*/*must*, etc.

Additional information not essential to the main report can be included at the end in the **appendices**.

Conclusion

It was generally felt that staff productivity is being reduced as a result of bad usage or misuse of the e-mail system. Furthermore, there are some important security and legal issues to be resolved.

These findings would indicate that an e-mail policy is a vital legal document that this company needs. It would set out our company's definition of acceptable use of the e-mail system for our employees, and help to solve many of the issues highlighted in the findings.

Recommendations

Therefore, I would like to make the following recommendations:

1 Employees should be made aware that while the company accepts their right to privacy, the company does have the legal right to open and read their e-mails if an employee is thought to be misusing the system.

2 The e-mail policy should be short, clear, concise and easy to understand. It is best to keep it to one side of A4, otherwise it will probably not be read.

3 The company should distribute this e-mail policy to all employees, and ask them to confirm that they have received, read, understood and agree to abide by the rules.

4 The policy should include these points:

 a) **Personal e-mails**
 It should be clear that the company e-mail is primarily for business purposes. While some personal e-mail may be acceptable, overuse or misuse is not. For instance, sending offensive jokes or chain letters must be prohibited.

 b) **Sending e-mails**
 We should restrict the general distribution of circulated material when only certain groups of people need to receive it.

 c) **Passwords**
 All employees should receive information on how to choose a secure password and should renew their passwords every 60 days. The IT team can set this up automatically.

 d) **Attachments**
 Large files should be transferred, wherever possible, at times of minimum usage out of office hours. Alternatively, the company should provide facilities for sharing data in larger files via an intranet, shared folders or file-compression programs.

 e) **Housekeeping**
 Staff should regularly delete unwanted messages and archive those that need to be kept. The IT department will automatically advise staff members when their account is getting too full.

5 Since the e-mail policy is a legally binding document, it is important that it is drafted or checked by a lawyer.

6 Employees should also receive guidelines outlining the preferred format and style for writing e-mails. For instance, how to write in a clear, concise, professional tone. For a suggested list of 'dos and don'ts' of e-mail etiquette, see Appendix A.

7 The e-mail policy should be closely monitored and reviewed at regular intervals. This should be done by the Human Resources Department in collaboration with the IT team.

Longer and more technical reports may include some of the following sections, although no report would probably use all of these:

Beginning	Middle	End
• Title page • Foreword • Preface • Acknowledgements • Contents page • Summary or Abstract • Introduction	• Main body including methods/procedures and detailed findings, organised into sub-sections	• Conclusions • Recommendations • Appendices • References • Bibliography • Glossary

Press releases

Date instructions

Write *For immediate release* in times of crisis, or provide other date instructions, e.g. *For release before* (*date*) or *For release after* (*date*).

The header for a press release should make clear who it comes from, what the subject is, and who it is aimed at.

The subject should preferably be in bold so that the media can immediately see if it is relevant to them. Longer press releases may include a sub-heading.

All the crucial information should be in the first paragraph so that the press can scan it quickly. It should spell out the five Ws – who, what, when, where and why.

Apologise when necessary. Briefly explain why the problem occurred and the reasons, if known, that led to the situation, even when only partial information is available.

The main body should include names of people who might be interesting for the press. And – if possible – a good quote which the media could report.

- Include future preventive actions.
- Add bullet points to highlight main points.
- Keep paragraphs short and concise.
- The press release should be no longer than one page or more than 300 words.

When you have finished, edit your release: do a spell check and check details such as the contact information.

Provide information as to how the media can get more information about the subject.

Press   Presse   Prensa

Horden Healthcare Products
Anti-Ageing Division
FOR IMMEDIATE RELEASE
For the medical and trade press
14 January, 13:30
Horden, UK

Horden withdraw anti-ageing drug from market

Horden Healthcare Products recall AAG anti-ageing capsules and apologise for unexpected side-effects

It has regrettably come to our notice that Horden's anti-ageing capsules, AAG, are NOT suitable for people with heart conditions. Since the product was first launched six months ago, there have been reports of a minority of users suffering from side effects such as increased heart rate and blood pressure, migraines, dizzy spells and poor vision. Horden is immediately withdrawing its anti-ageing drug from all points of sale.

'We apologise for any concern that AAG capsules may have caused among our customers. I would like, however, to reassure the public that we are recalling the product with immediate effect,' said Ms Anna Whittaker, Managing Director of Horden's anti-ageing division.

'Furthermore, Horden is committed to conducting further clinical research to fully investigate all possible side effects of the drug. I would like to add that, as yet, we have received no complaints of unexpected side effects among the under-45s.'

Horden advises all users to:

- cease taking AAG capsules immediately.
- consult a medical practitioner if they suspect they may be suffering from possible adverse side effects of the drug.

The matter is now subject to further investigation and an announcement will be made by Horden Pharmaceuticals in due course.

For additional information, visit our website
www.hordenpharma/aaginfo.co.uk
or contact Richard Hayes at the UK press office +44 (0)1754 493072

About us:
Horden Pharmaceuticals is a leading manufacturer of healthcare and dietary products and has been in the pharmaceuticals business since 1965.

Promise to report additional information until the matter is resolved.

Although it is not necessary, this is a good place to add some brief information about your company in the press release.

Activity file

1 First impressions, Business skills, Exercise G, page 10

Student A

You are one of the speakers at an international conference. It is now the coffee break. The person next to you suddenly starts a conversation with you. Ask them questions about themselves. Find three common interests or experiences and talk about someone you both know. You may want to talk about your presentation, your company's or organisation's activities, and your city. Unfortunately, you have run out of business cards. When you get the signal, introduce the person to a colleague, say something polite about meeting up again in the future and then move away and start talking to someone else.

2 Training, Business skills, Exercise E, page 18

Student B

You are a freelance trainer for Ashley Pharmaceuticals. Look at the information you have about the latest courses they require. Mel Van Der Horst, the Training Manager at the company, phones you to finalise the courses. Check and confirm the details, including the fees.

Course title	No. of participants	Date
Organisational skills	18?	13 May, full day?
Leadership skills	8?	17 May, full day?
Assertiveness training	22?	23 May, half day?
Team building	19?	To be confirmed

Fee schedule	Half day (3 hours)	Full day (6 hours)
Up to 12 participants	$900	$1,600
Up to 20 participants	$1,500	$2,800
Up to 30 participants	$2,200	$4,300

2 Training, Case study, Task 1, page 21

Student B

IT Project Manager (UK and Ireland)

- How long and what form should the training take, e.g. instructor-led, on-the-job, or a combination of training methods?

- Can the training be done internally? Will your small team of IT staff be able to train up 200 sales reps all over the UK and Ireland in a short period of time? What are the alternatives?

- The IT help desk is already overworked. Who will provide the support needed post-training?

2 Training, Case study, Breaking news, page 21

As a result of a downturn in the economy, people are starting to spend less money on branded consumer goods. Retailers' own brands are now competing for C&R's market share. The company has decided to reduce costs, and all training budgets have been cut by 25 per cent this year. Decide how you are going to apply these cuts to your training programme.

3 Energy, Business skills, Exercise F, page 26

Student B

Meeting 1

You are the Sales Manager. Your company provides all its top management and sales staff with luxury cars. You've heard rumours that the company now plans to replace these with smaller electric cars in order to be more environmentally friendly. Your staff have to travel hundreds of kilometres every week with lots of samples. You don't think this is a good idea. The other senior managers probably don't need big, powerful cars, but you and your staff do. Meet the CEO and the CFO to discuss your ideas and reach a decision with them.

Meeting 2

You are the Production Manager. Your company is thinking about relocating to new, larger offices outside the city centre. You think this is a good idea because it'll be cheaper, the offices and production area will be nicer, and the company is expanding, so you need the extra space. Meet to discuss your ideas and reach a decision with the Human Resources Manager and the CEO. You lead the discussion.

Meeting 3

You are going to share a new office with your two colleagues. There is only one desk by the window and you think you should have it. Talk to your colleagues and try to reach a decision.

8 Consultants, Reading and language, Exercise A, page 76

1 c) James Dyson is not a business guru. He is an English industrial designer, best known for the Dyson vacuum cleaner.

C.K. Prahalad, born in India, is a business professor at the University of Michigan, and specialises in corporate strategy.

Henry Mintzberg, Canadian professor and author, is an expert on business strategy.

Tom Peters, US consultant and best-selling author on business management practices, is best known for *In Search of Excellence*.

Rosabeth M. Kanter, author and professor in business at Harvard Business School, is an expert on management techniques, particularly change management.

3 The question of why manhole covers are typically round, at least in the US and UK, was made famous by Microsoft when they began asking it as a job interview question. Originally designed as a psychological assessment of how one approaches a question with more than one correct answer, the problem has produced a number of alternate explanations:

- A round manhole cover cannot fall through its circular opening, whereas a square manhole cover may fall in if it were inserted diagonally in the hole.

- Round tubes are the strongest and most efficient shape against the compression of the earth around them, and so it is natural that the cover of a round tube assume a circular shape.

- Circular covers do not need to be rotated to align them when covering a circular manhole.

- Human beings have a roughly circular cross-section.

- A round manhole cover can be more easily moved by being rolled.

- Tradition

- Supply. Most manhole covers are made by a few large companies. A different shape would have to be custom made.

3 Energy, Case study, Task, page 29

Student B

- Stopping staff business trips reduces CO_2 emissions and travel costs.

- Painting the surfaces of the rooms with light, bright colours maximises the use of light.

- Painting the roof white, or another highly reflective colour, minimises the amount of heat the building absorbs and can reduce peak cooling demand by 15 to 20 per cent.

5 Employment trends, Business skills, Exercise F, page 49

Student A

You discover that your colleague, Student B, has stolen a client from you by phoning and arranging a visit after you'd made first contact. You've come to the conclusion that the only way to stop your colleague is to fight for your clients, even though you can't prove you got there first. You decide to confront him/her about it.

5 Employment trends, Case study, Task 1, page 50

Student A

You are a team leader, and Student B is one of your agents. He/She has worked for the company for almost three years and, as such, is one of the longest serving agents. He/She is a very competent worker and a popular member of staff. However, he/she is off sick with minor ailments at least eight times a year, and all his/her sick days tend to fall on either a Friday or a Monday. Until now, you've decided to turn a blind eye to this situation, but management have asked you to conduct one-to-one interviews with all staff members with high levels of sickness leave in an attempt to monitor the situation and reduce absenteeism. Think about what you're going to say and hold a meeting with your agent.

6 Ethics, Language reference, Exercise 3, page 135

1   The businessman is the only man in the room. The rest of the poker players are women.

2   They are goldfish. A strong wind blew their fishbowl over.

3   Do you have a cure for hiccups?

4   He was walking.

6 Ethics, Business skills, Exercise H, page 57

Student A

You are the Human Resources Manager at Maynard Electronics.

- Your department always carries out thorough background checks with care when recruiting staff and you do not disclose information from referees.

- Many employees will resist the idea of security cameras and will accuse the company of spying on them.

- You have always found that having everyone sign a computer and Internet agreement policy is enough.

- Any new policies should be communicated to employees in advance.

6 Ethics, Case study, Task 2, page 59

Student A

You are Head of Marketing and Sales at Daybreak and you are chairing the meeting. Draw up a brief agenda before the meeting.

- The company should issue a press release with a public apology and hand out free samples of your children's cereals in major supermarkets throughout Europe.

- Daybreak should reduce its salt and sugar levels in children's cereals, increase the amount of fibre and label all the nutritional information accordingly on the packet per 100g as well as per 30g serving.

- It is vital these measures are communicated quickly and effectively to the press in order to regain consumer confidence.

3 Energy, Business skills, Exercise I, page 27

Plan

Working title: Relocation and transport concerns

Introduction
- The background to the report
- Who requested the report and why
- What the report aims to do

Findings
- What data was collected and how (transport and staff survey)
- Interpretation of the research results
- Refer readers to details in the appendices

Conclusions
- Review the main issue(s) in the findings
- Highlight the need for action

Recommendations
- Link to the conclusion and findings
- Recommend favoured options
- Mention cost/benefit to company and staff

A

How staff plan to travel

The data for this research was gathered by way of a written survey. Follow-up interviews were conducted with staff who did not know how they will travel to the new location.

A total of 310 staff will be based at the new premises. The following chart is a summary of the findings. More details are provided in Appendix 1.

Travel to existing premises

Walk or cycle	Bus	Train	Car, motorbike or car share	Total
70	101	64	75	310

Travel to Sunnydale Business Park

Walk or cycle	Train and cycle	Car, motorbike or car share	Don't know	Total
20	20	172	98	310

B

The main aims of the report are to find out how many staff will be adversely affected by the relocation, investigate transport links to the new premises and make recommendations in order to help staff get to and from Sunnydale Business Park.

C

The research indicates that more staff will be using private vehicles to get to work at the new location: 172 as opposed to the current figure of 75. The main reason for this is that the public transport options are very limited. There is no bus service, and the nearest train stations, Havington and Pachett, are six and four kilometres away respectively. Furthermore, the train services are not very frequent.

The findings also show that almost a third of staff (98) at all levels in the company do not know yet how they will travel to the new location. The main reasons for this were that they did not have use of a private vehicle (26) or did not know how they would travel between the train station and the business park (72). For more details, see Appendix 2.

D

Given the high cost of office space in the city centre, the company will be relocated to the new Sunnydale Business Park on the outskirts of the city in January next year. This move will provide more spacious facilities.

Despite these benefits, a major issue is the lack of public transport links to the business park. Therefore, I was requested by senior management to investigate this issue.

E

Car-sharing scheme

Due to the fact that many staff will now be using their cars to get to work, I would also recommend that the company provides staff with some incentives to set up a car-sharing scheme. This would be a very cost-effective, flexible option for many staff.

Both these solutions should be closely monitored and reviewed after three months in order to evaluate their effectiveness.

F

In light of these findings, these are my recommendations:

Taxi or shuttle bus service at Havington station
Given the distance from the train stations to the business park, the company could provide a morning and evening shuttle bus or taxi service to and from Havington train station. The timetable would be integrated with the train times from the station. A similar service at Pachett station would be less useful, as the train service is less frequent.

G

Transport options to the new location

This data is based on my experience of travelling from the city in my car, and on online research and telephone interviews with the local council and train and bus companies.

Car and private transport
The Sunnydale Business Park is approximately 30 kilometres from the city centre. The location has easy access by motorway to the city centre, although there is heavy traffic at rush hours.

Train services
The nearest train stations are in Havington and Pachett. Havington is six kilometres away. Mainline trains run every 30 minutes to this station at peak hours and every hour off-peak and at weekends. Pachett is only four kilometres away, but the service is less frequent, with trains stopping once an hour.

Bus services
There are currently no bus services from the city centre to the new premises.

H

The fact that almost a third of staff (98) do not know how they will travel to the new location is a major concern for them and the company. It can be concluded that the company will need to help staff with transport arrangements. To do nothing would adversely affect staff morale, and there is a risk that some staff would leave the company due to the relocation.

6 Ethics, Case study, Task 2, page 59

Student B

You are Daybreak's Head of Production.

- You are looking for a quick fix to avoid the present situation getting any worse.

- Labelling children's cereals correctly should be the priority, but you think it's best to lower the amount of sugar and salt in children's cereals only slightly. Children won't eat them otherwise, and Daybreak will lose sales.

- The company could also donate part of the profits, for example, to a child-friendly project in a developing country to appear to be more ethical.

7 Finance, Business skills, Exercise I, page 71

Student A

1 You start. Prepare one of the scenarios and be prepared to take any probing questions.

2 When you have finished, swap roles. Before your partner begins, prepare five questions using indirect forms.

- Two questions should be outside your partner's field of knowledge, but you insist on them.

- One question should be very long, including two or three 'sub-questions'.

- One question should be very direct and personal.

- One question should be completely irrelevant, but insist on it.

8 Consultants, Case study, Task 2, page 81

Students A and B

Keep the same roles as for Task 1. Make some preparatory notes and decide which negotiating tactics you might use before you negotiate.

Points to consider:

- The senior partner is not sure if there is time for Bajaj-tel to enter the market in 12 months' time. Negotiations with the government could be slow.

- The telecom market is a highly competitive one: the South African mobile operator SANphone is a profitable company, and other foreign operators are looking at setting up networks in Africa.

- You want to negotiate a high project fee. P.B. Bajaj is a billionaire entrepreneur, and it's a challenging project.

- The junior consultant thinks this project will be a brilliant career opportunity, which will secure his/her future in the firm.

11 New business, Listening and discussion, Exercise A, page 104

Count up the number of questions that you answered 'yes' to.

0–3   Although you might like the idea of setting up your own business, it's not really for you. You are much better off working for someone else and wouldn't be able to handle the risk or uncertainty. Who wants to work 24/7 anyway?

4–6   You probably have lots of initiative and good ideas, but remember you need to be fully committed before getting a business venture off the ground. You may need to work more on your entrepreneurial business skills or getting hold of some risk capital.

7–9   You are a serial entrepreneur in the making. Make sure you find a good mentor or a suitable business partner, and work on your sales pitch. If you haven't started your own company yet, what are you waiting for? Go for it!

8 Consultants, Business skills, Exercise F, page 79

Student A

Negotiate these situations with your partner. Make some preparatory notes about tactics before you start.

1 You want to go on holiday to Canada, but your friend/partner wants to go to Vietnam. Canada is going to cost €200 more per person, but you have relatives in Canada.

2 You are a buyer for a three-star hotel chain and you want to get better terms from your regular supplier of bathroom towels and accessories. You'd like them to deliver the same-quality product sooner, at the same price. But you're willing to renegotiate their payment terms and pay them 30 days sooner.

3 You are a first-time buyer and you have seen a flat which has the ideal number of bedrooms (two) and is in your preferred area of town. But the owner is asking for €50,000 more than you bargained for, and the kitchen needs a lot of work doing to it. Your moving costs will be minimal, as you have a cousin who owns an international removals company.

4 You work in sales for a toiletries company. Your products are low priced, although some are a little out of date. Your best-selling product, a shampoo, does quite well, but you want your customer to buy your suntan lotion range. He/She is a buyer for a low-cost supermarket chain. Persuade him/her to buy as many new products as possible for the holiday season – you mostly get paid on commission.

8 Consultants, Case study, Task 1, page 80

Students A and B

Student A: You are a senior partner at Heitinga T-com Consulting.

Student B: You are a junior consultant.

Decide which negotiating tactics you might use. Try to be tentative and diplomatic in your approach, as this project could bring a lot of money into the firm.

Points to consider:

- **Main concerns:** possible regulatory objections from the government; the challenges and timescale of a project this size – you estimate 18 months from the research stage to implementation of the new network.

- **Deliverables:** decide what you can offer, e.g. an in-depth feasibility study, a report on the South African mobile market, implementation, an advisory role once the project is up and running, etc.

- **The team:** decide how many senior and junior consultants you will need.

- **Consultancy fees:** confirm your fees, both for the feasibility study and time spent in meetings to date. Tentatively broach the subject of payment for any future work. Will you charge an hourly rate, e.g. US $230, or an overall fee on completion of the project?

- **Authority:** the other senior partner, Mr Heitinga, is away on business at the moment, but has given you authority to negotiate.

1 First impressions, Case study, Task, page 13

Student B

You are Sir Rufus/Lady Margaret Chesterton, an extremely successful media mogul. You have been advised by your PR officer to soften your public image. You are currently considering donating a substantial sum of money to a charity or NGO.

Network with as many people as possible and find someone who:

1 could help you to set up a children's foundation in your name (decide how much money you are prepared to give);

2 has done voluntary work for a charity or NGO;

3 shares one of your personal interests.

11 New business, Listening and discussion, Exercise C, page 105

The entrepreneurial quality check

1 **Self-confidence**

A self-belief and passion about your product or service – your enthusiasm should win people over to your ideas.

2 **Self-determination**

A belief that the outcome of events is down to your own actions, rather than external factors or other people's actions

3 **Being a self-starter**

The ability to be resourceful and take the initiative; also to be able to work independently and develop your ideas

4 **Judgement**

The ability to be open-minded when listening to other people's advice, while bearing in mind your objectives for the business

5 **Commitment**

The willingness to make personal sacrifices through long hours and loss of leisure time

6 **Perseverance**

The ability to continue despite setbacks, financial insecurity and risk

11 New business, Case study, Task 2, page 111

Student B

You represent a major chain of retail pharmacies in the UK. You know that OTC is a new company with little experience in distribution agreements and you can work this to your advantage.

Your company wants to:

- have a one-year distribution agreement – your company can give 30 days' notice of termination at any point during the year;
- make payment within 90 days of the date of invoice;
- fix product prices for one calendar year;
- pay for 40 per cent of marketing costs in the UK – you're not considering TV ads because they are too expensive;
- start selling its own-brand range of self-diagnosis products at a lower price than OTC's range. You'd like OTC to consider being the manufacturer.

10 Online business, Case study, Task 2, page 103

Student A

You are a consultant. Prepare your presentation, then hear from the client and adapt your proposal. Consider these points and add your own ideas about how to:

- manage the company's brand reputation – you think the business should avoid making false advertising claims, e.g. specify where the shirts are made;
- attract new online customers, e.g. improve the self-measuring experience on the site, include high-resolution photos and how-to sections with a step-by-step guide;
- dispel false rumours, e.g. use viral marketing;
- enhance a quality product and guarantee a customised service, e.g. maintain face-to-face contact with customers via measurings and fittings.

Listen to the Directors at Meerza Tailoring Fashions (Students C and D), then present your ideas for improving the online business.

12   Project management, Business skills, Exercise G, page 117

Student A

Meeting 1:   You lead this meeting.

Meeting 2:   Introduce lots of irrelevant issues and try to make casual
             conversation with your colleagues.

12   Project management, Case study, Task 2, page 119

Student A

You are the Project Manager from Australia. You host the teleconference. The items for
discussion are:

1   **Improving communication**

    You want a weekly progress teleconference with the team, along with a monthly face-
    to-face meeting. You want to know the best time for the teleconference for people
    based in India, Denmark and Holland.

2   **Record-keeping**

    It's important that the project team use your Internet-based application so everyone
    can keep track of things, otherwise work gets missed or duplicated.

3   **New schedule for the first phase**

    Finishing the first phase of the project within the next four months is the top priority.
    You're considering changing the contractor for phase two if this can't be done. As your
    consortium holds the concession to run the port, it will be losing money every day the
    facility is not operating.

4   **Cost overruns**

    The project is already 20 per cent over budget, so you can't tolerate any further cost
    increases.

5   **Improving morale**

    You want some solutions that don't cost much, or preferably nothing at all. You decide
    to start by asking the group for feedback on your management style.

Working across cultures 2: Ethical international business, Exercise E, page 61

Group B

Gift-giving

You are the Head Buyer for a well-known designer accessories brand and you go on a trip to
negotiate a deal with a new overseas supplier. You and your team have put a lot of effort into
the deal and have had to overcome various cultural barriers to date. The negotiations have
gone well, but before all the details are confirmed, your host takes you and your colleague
out for a meal. He presents you with a stunning pair of diamond earrings and your colleague
with an exquisite leather briefcase, both of which have been crafted locally. Bearing in mind
it is standard business practice to give key clients expensive gifts in some countries, your
colleague accepts the briefcase graciously. What do you do to maintain your integrity?

Compensation claims

Twenty years ago, there was a terrible accident involving a lethal gas in a chemical plant in
the poorest region in your country. Employees and thousands of local people were affected,
many of whom died, whilst survivors suffered irreparable damage to their eyesight or
went blind. Compensation to the victims was not paid for many years, although the courts
eventually ruled that a sum of $300–$500 should be paid to each injured party depending
on their disability. Ten former employees were sentenced to two years' imprisonment and
fined $2,000 each. Human-rights activists said this was not enough.

The multinational now wants to open a chemical plant in your town. Many people are
opposed to the idea. On the other hand, it would create much-needed jobs, and the
company has offered to contribute funds to local services. What do you, the local council,
do? What guarantees, checks and controls do you want to put in place? How else could the
company gain the trust of the local and international community?

1 First impressions, Case study, Task, page 13

Student F

You are Cal O'Leary, the middle-aged multi-millionaire lead singer of the well-known (90s) folk-rock band, Rockin' Grassroots. You are now something of a recluse and live in a huge mansion on an island, but occasionally attend events like these. You are currently writing a new solo album. You would also like to find someone to write your autobiography for you.

You usually can't stand networking, but make a big effort to find someone who:

1 knows someone who could house-sit for you on the island and look after your five dogs whilst you record your new album in Dublin;

2 knows a potential ghost writer for your autobiography;

3 shares your taste in music.

12 Project management, Business skills, Exercise G, page 117

Student C

Meeting 1: Try to dominate the conversation and use some acronyms unknown to your colleagues (e.g. BC = business consultant/case, CFO = Chief Financial Officer, HRO = human resources (HR) outsourcing; invent some of your own if necessary).

Meeting 2: Avoid making any contribution to this meeting. The issue does not really interest you, and you have come unprepared.

11 New business, Business skills, Exercise B, page 108

1 (first) name   2 relationship   3 numbers   4 paperwork/documents/documentation
5 show/indicate   6 person/speaker/caller/customer/client   7 understood
8 details/information   9 action   10 deadline

1 First impressions, Case study, Task, page 13

Student E

You are Chris Leibowitz, an incredibly popular US film director. You normally make action movies. You are looking for some business angels to back your latest project. This will be a 13-episode drama-documentary about the history of mankind. It will be incredibly costly to produce, as it involves filming all over the world. You would also like to cast some intelligent celebrities to present the film.

Network with as many people as possible and find someone who:

1 is prepared to finance your project;

2 has contacts regarding presenters for your film;

3 shares one of your personal interests.

12 Project management, Business skills, Exercise G, page 117

Student D

Meeting 1: Introduce lots of irrelevant issues and try to make casual conversation with your colleagues.

Meeting 2: Try to dominate the conversation and use lots of acronyms unknown to your colleagues (e.g. COE = centre of excellence/expertise, PM = project manager, POS = point of sale, ROI = return on investment; invent some of your own if necessary).

1 First impressions, Business skills, Exercise G, page 10

Student B

Prepare two or three business cards before you begin. You are attending an international conference in your field. It is now the coffee break. You really enjoyed the last talk and are standing next to the presenter. Think of a way to break the ice and start a conversation. Find three common interests or experiences and talk about someone you both know. You may want to talk about the last conference, your home town, your job or studies in brief. Suggest that you swap business cards – you are very interested in meeting this person again in the near future. Invite them for a meal or to a social event.

3 Energy, Business skills, Exercise F, page 26

Student C

Meeting 1
You are the Chief Financial Officer. Your company provides all its top management and sales staff with luxury cars. You think this is a complete waste of money and want to replace all of these with smaller electric cars in order to cut costs. What's more, you can argue it will be more environmentally friendly. Meet the CEO and the Sales Manager to discuss your ideas and reach a decision.

Meeting 2
You are the CEO. Your company is thinking about relocating to new, larger offices outside the city centre. You don't have any strong views on this, because you get to work by car, and the travelling time will be about the same for you every day. Meet the Human Resources Manager and the Production Manager to discuss your ideas and reach a decision.

Meeting 3
You are going to share a new office with your two colleagues. There is only one desk by the window and you think you should have it. Talk to your colleagues and try to reach a decision.

3 Energy, Case study, Task, page 29

Student C

- Companies are increasingly buying remote renewable energies, mainly solar energy and wind power, which reduce CO_2 emissions.
- City offices can also invest in embedded renewable energy, such as solar panels on the roof.
- The cost of solar panels is high, but increased demand and improvements in manufacturing techniques are bringing this down.

5 Employment trends, Business skills, Exercise F, page 49

Student B

You've often had colleagues steal new clients from under your nose, although you made first contact. You've come to the conclusion that the only way to survive in the company is to bend the rules a bit and do the same. All's fair in love and war, as they say. Now your colleague, Student A, has asked to speak to you.

5 Employment trends, Case study, Task 1, page 50

Student B

You are a call-centre agent. With almost three years' experience, you are one of the longest-serving agents. When the work gets too stressful, you tend to get bad headaches and have trouble sleeping well at night. When you take a day off sick from time to time, it helps you to cope with a job where you have no control over your workload and you're under constant supervision and pressure to meet targets. Your team leader has asked you for a one-to-one interview to discuss your sickness record for the past year – you've had eight days off in total, all on a Friday or Monday. Think about what you're going to say to your manager.

6   Ethics, Business skills, Exercise H, page 57

Student B

You are Head of Production at Maynard Electronics.

- You are the person who insisted on this meeting. You are very concerned about recent incidents, including theft of electronics goods from the warehouse. It has increased since new warehouse employees were taken on three months ago.

- The company should adopt tougher measures, e.g. surveillance cameras both in the warehouse and the offices. (Two weeks' notice to staff is required before installing any security cameras.)

- You are particularly concerned about the use of social media by staff in work time; the HR Department should also check out content of networking sites more thoroughly when recruiting new employees.

- The company should employ more security staff to carry out the new measures.

6   Ethics, Case study, Task 2, page 59

Student C

You are the Head of R&D at Daybreak.

- The current levels of sugar, salt, fibre and carbohydrates in children's cereals are unacceptable – you have two young children yourself.

- Daybreak could have avoided the present crisis. You tried to warn management and have been recommending a reduction in salt levels for some time, but you were told it wasn't cost-effective.

- Not only has the company's reputation been damaged, but your own professional credibility is at stake. If the worst comes to the worst, you will hand in your resignation and work for the competition.

7   Finance, Business skills, Exercise I, page 71

Student B

1   Before your partner begins, prepare five questions using indirect forms.
   - Two questions should be completely inaudible and/or incomprehensible.
   - One question should be outside your partner's field of knowledge, but you insist on it.
   - Ask and answer one question yourself without giving the interviewee the chance to answer.
   - One question should be completely irrelevant, but insist on it.

2   When you have finished, swap roles. Prepare one of the scenarios and be prepared to take any probing questions.

6   Ethics, Business skills, Exercise H, page 57

Student C

You are Head of IT at Maynard Electronics.

- The company should trust its employees; security cameras and similar measures only worsen staff relations.

- There should be no restrictions on portable technology and use of e-mail and the Internet, as this is essential for people to do their work. Firewalls already exist to limit access to certain sites.

- Studies of Internet use at work show that staff are much happier and more productive when they spend a certain amount of work time surfing.

- If there's going to be more computer surveillance, it needs to be said when it will occur and whether that will be on-going or temporary.

8   Consultants, Business skills, Exercise F, page 79

Student B

Negotiate these situations with your partner. Make some preparatory notes about tactics before you start.

1   You want to go on holiday to Vietnam, but your friend/partner wants to go to Canada. Canada is going to cost €200 more per person and you have always wanted to go to Vietnam.

2   Your client, a three-star hotel chain, wants to get better terms from you – you are their regular supplier of bathroom towels and accessories. They'd like you to deliver the same-quality product sooner, at the same price. This is going to be difficult and you already think the payment terms are unfair – you get paid after 90 days, or later.

3   You are going to work abroad and you want to sell your flat quickly. It only has two bedrooms and the kitchen needs a lot of work doing to it, but it is in a great area. Your initial asking price is €350,000. You are prepared to accept €25,000 less, but no more: you need to pay for your new property abroad (€300,000), as well as removal costs (€50,000 plus).

4   You work as a buyer for a chain of low-cost supermarkets. One of your suppliers is a toiletries company. Their products are very low priced and suit your customers. Their shampoo sells very well. Your supplier keeps insisting you buy their suntan lotions, which are cheap but of an inferior quality. You are prepared to try some of these in the holiday season on a sale-or-return basis.

8   Consultants, Case study, Task 1, page 80

Students C and D

Student C: You are the Chief of Finance at Bajaj-tel.

Student D: You are a manager at Bajaj-tel.

Decide which negotiating tactics you might use. Your aim is to 'test the ground' and see whether the consultancy is able to carry out the project.

Points to consider:

- **Main concerns:** the consultants' expertise in the telecoms field. Have they worked on a similar project? If so, ask for a case study. Timing is also crucial – insist on your desired timescale.

- **Deliverables:** decide on the deliverables you require, e.g. an in-depth research study, an extensive report on the South African mobile market, analysis of why the government previously refused a foreign operator; implementation of the new network and regular consultation with the consultancy thereafter.

- **The team:** you prefer to work with senior consultants – junior consultants tend to be young and inexperienced.

- **Consultancy fees:** negotiate the consultancy's fees for the feasibility study. You are prepared to pay up to US $160 per hour; you will pay an overall fee for any future work, but avoid talking about this at this stage.

- **Authority:** your CEO, Mr Bajaj, would prefer to negotiate with both senior partners at the consultancy.

12   Project management, Business skills, Exercise G, page 117

Student B

Meeting 1:   Avoid making any contribution to this meeting. The issue does not really interest you, and you have come unprepared.

Meeting 2:   You lead this meeting.

8 Consultants, Case study, Task 2, page 81

Students C and D

Student C: You are the Chief Executive of Bajaj-tel.

Student D: You are the Chief of Finance.

Make some preparatory notes and decide which negotiating tactics you might use. Remember, you have already changed your negotiating team once.

Points to consider:

- You only want to do business with Heitinga T-com Consulting if they are willing to set up operations in 12 months' time.

- The main advantage of Bajaj-tel is the low-cost model in India – with $4 or $5 average monthly revenue per user, you still have one of the highest profit margins in the world.

- You are prepared to pay generous fees on completion, but don't advertise this. You need guarantees that the consultancy will deliver on time, within budget and to performance.

- This is a preliminary negotiation, but you are willing to meet again over the weekend, depending on how your discussion evolves.

10 Online business, Business skills, Exercise G, page 101

Students C and D

Choose ONE of the topics below for your five-minute presentation. Work together; for example, Student C, present the introduction and conclusion; Student D, present one key point broken down into three main concepts. Be prepared to take questions either during the presentation or at the end. Be ready to think on your feet and answer the questions as best you can.

- How your company could attract more online business

- Why organisations should use social networking sites

- How social networking sites can improve your future job prospects

Listen to the other pair's presentation first. You may ask them serious questions during their talk, but at the end ask three irrelevant questions so that they have to think on their feet, e.g.

How would you weigh a plane without scales?

What's the best movie you've seen in the last year?

If you could be anywhere in the world right now, where would you be?

10 Online business, Case study, Task 2, page 103

Students C and D

You are the Directors at Meerza Tailoring Fashions. How can you improve the customer online experience and manage your brand reputation? Prepare your ideas, then outline your vision for the future, saying where you want to be in two years' time. Then listen to the consultants' proposals and ask them challenging questions. Consider these points and add your own ideas about how to:

- stay ahead of the competition;

- improve the online experience, e.g. help customers when taking their own measurements;

- manage the face-to-face measuring sessions;

- manage your brand reputation, e.g. complaints and rumours;

- retain control of website content.

Present your vision to Students A and B before they present their proposals.

12   Project management, Case study, Task 2, page 119

> **Student B**
>
> You are the civil engineer from Denmark. You're a firm believer in frank and direct communication. The items for discussion are:
>
> 1 **Improving communication**
>
>   You miss your family and don't want to spend all your time in India now that the project is up and running. You think you can manage things well from Denmark and visit the site once a month for a couple of days. Most issues can be dealt with via e-mail and teleconferences as far as you're concerned.
>
> 2 **Record-keeping**
>
>   You find the Project Manager's Internet-based application difficult to use. It doesn't really suit your needs. Some adjustments are required so that you can input vital information about your work.
>
> 3 **New schedule for the first phase**
>
>   You think the first phase of the project is going to take another eight months, mainly because the whole layout and design of the port has been unexpectedly changed by the client.
>
> 4 **Cost overruns**
>
>   You know the project is already 20 per cent over budget, but that was mostly due to delays in starting the project and the extra cost of materials for the bigger port that's now planned. You want to raise the subject of paying your staff overtime because of all the extra work you've had on the redesign. You also want to ask for return first- or business-class flights to India once a month.
>
> 5 **Improving morale**
>
>   You think it would help if the client noticed more what your group is doing right, i.e. providing excellent-quality work, and showed some appreciation.

1   First impressions, Case study, Task, page 13

> **Student C**
>
> You are Daniel(le) Blum, a hugely successful businessperson and also manager of your city's first-division football club. You have recently decided to go into politics and are standing as a candidate in the upcoming local elections. You are looking for a brilliant media relations advisor to help you become a 'caring politician' and put a spin on your public image.
>
> Network with as many people as possible and find someone who:
>
> 1 knows the right people in the media and/or politics;
>
> 2 could act as your public relations person or 'spin doctor';
>
> 3 shares one of your personal interests.

6   Ethics, Business skills, Exercise H, page 57

> **Student D**
>
> You are the Managing Director at Maynard Electronics. You want to consult an employment lawyer before taking any action, but you'd like to hear what the other managers think first.
>
> • The company needs to tread carefully on privacy issues – employers can be legally liable unless they deal correctly with information provided, e.g. from CVs, background checks or anything discovered during routine e-mail monitoring.
>
> • The legal position concerning monitoring employees' phone calls, e-mail and Internet usage is complex and unclear – the issue is currently under review by the government.
>
> • Another area is that of employees' records. Until now, companies have not been obliged to reveal this information to employees, but the law has changed, and the company needs a policy on this.

12 Project management, Case study, Task 2, page 119

Student C

You are the lead contractor from India. You would never openly disagree with or challenge the Project Manager or the rest of the group. The items for discussion are:

1 **Improving communication**

You'd really appreciate more regular face-to-face meetings, even informal meetings, especially with the civil engineer, who never seems to be on site.

2 **Record-keeping**

You can't see the point of the Project Manager's Internet-based application and you've just been ignoring requests to use it. Besides, you always use e-mail and phone calls to report on developments.

3 **New schedule for the first phase**

Slippage is inevitable, and you feel the client has unrealistic expectations. You wouldn't like to guess how long it will take now, especially as it's the monsoon season. And you always try to avoid giving a client bad news.

4 **Cost overruns**

You know the project is already 20 per cent over budget, but you're going to need to employ at least 100 more construction workers to get the job done. You'd also like to ask the Project Manager to provide more buses to transport workers to the site.

5 **Improving morale**

You think the consortium could think about providing accommodation and facilities on site for migrant construction workers and their families. Also, there's nothing like money to make people happier; bonuses on completion of work would boost morale.

---

1 First impressions, Case study, Task, page 13

Student D

You are Amy/Antoine de la Tour, a hugely successful film actor and businessperson. You have your own film company and a social conscience. You recently took a few years out of your career to spend more time with your children, but you are now missing your work. You don't want to start playing middle-aged characters in TV soap operas, but these are the kinds of parts your agent keeps offering you.

Network with as many people as possible and find someone who:

1 could give you an interesting part in a film;

2 could act as your agent;

3 shares one of your personal interests.

Working across cultures 3: Socialising, Task page 91

Student B

1 You are a member of an international delegation: greet your host, listen to the welcome speech, return any compliments if necessary and ask a few questions about the organisation and the week's schedule.

2 After a tour of the company, you are offered some light refreshments and local dishes that you do not like the look of. Refuse politely in as many different ways as possible. In fact, you are feeling rather unwell after your journey.

3 You are making small talk at lunch. Answer your host's questions politely, although you are not used to talking about your family with people you don't know very well and hate talking about the weather. Try to introduce other topics of conversation such as sport, cinema, local sightseeing, etc.

4 Your host invites you out for dinner with all the team this evening, but you have an urgent work assignment and you are exhausted after your long-haul flight. Turn down the invitation politely and suggest an alternative.

---

12   Project management, Case study, Task 2, page 119

> **Student D**
>
> You are the head of the dredging company from Holland which is responsible for reclaiming land for the sea in order to build part of the port. You'd like to use this opportunity to get to know the other team members a bit better, so ask them questions about themselves. The items for discussion are:
>
> 1   **Improving communication**
>
>   You can't see the point of regular meetings. You know what you have to do, and meetings are only necessary once a month, or if there's an urgent issue to discuss.
>
> 2   **Record-keeping**
>
>   You have your own system, so you don't need to use the Project Manager's Internet-based application. It's just extra work for you.
>
> 3   **New schedule for the first phase**
>
>   The work has run into complications and a different dredging machine is needed. It will take several weeks to arrive and that will delay the work of the contractor as well.
>
> 4   **Cost overruns**
>
>   You know the project is already 20 per cent over budget, but the new dredging machine is an expensive piece of equipment. You're going to have to ask for another $200,000.
>
> 5   **Improving morale**
>
>   You think there should be some social events so people can get to know each other better. A party would be a good start.

10   Online business, Case study, Task 2, page 103

> **Student B**
>
> You are a consultant. Prepare your presentation, then hear from the client and adapt your proposal. Consider these points and add your own ideas about how to:
>
> - manage the company's brand reputation, e.g. the Social Media Manager should trawl blogs and social networking sites on the Internet, and the company could offer real-time unfiltered customer reviews
>
> - handle customer complaints effectively, e.g. the Social Media Manager should have the authority to reply to any critical posts immediately
>
> - attract new online customers, e.g. use viral marketing
>
> - concentrate on online sales, e.g. face-to-face contact with customers will slow down the online business and should be abandoned.
>
> Listen to the Directors at Meerza Tailoring Fashions (Students C and D), then present your ideas for improving the online business.

11   New business, Business skills, Exercise G, page 109

> **Student B**
>
> You are Max Bryson, the Accounts Manager at Carswell Department Stores. Dunbarry Jewellers, a new company, is just one of many small suppliers you deal with. You have a good working relationship with the company; they are reliable, and their products are good quality and sell well. You feel bad that sometimes you have to make them promises you can't keep.
>
> - It's late July. You've paid one of the two invoices (BJ1698, dated 28 May) that you promised Val Bailey at Dunbarry Jewellers, but not the other one (BJ1712, dated 8 June).
>
> - There are also two more invoices which are now overdue for payment: BJ1728, dated 13 June, and BJ1735, dated 22 June.
>
> - You're hoping Val will accept payment of all three invoices at the end of August. Think of a convincing reason why you've been paying your bills so late – you can't afford to let any suppliers know that you're having cashflow problems.

11   New business, Reading and language, Exercise E, page 107

Article 2

FT

Work longer, work older

by Luke Johnson

This decade will see older people working longer. That is not surprising. In addition to governments from Britain to Greece raising the retirement age, low interest rates and the reduction in pension benefits mean many people will not have enough money at age 65 to enjoy their sunset years. They will be forced to work to make ends meet.

What I find interesting – and what could change the face of business – is that they may prefer to do that working for themselves. A recent study suggests that one in six Britons aged 46–65 hopes to embark on a new business venture rather than retire. This is seven times more than the number of possible start-ups from their parents' generation – and could amount to a million new businesses in the UK.

Their experience, wisdom and connections will be their secret weapons. But they are also likely to have more time and money to spare than current entrepreneurs. The typical age today for someone to start his/her own business is between 30 and 45. Inconveniently, this is also when you are likely to have young children and a mortgage. 'Olderpreneurs', meanwhile, will often be close to seeing off these responsibilities – as well as eager for ways to stay in touch with people from all generations, as customers, partners, suppliers or perhaps staff. I predict many great companies will be started in the next few years.

10   Online business, Business skills, Exercise G, page 101

Students A and B

Choose ONE of the topics below for your five-minute presentation. Work together: for example, Student A, present the introduction and conclusion; Student B, present one key point broken down into three main concepts. Be prepared to take questions either during the presentation or at the end. Be ready to think on your feet and answer the questions as best you can.

- How your company or organisation could improve its website

- Your favourite website and why you think it's effective

- A comparison between the content and usability of three similar websites

When you have finished, listen to the other pair's presentation. You may ask them serious questions at the end, but interrupt them during their talk, asking three irrelevant questions so that they have to think on their feet, e.g.

If you were at a business lunch, and you ordered rare steak and they brought it to you well done, what would you do?

How many times do a clock's hands overlap in a day?

If you could choose one superhero power, what would it be, and why?

Audio scripts

UNIT 1 FIRST IMPRESSIONS

CD1 TRACK 1 (I = INTERVIEWER, AG = ANNELIESE GUÉRIN-LETENDRE)

I People say the first two minutes of a presentation are the hardest part. What advice do you give to presenters?

AG I think, yes, maybe even less than two minutes, actually, to make that vital first impression. Um, and I think I would want to work with my client to try and break that down a little bit into what's really going on with the audience and, indeed, what happens when we communicate with people. A lot is based on body language, non-verbal communication. Um, that may be as much as 60 to, some people say even 90 per cent of our communication is non-verbal communication, er, which is rather an amazing statistic. Um, but certainly, we do take in impressions from the sound of the person's voice; their facial expression, for example; their posture; the way in which they use the room, the space that they have. Um, all of those things combine, really … the way they dress. Um, we will put together a composite picture. Usually these messages are not viewed independently; they're usually seen as clusters of behaviour. And we will build up an image very, very quickly of who we think that person is and what they are and who they are, um, before we really even take in much of what they've got to say, although, of course, those first few words are also essential.

CD1 TRACK 2 (AG = ANNELIESE GUÉRIN-LETENDRE)

AG We think about posture, for example, um, the way one stands, er, the way in which you can be upright but not rigid, um, the way you take charge of the space. For example, rather than hiding behind a table or a lectern, um, you try to get that direct contact with your audience. A problem comes, of course, with PowerPoint, where people want to stay near their laptop to change the slides, and obviously, the, the message is very simple, just use a remote and that will liberate you from your laptop. Um, but also the way that we use our eye contact to scan the room, rather than just look at the first few rows, so that everybody feels as though there's a conversation going on, no matter how far back they are or whether they're at the sides of the room. Um, the way in which we use modulation in our voices. You know, the, the, the kind of intonation that we use. There is also sometimes perhaps a tendency to want to shout in order to be heard in a large room. If there's a microphone, try it out before the audience arrives, see how your voice sounds, get that feel for how you're going to sound, how you're going to come across, and modulate your voice accordingly. But also remember how important intonation is. Um, English is the language of Shakespeare after all, so we have that capacity to produce all sorts of light and dark shades in our voices that add interest and get the audience really paying attention. Um, and I think also we need to think very carefully about how we control our gestures. Um, certainly all of us have, perhaps, particular mannerisms that we might use. Um, but, you know, the flicking of the hair, um, or the nervous fidgeting with a bracelet or a ring, or the constant adjustment of the suit jacket, or the nervous cough can become a distraction to the audience, and all of that can happen in the first minute or so. A minute is a long time when you're speaking.

CD1 TRACK 3 (Y = YASMIN, E = ERIK)

CONVERSATION 1

Y Oh, excuse me, could you do me a favour and pass the milk jug?

E Yes, of course. Here you are.

Y So, what did you think of the last presentation?

E Great, wasn't it? I always enjoy her talks, don't you?

Y Yes, she really knows how to captivate an audience, doesn't she? But it wasn't exactly what I was expecting.

E No? Why's that?

Y Well, I thought there was going to be a panel discussion at the end …

E Oh, I think that's coming up after the coffee break.

Y Oh, I see. And what do you think of the conference so far?

E Not bad. Fewer people than last year, aren't there?

Y Yes, it must be the venue. Copenhagen isn't exactly the cheapest city to get to, is it?

E No, that's true. Do you mind me asking where you are from?

Y Oh, I'm from the UK, Birmingham. And yourself?

E I'm Danish.

Y Really? Oh, sorry, I didn't realise …

E No, no, that's all right. Copenhagen is expensive, I know.

Y Well, you speak excellent English, if you don't mind me saying.

E Thanks. Actually, my sister's doing research at Cambridge University. So, you know, I visit her often.

Y Oh, really?

E Uh-huh. My name is Erik, by the way.

Y Nice to meet you, Erik. I'm Yasmin.

E Oh, I think we're starting again. Shall we go through?

CD1 TRACK 4 (S = SERGI, V = VAL, T = TONY)

CONVERSATION 2

S That's a great calling card, if you don't mind me saying.

V Oh, thanks. Our company thought these cute figures would get us noticed at conferences.

S Great idea. I think I'll ask for one when I get back.

V They're certainly eye-catching, but they're a bit bulky to carry around, you know.

S Do you mind if I take a look at one?

V Sure, here you go.

S Thanks, that's great. Valerie, er, Valerie Car… Sorry, how do you say your name?

V Ah, it's Valerie Carlyle. From Lennox, the pharmaceutical division.

S And how's business in your part of the world, Valerie?

V Oh, just call me Val. Not bad. Sales have picked up again in the US.

S So I hear. That must be a relief. Oh, look, have you seen the menu for dinner this evening?

V Mmm, yes, but I didn't enjoy the dinner very much last night. Did you?

S Well, it's always good to try some of the local dishes, but, frankly, I'm not too keen on very rich food.

V I know what you mean. Neither am I.

S I don't suppose you know of any good places to eat near here, do you?

V It's funny you should say that, I think my colleague might. Excuse me, Tony, did the hotel clerk recommend somewhere to eat out?

T Uh, hang on a sec. I think I have a card here somewhere. Yeah, the Oslo Fish Bar! They do great, er … fish, apparently.

V Sounds perfect. Do you want to eat there this evening? Oh, sorry, I didn't catch your name …

S It's Sergei.

V Hi, Sergei. As you know, I'm Val, and this is Tony.

S Good to meet you, Val, Tony. Here is my business card.

V Wow! That's an impressive name! How do you say it?

S Actually, it's Leyushenko, but just call me Sergei.

V OK, Sergei. Good talking to you. Oh, excuse me, but I've just seen a friend. I'll see you later, hopefully.

S Sure.

V Hi, Petra! How *are* you?

T So, you're based in Saint Petersburg …

S That's right.

T I was there not so long ago, actually. For the Medical Fair.

S Really? I thought your face looked familiar! Didn't you give a talk on medical aid in developing countries? You got a standing ovation if I remember rightly.

T Well, I think a few people stood up, but they were mostly colleagues. Anyway, er, would you like to join us for dinner tonight, Sergei?

S Well, that's very kind of you. Thanks. Actually, do you mind if I invite one of my team?

T No, not at all. The more, the merrier!

S That will be great. Excuse me a moment, Tony. I'm afraid I have to make a quick call.

V Tony! Tony, I don't think you've met Petra from the Hamburg office, have you?

T Ah, so *you're* the famous Petra!

V Tony! Petra, this is Dr Anthony Clarke.

T Er, it's great to meet you at last, Petra.

CD1 TRACK 5 (EK = ED KAMINSKI)

EK First of all, I'd like to say, thank you for coming this evening. I'm sure you'll agree we've enjoyed good food, good company and excellent wine. The question I've been asked most this evening is, when did you first get involved with Logistaid? The answer's simple. When I was a young student of engineering, I decided to take a gap year, a year out to travel the world. And the second question I get asked is why? And what I say is, the thing that impressed me most about the world at that time wasn't Venice or the Sydney Opera House; it wasn't the Taj Mahal or the Statue of Liberty, or even the ancient pyramids of Egypt. These, of course, are all brilliant tributes to our capacity for creativity and construction. What impressed me most of all was that, despite our wonderful ability to design and build magnificent monuments and beautiful cities, there were still many, many people in the world without a roof over their heads, sick people without a local hospital, and children without a school. So, that was why I decided to get involved with Logistaid and do something about it. I'd like to stand here and tell you about all the good work that we've done at Logistaid; I'd like to stand here and tell you about the number of refugees we've helped to re-house, or the number of vaccinations we've managed to give, or the number of teachers we've managed to send out to remote areas to educate enthusiastic kids ... but I won't. That would defeat the purpose of tonight's Gala Dinner. The reason I am here tonight, the reason you have been invited here tonight, is because there are still many parts of the world where people live without decent housing, where people don't have access to basic medical treatment, and where children still can't go to school because one doesn't exist. So, ladies and gentlemen, I'd like to ask you, when did you get involved with Logistaid? And I'd like to hear you say, it was tonight, here at our first celebrity Gala Dinner, rubbing shoulders with some of the country's most distinguished public figures, surrounded by some of society's most influential movers and shakers. Well, let's see you moving and shaking now! Let's see you get involved! Let's see how you can help us to help them. Thank you.

UNIT 2 TRAINING

CD1 TRACK 6 (I = INTERVIEWER, BA = DR BERND ATENSTAEDT)

I What are apprenticeships, and why are they useful?

BA An apprentice is a young person training at, er, an office, or in a factory, or in a warehouse. And they are useful because their employers, hopefully, er, train them to become permanent employees. They will then show loyalty to the company because they have been trained by the company. And, er, and overall, er, it gives the young apprentice, er, a focus in life. Er, they get an allowance, certainly in Germany, er, a monthly allowance, er, to keep them going. So, overall, certainly we in German industry feel, er, the whole idea of apprenticeships is a worthwhile exercise for both employers and for the young apprentices.

CD1 TRACK 7 (I = INTERVIEWER, BA = DR BERND ATENSTAEDT)

I Can you give us some examples of how apprenticeships work in Germany?

BA Apprentices in Germany are usually school leavers aged 16. And about, er, 60 per cent of all school leavers, aged 16, become apprentice[s]. The, the rest goes into higher education either, er, into, er, colleges or into universities, so the majority become apprentices. Er, most of them want, er, to go into well-known companies like BMW, er, Mercedes, Siemens. Once they get, er, a training, er, job, or employment as an apprentice, they then, er, sign an employment contract, er, which, er, tells them how many hours they have to work, how long the employment period is, er, usually two years ... you can extend to, extend to three and a half years. And then it sets down how much allowances the company pays, pays them. And they spend usually three to four days in the company and one to two days, er, in a vocational school, which is, er, usually in the same, er, place, er, town or city.

I How does your organisation promote apprenticeships in the UK?

BA There's no solid, er, training programme for all apprentices right across the UK, which we have in Germany. We have, er, a Training Act, er, we have 340 recognised skills in Germany, from apprentices in offices, er, to apprentices in a factory, on the conveyor belt. And, and we have a, a recognised, so to speak, profession, skills profession, which, er, we are very proud of. Ah, we have, er, two labels, er, we are proud of in industry: *Trained in Germany* and *Made in Germany*. And we would like, all of us in German Industry-UK, would like to have the dual training system as described. And we are now working with the government here on some sort of system which is similar to our dual training system.

CD1 TRACK 8 (B = BRENDAN)

B I initially spent two days' work experience while still at school and then a further week at an electronics company when I was 16 years old. It was then that I decided to pursue an apprenticeship. I started working in 1992 as an apprentice technician. I was one of the first interns on the newly established apprentice scheme. I then spent four years in the workshop completing the apprenticeship, and two more years working in the same company as a qualified technician. Since then, I've taken on numerous roles across different areas of the organisation, including Technical Service, Parts, Marketing, Sales, and the Product department in Munich. What advice would I give to people starting out? Challenge yourself, don't be afraid to take risks and, more importantly, do something you'll enjoy and believe in. I always get a buzz out of playing with the new technology.

CD1 TRACK 9 (F = FALAK)

F It was pure chance! I'd just finished my GCSEs and had enrolled into college to start studying for A Levels and take the normal degree route, hoping I would find a job to do with engineering when I'd finished. But then I saw an ad in an aeronautical magazine about apprenticeships at Rolls Royce. At first, my parents were worried that I'd be missing out on a decent education, going off to work when I'd just turned 16. But I'd be going to college, getting good qualifications and spending time working on planes – all whilst being paid! I completed my apprenticeship in 2001. I then progressed to senior technician and I'm now a master technician. The thing I find most rewarding is the satisfaction of knowing that you've fixed something. I love working at the head office because I'm involved in R&D – research and development and testing. I also get to work on some special models – it's just so innovative and hi-tech. If you want to work in the aeronautical industry, you have to aim high and go for it. Having a lot of enthusiasm is important, too, and will take you far.

CD1 TRACK 10 (R = RACHEL)

R After I left school with four A Levels, I went to do a degree in French with Business Studies at York University. My university studies also included a 12-month placement working for a Swiss drinks company in their Research and Technology department in Zurich. After graduating in 2002, I joined the UK graduate programme.
What's my advice? Um, I'd say you need to have passion for what you do, as well as having a good understanding of what's going on in the marketplace – this applies to anything you want to do, not just the food and beverages industry. I think it's important to explore all avenues open to you. You need to do lots of research to find out what options are available to you before you can make your mind up.

CD1 TRACK 11 (M = MARIEKE)

M I've just finished studying for a Linguistics degree at Madrid University. Um, I speak English and Spanish, as well as German. Tomorrow I've got an interview lined up with an international marketing company here in Madrid for a work placement, an internship for the summer. It's only for three months, and I'm not sure how much I'll get paid yet. Interns back home get paid on average about 500 euros per month, which is quite good really. But I'm prepared to accept this internship for less.
I'm also thinking about doing a Master's degree in marketing, so I'll ask them about future prospects, um, training and job opportunities. Perhaps they might offer me a part-time job in the afternoons while I'm studying next year. I haven't got a clue about marketing, but I'm willing to learn and I hope they don't expect me just to make photocopies and answer the phone. I think there are about 25 applicants for this post. So any advice would be welcome!

CD1 TRACK 12 (M = MEL, N = NAOMI)

M Human Resources. Mel Van Der Horst speaking.

N Oh, hello, this is Naomi Taylor. I'm coming to the staff induction day this Thursday.

M Sorry, could you give me your name again?

N Yes, it's Naomi Taylor. I've just started working at the Richmond office.

M Hello, Ms Taylor. How can I help you?

N Well, I'm coming to head office for the induction course on, er, Thursday, and I don't know what time it starts, or even which room to go to.

M So, you didn't receive the programme we e-mailed you?

N Well, no, not exactly ... um, I think I might have deleted your e-mail, sorry.

M Not to worry, I'll give you the details now. It starts at nine-thirty in meeting room B15.

N Uh, OK, can I just check that? Did you say half past nine?

M Yes, that's right. But get here a bit earlier to sign in at reception and get your security pass and things.

N And the room was, er ...?

M Meeting room B15. Just ask at reception, they'll give you directions.

N So, that's B15, thanks. And it doesn't matter if I haven't got a copy of the programme?

M No, don't worry. Look, I'll e-mail you another one now, and I'll bring some extra copies on Thursday.

N Oh, thank you very much.

M Can I help you with anything else?

N No, you've been really helpful. Thanks.

M See you on Thursday, Ms Taylor. Bye-bye.

N Bye, thanks.

CD1 TRACK 13 (P = PIERRE, M = MEL)

M Human Resources. Mel Van Der Horst speaking.

P Hi, Mel. It's Pierre in reception. I'm very sorry, but there is a problem with the room bookings for Thursday. It looks like B15 is double-booked.

M What? You mean we can't have that room at all?

P No, what I meant was, we can't really ask the CEO to shift her meeting. But it's only occupied till 11. You could have it afterwards.

M After 11? What about the other meeting rooms?

P Well, there's nothing free all day. Uh, we could put you in B13 or C2 in the morning.

M C2's the one next to the vending machines on the third floor? Right?

P Yes, that's the one.

M Yeah, I think it's a slightly smaller room than B13, isn't it? We're going to need the space.

P Look, I'm not sure which room would be better for you. Why don't you come down to reception, get the keys to both, and you can see for yourself?

M Er, no, thanks. I'm sure B13 will be fine for a few hours.

P Do you want to book it till 11, then?

M No, er, better put us down till noon, in case the CEO's meeting overruns.

P OK, I'll put you in B13 from nine to midday, and B15 for the rest of the day. Thanks, Mel, for being so understanding.

M Don't mention it. One thing though, I'll e-mail the people who are coming about the change, but they might not all read my message. Um, could you make sure that they know where to go when they arrive on Thursday morning?

P Sure, Mel. I'll tell the others, and leave a note in reception with the attendance list.

M Thank you, Pierre.

CD1 TRACK 14 (AC = AMY CHENG)

AC I've been working for C&R for over two years now. The training programme for new graduates in the first year was one of the main reasons why I wanted to work here. It's famous throughout the industry, and I can see why now – the training and support is first rate. It helped me to build up confidence in key skills like customer service and sales techniques before I went into the field to put it into practice. Um, the thing is that the training just sort of stopped after that. I mean, there are a lot of training modules on the intranet, but I'd really like to take some ownership of my learning, and develop particular skills. I'd be interested in attending a leadership course, for instance.

CD1 TRACK 15 (CT = CHARLIE TURNER)

CT I've got over 20 years of sales experience, so there's not much you can teach me about selling. And I've got a good relationship with my customers. We always have a good laugh. I know they talk about life-long learning these days, but when are you supposed to find the time if you've got a full-time job and a family? My biggest problem is the technology. I can't keep up with all these new applications and software, and the training is always so ad-hoc and informal. It seems as soon as I get used to something, they go and change the processes again. It's also a struggle to keep up with all the new products they keep launching. To be honest, I do very well just selling the old favourites. Why change for the sake of it?

CD1 TRACK 16 (KS = KAMAL SATINDER)

KS I'd like some help with my sales team. Since C&R bought out a rival company, Kelman Shavers, and the sales teams merged, I've been trying to develop a culture of cooperation and teamwork, but I get the feeling the teams aren't integrating well. It's a bit hard when you put two rival teams of aggressive sales reps together. I know it's difficult for them to adapt to working with people who used to work for the competition, and there's sometimes a distinct, well, tension in the air. It could become a problem for staff motivation and morale. I wonder if there's some way to accelerate the whole team-building process and get them to be 'externally competitive but internally cooperative', as they say.

CD1 TRACK 17 (JA = JESSICA ARMSTRONG)

JA Well, one major challenge we're facing is the pace of innovation in consumer goods. There are just more and more new products coming out. I know we need to stay ahead of the competition, so the sales reps have to be able to familiarise themselves quickly with new products without losing too much valuable time in the field. They need to be out there selling, not listening to product presentations all day. Oh, and another issue is … don't get me wrong, I'm proud to manage some really experienced sales reps, but I've noticed a few of them could do with updating their skills, in particular customer awareness training. You know, something that will help them better listeners, and become a bit more, um, sort of, I don't know, responsive to customers' needs, and 'pro-active' in their approach to selling.

UNIT 3 ENERGY

CD1 TRACK 18 (I = INTERVIEWER, AM = ANGUS MCCRONE)

I Can you tell us what your company does?

AM New Energy Finance is an international company that, er, provides news, data and deep analysis on all sectors of clean energy. So that's everything from wind and solar, small hydro, up to 50 megawatts, er, marine, wave and tidal, geothermal and then, er, other low-carbon technologies like um, carbon capture and storage and energy efficiency. And we also look at the carbon markets in great detail and what the carbon price is going to be in the future. On the data side, um, the, we, er, put together data on all the deals and projects in the world and that enables us to calculate, for instance, that there was 155 billion dollars invested in clean energy worldwide in 2008. And in analysis, we look at things like, what happens if the gas price falls. Does that deter people from investing in renewable energy, or will that have more effect, for instance, on coal and nuclear than it will on renewable energy?

CD1 TRACK 19 (I = INTERVIEWER, AM = ANGUS MCCRONE)

I Which do you think will be the most viable alternative energy supply?

AM Well, right now, the most mature, um, of the *main* clean energy sectors is wind, er, because the, er, the technologies have basically been standardised for 20, 25, 30 years, through bladed turbine. And people know exactly how much it costs to generate power with, with that technology. They know where the, the best geographical locations are to base wind farms, so it's regarded as a mature technology and often an alternative to things like gas and coal. Um, but I think in the long term, solar is the, er, clean energy technology will probably get the widest, um, er, uptake, both, er, er, putting, er, plants in places like deserts and in very sunny areas, um, taking advantage of land that hasn't got a lot of other use. Er, but also micro-generation, people putting solar panels on roofs. Once the technology comes down enough, it's not there yet, but once it comes down enough, then it'll be something that people do routinely as a way of actually, um, dealing with some of their power needs, um, during the course of the year. And solar panels will have a huge market for that.

CD1 TRACK 20 (I = INTERVIEWER, S = SPEAKER)

I Do you think carbon emissions are a cause for concern? I mean, the general public seems to be more concerned about other social and economic issues at the moment.

S1 Yes, I do think it's a major cause for concern, and it's *vital* we reduce carbon emissions. It's one of the main causes of global warming. I think the goal of the world's governments should be to prevent the Earth's temperature from increasing. The real question, of course, is how we go about doing that and whether people are prepared to consume less energy and stop wasting it. After all, it was the environmentalist Paul Ehrlich who said, 'We're not running out of fossil fuels. We're running out of environment.'

I What role can business play in the reduction of CO_2 emissions?

S2 Well, I think the role of business, and especially manufacturing companies, is to reduce energy consumption and to use greener production processes, not only involving solar and wind energy, but also hydrogen, fuel-cell technology and so on, and that way cut down on CO_2 emissions. But it's complicated and it's going to take time and money to get certain industries to swap from fossil fuels – oil and gas – to a viable alternative.

I What do you think the government can do to promote the use of clean energy?

S3 I think the government should invest more in green products like hydrogen-powered or electric cars. As a matter of fact, I've already driven a hydrogen-powered car myself. It works! But I realise we might have to wait another five years or so before we see these kinds of green cars on the road in any significant number. And the government should be leading by example, using renewable energy, particularly photovoltaic energy – that is, using solar panels, to heat public buildings, schools and offices … that kind of thing.

CD1 TRACK 21 (I = INTERVIEWER, S = SPEAKER)

I Do you think the government should charge a carbon tax?

S1 A carbon tax? What do you mean exactly?

I Well, whether companies and individual citizens should pay some kind of carbon tax in proportion to the amount of carbon they use, to offset carbon emissions.

S1 No, I don't think so. But it could be voluntary, in the same way when you book a flight with certain airlines, you can choose to pay carbon offset, or not. A carbon tax wouldn't be at all popular here in the UK, although I do think more manufacturing companies could make regular donations to offset their carbon emissions.

I Do you think the government should charge taxpayers a carbon tax?

S2 No. Not if it's just another tax. I think it'll fail. But if it's a tax which makes industry and people really behave differently, that's all to the good. Even so, I think it should come with some kind of tax deduction or tax relief elsewhere, especially for new businesses, so that they don't end up paying higher taxes.

I How do you think developing countries should reduce their carbon emissions?

S3 Firstly, I think the richer countries should stop making these demands on developing countries. People in developing countries have just the same rights to basic energy as we have. You know, many people in the developing world still don't have access to piped gas and electricity: they cook over wood fires; they don't have tractors to farm the land; and they walk or cycle to work. Secondly, richer countries should help developing countries obtain their basic energy needs, at the lowest possible price and in the greenest possible way. Yes, China and India need to adopt national targets for reducing carbon emissions. I understand China has already moved in this direction, and India is also considering such a move. So *all* countries should have international targets for reducing carbon emissions, not just developing ones.

I Would you live in the same area as a wind farm?

S1 Yes, if the wind turbines were located in the right position without damaging the local environment, although I'd also have solar panels on my house.

S2 Well, the countryside where I live is very picturesque, so I can see how some locals might object to it. But there is very high unemployment, so if it brought jobs and improved services to the area, why not?

S3 The trouble with wind power is that, although it's a clean energy, some people don't want turbines in their local area because, well, they obviously spoil the scenery. But it's now typical in many parts of the US and Europe for landowners to lease their land to wind-energy developers, and there are few complaints. At the end of the day, it's certainly more preferable to living next door to a nuclear power station!

CD1 TRACK 22 (A = ALAIN, T = TONY, C = CAROLINE)

A Right, as you know, there's been an oil spill at one of our refineries in the Philippines.

T Do you know what happened exactly?

A Well, we don't have all the details yet. But it looks like there was a leak in an underground pipeline. It turned out to be a minor one and it was plugged within hours. It seems a few thousand litres apparently seeped out of a damaged pipeline. We don't know what caused the leak yet. So, I'd like your take on this, please. What's the best course of action?

T Would it be an idea to close the refinery for a while until we've conducted a full investigation?

C Well, I'm in two …

A I'm not so sure …

C Sorry, Alain, go ahead.

A Thanks, Caroline. Now, where was I? Ah, yes. I'm not entirely sure we want to disrupt production at this stage. The leak has been dealt with, so there's no immediate issue. Caroline, what were you going to say?

C Well, I'd say we should think it through a bit more. Yes, there was another spillage a month and a half ago at the same refinery. So, we do have to look into what's going on there urgently. That said, I don't think we should rush into a decision until we have all the facts.

A Yes, that's right. Our priorities are to ensure people's safety, and to minimise any impact on the environment and property. However, closing the refinery, even for a short time, would be a costly solution. Here's a suggestion: we could set up an investigation team first, and then act according to their findings.

T Sounds reasonable to me.

C Yes, me too.

T The team needs to work quickly, though. I'm really concerned that another incident may not be so minor, and we just can't afford any more bad publicity.

A Very true, Tony. Would you like to lead the investigation?

T Me? Oh, I … well, yes, sure.

CD1 TRACK 23 (J = JOANNE, B = BILL, R = RAJIV)

J OK, OK, guys, everybody, let's get down to business. Did you all get a chance to read the latest reports I sent you?

B Yeah, some of it. There was kind of a lot of stuff there.

J Right, um, I would, er … I'd really like your input on new ideas for projects and it would be good if we could make some decisions today.

B Well, I'd say we've implemented most of the low-cost, quick fixes, and we have to start looking at longer-term solutions now, but that'll cost money.

R Bill's right. The, er, the low-hanging fruit is long gone. We've reduced our lighting bills and saved on office costs by powering down our equipment. All our new printers and copiers can be set to 'standby' mode after 20 minutes of non-use. But it'll be expensive to replace all the old equipment in one go. Maybe it's better to, er, phase things out.

J Perhaps. We could look at reducing the amount of equipment we have in the offices as well. I mean, does everyone need a printer by their desk?

B Well, no, but there might be some resistance from people.

J How so?

B Well, they might feel we're trying to take away entitlements. Who gets to have their own printer, and who doesn't? Employees might find it inconvenient.

J I take your point. Some employees might feel left out of the decision-making and we … we wanna figure out some ways to get them all on board. You know, make energy efficiency a priority for everyone.

B Well, we can try.

J Bill, what kind of long-term solutions did you have in mind?

B Well, I hear that some companies now have all the building systems centrally controlled. And there are sensors to monitor and regulate office lighting, air conditioning and pretty much anything that uses electricity. One company alone has managed to reduce electricity use per person by 35 per cent and natural gas use by 40 per cent.

J Really? That sounds cool. I wonder if we could do something similar. The potential cost savings should convince the management team that it's a good investment.

R I agree. Another idea is to start buying some of our energy from renewable sources.

J Do you know which renewable energies we can buy?

R No, but I can look into it.

J OK, thanks, Rajiv. All right, let's go over what we've said so far. So we've agreed that we'll look at reducing …

WORKING ACROSS CULTURES 1:
INTERNATIONAL PRESENTATIONS

CD1 TRACK 24

1 Last week, I was in Geneva giving a talk to some of our company executives from all over the world. And, you know, you simply can't take anything for granted in that situation. Speaking with an international audience made me realise just how much slang I use to explain myself. Um, I've always felt that it gives me a casual style that I think is fun and adds a personal touch, and it always goes down well here in the States. But after seeing their faces, I realised just how inappropriate and insensitive it is for those who don't get what I'm saying. It also means that I've lost a valuable opportunity to get my message across.

Next time I have to do that again, I'm definitely going to simplify my language and try to avoid words and expressions that might mean nothing to my listeners. But it's actually very hard for me to know when I'm using slang. So I'll just have to remember to schedule some time with, er, one of my international colleagues to help me review my talk.

CD1 TRACK 25

2 One valuable lesson I've learned is that people around the world respond differently to presentations. I remember once I was in Japan and I noticed some people in the audience were closing their eyes and nodding their head up and down slightly. I thought 'What have I done wrong?', but later someone told me that it's a sign of concentration. Then again, who knows? Maybe I really *was* putting them to sleep!

Then there is the level of interaction with the audience. In North America and the UK, audiences will almost always ask me questions, but in Japan, people are more likely to be silent.

And I used to think that clapping was a universal reaction at the end of a speech, but I've found that in parts of Germany and Austria, people sitting around a table may knock on the table instead. It startled me the first time that it happened.

CD1 TRACK 26

3 I've found that when I'm talking to an international group, people need more time to digest numbers and figures, especially when they're not native English speakers. I remember one time there was a confusion when I said 'a billion' – which used to mean 'a million million' in the UK with 12 noughts. But now everyone uses it to mean 'a thousand million'. And I only picked up on the misunderstanding much further down the road.

I also find people are often unfamiliar with my pronunciation of names and places, like Levi's and Moscow. I've seen it throw some people, and lead to a bit of a misunderstanding. My tips? I think using visuals can help compensate for these sorts of language problems. Also, if you ever have to use any foreign names, do some research on the pronunciation before running the risk of amusing, confusing or offending other people.

CD1 TRACK 27 (I = INTERVIEWER, AG = ANNELIESE GUÉRIN-LETENDRE)

I How do you begin preparing people to be international presenters?

AG Well, of course, it does depend very much on the individual client; what their own cultural background is; whether English is their first language or not; who their audience is likely to be, and of the objective, of course, of the presentation. But generally speaking, I suppose I would work through a series of four main components. Um, there would be an introduction, a general introduction, to really explore what we mean by 'culture' in the first place. What do we mean by cultural difference? The norms, the values, the basic assumptions of that culture; what's often referred to as the 'culture iceberg' – the difference between what we can see and what is underlying.

And we move on from there to thinking in more detail about what the expectations of this particular audience might be, and what the expectations of the presenter might be. Er, and how does the presenter, for example, establish credibility with the audience? What's the audience looking for? Are they interested in knowing about the presenter's expertise, perhaps? Does age, class, education, sex and dress matter? If so, to what extent? Um, what about the listening styles of the audience? What, what does that particular culture prefer in terms of communication? Is it a culture that values the spoken word, the visual, or even the written word more in terms of communication? To what extent will the audience value and appreciate an interactive approach? Some audiences actually don't want the kind of interaction that Anglo-Saxons, for example, very often appreciate. Um, what about humour? What about humour and whether it's considered appropriate for business at all? Sometimes it can be interpreted as being quite frivolous, even cynical sometimes. And yet, on the other hand, we often see it being used to create a relaxed atmosphere and diffuse tensions. So, that's a big question. And I suppose also how to read, er, the audience: how to read their body language; how to read, er, their silence sometimes – is that an appreciative silence or a bored silence? Um, how to read their facial expressions; how to know the degree of formality. Here we have all sorts of ideas to think about. And lastly, and of course, very importantly, what level of detail do they expect? Some cultures prefer to have a lot of detail, a lot of what's called 'context'. Others, the Anglo-Saxon nations being a case in point, really appreciate presentations that are concise and get straight to the point.

Then, we move on to the third part of this, um, awareness training session, which is thinking about the use of English, use of English as a global language, um, and trying to be aware that we need to make our English as transparent and culture neutral as possible.

And then lastly, we move on to the typical presentation style of the client, so that that person is aware of their typical delivery techniques. Invariably, this will be somebody who has a lot of experience, and knows what works well with a particular audience, but of course, as the audience changes, some of those techniques may need to be re-evaluated. What's successful in the home culture where everybody understands the context may not always work elsewhere, may need to be modified or adapted to suit the context.

UNIT 4 MARKETING

CD1 TRACK 28 (I = INTERVIEWER, JR = JONATHAN REYNOLDS)

I   What is customer relationship management, and why is it important?

JR Customer relationship management, or CRM as it's known for short, is, is really the whole collection of systems and processes that companies use to interact with customers. In some people's minds, CRM has been associated with, um, software, and certainly, the software that companies use to manage their interactions, through e-mail, telesales calling and so on, is very important. But increasingly, I think we need to think about customer relationship management as being a much broader set of responsibilities for organisations; creating, if you like, customer-centric businesses, er, where the customer is at the heart of everything that an organisation thinks and feels about its market. Certainly, systematising the way in we think about customers might be thought of as a little mechanical. When you're dealing with a mass market, when you're trying to record, perhaps, very important personal differences and preferences, using some kind of systematic piece of CRM software, it's very important to, er, provide a consistent service to the customer.

CD1 TRACK 29 (I = INTERVIEWER, JR = JONATHAN REYNOLDS)

I   With so much competition in retail these days, how are companies managing to retain their customers?

JR I think there are several ways that are being used at the moment. The most obvious one is to invest in loyalty cards or loyalty marketing schemes. And we can think of companies like Tesco, which have invested a lot of money in their Club Card scheme over the last 10 to 15 years. This is a way of gathering intelligence about customers, their buying behaviour and then using that to try and create promotions and offers, er, which will, er, better meet their needs, and therefore encourage them to come back again and again.

Er, we can also see, though, companies investing more significantly in the customer value that their brand represents. In the longer term, that's a better bet because, again, if we can understand precisely why customers are using our brand and how important it is, it is to them and invest in those aspects of it, then we have a better chance of retaining customers over the longer term.

But we can also see, I think, companies, er, investing in price promotion activity, and absolutely this retains customers whilst the price is low, but, of course, there is only ever one lowest-cost provider. And the key issue for those companies is: can they retain that low-cost position in the marketplace?

CD1 TRACK 30 (I = INTERVIEWER, JR = JONATHAN REYNOLDS)

I   How much data should companies have about their customers, and should we be concerned about privacy?

JR There's a lot of discussion about privacy and its relevance to customers, given that more and more data is being collected by all sorts of organisations. Certainly, the e-mails I get coming through every day from everyone from airlines through to banks to, er, grocers and booksellers, advertising things and knowing something about my buying behaviour, can be quite concerning. Er, indeed, it's been suggested that we're all 'glass consumers', that, er, you know, companies can see through us and know exactly how we behave and how we think. On the one hand, that's concerning. On the other hand, in a sense, perhaps that helps companies to serve us better. One of the ways we can think about this is that there are three attitudes to privacy: there are the 'privacy fundamentalists' who are desperately concerned about the amount and quality of information that is held about them by companies, and really don't want that to, to continue, and want that to be legislated against. We then see the 'privacy pragmatists' who actually recognise, well, the reality is companies collect data about us, that's fine, we can live with that. It may even help us in terms of getting better offers in the long term. And then finally, there are the 'privacy indifferents' who actually, you know, couldn't care less about what information is collected about them, and er, er, really, er, often are very unaware of what is collected.

CD1 TRACK 31

PRESENTER 1

Hello, everyone. As you probably know, I'm Carol Hughes, and today I'm going to be talking about the principles of marketing.

Marketing is too often confused with selling. Selling is only the tip of the marketing iceberg. What is *unseen* is the extensive market research and development of products, the challenge of pricing them right, of opening up distribution, and of letting the market know about the product. So, marketing is a far more complex process than selling.

But what *is* marketing? According to marketing guru Philip Kotler, there are five key processes in marketing. First, there's opportunity identification; second is new product development; third, there's customer attraction; the fourth process is customer retention and loyalty building; and last but not least, order fulfilment.

Now, you're probably wondering, what's the significance of all of this? Well, Kotler would argue that a company that handles all of these processes *well* will probably be successful. But a company that *fails* at any one of these processes will *not* survive. Let's take a look at a couple of case studies …

CD1 TRACK 32

PRESENTER 2

You know, a funny thing happened to me the other day. I was looking for a present to buy for my wife. Don't laugh! I'm the kind of guy who remembers his wife's birthday. But I'd been looking and looking and I hadn't been able to find anything on her wish list. Well, of course, she gave me a list … And the sales assistant said, 'There's something I'd like to show you, sir'. 'Here. Have you seen this coat? It may *look* like an Armani, it may *feel* like an Armani, but if you look at the price tag, you'll see it costs a fraction of the price of an Armani.'

Anyway, I'm not here to tell you about my wife's new coat. I'm here to tell you how this new campaign is going to give us a competitive advantage. For instance, did you know that China's fashion market will probably grow to around 12.4 *billion* US dollars over the next two years? I bet you didn't know that, did you?

CD1 TRACK 33

PRESENTER 1

So, to go back to what I was saying earlier, even social media marketing, like, say, the Axe campaign, is taking the same old ideas and just adding new technology. So, you know, *Houston, we have an innovation problem*. Marketers are pushing the *same* old buttons to sell more variations of the *same* old products. It's a negative-sum game. Think about it. Right, let's just go back to that slide. Now, we've seen how product variations increase cost without enlarging the overall market. And with increased competition, prices are pushed down, inviting more competitors, such as supermarket low-cost home brands. This means consumers are just overloaded with more choice of very similar products.

Clearly, we've got to do something different here. So, to sum up the key points, marketing needs to pull back from its focus on distribution, packaging and communication, and refocus on helping create great new products that deliver distinctive value and make people's lives better. Then it'll be easy to communicate that to prospective customers. And that's what I'd like *you* to do for your next assignment: *innovate*. Work in groups and come up with a brand-new product or service. Think about a product that will make *your* life easier. Oh, sorry, folks, but that's all we have time for today. See you on Thursday.

CD1 TRACK 34
PRESENTER 2

Right then, let's take another look at those figures, shall we? If you look at this chart a moment showing the projected figures for China's fashion market, you'll see we're talking about over *five billion* euros. That's a huge increase in growth, isn't it? It's a massive market that's there for the taking.

We've got to produce quality sports clothing at competitive prices that both look good and feel good. Yes, the Chinese market is excellent at imitation. But if you can't beat them, join them! I'd like to quote the words of a journalist from the *FT* here: 'Customers may not always be right, but they certainly matter.' And unless we can give them what our competitors can't, we have no business.

If there's just one thing I'd like you all to remember, it's focus on our customer base. Not by generating business in the short term, but by positioning ourselves for the future. And finally, I'd like to reveal our new marketing strapline. Here we go ... I think you'll all agree, that sums us up perfectly.

CD1 TRACK 35 (J = JODIE, E = EMILIO)

J So, how are you doing with the recruitment, Emilio? Did you manage to get Vanessa Flores booked for our TV commercial?

E Sorry, Jodie. No can do.

J No way! What happened?

E She just went on an international tour – LA, London, Madrid. But maybe it was for the best.

J Oh, how's that?

E Well, she'd been having boyfriend trouble. I figured she'd bring you bad publicity.

J Oh! But I thought her and Kurt were going to settle down. What about the actress? Olinda something or other – the one who endorsed that cereals brand in Europe.

E Elvira Olivas? Yeah, she would have been great. I spoke to her agent ...

J And?

E Well, they started making noises about her wanting endorsement deals further away from home. I got a bad feeling about her. She'd be a real prima donna.

J She's a big name, Emilio. She'd be calling the shots.

E You mean she'd raise the fees and turn up late all the time. Nah, it wouldn't work.

J Hmm. So, who does that leave us with? Er, Eddie, the Latin rapper?

E Eddie's an interesting guy and he's photogenic ...

J But ...?

E Jodie, let's face it, he's pushing 40.

J I guess so. OK, who do we have, Emilio? We've got a studio booked a week on Monday!

E Looks like Leona's the hot favourite.

J The golfer pro? But ... but she just came out of high school!

E She's 24. She's gonna be great.

J You gotta be kidding me, Emilio. Who's heard of her, except for a couple of college kids?

E The twenty-somethings and all the moms love her. Trust me. We did the research.

J She looks like the girl next door. We wanted someone with more charisma.

E Leona's a role model. Her image is: 'Hey, I've made it'. Ambitious young woman finds the American dream. And she's not another would-be singer or actress.

J You think? Does she know what we do?

E Sure! She says she bought your paints and did up her bedroom herself when she was 16. Come along to the casting and check her out for yourself.

J Don't worry, I will. We gotta get this absolutely right.

E Is that the time? Sorry, Jodie. I have a briefing with the TV director now. By the way, how are you doing?

J Well, as you can see, I'm looking and feeling huge.

E The little one's due any day now, right?

J Any day now.

E You take care of yourself.

J Thanks, Emilio. Adiós!

CD1 TRACK 36 (C = CLAPPERBOARD BOY, L = LEONA, D = DIRECTOR)

C Leona Pedraza for Home2u, take five.

L Hi, I'm Leona Pedraza, and like any professional woman, I like to call the shots. And er ..., not just on the course – sorry, I mean, the golf course.

D No, no, Leona, you need to be quicker on that line. Straight after the shot, right? Pow! 'And not just on the golf course.' Let's take it from the top!

L Er, yeah, whatever. It's just that ... it sounds a bit weird.

D I know. But it's the script, OK, hon? Just think Home2u, it's your ideal store. The store you always visit when you go to the mall. Like a second

home. Can we do another take, everybody? And Leona, if you fluff your lines this time, we'll just edit it, OK? Just relax. Don't worry.

C I'm worried ... Leona Pedraza for Home2u, take six.

L Hi, I'm Leona Pedraza, and like any professional woman, I like to call the shots. And not just on the golf course. So, if you've rented a new apartment, or you have *la familia* round for a barbecue, or just, just fixing something at home for your *mamá*, you can find it all here at Home2u, the store with a Latin touch.

D OK!

L Is that a take?

D Uh, can we do it just one more time, Leona? And you know that marketing strapline? Could you, well, could we have a little more oomph on it? A bit more sassy. Say it like you mean it. I dunno, I'm thinking, 'The store with a Latin touch'.

L I'll try.

UNIT 5 EMPLOYMENT TRENDS

CD2 TRACK 1

1 I'm covering for sick leave until the end of the month. Then I hope the agency has something else lined up for me.

CD2 TRACK 2

2 You see, after I had the baby, it was getting to be impossible to combine full-time work with my family commitments. So when my maternity leave was up, they agreed to let me finish at three o'clock instead of five.

CD2 TRACK 3

3 The company wanted to reduce the office costs, and I jumped at the chance to work from home. I don't miss travelling to the office every day, but I do miss my colleagues ... sometimes!

CD2 TRACK 4

4 Like most of my colleagues at the hospital, we have to work on a 24-hour rota, and it's a real problem getting enough sleep, given the strange hours that we sometimes work. It's especially hard when you're working nights.

CD2 TRACK 5

5 I always wanted to start my own business, so when the opportunity came up to take the redundancy package, the time seemed right. It's great being my own boss.

CD2 TRACK 6

6 There's always a group of men at the gates of the construction site in the morning, and a supervisor comes out and picks the people they want to work that day. It's all cash-in-hand, of course.

CD2 TRACK 7

7 It's good to get some money together before I go back to university, so I'm going to be working in a holiday resort this summer.

CD2 TRACK 8

8 My sister came to the USA a few years ago for work and I followed her over. We both clean houses. My son and daughter are still in Mexico with my mother, but I want to bring them here as soon as I can.

CD2 TRACK 9 (I = INTERVIEWER, IB = IAN BRINKLEY)

I What recent trends have you noticed in employment?

IB I think there are three big ones. The first one is that jobs have become much more skilled. If you look at the increases in employment, they're all for jobs with high levels of skills. This is a very, very constant change that we've seen over time both in this country, and in other countries.
The second big change has been the industries. The new jobs have come through in service industries, and they've come through particularly in what we call the 'high-value' service industries, and by those we mean hi-tech industries, we mean business services, we mean education services, we mean health services, and we mean the cultural and creative sectors. And these have been the big generators of new jobs, again here, and in other countries.
And a third thing we've noticed, is a lot of this job growth is taking place in major cities, and in particular, we're seeing a big gap open up between those cities that were doing well, and those cities doing badly. And so, this is a big problem because the new jobs are occurring only in certain parts of the country, and other parts of the country they're really seeing little benefit from this job growth.

CD2 TRACK 10 (I = INTERVIEWER, IB = IAN BRINKLEY)

I How has technology changed the world of work?

IB One is, it's made things much faster, so the response times of businesses and individuals, that's all speeded up, and so people are expected now to work at a much faster pace than they did in the past.
Secondly, it's placed a big emphasis on communication skills. If you think about all the changes in new technology, most of them are related to communications in some way or another. And so, businesses and individuals who have good communication skills, these are the ones which we've seen develop most.

CD2 TRACK 11 (I = INTERVIEWER, IB = IAN BRINKLEY)

I What advice, in terms of skills preparation, would you give those starting out on their careers now?

IB I think the most important thing is to get the widest set of skills and experiences that you possibly can. Most employers now are not looking for deep specialists, they want people who can work across a wide variety of tasks within the workplace. So particularly, communication skills, the ability to get on with other people and work in a team, as well as some technical competence. But the most important thing is to make sure that you have got a wide set of skills, rather than just skills in a very, very narrow area.

CD2 TRACK 12 (C = CARL, Y = YOLANDA)

C Listen, before you go, I got another one for you. This old woman is driving at a hundred miles an hour down the road and she's knitting … yeah, knitting. So, anyway, a policeman in a patrol car spots her and goes after her. He drives up, winds down his window and shouts, 'Pull over! Pull over!' And she turns round and shouts back, 'No, cardigan!' Yeah, right. Gotta go. Speak to you soon.

Y Look, Carl, I'm sorry, but this is really driving me up the wall.

C Sorry, Yolanda, I wasn't listening, just checking my e-mail. Could you say that again?

Y I'm trying to get some work done here, and some days it's just impossible.

C Poor you. Got too much to do? I know the feeling.

Y What? No … no, that's not it. I'm saying that I can't concentrate with you there.

C So, what you're saying is, my incredible good looks keep distracting you.

Y Carl, could you just be serious for one minute and listen to me?

C I'm sorry, I'm sorry. You were saying …

Y I was saying, could you keep it down?

C Keep what down?

Y The noise! You're on the phone all day and … oh, it doesn't matter.

C No, no, I'm listening. Please go on.

Y Well, if I'm trying to concentrate on something, and you're on the phone, I can't work.

C I appreciate how you feel, Yolanda. The thing is, it's important for me to talk to clients and engage in some friendly banter. It really helps to get the sales.

Y Well, it's not just that. You see, sometimes you're a bit loud on the phone.

C Oh, I see. Don't worry – I'll be as quiet as a mouse, in future, quiet as a mouse. You won't even know I'm here. Mike, how you doing? Yeah, yeah, I got your e-mail … yeah, I'm working on the report right now …

CD2 TRACK 13 (I = INTERVIEWER, RG = ROB GIARDINA)

I So, Rob, why are there so many problems and misunderstandings when people write e-mails to each other?

RG Primarily because you don't have the, the visual information and feedback that you have in a face-to-face conversation. You know, things like smiles or nods, or even being able to say 'I don't understand'. An… and that also makes it easier to get nasty, to … uh, to do what they call 'flaming' – sending angry or insulting e-mails to people. Another factor is that your context when you write it is different from their context when they read it. So, for example, you're in a rush, you write a quick e-mail, their context is different, they don't see it that way, they see it as brusque and direct. An… and finally, you know the truth is some people just don't express themselves so well in writing.

I So what can we do?

RG Well, first, keep those things in mind when you read and write. So when you read an e-mail, don't always believe your first impression. If something doesn't seem right or appropriate to you, think about other possible interpretations. And when you write e-mails, think about how the other person could maybe misinterpret what you're writing and then make it clear that you don't mean that. You know, those emoticons seem so silly, but sometimes they help express the tone that you want. Really, as with any conflict, the best advice is to take into account the other person's perceptions and context – what they think and where they're coming from. And to ask questions if you don't know – open, neutral questions, not the type that begin 'How could you possibly …?'

I So, when there's obviously a problem, is it best to talk about it face to face or on the phone?

RG Well, for small disputes or misunderstandings, yes. But if you know how to use it, e-mail can be an effective tool to avoid and even resolve conflicts.

I And how's that?

RG Well, again, it takes out the visual information; that can be particularly useful for multicultural teams because you can avoid the misunderstandings that can be caused by … by different communication styles and differences in things like body space or eye contact. Also, if a conflict already exists, well, they can't see if you're angry or frustrated, so you have more control over what you actually communicate. Secondly, you ha… have the time to make your

e-mails more rational and less emotional if you choose. You know, they say that you should count to 10 when you're angry, and e-mail forces you to do that. Uh … finally, um, you know, it's a basic but important factor, you can't interrupt and you can't be interrupted.

CD2 TRACK 14

1 There are strict performance targets, and we lose the bonus if we don't meet them every month, plus we get a rude e-mail from the team leader about our work. They don't take anything into consideration.

CD2 TRACK 15

2 It's sometimes impossible to meet the targets. We only have five minutes to deal with each caller, and if there's a tricky booking or the customer can't decide what he wants, then you're stuck. The team leader just doesn't appreciate this.

CD2 TRACK 16

3 It makes me feel bad that I'm being unhelpful to callers, rushing them through the bookings, and I think they get angry and resentful sometimes for that reason.

CD2 TRACK 17

4 If a caller's rude or aggressive, which sometimes happens, I don't feel supported by management. I'm desperate for a break sometimes after dealing with a difficult customer, but there's nowhere to go and chill out, and you'd be in trouble anyway for leaving your workstation.

CD2 TRACK 18

5 As a team leader, I'm under constant pressure from my manager to make sure my staff are meeting the targets. There's absolutely no flexibility, no room for manoeuvre or individual decision-making.

CD2 TRACK 19

6 Call-monitoring is a major source of stress. I feel like I'm being spied on and that the team leader doesn't trust me to do my job. I have to watch every word I say.

UNIT 6 ETHICS

CD2 TRACK 20 (I = INTERVIEWER; PFB = PHILIPPA FOSTER BACK)

I How have attitudes to corporate responsibility changed in recent years?

PFB I think there's been a sea change in attitudes because of the level of awareness that there is throughout the world now in how companies do their business. It started, I would say, 15, 20 years ago when there was a first level of interest in how the oil and gas industries were actually extracting oil and gas, and the effect that they were having on the local communities and this raised the level of awareness.
From that time, it has developed quite significantly because with the growing 24/7 media world, er, the growth of the Internet, er, there are very few places that a company can hide what it's doing. And companies are being brought to account for how they do their business. Not only in environmental issues, but also it's moved on into how companies, um, deal with companies in their supply chain. Um, an example would be a company that perhaps has, um, a long supply chain. It might be manufacturing clothes, it might be manufacturing shoes, and it's outsourced that work so others, people are doing the work for them. Um, and unless they control how that work is done, er, sadly, in some cases, it's done by child labour. Nowadays, this is being exposed.

CD2 TRACK 21 (I = INTERVIEWER; PFB = PHILIPPA FOSTER BACK)

I How have *companies'* attitudes to accountability changed?

PFB I think they've changed in the sense that in the old days when they were family-run companies – and I'm going back now a hundred years – um, there was a great deal of *trust* around the way that the companies were being run. Companies were quite paternalistic, so there was an attitude of 'Don't worry, we'll look after you', er, both of the customers, obviously, but also of employees. And, that model, that business model, I would call a *trust* model.
And that carried on for many, many years, and it's really only until the 1980s, 1990s when there were some quite significant corporate scandals that caused people to doubt this. And, married with what, er, the growing media attention on how companies were behaving, the growing attention around environmental issues – back in the oil and gas industry – led again to this, er, raising of awareness, to the extent that companies thought, 'Mm, maybe this isn't the model any more.' And certainly from their customers and people interested in business they said, 'No, we don't trust you. Er, please involve us.' So we moved to more of a model of, 'Involve us in how you do your business. We would like to help you to do it better.'
Um, that worked with many companies, with others it didn't, so that model then evolved to *show* us: 'Show us you are doing business in the right way.' Um, and that, for many companies, is where it stopped for quite a number of years.

CD2 TRACK 22 (PFB = PHILIPPA FOSTER BACK)

PFB Around 2000 at the, er, again a change of the language that was being used by stakeholders, people who have an interest in how the company's run, er, where they started talking about corporate responsibility. They asked companies actually to *prove* to those *outside* the company that this was, er, the way that they were doing their business.

At that time, we had a number of companies beginning to produce, in addition to their annual report accounts, their corporate social responsibility reports, or corporate responsibility reports. These names have been changed over the years. Typically now it's corporate responsibility, or indeed sustainability reports. And so the model at the moment, as we look at it, is *prove* to me. Companies are being asked to prove to the people, not only their, er, customers, their shareholders, their employees, their suppliers *how* they do their business.

There is one further stage that *might* happen, and indeed it has in some areas and that is, *obey* me. And this is where society deems through the democratic process that companies are *not* behaving and therefore they encourage their governments to bring in law to make them behave and, and to enforce that law. And that is what I would call at the end of this: 'trust me', um, 'involve me, show me, prove to me'. The ultimate is, 'obey me'.

CD2 TRACK 23

Of course, it's not always easy to do the right thing, especially when friends and family are involved. As the saying goes, we prefer to do business with people we like. But from the company's perspective, whether one of the suppliers is a friend or not is neither here nor there. In the first place, you need to ask yourself what is in the best interest of the company. If it was up to me, I'd want to go for the best price.

In this situation, you have two duties of fairness: to your company and to your supplier friend – but it depends on what you've already promised. You say you're in danger of losing a close friend over this deal. On the other hand, your friend should understand that you're in a tricky situation. Is he prepared to lower his prices? If not, and he reacts badly to a negative decision, maybe he's not the kind of person you want to socialise with anyway. But if he's a level-headed guy, I'm sure you'll be able to sort something out.

Another thing you could do is to speak to your boss, who might talk to your friend so that you avoid any direct confrontation. The important thing is that you show your friend that you are acting fairly at the same time as demonstrating to your boss that you can make business decisions without being swayed by any personal interests.

CD2 TRACK 24

Most readers seem to think this is a clear-cut case. There can be no contest, they say, between getting a job through nepotism and working for a fair-trade company.

However, I don't see it that way. This is simply the first in a series of make-or-break decisions you'll have to make in your working life, where you have to weigh up the pros and cons, such as the company you want to work for, your salary, chances of promotion, workmates, and family commitments.

Firstly, you should ask yourself whether you have any reservations about working for a tobacco company. Apart from anything else, you're likely to start smoking again. Do you *really* want to put your reputation at risk by working for an unethical company?

With your second option, you have the opportunity of a career in the family firm, although working with family members is never easy. And, you may end up hating going to work somewhere where you are despised for being the director's favourite niece. On the other hand, I doubt if you'll be happy at the fair-trade company for long, as you sound like an ambitious young woman.

What you finally decide is up to you. But you need to ask yourself what you want from a job and where you want to be in the future. What I would say, though, is your first job won't be your last. There are a number of other job offers that will follow once you have some solid experience under your belt.

CD2 TRACK 25 (B = BECKY, J = JOHN, V = VINCENT, A = ANDREA)

B Right, shall we start then? John, do you mind taking the minutes?

J Er … sure.

B OK. You've all seen the agenda. The question today is how are we going to communicate these redundancies to employees? It's in everyone's interest to make this as smooth and painless as possible.

J Well, *that's* an understatement.

B John?

J Uh, well, it's not going to be exactly painless, is it? The Human Resources Department is going to have to tell a dozen people they're not coming back to work after the holiday.

V Some vacation, huh?

J Precisely.

A But we discussed this in our last meeting. We said *today's* meeting was going to be about *communicating* the redundancies to the people in question.

B Andrea's right. The decision's already been made … if I could just finish, please – and what we need to focus on now is the *how*.

J Well, I don't see why Human Resources always needs to do everyone else's dirty work. If some people from the Sales Department are losing their jobs, then I think it'd be better if it came from their Sales Manager.

V Oh, great, so now *I'm* the bad guy? You should never have taken on half a dozen new people in Production at the start of the year!

J Oh, come on, Vincent! You know we needed temporary staff in Production to cover those orders.

B OK, OK, let's not get personal here. Redundancies have to be made. The company will, of course, be very sorry to see some of our staff go. What I would say, though, is we need to let them know soon because these rumours are going to create bad feeling …

J There's already bad feeling, Becky. People are whispering in corridors, staff morale is low …

A The way I see it, there's an economic downturn, orders are down. Everyone's heard the company is restructuring …

B OK, hold on a minute. Let's go round the table. Vincent, what do you think?

V I think we should have told it to them straight, after our last meeting. But now – if you'd just let me finish – but now we gotta to devise a communications plan to let *all* staff know about the restructuring asap.

B Uh-huh. John, do you think it's necessary to inform *all* members of staff?

J At this stage, we should just talk to individuals. We can send a general memo after that informing everyone of the redundancies. You know, minimise unnecessary concern.

V *Minimise unnecessary concern?* John, they're losing their jobs! Half my team are going to be out on the street!

B Can we all just calm down a moment? Vincent, please go on.

V Would someone like to tell me why we're *having* a meeting if the decision has already been made?

B Vincent, I appreciate your concerns. And John *has* got a point about talking to people on a one-to-one basis. But we need to keep the rest of staff informed, too. So I say John prepares an internal memo. OK? Something along the lines of 'We are taking prudent measures in tough times in order to protect the long-term interests of …'

J … prudent measures in tough times, er, sorry, what else?

B The main thing is to communicate this in a transparent way. I'll give you a hand with the internal memo later, John.

J OK, thanks.

B Listen, I think it best if we go ahead with this in the next day or two. I know this isn't going to be easy … John, I'd like *you* to conduct these interviews, but you'll need to liaise with Vincent beforehand. Is that all right?

V/J Sure./Fine.

CD2 TRACK 26 (P = PRESENTER, HW = HELEN WHEATFIELD)

P Most kids love cereals in the morning. But according to a recent report, some breakfast cereals for children are more than 50-per-cent sugar by weight. The study, published in the *Journal of Nutrition*, found that children's cereals have more sugar, salt, carbohydrates and calories per gram than cereals that are *not* marketed at kids.

A single serving of 10 popular cereals, including brands such as Ready-to-go by Daybreak, can have as much sugar as a doughnut. Two of the brands were found to be more than 50-per-cent sugar by weight, while eight brands were at least 40-per-cent sugar.

The food industry spends about £145 million annually advertising these cereals to children. Colourful characters and collectable gifts inside the packs are meant to stimulate your child into wanting these 'fun' foods, but the damage they can do to your child's health is no laughing matter. We spoke to Helen Wheatfield, an expert nutritionist from The National Food Council.

HW Child obesity has become a major concern, with excess sugar and carbohydrates being the two main culprits. In our study, we found that most kids usually serve themselves over 50 per cent more than the suggested serving of 30 grams. But we also found two cereal brands that scored very well in our nutrition rating. Mini-oats and Barley-bites had only *one* gram of sugar per serving and a healthy three grams of fibre.

P So, if you don't want your children eating a sugary breakfast, check the nutritional information on the side of the cereal pack. Jonathan Oates, Healthwatch.

CD2 TRACK 27 (P = PRESENTER, N = NUTRITIONIST)

P According to a recent report, food manufacturers still continue to mislead consumers. Daybreak, for example, has said it has now standardised its food labels and claims that its children's cereals are healthier than ever. But when nutritional experts checked Ready-to-go cereals, they found that sugar content had only been reduced by 10 per cent. At 40 per cent, or 12 grams, critics say Daybreak's sugar content is still higher than it should be. In contrast, other brands of cereals only have *one* gram, or about *three* per cent, of sugar.
Sales of Ready-to-go have continued to drop, despite the company giving away thousands of its cereal packs in supermarkets last week as part of a promotional campaign. We spoke to one of their former employees, an expert nutritionist who prefers to remain anonymous.

N Daybreak should have reduced its levels of sugar, salt and carbohydrates in children's cereals, and increased the fibre content, too. This was my recommendation, but the company told me kids wouldn't eat cereals without sugar. At the end of the day, it's a question of common sense and kids learning to make better food choices. I mean, do you want your child to eat the equivalent of a sugary doughnut for breakfast?

P A spokesperson for Daybreak told Healthwatch that the company is donating part of its profits to a children's project in Mali. But parents back home, who just want their kids to eat a healthy breakfast, might take a bit more convincing. Jonathan Oates, Healthwatch.

WORKING ACROSS CULTURES 2
ETHICAL INTERNATIONAL BUSINESS

CD2 TRACK 28 (I = INTERVIEWER, E = EXPERT)

I Are companies more accountable than they used to be? If not, how can they become so?

E In the main, companies are more accountable, particularly those that are listed on a public stock exchange. The laws nowadays require them to be more accountable, and that's on an international scale. And I think that's very healthy. Some companies have gone further and have signed up to international standards of accountability. These tend to be run by institutions which have developed frameworks whereby the company can check its activities against these frameworks to prove to stakeholders and the outside world that they *are* behaving and that they *are* doing business in the right way. However, there are some flaws in those frameworks in that they tend to be a 'one size fits all'. So, if you're a company in the oil and gas industry, or, um, you're a pharmaceutical company, or you're in financial services, you're faced with the same set of questions. And that might not be entirely appropriate because obviously those are very different types of industries and activities. So … but there are opportunities to demonstrate accountability, and the more enlightened companies are certainly doing so. Some responsible companies are listed on the Dow Jones Sustainability Index in the States, or the FTSE4Good index that's run on the same lines in the UK.

CD2 TRACK 29 (I = INTERVIEWER, E = EXPERT)

I How can institutions go about rebuilding trust when things go wrong?

E Trust has to be earned. And it takes a long time for companies to earn that trust from its customers and employees, but it can be so easily lost. It can be lost by saying something misleading or wrong about your product, which then gets spread through the rumour mill. Trust can be lost by the unethical actions of a company itself, or, um, an individual within it: an employee bribing someone, or being accused of corruption. But once lost, you have to work very hard at regaining it. The easiest way to regain that trust is, um, just to be very open and honest about what went wrong and try and address the issues, and get it right in the future. Um, I'd say the key is being frank, and being transparent about what you do.
One sector that has recently been going through this is the defence and aerospace industry. For many years, um, it saw itself as an industry apart. You know, they dealt with governments; they were selling their products to governments, on behalf of governments. And they felt that they needn't be worried about corporate responsibility. With accusations that have been made against the defence industry, things have changed. One of the first companies to deal with this was BAE Systems which appointed a special ethical committee called the Woolf Committee, which actually looked into their ethical business conduct, and made recommendations for how they should behave in the future.
Then the defence industry together created a code of conduct, first in Europe, called the Common Industry Standard, and, um, then another was created at an international level, bringing together European as well as American defence and aerospace companies. And, um, this is how the defence industry is trying to rebuild trust with the wider public. You know, so they are now more aware of *how* they do business. And I think that's a very positive move.

UNIT 7 FINANCE

CD2 TRACK 30 (I = INTERVIEWER, CM = CHARLES MIDDLETON)

I Triodos Bank recently won the *Financial Times* Sustainable Bank of the Year Award. What exactly is sustainable banking?

CM When we were given the award, the, the people who, who presented it made it very clear that it was a mixture of two things – er, which is, er, you know, what we do, but also how we do it. And I think in terms of what we do, as a bank we are purely focused, and always have been, on supporting projects that are delivering a social, environmental positive impact, that's what the sort of, the mission is built on. So, all the projects that we lend to, whether they be individuals or companies, businesses, are all doing something that in some way is delivering a positive impact, er, socially and environmentally.
Um, in terms of how we do it, er, which is equally important, er, our business model is built on, er, working with the real economy, so we fund ourselves with deposits from real people, er, mostly individuals, but some businesses, er, and then we *lend* that money to real projects, projects that are actually *doing* things. Er, we know them well, we work with them closely, we have an expertise in the various sectors, er, to which we lend. Um, and what that means is, we're *not* exposed in terms of lending, er, to some third party removed, um, derivative project … product, the risk of which is not really understood, and when that goes wrong, the repercussions are enormous. All of that builds up to, er, an understanding that the return that we seek to achieve is not just about finance. It's about the social, environmental impact as well. And so people talk about the triple bottom line that is really important to us. And that I think is a great feature of a truly sustainable bank.

CD2 TRACK 31 (I = INTERVIEWER, CM = CHARLES MIDDLETON)

I Triodos invests in over nine-and-a-half thousand projects. What sorts of project are these, and which are giving the best returns?

CM They're very exciting projects, that's one of the things I would like to say. I mean, they cover a, a huge range of activity. Er, as I said earlier, they are all focused on making a difference in a social and environmental way, er, so they're all pursuing social and environmental aims. Um, but if you look across the range of things that we're involved in – so, in renewable energy, er, we're lending to some of the major renewable energy providers in the UK. Um, in, in social, er, in social housing, we're financing some of the big providers of social housing in the UK, such as Mencap and their subsidiaries. And then we're also involved in trading activity which has a fair-trade, er, focus to it – er, organisations like Café Direct, who are the sort of major hot-drinks fair-trade provider in the UK. So, a vast range of organisations, all with that firm social and environmental focus.
In terms of return, um, as a, as a provider of, of debt funding, um, the return for us is merely the interest that we are paid on the loan.

CD2 TRACK 32 (I = INTERVIEWER, CM = CHARLES MIDDLETON)

I Do you think that changes in the banking system are necessary? And, if so, why?

CM I think the sort of changes that we'd like to see are this, er, focus on banking in what I said before, the real economy, as opposed to creating, er, products and services that are several, er, places removed from the, er, from the bank that is involved in the business. Er, this notion that, um, that we can then, or the banks can then manage that risk in a way that, er, avoids any, any danger, er, has clearly been proven to be, to be entirely incorrect and the consequence was, we nearly saw a complete failure of the banking sector.
So I think more engagement with the, with the real economies, er, in whichever sectors the banks are operating, and also I think some separation of activities. Er, we've seen various ideas put forward about separating the more esoteric, the more investment-banking type activity from the more straightforward, commercial banking. We *all* need banks to go about our everyday business, er, we're all therefore engaged with banks, we are at risk of those banks failing. Er, if those banks are more likely to fail because they're *also* doing business which is a lot more risky in nature, that seems to me to be entirely inappropriate, er, and I think some recognition of separation there will be very helpful, er, going forward.

CD2 TRACK 33 (J = JOURNALIST, M = MINISTER)
SPEAKER 1

J Minister, on the subject of tax evasion, I was wondering whether the minister could confirm whether it's true that the tax authorities bought copies of confidential banking data from a former employee of the National Bank of Liechtenstein?

M Well, I'm afraid I'm not in a position to comment on that at this point in time.

J But surely the public has a right to know …

M Well, if you'd just let me finish, the government will be issuing a press statement later in the day concerning that matter.

CD2 TRACK 34 (P = PRESENTER, Q = QUESTIONER)

SPEAKER 2

P … and I think we still have five minutes for questions. Yes, the gentleman at the back.

Q What would you say were the secrets of fraud accounting? I mean, um, how do you decide whether to take on a client or not?

P I'm, I'm sorry, do you mind using the microphone? And can you tell us your name, please?

Q Sorry, yeah, er, Peter Guthrie, accountant. My question concerns fraud in accounting. I'd like to know more about your policy for taking on clients when it comes to investigating fraud.

P Thanks, Peter. So your question is about how we take on new clients. Well, speaking from our experience, I can say we turn down two jobs out of 10 because we are not comfortable with the prospective clients. I hope that answers your question.

CD2 TRACK 35 (Q = QUESTIONER, P = PRESENTER)

SPEAKER 3

Q I have 100,000 euros, but I'm not sure how to invest the money.

P If I understand you correctly, you'd like me to advise you on how to invest your money?

Q Yes, could you tell us what makes a good investment?

P Well, I'm often asked that question. To be honest, Anne-Marie, sometimes it's just instinct or a personal recommendation. But I *can* tell you what is *not* a good investment. I would avoid any family businesses, any business that claims to be number one, or any business that has already peaked.

Q Thanks. That's very useful.

CD2 TRACK 36 (P = PRESENTER, Q = QUESTIONER)

SPEAKER 4

P OK, so that's an overview of investment in start-ups in Europe. Are there any questions before I move on?

Q I'd like to ask you why you think most financiers are *not* investing in technology in Russia.

P Well, that's difficult to say, and it's not my field of expertise as such. But I would hazard a guess it's, er … too risky, despite the large pool of science and maths talent.

Q So you are saying Russia is too *risky*?

P Well, not exactly, no. In fact, the unpopularity of high-risk investment is an *advantage* for those investors interested in the region.

Q And the fact that business start-ups in Silicon Valley have dozens of venture capital companies to choose from, whereas in Russia we have relatively few.

P Yes, that's a good point. In fact, one Russian businessman told me that there are three types of investors. The first are the three Fs – friends, family and fools. Then you have the so-called *angel* investors, the individual investors and the venture capitalists who take a project to the next level, to the *strategic* investors.

Q *Strategic* investors?

P Yes, if I could just finish what I was saying. At the last stage, the *strategic* investors are governments, big multinationals, that kind of thing. But it's the angels, with the highest risk and highest reward, that are lacking in Russia.

CD2 TRACK 37 (I = INTERVIEWER, F = FINANCIER)

I Do you think you could describe what you do in 10 words?

F I evaluate investment proposals and assess their management teams.

I And how do you think your personal assistant would describe you?

F Determined, a bit insensitive … but with a sense of humour.

I Did you ever predict you would end up where you are today?

F No. I've ended up a great deal richer than I ever imagined. When I was a young lad, I had no idea what I wanted to do and someone advised me to go into private equity. Things just took off from there, really.

I Ah! I'd like to know who has been your biggest influence.

F My grandfather, without a doubt. He built himself up out of nothing.

I And can you tell me, what's the worst job you've ever done?

F Working in a motorway service station.

I Would you mind telling me what's the worst thing you've ever had to do at work?

F Fire people. I hate doing it, but sometimes it's a necessary evil.

I And, um, I was wondering if you had any guilty pleasures.

F Guilty pleasures? Oh, lots – no, no, I'm only joking. Um, it would have to be … taking it easy – I don't do it very often and then I feel guilty.

I And what would you say was your number-one rule?

F Be open and honest. It works in the long term.

I Right. And I have to ask you: have you ever lied at work?

F Er … no. My wife tells me I'm a very bad liar!

I Ah! And have you ever praised someone and not meant it?

F No. Though a woman once threw a cup of coffee at me during her investment proposal, so she probably wished I had.

I Oh. Um, so how important is money to you?

F Less than family, but more than sport.

I Right, and if you hadn't gone into finance, have you any idea what you would have done?

F I'd have been a dentist.

I Oh! And finally, I'd like to ask how you'd like to be remembered.

F As a loving husband and father who lived life to the full.

CD2 TRACK 38 (I = INVESTOR, EG = EVAN GRIFFITHS)

I Can you tell me about your business idea, in a nutshell?

EG I set up my own e-book publishing company, E-sellers, which led me to create an online bookstore. I've now developed my own e-reader, also called the E-seller. The idea is to make the E-seller reader smaller and smarter so that it fits easily into a pocket or handbag.

I We'd like to know a little more about your professional background. What kind of knowledge and expertise have you got?

EG I'm a former management consultant turned serial entrepreneur. So, I'm good at maths and I know how to run a business. I'm also a big thriller reader and I'm writing my own e-thriller at the moment.

I Give me three good reasons why we should invest in you.

EG First of all, I've already set up two businesses successfully. Secondly, when I set up the company last year, I would've been happy for E-sellers to rank fifth by sales worldwide. But now we have an eight-per-cent share of the e-book market and, with some venture capital, I think we can be number two.

I So, you're pretty ambitious then?

EG Yes, definitely. And, and thirdly, I'm convinced this will be the year of the e-book.

CD2 TRACK 39 (I = INVESTOR, AM = AGNES McQUEEN)

I What makes you think people are going to buy an expensive *Scottish* goat's cheese?

AM Because it's a quality product and people are basically willing to pay a bit extra because it's produced by a carbon-neutral company. Green consumer products are in demand again, that's a fact.

I/AM Do you mind me … / The Scottish government, … sorry?

I No, please, carry on.

AM You know, the Scottish government hopes there will be 200,000 new jobs created in green industries over the next five years, and we want to be a part of that new economy.

I Do you mind me asking why your partner isn't here today? She's your sister, right? How do you work together?

AM Um, we're co-directors and one of us needed to stay in the office today. People say I'm more the public-relations person, whereas Morag's a bit shy. But she's absolutely brilliant at the nitty-gritty and the figures. We make a great team.

I You say you're passionate about your business. Being passionate as an entrepreneur is all very well, but what about the money? I get the impression you're not in this for the money, are you, Agnes?

AM Well, of course, you know there *are* financial benefits, both for us and for you as investors, but I wouldn't say we're *only* in it for the money. It's a family business and, most importantly, we pride ourselves on being a carbon-neutral company.

CD2 TRACK 40 (I = INVESTOR, TM = TROELS MCCLINTOCK)

I We were wondering what kind of investment you were looking at. We obviously haven't got £55 million to spare!

TM Well, yes, I realise you're a small syndicate. But I heard that Scotland was investing in early-stage risk capital. I've also been talking to Edinburgh University, and they're prepared to co-invest in this venture. Actually, I'll be going to the States soon to talk to some aircraft manufacturers there, as well as a ship-building company. I think people are very excited about being involved in a venture of this scale.

I I'd like you to be honest here and tell me whether you've ever done anything like this before.

TM Well, I'm an aeronautical engineer and an expert ballooner. I've set several world records for travelling by hot-air balloon. Of course, this is a completely new venture – so yes, I accept it's risky. But we've got to start thinking outside the box if we want to change the world. We can't rely on oil like we've done in the past. The future is renewable energy.

I To tell the truth, it sounds completely crazy. Do you really think you'll be able to carry it through?

TM What can I say? My family are adventurers and we've always taken risks. My father was a mountain climber. And my grandfather, who was a Scot, was a pilot. If you invest in Soul-air, you'll be part of an amazing solar-powered adventure!

UNIT 8 CONSULTANTS

CD2 TRACK 41 (I = INTERVIEWER, PS = PETER SIRMAN)

I When you're advising a company on its operational efficiency, what are your first steps?

PS Let me start by defining what we mean by 'operations'. So, we refer to 'order to cash,' um, meaning the point from which an order is placed by a customer, through to the point at which that order, er, is delivered to the customer and cash is paid for the product. So that's the domain in which we're operating.

Um, the first thing we want to do is to understand what it is, um, the company should be delivering to its customer and how well they're actually delivering. Um, and we un– we try to understand that through a series of techniques and methods, and I'll give you an overview of those. Um, the first thing is, operations is all about serving customers, so we have to start by understanding what it is that the customers want. Er, we want to be sure that we're delivering a service they value, a product that they like and that that's being done every time, to, to the right level of quality.

So we start by talking to customers. And those, um, conversations will be quite detailed, they'll be quite specific about, um, the, the features of the product that the customer values. What is it about the service that's given to them that they like? What is it that they don't like? Not in a sort of very broad, general sense, but in quite a detailed way, so that we can take those points of view back to our client and, and we can use that information to shape the way that they're delivering services and products.

CD2 TRACK 42 (PS = PETER SIRMAN)

PS The second point is that we then want to understand the work that the company is doing to deliver those services and products. Um, we use a technique called 'value stream mapping' – um, that many people will be familiar with – but it looks at the complete process, at all of the activities required to deliver the service or product, linked together so that we can see, um, how the whole organisation is working together, um, to deliver those services.

Um, we then start to analyse the work in more detail: we're interested in the amount of time that each step takes; um, we're interested in levels of quality at each stage of the process; we want to know where things go wrong; why they go wrong; we look at all of the work that's done, um, in that process and we ask 'is this work valuable to the customer? Is this just internal bureaucracy? Are we doing things twice or three ti– three times and not adding value to the customer?' Um, so that we have a real understanding of the efficiency with which services are delivered in terms of the quality, the cost, um, and the delivery effectiveness of those services.

CD2 TRACK 43 (I = INTERVIEWER, PS = PETER SIRMAN)

I And once you've learned about how the company operates, what are your next steps?

PS Well, we move quickly into starting to redesign the work. The, the client company is interested in the solution rather than a long diagnosis. So phase one is all about helping to understand what's going wrong. The real interest is in coming up with a better way of doing things. Um, and this is all about applying creative techniques to improving the way that the work is delivered. And again, this is where the input from the customers is particularly important. It helps us to reshape the way that the services and products are defined and the way they're delivered. We'll very often say to our clients: 'There are things that you should stop doing because your customer does not value them at all, and it's a waste of people's time and money.' Or 'There are things that you should do differently.'

Um, so, that's a starting point. We, so, we look at service features; we look at lead times; we use, um, reduced lead times as a driver for efficiency in an organisation. So if, for example, a customer wants something within one day instead of the four days that it's currently taking, we'll lay that down as a target and say, 'Our target is to design a process that allows us to deliver to customers within a day. How are we going to make that happen?'

So, the, the, our second step here is to identify the drivers of improved performance, which might be, as I said, lead time; it might be about driving costs down; it might be about driving quality up.

CD2 TRACK 44 (PS = PETER SIRMAN)

PS And then we start to redesign the work, at a detailed level, um, to ensure that we can deliver, um, improved performance. And that will include taking out unnecessary steps. It might include looking and saying … looking at a particular set of activities and saying, 'Well, this is something you could outsource because another company can do this cheaper or better than you.' Um, we might look at restructuring the company, at simplifying its structure, so that instead of having a lot of small sites, um, we consolidate into a larger site to increase efficiency. Er, we might look at the management infrastructure; the way that people are managed; the way that, er, targets are set and performance indicators are used, to try and help managers get a better understanding of their performance and therefore to help them improve their performance. So we look at a whole range of things within what we refer to as 'the management system': all of the activities and influences in a company that affect performance.

Um, and then during that process, we'll, we'll run a series of workshops and meetings with client staff, um, and during that process we start to see a new design evolving from all of those discussions and all of that analysis. Um… Until we gradually come up with a consensus around something that we think is going to be better. Um, and at that stage, we start looking at the business case and building a strong financial case for making the changes that we're recommending.

CD2 TRACK 45 (I = IRENE, K = MR KHILAWALA)

I So, Mr Khilawala. I was wondering if you could deliver, um, a bit sooner.

K Sooner? How much sooner?

I Ideally, a fortnight sooner. As you know, we've been doing business now for a year, so we'd expect your usual standards of course! … And, um, we hope that wouldn't, er, change your prices or anything … OK, er, maybe we could talk a little about terms of payment at this point?

K We could deliver sooner, provided you paid in cash.

I Cash? I suppose I could look into it. But I'd have to check with my supervisor first.

K Your supervisor?

I That's right. You know, John.

K Mr John Himona? I've never met him.

I Ah yes, well, he'd have to confirm the payment terms, you see. I'm afraid I don't have the authority.

K Mmm.

I Some more tea?

K Don't mind if I do. We've had 60-day credit terms to date, as you know. But late payments are no good for our cashflow. I'd have to check with our manager in the warehouse.

I No problem.

K What if we delivered one week earlier and you gave us, say, … 30-day credit terms? How does that sound?

I Thirty-day credit? I think that should be do-able. Leave it with me. I'll see what I can do.

K I'll wait to hear from you, then, Irene … Or will that be from John Himona?

CD2 TRACK 46 (C = CLAUDE, K = KEVIN)

C Hello! How's business, Kevin, my friend?

K Not bad, not bad, Claude. But now that you mention it, I was talking to our sales team the other day …

C All good news, I hope …

K Actually, it seems a couple of the products aren't doing that well.

C I'm sorry to hear that. Which ones would those be?

K Well, you know I've mentioned this to you before – the talc, baby talcum powder …

C But in my country, it's one of our bestsellers!

K I know. It might do better if it wasn't in a 500-gram container. But it's the lavender body spray that is a real no-go …

C Our lavender *eau de cologne*? I don't believe it.

K I'm sorry, but I think our customers tend to associate that kind of smell with … well, their grandmothers or something.

C Are you saying it smells *old-fashioned*?

K Er, yes. So, we were wondering whether you'd be able to send us some samples of your, how can I put it, *trendier* products.

C Trendier?

K More 'hip', you know?

C *Eau de cologne* for hip-hop fans?

K No.

C Do you mean a perfume with technological notes?

K Not exactly. I mean modern, less of the old ladies.

C More cool?

K Yes!

C Sure. I've brought some new samples with me. Try this. What does that remind you of?

K I dunno. Tangerines?

C Very good. Citric base notes with a splash of bergamot and, um, how do you call it, a dash of cinnamon.

K It's quite strong, isn't it?

C For strong-minded British ladies. And economical, too.

K Really?

C Really! Now, our usual price is 10 euros per 50 millilitres. But for *you*, we're offering it at nine euros fifty! That's a five-per-cent saving, Kevin.

K What would you say to a 10-per-cent discount?

C Ah, you ride a hard bargain, Kevin.

K Sorry?

C Oh, I mean you *drive* a hard bargain.

K So, do we agree on nine euros per bottle, then?

C Sure. It's always good doing business with you, Kevin. I'll leave you these free samples. And you'll put it all in writing, won't you?

K Consider it a deal. Take care, Claude! Nine euros per bottle. Brilliant. Hang on, this is a *30-millilitre* bottle!

CD2 TRACK 47 (SS = SUNIL SUKKAWALA, JC = JEFF CARSTENS, AK = ANNABEL KUPER)

SS So, you see, we saw mobile phones were only available for the super-rich. We've invested millions in India building a full-scale network and started selling pre-paid mobile phones that cost just 15 US dollars.

JC And do you think you can sell a phone at 15 dollars and still make money?

SS Absolutely. We subsidise them, of course, but typically we have a three-month payback on our subsidy.

AK I understand most of your customers are pre-paid, Mr Sukkawala.

SS Yes, about 90 per cent of our customer base is pre-paid. But in wealthier cities like Delhi and Mumbai, about 60 per cent of our customers are on contract.

AK How interested are they in the latest handsets?

SS Well, people might not own a car, but having the latest mobile phone is very much a status symbol.

JC And why South Africa?

SS Basically, we look at opportunities where existing operators are under-serving the population. And we see a lot of opportunities in South Africa. Our goal is to implement a new mobile network here over the next 12 or 18 months.

JC Twelve months? You mean in time for the World Athletics Championships next year?

SS Exactly.

JC Twelve months? That's going to be a … a challenge.

SS Yes, and it's also going to be a great media opportunity.

AK I hear you are big sponsors of cricket and sport in general.

SS Absolutely.

AK Well, I think Bajaj-tel is in a pretty strong position. I've read your annual growth rate has been over 50 per cent.

SS That's right.

JC Um, by the way, I thought we were expecting Mr Bajaj in today's meeting?

SS Ah! That must be him now. Excuse me … Yes? … Twenty minutes? … I'll let them know … Bye.

JC Mr Bajaj?

SS Yes. He sends his apologies. He's been having lunch with, er, some important people. He'll be here in 20 minutes. Mr Carstens, you said earlier there could be objections from the government?

AK/JC Yes, possibly. / More than likely.

AK But we are hoping that a mobile operator from India would stand more of a chance than some of the other foreign operators.

SS Ah! My question is, Mr Carstens, is how can Heitinga T-com Consulting help us in the *political* arena?

JC Well, er, my partner, Andrew Heitinga, has one or two well-placed contacts.

SS That's good to hear. Actually, I was wondering whether we'll be meeting Mr Heitinga later …

JC Oh, I'm afraid Andrew is away on business. He'll be back Friday.

SS That's a pity! Mmm, maybe we could catch up with him at the weekend, then? Over some cricket, perhaps? Do you enjoy cricket?

JC Actually, I'm more of a rugby man myself.

AK I'm a big cricket fan!

SS/JC Really? / You are?

JC Shall we take a short break? I'd like to give Andrew a call. Annabel, would you mind, er … checking up on the refreshments?

AK Refreshments? I thought lunch was … Oh, yeah, got it.

UNIT 9 STRATEGY

CD3 TRACK 1 (MS = MARJORIE SCARDINO, I = INTERVIEWER)

MS We decided a long time ago, maybe 10 years ago, that, um, as a media company, we were, er, devoted to content, to high-quality content, but content was never going to be enough on its own. Um, we felt that we had to add services to that content to make it more helpful to users. So we added technology in most cases. We added different ways for our customers to use that content. Um, if you are a child studying math, we added new kinds of interactive tools, for instance. Those kinds of things have changed our strategy. And now, much of what we sell is digital, or digitally enabled in some way.

I How do you develop and communicate a strategy in a large multinational organisation like Pearson?

MS We start with the idea that you have to communicate more than strategy. You have to first communicate what the company's goals are and what its values are. Um, and that for us has been the making of our culture, I think. And I think the best companies do have a strong culture. So we have tried to communicate our … goals first, and then our strategy for achieving those goals. Um, I think I have to communicate directly with everybody. Pearson has 35,000 people in it. But I try to … and, and the Internet allows me to do that, so I try to write letters to everybody every time I think there's something important to say. And the people who run different parts of our company try to do the very same, to communicate directly with the people they work with.

And we *try*, though not always do we succeed, but we try to communicate in a colourful way but in a simple and, um, down-to-earth way, so that everyone feels that we're all on the same plain. And I think that really helps to communicate the strategy. Er, it helps to communicate *anything* if you communicate it in simple words, in clear language so that everybody understands.

CD3 TRACK 2 (MS = MARJORIE SCARDINO)

MS Our company's goal is to help individuals make progress in their lives through education. And that's a powerful goal. But it allows everybody to be able to get out of bed ready to do something larger than themselves. So the strategies that help us to accomplish that goal are the ones that excite me more. Um, they're bigger-thinking strategies. They are things about how you change the world, how you influence maybe person by person, or maybe in large schools or, or in countries. How you deliver education in a way that is able to teach every person in his own way, in his own time. Those are the strategies that we've employed to, er, move our education company along.

CD3 TRACK 3

1   When it comes to quality, the company I most admire is the chipmaker, Intel. They have about 80 per cent of the world's PC microprocessor market. Like Apple, they just keep innovating. Intel has just launched a smaller, faster, more powerful chip. Every year, their goal is to introduce new cutting-edge products. Intel calls this its 'tick-tock' strategy.

CD3 TRACK 4

2   I'm a big fan of the Spanish supermarket, Mercadona. Um, I think their strategy has been to offer quality produce like fresh fruit and vegetables, and develop their own brand at competitive prices. They say they source directly without any go-betweens. Um, the business strategy is called ALP – that stands for Always Low Prices. What really impresses me, though, is the way they treat their employees. The company website says they regard workers as their second priority after customers and offer all of them permanent work contracts. From what I can see, I think that's true: from cashiers to shelf-packers, everyone's friendly and helpful, and there doesn't seem to be a high staff turnover. That's something you don't always see in a lot of supermarkets.

CD3 TRACK 5

3   I'd say, Toyota any day. Why? For its product quality, customer care and corporate citizenship. I've been reading about their company philosophy, and it was Taiichi Ohno who developed what's known as the 'Toyota production system'. Ohno believed in producing perfect goods and said, 'If a machine is not producing perfect goods, it is not working.' Now, I've driven plenty of American models, but the most reliable cars I've ever had have all been Toyotas. If I want to pop across town, I might take my daughter's hybrid. And if I had to drive across the country today, I'd take my Toyota pickup. Toyota has never let me down, unlike other vehicles I've owned that have broken down and have had to be towed.

CD3 TRACK 6

4   I'm a store manager for H&M and I can safely say I've never had a bad day at work. I look forward to every day with H&M and I'm not simply saying that because I work for them. H&M offers customers the latest fashions at affordable prices *and* we're socially responsible. We ensure quality merchandise by carrying out regular quality controls, and the company manufactures garments with the least possible impact on the environment. Um, the way we offer best prices is by buying in large volumes and limiting the number of middlemen: the strategy is basically very cost-conscious. I also love the way we sometimes get top fashion designers to design exclusive collections. That's smart marketing for you.

CD3 TRACK 7 (T = TRAINER, S = SARAH, M = MARTIN)

T So, what's your view of brainstorming sessions, Sarah?

S I just don't see the point of them sometimes.

T Yes, that can happen if the group hasn't clearly defined the issue to be solved, or the session doesn't stay focused on that issue. Ideally, there shouldn't be more than eight to 10 people per session, and they should be the right people for the task.

S And I don't think that I'm at my most creative when I'm in a large group. You know, I prefer to work on my own, like first thing in the morning when the office is still quiet.

T That's not an uncommon feeling, but you know, when it's done well, brainstorming is a powerful tool. Yes, Martin …

M I really like working in groups 'cause the dynamics are different. I think it's a really helpful way of, well, generating lots of new ideas in a short amount of time.

T Well, essentially the idea is just that, to generate as many ideas as possible.

M In our meetings, it's always the same people who do all the talking, though.

T Mmm, the facilitator or chairperson should try to get everyone to contribute, even the quietest people. It's also crucial that he or she encourages all the ideas, as wild as they may seem.

S Yes, but most of the ideas people come up with are completely impractical or just stupid. I think we waste a lot of time in these kinds of meetings.

T Don't spend too long discussing any one suggestion to keep things moving. And all participants should try to have an enthusiastic and uncritical attitude to others' contributions. If someone is too critical, the others aren't going to feel comfortable about being creative. So try and suspend judgement until later, after the session. Then you can study and evaluate the ideas. Let's try a short practical exercise. I'd like you all to think of new ways to promote your brand. And Sarah, could you write all the ideas on the flip chart?

S Sure.

T Thanks. So, who'd like to get the ball rolling?

M I've got one. How about adverts on the sides of all the buses and bus stops around the city centre? It could be good for business.

S That's been done before.

M I just thought I'd make a start.

T Thanks, Martin. Remember, as I was saying earlier, the rule is there are no bad ideas when we're brainstorming.

CD3 TRACK 8 (T = TRAINER, S = SARAH)

T Before we go on, just let me interrupt you for a minute to tell you about Einstein and his colleagues. They spent years brainstorming with each other, sharing their ideas openly and honestly by using some ancient principles of group communication. It seems that Socrates and other Greek philosophers used to sit around brainstorming and debating issues, but their discussions didn't usually get out of hand. Why? Because the participants followed the seven principles of discussion established by Socrates. He called these principles *Koinonia*, meaning 'spirit of fellowship'. They were:

1 Establish dialogue.
2 Exchange ideas.
3 Don't argue.
4 Don't interrupt.
5 Listen carefully.
6 Clarify your thinking.

And finally, number 7, be honest.

M Makes sense.

S Yeah, but I'm no Einstein.

T Yes, well. Back to where we left off. Does anyone have any more promotion ideas?

CD3 TRACK 9 (DM = DIRECTOR OF MARKETING, HCC = HEAD OF CORPORATE COMMUNICATIONS, CEO = CHIEF EXECUTIVE OFFICER)

DM As I was saying, we can't just carry on with business as usual. The main issue here is that we have an image problem. The research says it loud and clear: people think our stores and our products are old-fashioned.

HCC Yes, we've relied too heavily on our reputation for quality, value and service over the years, and that just isn't sexy any more.

CEO Hang on, those are our core values. It's what's made R&F what it is today.

DM Absolutely, and I'm not suggesting at all that we lose those values. It's more a case of adding to them. I'm thinking of innovation. We need to move with the times. Show that we have new ideas.

CEO Yes, I like that.

HCC Our challenge is to meet the needs of the loyal older customer while anticipating trends in younger fashions and lifestyles. Women especially are shopping by attitude rather than age these days and are far more willing to experiment, for instance by shopping online.

DM I think advertising is key to our recovery plan. I'll admit we've made some disastrous decisions in the past that have probably added to our outdated image.

CEO Yes, and maybe we need to hire a new advertising agency for this one. Get some fresh ideas. I really believe a good advertising campaign will go a long way to reviving our fortunes.

DM That and innovation in our furnishings, food and clothing brands. Drop some of the old brands and introduce new lines. Get celebrities to advertise our new ranges.

HCC And, and let's communicate ideas through the campaign. Remind people what we stand for, that they can always trust our brand. R&F is the same but better, you know?

CEO I think so.

DM It's also important that the marketing strategy focuses on multiple key areas, including food – that accounts for 30 per cent of our turnover – and womenswear and home furnishings.

CEO Good idea. OK, since you guys have started, let's brainstorm some more ideas for our new marketing strategy.

CD3 TRACK 10
MANAGER 1

Our operating costs are always going to be higher than the LCCs – for one thing, we're flying to popular destinations that involve higher airport taxes and route costs. But we could try and weed out some of the poorer routes and reduce the number of landing slots in low season. Then we could switch our aircraft to new opportunities, like having more slots on popular routes in Europe and the US, and expand into the Asian markets. We could also think about having a 'dual brand' structure. I mean, we could develop a low-cost subsidiary airline aside from our own main brand. That would allow us to protect valuable European routes from being lost to competitors.

CD3 TRACK 11
MANAGER 2

We have to reduce maintenance costs on our fleet. If we ordered more of the same models, it would be cheaper in terms of spare parts and staff training. We've been trying to negotiate prices with our main aircraft manufacturer, but I wonder if we should change supplier.

CD3 TRACK 12
MANAGER 3

Stella has been operating for more than 40 years – the airline has an excellent safety record. We've also got experience and expertise that the low-cost airlines just can't match. And we've built our reputation on a quality service to our customers. We need to focus on the passengers who don't mind paying a bit more to travel in comfort, especially on the key long-haul routes where the European LCCs can't compete … well, not yet, anyway.

CD3 TRACK 13
STAFF MEMBER 1

We could generate ancillary revenue streams in the same way that the LCCs do. I'd charge for in-flight catering. After all, you'd never expect any other form of transport to provide you with free food and drinks. I'd also start charging for more than one piece of check-in luggage; that would offset some fuel costs. And some passengers will be prepared to pay for advanced seat booking and for upgrades. It needs to be done carefully, though. I mean, passengers will just downgrade to the LCCs if we're seen as being just the same as them.

CD3 TRACK 14
STAFF MEMBER 2

This is not the first time the airline has restructured, and I doubt it'll be the last. Morale is rock bottom right now. We know what 'cost reductions' mean – job losses and worse pay and conditions for the rest of us.

CD3 TRACK 15
STAFF MEMBER 3

We need to hook up with an airline in the expanding North Asia and Asia–Pacific markets, where we have very few routes. In fact, I hear that we're already in discussions with Victoria Jets, the Australian carrier. Both airlines could do with a bigger network so we can compete with larger rivals.

WORKING ACROSS CULTURES 3: SOCIALISING

CD3 TRACK 16 (GD = GARY DAVIES)

GD Good morning, good morning, I'm Gary Davies and welcome to Swindon Securities and our annual strategy convention. I hope the, er, wet weather won't spoil your visit too much! Now, we know some of you have come from as far afield as South Korea, Brazil, the USA … and Gloucester! So we've tried to keep the schedule simple today: a tour of the premises, a few meetings, a working lunch and a training session. Only joking!
Right then, um, as you all know, I'm the Manufacturing Manager. It's my job to make the product. It's Sandra's job to design the product. And it's Nathan's job to sell the product. They both think I've got the easiest job! Well, I'll be taking you on a tour shortly. If you have any questions, please just ask. And in case you're still wondering, this is Sandra and that's Nathan. OK, would you like to follow me through? You'll need to have your security passes at the ready.

CD3 TRACK 17 (GD = GARY DAVIES, EA = ELVIRA ALVES, ND = NATHAN DONOVAN)

GD Elvira, I'm so glad you could make it. What was the flight like from Brazil?

EA Oh, it was a complete nightmare! There were delays because of the air-traffic controllers' strike.

GD Oh dear, I'm sorry to hear that.

EA Don't worry. I'm here now.

GD Right. Oh, by the way, I don't think you've met Nathan, Nathan Donovan. He's the International Sales Manager at our California office.

ND Hi. Sorry, I didn't catch your name.

EA Elvira Alves. Nice to meet you, Nathan.

GD Elvira was made Head of the São Paulo office this year.

ND No way! I hear you've been doing great things there.

EA We try to do our best. Thanks.

GD Yes, and Elvira is leading the meeting tomorrow on our global strategy.

ND I see.

GD I thought we could meet up later with all the team for dinner this evening. How does that sound?

ND Dinner? Er, tonight?

GD That's right. Some of the team know each other. But our overseas partners are a bit out on a limb, so to speak. It's booked for seven. Elvira?

EA Sure.

GD Great. I can meet you in the hotel foyer at half six.

ND Er, Gary, actually, I'd prefer to stay in this evening, if it's all the same to you.

GD You're not coming out for dinner this evening?

ND The thing is, er, I'd really like to fine-tune my presentation for tomorrow's meeting.

GD It's just that I thought we could get to know all the partners a bit better.

ND I know. I'm sorry to let you down. I'm sure Belinda from the Baltimore office will be happy to come along.

GD Sure.

ND Tell you what ... perhaps I'll try to make it later for coffee and drinks?

GD Fine. This sales presentation of yours had better be something, Nathan!

ND It will be! Catch you later, Gary.

EA Excuse me, Gary. Did you say we're eating at the hotel at seven?

GD Uh, no, dinner's at seven, but I'll meet you in the foyer at six thirty.

EA Oh, OK, no problem. By the way, I'd just like to say you've done a great job, Gary.

GD Oh, thanks.

EA All of this organisation. It must have been a lot of work.

GD Oh, it was nothing really.

EA You're too modest. The programme for this week looks great. I'm looking forward to the nightlife in Swindon!

GD Well, I wouldn't want to raise your hopes. Swindon's not exactly Rio.

CD3 TRACK 18 (EA = ELVIRA ALVES, GD = GARY DAVIES, ND = NATHAN DONOVAN)

EA That was a fabulous meal, Gary. People always complain about the food in the UK, but this evening's meal was surprisingly good.

GD Well, we like to bring visitors here. It's a shame we couldn't sit outside on the terrace, though.

EA Typical British weather, huh?

GD I know. I've been thinking, Elvira, we should go to Brazil for our next annual meeting.

EA Ah, yeah, let's organise it in Brazil!

GD Just as long as it isn't during the carnival.

EA Why's that?

GD Oh, I heard it's extremely noisy, and some friends once got mugged there ...

EA Ah, really? Well, the carnival, unfortunately, attracts huge crowds.

GD Yes, it absolutely ruined my friends' holiday.

EA That's a pity.

GD They ended up spending most of their holiday in a police station because their passports had been stolen, too.

EA That's awful ... Um, so, how's your family, Gary?

GD What? Oh, fine, thanks. My son's doing his exams at the moment, and we're hoping he's going to study economics at university.

EA That's great. You must be very proud.

GD Well, we do what we can. And, er, what are your kids up to?

EA Kids? Oh, no, I don't have any children.

GD Oh, I'm sorry. I didn't realise ...

EA That's all right. You must be thinking of my predecessor, Gilberto. He has *five* children.

GD Right.

EA Gary, excuse me. I'm just going outside for a cigarette.

GD But it's still raining. Shall I order you a coffee?

EA Um, do they have espresso?

GD Uh, I think it's filter.

EA No, I'm fine, thanks. I won't be long.

ND Hi, Gary. What's up?

GD I think I may have put my foot in it ...

ND What, with Elvira?

GD Yes, I might have offended our new chief strategist.

ND Oh? Nice shirt, by the way.

GD What? Oh, thanks. I got it tailor-made ... Nathan, are you fishing for something?

ND Um ... what are you doing tomorrow at breakfast?

GD Why?

ND I was just wondering if you wanted to take a quick look at my presentation?

GD Sure. But I'm relying on you to wow them. No pressure or anything.

ND Right.

CD3 TRACK 19 (EA = ELVIRA ALVES)

EA I know our British host was trying to be hospitable, but his jokes didn't go down well with everybody. The Korean visitors didn't understand his sense of humour at all. And some of the other delegates wouldn't tell jokes in this way at work, especially in a formal speech. Most of the visitors spoke English, but I think Gary needed to slow down and use less colloquial language.

CD3 TRACK 20 (ND = NATHAN DONOVAN)

ND I guess Gary was a little put-out when I turned down his invitation for dinner. Sure, people socialise with work colleagues in the States. The thing is, most of my British and Brazilian colleagues always want to go out and party, but I'm teetotal, so that's a bit awkward at times. They say socialising is good for team building, but why can't we just celebrate the end of a successful meeting? Anyway, Gary should have realised I needed time to prepare for the next day. It was a key presentation.

CD3 TRACK 21 (EA = ELVIRA ALVES)

EA I wish Gary hadn't mentioned the carnival. *Everyone* talks about the carnival when they find out I'm from Brazil. Some of my international colleagues think we're partying all the time when in fact I work really hard. Don't get me wrong: I'm enjoying getting to know the team in England, but all this rain, no smoking in restaurants and watery coffee, it's getting me down.

UNIT 10 ONLINE BUSINESS

CD3 TRACK 22 (I = INTERVIEWER, DB = DAVID BOWEN)

I What sort of companies have been the main winners in terms of doing business online?

DB Well, the first and most obvious group are companies that were set up specifically to *do* business online; er, the giant booksellers, like Amazon. And also some companies who, er, couldn't have existed in the old days, like eBay, the auction site. Um, I think second are *small* companies that have been able to sell *outside* their traditional markets. That's now much easier for them. Um, and the third point is that companies are able to *buy* things around the world online, er, much more cheaply than they could in the past; both large companies and also your local plumber might be able to buy something in Hong Kong, er, when he never could have before.

CD3 TRACK 23 (I = INTERVIEWER, DB = DAVID BOWEN)

I Your work involves helping organisations to build truly global websites. What are the key features of such websites?

DB The first feature of the global website is its complexity. It has to serve a huge number of audiences, both geographically dispersed and also different types of people: um, they could be customers, shareholders, journalists, governments, all sorts. So, the signposting, the navigation and the usability of those websites are all *extremely* important. I think the second point is to do with branding. Er, you can no longer come across with a look and feel, er, in Bolivia that's different from one in Bulgaria, for example. So, everything has to be much, much more homogeneous. It *pulls* the whole company together in a way that really wasn't necessary in the past.

CD3 TRACK 24 (I = INTERVIEWER, DB = DAVID BOWEN)

I How are companies benefiting from the use of social media?

DB I think the first area is in marketing; that by very, very subtle use of social networking sites like Facebook, and also what they call micro-blogging sites, like Twitter, um, they can get their messages across in a, a rather different way from the way that they do, um, on the Web itself. It's more engaging, they can have more two-way conversations with their customers. Um, and so I think that, that's an, an important point. The second one is that actually they can talk to *other* groups, for example people looking for jobs. Young people typically will spend a lot of time on Facebook, so why not go to Facebook to talk to them?

I What problems can social media cause for companies?

DB There's a big reputation risk from social media. If a story gets out, um, which may be false, it can spread very, very fast indeed on Twitter, on blogs, um, even on YouTube. And it's very, very difficult for companies to, er, to deal with that. They have to move much faster than they've been traditionally used to. They can't just ring up journalists, they have to get out there, and try and counter the reputation-management issue very, very early on.

I Can you give us an example?

DB There's a rare example of a company dealing successfully with a, with a reputation management crisis when, er, Ford has a Social Media Manager. His job is to look after Twitter and things like that. And he discovered that a story was going around that Ford had tried to close down, er, a very small dealership's website. Um, and it appeared that this was Ford behaving quite badly. He send out, sent out messages on Twitter to his followers saying, 'I'm trying to find out about this. I'm trying to find out about this.' Eventually, he discovered that there was a Ford side to the story. He put that out, and what could have been quite a nasty fire was put out at the very beginning, within a few hours.

CD3 TRACK 25 (I = INTERVIEWER, DB = DAVID BOWEN)

I And where is online business heading? What developments do you see over the next few years?

DB Well, I think the developments that are already starting where companies are having to be much more responsive, er, to their customers, because customers no longer necessarily listen to what a company says to them. They'll go and ask *other* customers of their experience. It's something that's happening with social media and that's going to develop enormously. Er, from a more, if you like, exciting point of view, I think we're going to get 3D, so we'll get quite a lot more, you know, going into a, a virtual shop. Er, I think that's going to become quite big. Um, and also, we're going to get the convergence of television and computers. So in a few years' time, you really won't notice whether you're using a television or a computer. They will be the same thing.

CD3 TRACK 26 (SR = SOPHIE RAWLINGS, S = SPEAKER)

SR I think that gives us time for a couple of questions before the break. Um, oh yes?

S1 I was, er, just wondering what you thought were the main differences between, um, er, government websites and those in the private business sector?

SR Right. Well, it's really what I was talking about at the start of my presentation. One of the main differences used to be that business websites were aimed at selling online, whereas government sites were simply offering information and access to services. But a new online business might start off by offering its products or services for free, while some government sites might be taking payment for certain services. Um, I don't really want to go into too much detail at this stage, as Peter Adams will be dealing with commercial sites and credit-card security in the next session.

S2 Excuse me.

SR Yeah?

S2 Um … er, yeah, I'd, I'd like to know how a company can improve its online sales through web-page design.

SR I'm really sorry, could you just repeat that question because I don't think everyone heard.

S2 Oh, sure, sorry. I'd like to know how a company can actually improve its online sales through web-page design. I mean, what is it exactly that makes it more effective?

SR Um, well, as I've already said, Peter will be dealing with those kinds of issues later, but what I would say is, think of eBay and Amazon. You know, what makes those sites so effective? Making the online experience quick, easy and user-friendly is the key. Otherwise users will just click off the site. And build in flexibility. I mean, allow your user to change her mind and order two items instead of three without going all the way back to the beginning. When you think of the most successful sites, they have very user-focused design, provide information without overloading the user and are just simple to use. I hope that answers your question.

S2 Yes, thanks.

SR Good.

S3 I'd be interested to know more about copywriting. I mean to say, could you tell us what kind of language you think works well on websites?

SR That's a really interesting question. Um, the language, tone and look of a business site is going to be quite different, although government sites should also be open, friendly and clearly written. And we've seen the increasing use of social media such as wikis and blogs for both company and government sites. But on the whole, commercial sites use language that's what I'd call punchy, or young and trendy. And copy, or the language used on websites, is primarily designed to encourage users to spend money!

S3 Yes, but I was wondering whether there was any kind of language that you would *avoid* using?

SR So, your question is what kind of language should we avoid? Well, apart from the obvious, you know, offensive language, the sort of language depends on the industry and the purpose of the website. Is it aimed at customers, members of staff or shareholders? What I usually say is don't use very technical terminology: jargon, abbreviations and acronyms should all be avoided. You'll find some guidelines on copywriting in the handout. Is that all? OK, great, well, let's break for 15 minutes, then …

CD3 TRACK 27 (LC = LEA CHIU, ZM = ZAYNA MEERZA)

LC I'm Lea Chiu, and our special guest today is award-winning tailor, Zayna Meerza. Zayna, you're one of the top five tailors in Paris, if not Europe. What do you think you owe your success to?

ZM Well, we always try to personalise our suits. I don't offer a standard two-button suit – people want special touches. And once a client has worn a tailored suit, they can't bear to buy clothes off the peg.

LC Sure, but the, er, competition in the industry is extremely tough. I mean, with so many online retailers offering top brands at cut prices, do you think your success is, um, going to last?

ZM Of course trends come and go. But at Meerza, we're using new media tools to find key trends, to, to find out what our clients really want.

LC Mm-hm. And I hear you've expanded the business to include tailored shirts. Tell us a bit about that.

ZM Well, customers can choose styles, submit their measurements and mix and match fabrics online. And after the first order, we offer a 10-per-cent discount on subsequent orders.

LC Cool! You mentioned new media – how are you using digital media in your business? Customers are soooo fickle nowadays – they're quick to complain and, um, change brands.

ZM I'm sorry, I, I'm not sure what … I'm not sure I follow you.

LC Um, what I'm asking is, how are you adapting your online business? I suppose you must have a social media team, someone trawling the Internet?

ZM Oh, er, yes … That's an interesting point. Well, up to now, I can safely say we've had hardly any complaints. But having a social media manager is, um, it's something I'm considering.

LC Right, and, um, what would you say to critics who think your suits are not all they claim to be?

ZM Excuse me?

LC Your garments are advertised as made in Paris. But bloggers are saying they're made in Frankfurt, China or … who knows where!

ZM Really? I didn't realise, I mean that's a false accusation. Our suits are mostly made in Paris, but it could be Frankfurt, depending on the customer's location …

LC Mostly? So, um, are you saying they're made in Paris, or not?

ZM Well, it depends …

LC So, 'Made in Paris', is what, just a marketing slogan?

ZM No, I didn't say that …

LC And what about your business finance. Is it true that the company is experiencing some financial difficulty?

ZM Those are just rumours.

LC Right.

ZM Meerza Tailoring Fashions is going from strength to strength.

LC And finally, I'm sure all our viewers have been following the *don't-shop-sweatshop* campaign. What's your position on that, Zayna?

ZM Well, at Meerza, we're opposed to sweatshop labour, obviously.

LC Yes, but a little birdie tells me you haven't yet signed the petition.

ZM No, not yet. But it's something I'm seriously thinking about.

LC You heard it here first on our show – Zayna Meerza is going to sign the petition! And next we have *l'enfant terrible* of the fashion world, Vincent Selz! Let's take a look at Vincent's digitally inspired *Futura* collection. It's to die for!

UNIT 11 NEW BUSINESS

CD3 TRACK 28 (I = INTERVIEWER, MS = MIKE SOUTHON)

I What kind of start-ups are the most popular with first-time entrepreneurs?

MS Well, really there's two types of start-ups which people do nowadays. One is something that solves a problem in a local area. So, for example, there's a local entrepreneur and notices there's a problem, so may start a plumbing company, or an accounting company, or just something that brings services to the local area that aren't there already, so that's a, some kind of physical business, usually a services business. And the other one, of course, are Internet businesses, where anybody in theory can have a website and, er, drive people to there and then sell things from it. It could be selling information, it could be selling products. So I'd say there are two types: there's local businesses and Internet businesses.

CD3 TRACK 29 (I = INTERVIEWER, MS = MIKE SOUTHON)

I What are some of the classic mistakes that first-time entrepreneurs make?

MS Well, the difference between a good start-up and a bad start-up is whether you can actually sell your stuff. So, a big mistake that people make is spending too much time developing their product and service without going out to sell it. So the key thing is find customers first, then worry about delivery second. And I'd say the other thing that really holds people back is lack of a team, because it's a great myth that entrepreneurship is a solo activity. Actually, it's a team game. In fact, the first advice that I give to budding entrepreneurs is, before they even have an idea, is to find what I call a foil, that's somebody with the opposite set of skills to themselves. So if they're good at delivery, then it's somebody who is good at sales, or if they're good at sales, somebody good at delivery, an introvert and an extrovert perhaps. So, build a team is the main thing. And also make sure there are people who actually want to spend money on your product or service.

CD3 TRACK 30 (I = INTERVIEWER, MS = MIKE SOUTHON)

I What advice would you give to someone starting a new business?

MS Well, after you've put a bit of a team together, er, and again before you start spending any money, er, we spend a lot of time advising people to get a good mentor, that's somebody who can give you good advice. This is probably somebody you know, maybe a family friend who's got some business experience and contacts. Because mentors do two things: first they can test your idea to see if it's a good idea, they can give you practical advice on how to make your product or service better, or how to get customers. The, the second thing they do is they can pick up the phone, or start writing letters for you, they can make contacts for you, they can open doors, which is very important, especially for that elusive first customer. I always say that everybody should always have a good 'elevator pitch'. And that comes from the expression when you're in an elevator or a lift, and you're pitching your idea to somebody important, perhaps a customer, or someone who might invest in your company. I always say there's five Ps that people should remember. The first P is, stands for pain, where is the pain or problem that you solve? That's the first question you must ask yourself. The second P is fairly straightforward, what is the premise of your business? What does your business actually do? What products or services do you sell? The third P is all about people because, whatever business you have, there's lots of different people competing with you. So what makes your people better than somebody else's people? It's all about the people in your organisation.

The fourth P is P for proof which is it … sounds really good, a good business idea. But you have to have some proof, and the best proof is some happy customers that you can direct potential customers to. So successful customers is very good proof. The last P is bit more, sort of philosophical, what is the purpose of your business? Now, you could say a very obvious purpose would be to make money, and that's absolutely true. But the second purpose is why are you doing this business and not something else? Are you making the world a better place? Are you enjoying yourself? Are you having fun? And those are the five Ps. So it's pain, premise, people, proof and then purpose.

CD3 TRACK 31 (VB = VAL BAILEY, MB = MAX BRYSON)

VB Dunbarry Jewellers, Val Bailey speaking.

MB Hello, this is Max Bryson, calling on behalf of Carswell Department Stores. I'd like to query a bill we received.

VB I see, Mr Bryson. Could you give me the invoice number, please?

MB Yes, um, it's, um, I think … er, I have it here somewhere. Um, er, yes, here it is. Um, I'm not sure which number … um …

VB It's on the top right-hand side, below the date.

MB Ah, yes. Sorry about that. Yes, it's BJ1687, dated 22nd of May.

VB BJ1687, I'll just check that … Oh, yes, I have it here on screen. What seems to be the problem?

MB Er, well, we've been overcharged. You see, the invoice is for 300 units, but our original order was, er, for 260.

VB Let me see if I have that right. You asked for 260 units, and we've billed you for 300. Is that correct?

MB Yes, that's it.

VB Do you have a copy of the delivery note?

MB Um, it must be somewhere around here. Let me see, um … Hang on just a sec. Um, Jean, pass that file over here … no, no, the one on your right. Yeah, yeah … here it is. We definitely signed for 260.

VB Well, I'll need to confirm that with our records, too, Mr Bryson.

MB Please, call me Max.

VB Certainly, Max. As I say, I'll need to check the original purchase order and issue a new invoice if we have made a mistake. Can I take your number and call you back?

MB Yes, the number here is 020 9658 5518. When will you call me back, Val?

VB Um, it shouldn't take long. I'll, I'll ring you later this morning.

MB OK, fine, thank you. I'll be in the office until one o'clock.

VB One p.m.? OK, Max. I'll give you a call before then. Bye.

CD3 TRACK 32 (VB = VAL BAILEY, MB = MAX BRYSON)

MB Hello?

VB Oh, hello, could I speak to Max Bryson, please?

MB Speaking.

VB Hello, Max, this is Val Bailey calling from Dunbarry Jewellers. I'm phoning about the outstanding payments on two of our invoices.

MB Ah, right, yeah. Um … could you give me the invoice numbers?

VB Yeah, sure. There's BJ1698, dated 28th of May, and BJ1712 dated 8th of June. I also sent you an e-mail reminder on the 10th of July.

MB Yes, I'm sure.

VB As you know, our credit terms are 30 days, and payment is now way overdue on both of these bills.

MB Yeah, sure. I … I must apologise for the delay, Val, you know what it's like in a busy office. I'll authorise payment as soon as possible.

VB I understand. Could you tell me when that will be?

MB Um … on the last banking day of the month.

VB I'm sorry, but we'd expect payment sooner. Given the situation, we'll have to consider withdrawing credit terms if these invoices aren't settled within seven days.

MB Look, I'm … I'm sure we can sort this out, Val. I can make an exception and settle the invoice for the 28th of May this week, but the other invoice will be paid as part of our normal monthly payment procedures. Would that be acceptable?

VB So, are you saying that you can pay us this week?

MB Um … I'm saying that we can pay you for the invoice from the 28th of May, yes.

VB I see. Well, we would prefer payment of the other outstanding invoice within 15 days.

MB Um, let me see. Fine, I … I think we can work with that.

VB OK, Max, I'll get back to you on the 30th of July if we haven't received both payments.

MB Yeah, of course. Thanks for calling, Val. Bye.

CD3 TRACK 33 (AL = ANDERS LARSEN, EB = EMILY BROOKES, UH = ULLA HOFMANN)

AL Well, to be honest, um, I'm happy with our current performance. We don't have the sales volumes we'd anticipated by this stage, but our profit margins are reasonably high. I'm inclined to let things, you know, continue as they are.

EB Even if you're happy with your present situation, Anders, it's important to keep looking for ways to develop. If you don't, you risk giving your competitors the room to grow and taking market share from you, and that could seriously weaken your position.

UH Ah, well, yes, you're right.

EB First off, if you're looking to increase market share, it's important to make sure your business is in good shape.

UH Well, we've definitely improved our production processes since we started, and managed to reduce costs, production and delivery times. We've also developed an excellent quality-control system, and our pricing is competitive.

EB OK, what about marketing?

AL Well, you know, we thought if we had good products, they'd pretty much sell themselves.

EB I'm afraid life's not like that. The focus groups we've held have produced some interesting findings. Most people in your target markets have never heard of your products. And those who had bought a home testing kit, or said they would consider buying one, generally felt that the instructions for use were too long and complicated.

UH Yes, it's true, Emily. But, um, we need to do something about that. I did wonder about putting short instruction videos on the website, and maybe starting a customer blog.

EB I, I think essentially you need publicity. A launch event is one thing that would have created greater impact and perhaps a bigger initial marketing push for your products.

AL Well, you know, to be honest with you, neither of us has got any experience in the marketing field. We've just left the sales team to get on with it. I'm afraid we just hoped for the best. But yeah, I can see now we need someone to help us with that.

EB Yes, um, to increase your market share, you're going to have to find ways to get your customers to want to buy more, or take customers from your competitors, or attract new customers – or preferably all three. And I think if we can get pharmacies and shops to, um, display your products more prominently, that would help. Um, I mean, on the counter rather than behind the counter, so people can help themselves.

AL That's an excellent idea!!

CD3 TRACK 34

Coming up next on today's programme, we have three special features for you. Our first report is about the work of the Hazlett Foundation, which is dedicated to bringing innovations in health to global communities. The Foundation, set up by billionaire businessman Paul Hazlett and his wife Miriam, offers grants to organisations working in the field of medical technologies for developing countries where easy-to-use, low-tech solutions are desperately needed.

Our second report investigates the work of the Food and Drug Administration in the United States. Medical suppliers need FDA approval to sell medical products in the US, but, as our reporter discovered, the approval process can be complicated and drawn-out. For our final report, we go to India, where the prevalence of type-two diabetes is set to grow more rapidly than in any other nation. There are expected to be more than 60 million cases by 2017. So, more on these stories coming up after the break.

UNIT 12 PROJECT MANAGEMENT

CD3 TRACK 35 (I = INTERVIEWER, PM1 = PROJECT MANAGER 1, PM2 = PROJECT MANAGER 2)

I What are the qualities of a good project manager?

PM1 Er, I think you need to have very good interpersonal skills, to be very good at communicating and to clarify people's roles in the team, so they know exactly what they're supposed to be doing. Um, it's not like saying that the project manager gives the orders and the others follow – no, it's, it's not like that. The project manager isn't necessarily the boss, because the team members may come from different departments, and the project manager may not be directly in charge of them. This is why he or she should discuss issues with all members of the team and then make decisions together with them, setting achievable goals, but without telling people what they have to do.

PM2 Really, to be a good project manager, you need to know how to delegate. You need to be able to juggle different issues all at the same time – you know, be good at multi-tasking. On the other hand, you're the person who can stand back and see the big picture, have a general overview of everything. And seeing the details and the complexities of issues is part of the job, so you understand exactly what people are doing and what they're talking about. But most of all, a project manager has got to know how to organise a team, direct them and motivate them, so that they are 100 per cent clear about the goals that you're aiming for.

CD3 TRACK 36 (TT = TOM TAYLOR)

TT I think successful project managers work on successful projects. I think that's a good start. And successful projects, well, people say three things: on time, on budget, to performance. Some people say 'to scope' or 'to quality', but I like 'to performance'. I think those three things generally are understood to be a successful project. But there is something else and that is, success. What is success? And it's those three things, but usually something else as well. So if my project is ... a wedding: on time, on budget, to performance. They get married, that sounds like it's good enough. But it's not. And if you talk to people, then they will say something else, like, 'We'd like a nice day. We'd like some nice photographs or a video. We'd like everybody who should come to arrive.' And therefore the project manager has the job of getting those other things done.

If we had a power station, which is at the other end of the story, then on time, on budget, to performance – that sounds good, but there may be other things as well. So if you talk to the stakeholders, you will find things like, 'We'd like it to be safe. We'd like it to have minimum environmental impact,' something like that. 'We'd like it to last for 50 years.' So the project manager needs to know what is success, for themselves, for their team.

CD3 TRACK 37 (I = INTERVIEWER, TT = TOM TAYLOR)

I What are some of the main issues for project managers today?

TT I think it's mainly about change. Projects are about change. Society wants change. I think the challenges really are no different in projects to what everybody is facing. Tight budgets, value-for-money requirements, needing things to be delivered on time, maybe not just at the end of the project but at the stages during the project, things like that. The best use of technology, technology appropriate to the project – it might be a heavy technology project, it might be a light one, and you use the technology to suit, suit the people and their capabilities. There's an interest everywhere in sustainability, the environment and green issues. A lot of that is appearing in projects, to make things better, to overcome some of the problems and damage that has occurred in the world, um, that's, that's an important issue for people.

And probably the biggest other area is just dealing with people. Um, you can't project-manage from behind a computer, you will have to come out and deal with people.

CD3 TRACK 38 (BA = BILL ANDERSON, MP = MIRIAM PARKER, GH = GEORGES HUBERT)

EXTRACT 1

BA So, are you ready? Want to lead today?

MP Sure. Here we go.
*Welcome to the conference centre. Please enter your password and hash sign ...
Please state your name.*

MP Miriam Parker and Bill Anderson.
You are the first caller to this conference. Please wait while others join.

BA Why are we always the first ones to ...?
Suzanne Fossey has now joined the conference call.

MP Good afternoon, Suzanne. How are ...?
Georges Hubert has now joined the conference call.

BA Good afternoon, Georges.

GH Hello, Miriam. Are Bill and Suzanne there?

MP Yes, we're all here now. Thanks for joining ...
Suzanne Fossey has left the conference call.

CD3 TRACK 39

EXTRACT 2

A I know we weren't due to discuss this today, but I think it's important to bring the issue up. We've been trying to get these trials off the ground for weeks now, but the people at the Albany plant can't tell us when we can start. I think we should look for an alternative location. Does anyone have any suggestions?

B I can see that's a problem for you, but we have a lot to get through today. Let's come back to that question at the end of the meeting if we have time. What's ... what's that noise?

C Whoops, sorry, I was just checking my e-mail.

CD3 TRACK 40

EXTRACT 3

A As you can see from the report, the projected sales figures are looking very promising.

B Yves, do we have a detailed breakdown by country?

C Sorry, who was that speaking?

B Me, Martha from the Phoenix office.

A Thanks for your question, Martha. We haven't gone into that level of detail at this stage.

C What's that?

B Sorry, guys. Forgot to turn my cell phone off.

CD3 TRACK 41 (L = LAUREN, S = STAN, A = ABIGAIL)

EXTRACT 4

L Right then, final item; as you all know, we had an outage in the production plant yesterday for three hours. Stan, can you bring us up to speed on that?

S Well, everything's working fine again now.

L Do we know what the problem was?

S No, sorry, Lauren, not yet. There's obviously a glitch in the system, but I can't say how long it'll take to find it.

A Abigail here. Sorry, I'm confused. A glit??

S Yeah, some sort of glitch in the software. We'll prep. an incident report asap and I'll cc you all in on it, as soon as it's ready.

L OK, thanks, Stan. I think that's as far as we can get today. So, any comments anyone? Great! Thanks for the input, you guys.

S BFN, everybody.

A BFN?

CD3 TRACK 42 (RS = RACHEL STEADMAN, EH = ESTHER HOLMES, DC = DONG CHEN, DM = DANIEL MATTHEWS)

RS Hello, everybody. This Rachel Steadman from Melbourne HQ. Today we'll be getting an update on the project to introduce our biscuits into the Chinese market. Let's start by taking the roll call.

DC Hi, all. This is Dong Chen in Hong Kong speaking.

EH Esther Holmes from Marketing in Singapore here.

RS And Daniel Matthews from R&D has just joined us. I don't think you know him. Daniel?

DM Hi, guys. Sorry I'm a bit late. My last meeting overran.

EH Daniel, is that a British accent I hear?

DM Yes, that's right.

EH It must be very late, or is it early, over there. Is it raining in England?

DM Um, I'm in Melbourne, Esther.

EH Oh, sorry, I see.

RS Rachel here. Let's look at the items for discussion today. First is Esther's report.

DM Actually, I only got the report this morning, and I haven't really had time to look at it.

RS Don't worry, Daniel. Esther will go over the main points now, and you can read it in detail later. Next on the agenda, Dong Chen will talk about production capacity. To finish, I'll say something about consumer testing. We only have 45 minutes, so let's make a start. Esther?

EH Well, we've already done the first round of trials and ironed out a few issues. And, um, I think we've come up with a much better biscuit.

DC Sorry, Esther, I didn't quite catch all that. Did you say that there were problems with the trials?

EH Well, no. In fact, we solved some of the earlier problems.

DM Daniel again. I have a question. What were the issues initially, Esther?

EH Seems our biscuit was too sweet. The Chinese aren't used to the amount of sugar we use in our processed foods.

DM Do you know when…?

DC Dong Chen here … Sorry, Daniel, go ahead.

DM No, please, after you.

RS OK, Dong Chen, what were you going to say?

DC When is the next round of trials due, Esther?

EH Next week, but I think Rachel will be saying more about that later.

RS Yes, that's right, we'll be talking about that at the end of our call. So, can we concentrate for now …

CD3 TRACK 43

Well, we wanted everyone to use our Internet-based application so that all the team members could collaborate and manage their part of the project more efficiently. It was a good idea, in theory, but frankly, some people aren't as familiar with this software as others, and it's causing problems with communication. Some people in India and Denmark prefer to use e-mail, telephone and their own IT solutions and even paper-based systems. It makes it difficult to keep track of who's doing what. And it's frustrating, because work gets duplicated or missed, and that's causing more delays. But, but I'd say that our biggest obstacle isn't the technology – it's the way we work together. I think the team should be more task-driven and deadline-oriented. We should, well, we should, we should go for effective time-management over other aspects such as quality. It's what I call a 'good enough' approach so that we can get the work done on time. But the engineers seem to be focused on maintaining an excessively high quality, which is causing more delays.

CD3 TRACK 44

Teleconferences aren't easy. You see, first there are the time differences. The people in Sydney are four-and-a-half hours ahead of us, so we can only communicate for half a day. It seems that the time for a teleconference is always set at the Australian team's convenience. And another thing, I personally don't like speaking in teleconferences. I don't like confrontation and I feel like I'm confronting the client by discussing schedule slippage or other potential risks and problems. I can see it's creating misunderstandings and friction.

And the feedback we get from the client is always so negative. I know that we're running behind schedule and that the costs have run over, especially with steel supply, but let's not forget we've achieved a lot, too, in these 12 months. It's not a total disaster.

CD3 TRACK 45

Designing the civil infrastructure for a new port would have been enough of a challenge, without the client revising the scope of the project. The whole layout had to change to accommodate the increased traffic that was expected. And the client wants the construction to be completed within the original timeframe. There really hasn't been enough time allocated for quality design and revisions to the plans. My staff are up in arms about the schedule changes. Why should they be asked to give up their holidays? Postponing vacations was not an option, and I told the client that. Now they're blaming us, saying the redesigns were late. Um, and working with a 'virtual team' means there's no real sense of working towards a common goal. This team really suffers from poor communication. More teleconferences would help, so we can have regular progress reports.

WORKING ACROSS CULTURES 4: MANAGING AN INTERNATIONAL TEAM

CD3 TRACK 46

Within a few days of their arrival, the Japanese engineers were in a state of shock. They found their German collaborators to be rude, inconsiderate and lazy. The Germans interrupted during meetings and presentations, and showed no interest in reaching consensus through the numerous 'pre-meeting' meetings, or very small group meetings, that are an integral part of Japanese business culture. The Japanese were intensely uncomfortable with the German way of arguing everything out in front of everybody: for the Japanese, the potential for loss of face was just too big. They also disliked what they saw as the Germans' willingness to go home even when tasks were unfinished.

As for the Germans, they were equally unhappy with the Japanese, who seemed very uncommunicative. They complained that even those who did speak didn't state their opinions clearly and frankly. By the time I was called in, the two sides were hardly speaking to each other. Communication had completely broken down. I did what I could, but it was too late. And sadly, the team was disbanded a few months later.

CD3 TRACK 47

The two organisations should from the outset have been alive to the dangers
that can arise when teams – or individuals – from different cultures are suddenly brought together in the workplace. There's plenty of evidence that cross-cultural differences are a major reason why so many of these cross-border joint ventures or other types of business agreements fail. Unfortunately, it's extremely rare for organisations to bother with the nitty-gritty details of how the people lower down the hierarchy, or in the new project team, will run meetings, make decisions, solve problems, manage staff and communicate. Yet all these 'standard operating procedures', what's known as SOPs, are carried out in lots of different ways by people from different cultures.

The trouble is, each culture assumes their way is the 'normal' one. Unexplained deviations from these norms are perceived as – well, deviant or even devious. People start to think: can we trust people from other countries who do things in this strange way?

In the case of the German and Japanese companies, neither organisation bothered to give their people any understanding of the cultural attitudes and behaviour of the other side. No attempt was made to get the new team to discuss their differences *and* similarities – for instance, both the Japanese and Germans generally expect punctuality and clear, detailed agendas. The team should have had a chance to explore their similarities and differences and establish the best way to work together through a code of practice or SOPs.

CD3 TRACK 48

Different types of international teams will require a variety of solutions. Sometimes, for example, the answer can lie in providing a, a combination of intensive language training and cross-cultural training for key personnel. Or a kick-off meeting for a new multinational team that helps team members learn about the cross-cultural differences and similarities of their new colleagues, so all team members get useful insights into how they can best work together.

Renault, for example, decided very early on in its alliance with Nissan to invest massively in cross-cultural training, team building and consultancy for managers at all levels of the company. They wanted to be sure that both the French and Japanese staff had a good understanding of the cultural norms and expectations of their partners. Respect for cultural identity was critical in order to build trust and create a harmonious partnership. As a result, the Renault–Nissan alliance has been hugely successful. English is now the official language of the alliance and is used in meetings and communication. There is also a systematic exchange of people between companies and a strict culture of equality between partners. The alliance is also sensitive to cultural practices, for instance vacations such as the Fourteenth of July in France and Golden Week in Japan. After over a decade of partnership, the companies are still learning about each other.

Market Leader Extra: Business skills
Audio script Advanced

1.1 E-MAILS

BSA1.1.1 (B = Bruno, P = Patrick)

B: So Patrick, what's the problem?

P: What's the problem? To be honest, I'm really irritated. I just got this e-mail from Anita. I forwarded it to you …

B: Yes, I had a look.

P: Well, then, you know. They've already gone into the additional budget, without consultation. That's just not on; it's unprofessional. And then they're accusing me of withholding information about data migration issues. In other words, blaming me for the fact that they can't do their job on time. And again, using complex English to confuse me … it's not fair. I'm not exactly sure how to respond, to be honest.

B: Hang on, Patrick.

P: What?

B: Well, let's just take a bit of time to think about this. I've seen these issues before, and it's not always what you think. I mean, on the use of budget, I'm not sure if I've seen all the e-mails on this, but I don't remember seeing anywhere a clear protocol on how to use this budget.

P: Erm, well, not exactly. You saw Anita's minutes from the meeting three weeks ago. I think that's it. But it was clear in the meeting.

B: I'm not sure. It was clear to you but you didn't clarify her original e-mail in any detail, so I think she's acting from her side in good faith. Probably just being proactive to get problems solved asap, because she knows deadlines are important to you.

P: OK, but accusing our engineers of disguising problems. It's not on.

B: Again, to be fair, can you really be certain she's accusing you, really?

P: Erm, well … it feels like it anyway.

B: Exactly. Yes, she's assuming you had the information and it was not passed on, and in some ways she's not taking responsibility – she should have asked more questions – but I think that's also natural in some ways. I don't see it so negatively. You just need to write back and set up a meeting to talk it through.

P: So what strategy should I follow?

B: Well, on the budget issue, I think it's fair to say you are surprised by the use of the budget without consultation, and point out what your understanding was. You should be able to reduce our cost liability here, as they should really have consulted you. On the migration issue, Anita … let me see, yes, she's kind of assuming that a delay is acceptable, so you need to put her right on that. We have to hit the deadline. And then you, or we, need to negotiate how we manage the additional costs. Patrick, honestly, I would take a collaborative approach. If you cause bad feeling, it might push back the go-live even more.

P: Yes, you're right. OK, thanks. If I draft the e-mail, can I run it past you, just to check I don't go overboard as I usually do?

B: Sure, happy to take a look.

P: Thanks, Bruno. OK, I'll get on with it now. See you later.

B: Ciao, Patrick.

1.2 SMALL TALK

BSA1.2.2 (SB = Steve Benton, HL = Hans Lehmann, IM = Ines Moya)

SB: Excuse me, do you mind me asking where you're from?

HL: Munich, Germany.

SB: Oh, thanks. I couldn't quite place your accent. Hi, I'm Steve Benton, CEO of Benton Seals, Chicago.

HL: Pleased to meet you. Hans Lehmann of Lehmann Boilers and Heating.

SB: Sorry, I didn't quite catch your surname.

HL: Lehmann. Here's my card. Please call me Hans. And this is Ines Moya from Spain.

SB: Hello, Ines. Pleased to meet you.

IM: And you, too.

SB: What line of business are you in, Ines?

IM: Advertising.

SB: Not heating or engineering then?

IM: No, not at all. My company has done some work for Hans in the past.

SB: Oh, I see. What do you both think of the seminar so far?

HL: Not bad, but not exactly what I expected. I haven't learned anything new yet.

IM: Haven't you? I found the workshop on inter-culturalism very useful.

SB: So did I. I'm looking forward to Sara Walters' talk on communication efficiency this evening.

IM: Oh, she's very good, isn't she? I've heard her before.

HL: I wasn't going to go to that but if you recommend it perhaps I should. Ines, could you do me a favour and pass me the leaflet over there on Sara's talk?

IM: Of course. Here you are.

SB: And why did you decide to come to this particular seminar, Hans?

HL: Well, I want to improve my inter-cultural communication skills and I was hoping to make some good contacts, too. I'm looking for new suppliers.

SB: Ah, well, it's funny you should say that because I'm looking for European customers. I think we should get together later and discuss this in more detail.

IM: Sorry, but the next talk is about to start. I think we should go in.

HL: Perhaps we could discuss business over dinner after the talk?

SB: Great! Look forward to it!

BSA1.2.3 (HS = Henrik Schulz, SB = Steve Benton, IO = Ilya Orlov)

HS: Excuse me, I couldn't help overhearing what you were saying about finding new European customers. I think we may be interested in doing business with you, Mr Benton.

SB: Sorry, have we met before?

HS: Henrik Schulz. It was when I heard you talking about the Sara Walters' talk that I remembered you. We were at her talk in Rome. You asked her lots of questions.

SB: Of course. I thought your face looked familiar but I just couldn't place it. And I complimented you on your excellent English. You manufacture small engines, don't you, if I recall correctly?

HS: Indeed we do and your seals might be just what we need.

SB: Really?

HS: I don't think you've met my colleague, Ilya Orlov. He's based in Boston at the moment.

SB: Nice to meet you, Ilya. I was there just last month. Great city, isn't it? Do you like being based there?

IO: Yes, I do, very much.

SB: How long have you been there?

IO: Just over a year now.

HS: Perhaps you and Ilya should arrange to meet up when you're both back in the States and discuss our requirements. See if we can come to a mutually agreeable arrangement?

SB: Good idea. Here's my card and I'll write down my home contact details for you, too. Do give me a ring when you get back and we'll organise it. It'll be great to hear from you.

HS: Oh, excuse me. I'm afraid I've got to make a quick call. I'll see you later.

SB and IO: Bye. See you.

SB: It's been good seeing you again, Henrik.

IO: I don't suppose you know of any good places to eat around here, do you?

SB: Actually, I do. There's a …

BSA1.2.4 (SB = Steve Benton, JG = Julia Godfrey, IO = Ilya Orlov)

SB: Ilya, you might like to meet my production director. She's here somewhere. Ah yes, there she is. Julia, meet Ilya Orlov. He's interested in doing business with us. We're going to arrange a meeting when we return to the States.

JG: Julia Godfrey. Hi, Ilya. Good to meet you. Are you enjoying the seminars and workshops here?

IO: Yes, I am. I've met some very interesting people we can do business with.

JG: You mean we've got competition?

IO: Well, you're not the only company we'll be talking to.

JG: I understand that but I think we can offer you the best deal you're going to get anywhere.

IO: Maybe. We'll have to see, won't we?

JG: Let's get together before you return to the States. Perhaps we could come to some agreement before we leave.

SB: I think you're getting ahead of yourself, Julia.

JG: I'm not sure I agree with you there, Steve.

SB: How's the economic situation affected your business, Ilya?

IO: I think it's worse back in Russia than in the States. We've seen steady growth in the States.

SB: That's good to hear.

IO: But it's always a battle, isn't it? We're constantly looking for ways to cut costs and increase sales.

SB: So are we. …

JG: Do you have your family with you in the States, Ilya?

IO: Actually, my wife is there too and she works at the university. Our sons stayed in Russia with their grandparents.

JG: Oh, that must be difficult for you.

IO: No, not at all. They've been at boarding school since they were seven, so they don't notice any difference. They come over for the holidays. What about you, Julia?

JG: What? Am I married?

IO: Yes.

JG: No. I'm divorced, but I don't have any children.

SB: Right, shall we get back to business.

IO: We'll do that back in the States. Let's find Henrik and have a drink together.

SB and JG: Good idea!

2.1 PRESENTATIONS

BSA2.1.5 (P = Presenter)

P: So what's the main argument for compulsory quotas? Well, corporate boards are male-dominated, and I believe will always promote people like themselves, ignoring female talent. Let's just look at the evidence. In reality, there are many, many talented women out there and yet the number of women with boardroom seats remains alarmingly low today. For instance, in the UK London Stock Exchange's top 100 companies, a mere 22.8% of directors are women. The only answer is quotas, which will break the vicious cycle by putting lots of women at the top. In other words, quotas force the breakup of male elites. This is about equality in our society and fairness for women. Another point in favour of quotas is that women board members will act as positive role models for others. It is true that the proportion of female employees falls off dramatically at the higher levels of corporate hierarchy, but that is where organisations recruit the majority of future board members. Greater representation at board level will actually help other women climb the executive ladder. But actually, I believe there are wider issues at stake here. This is not just about male versus female. Diversity helps to address the dangers of groupthink. The contemporary boardroom needs to incorporate a good range of viewpoints, expertise and international backgrounds to ensure independent and creative thinking. Most importantly, change needs to happen fast – things will not just improve by themselves. Legally enforced quotas, with set time limits, are the fastest, most effective way to ensure more equal numbers of men and women on boards. A case in point is France, which let companies self-regulate until 2011. As no change was observed, the country passed a quotas law the same year and the intermediate goal of 20% was reached in 2014. Boards now have more than enough time to recruit well-qualified women and reach the goal of 40% by 2020.

On the other side of the argument, there's no doubt that quotas have generated an outcry against 'reverse discrimination'. And it is true that individual male candidates for jobs may lose out when they run against equally talented women. Some predict dire consequences for the competitiveness of the economy because inexperienced, under-qualified women will end up on boards. Investors don't want quotas; a board director must be chosen on merit, not gender. Shareholder value, they argue, can be undermined. Recruiting talented women is, I believe, the real challenge for companies – it will mean that boards and head-hunters have to look beyond their closed male-dominated networks and look for people across the widest possible talent pool. And in terms of those already at board level, quotas damage the credibility of the small number of individual women who have managed to battle their way to the top thanks to their skills and hard work. It may be seen as tokenism. It may be written off as nepotism. Women whose appointments are known to be quota-driven will find it difficult to earn respect.

I know there is an argument for company self-regulation. The fact is, quotas aren't perfect, but at least they break down unofficial barriers to access. In an ideal world, interference would not be necessary, but that said, I'm convinced we're on the right path – quotas will be necessary for years to come in order to make change happen. Not only is Norway's solution simple, but it is also effective. It is a revolutionary breakthrough. So far, nothing else has worked. After years of little or no change, the time has come to simply make it happen. Thank you.

BSA2.1.6

1 In reality there are many, many talented women out there …

2 … and yet the number of women with boardroom seats remains alarmingly low today.

3 Greater representation at board level will actually help other women climb the executive ladder.

4 It will mean that boards and headhunters have to look for people across the widest possible talent pool.

5 Not only is Norway's solution simple, but it is also effective.

6 So far, nothing else has worked.

2.2 MEETINGS

BSA2.2.7 (ML = MEETING LEADER)

Version A

ML: OK, welcome everybody. Let's get this meeting underway. We need to talk about some big problems today. This is a difficult time for the company. There are quite a few problems so it's going to be quite a long day, I'm afraid.

BSA2.2.8 (ML = MEETING LEADER)

Version B

ML: OK, welcome everybody. Let's get this meeting underway. What we need to deal with today is a number of very serious issues. This is one of the most challenging times we've ever faced as a company, to say the least. It isn't simply a question of looking at what we do well and what we need to improve. In fact, we won't be looking at what we're doing well at all. I'm afraid it's going to be quite a long day!

BSA2.2.9 (ML = MEETING LEADER, P = PARTICIPANT)

ML: Right, so let's start with the first item on the agenda: sales turnover. This is the largest drop in turnover I've ever witnessed in this company. In fact, we've only ever had one other downturn in sales in the entire 20-year history of the company! What I'd really like to understand is how it could possibly have dropped by as much as 35%. Any comments?

P: Yes, that comes as no surprise, actually. We've made any number of mistakes, as I see it. Crucially, it was our products that should have been upgraded two years ago, not our CRM system. We should have followed our competitors' example. In my opinion, if we had done that, we wouldn't have plummeted from second to fifth position in the market.

3.1 NEGOTIATION

BSA3.1.10 (CB = CHARLOTTE BAKER, MA = MAYOR, MT = MINISTER OF TOURISM, CJ = CAMILA JONES, JM = JOSÉ MORENO)

CB: This busy international port receives thousands of cruise passengers in the summer months. Tourism is the main source of income in this region. But some members of the local community are unhappy about thousands of passengers coming into their city centre. We asked the key members of the city's Committee for Sustainable Tourism for their views.

As the new Mayor of the city, you've already put some tourism projects on hold. The City Council now wants to ban some international conferences that are hosted here, as well as the number of cruise passengers visiting this port. Why is that?

MA: Well, to answer your first point, as I said before, we're not going to ban any major congresses from the city. We recognise they are an important source of income, but we do want to manage them better. Secondly, we're not going to ban cruise passengers, but we do want to reduce the number of visitors in the centre, as well as oversee any new developments around the city. Local residents are simply unable to enjoy living and working in their city as they used to do.

CB: And what would you say to critics who claim that you don't have the experience to govern this city?

MA: I'd say the previous City Council had plenty of experience in politics, but all they did was to systematically destroy the historic nature of our city, and make its people feel like second-class citizens.

CB: Minister, as Minister of Tourism, I'm sure we'd all like to hear from you why this historic city is being over-run by cruise passengers.

MT: Well, I have to say that's just nonsense! Our beautiful city is a major destination but it's also maintained its original character. The previous Mayor and local businesses have simply developed this unique city into a more profitable one. If you were a Londoner, would you complain there were too many tourists going to Buckingham Palace? Of course not! What we're seeing now is the over-reaction by a few left-wing political activists, in response to a couple of unfortunate incidents in a very localised area last summer …

CB: Yes, but those incidents led to a significant demonstration of thousands of residents in the centre, who are not happy with the situation.

MT: With all due respect, Charlotte …

CB: Are you denying that many local residents simply don't want so many visitors?

MT: If you'd just let me finish, we have to be realistic. You cannot have your cake and eat it! You can't open local businesses, shops and restaurants, and rent rooms privately to tourists and then complain about it. Yes, of course, it needs to be controlled, but as Minister of Tourism, first of all, I need to ensure we invest in businesses that are going to profit both the local and national economies. Secondly, we've worked very closely with Public Transport to make it easier to get around. And thirdly, we need to create jobs, all-year-round jobs, and that's going to benefit everybody!

CB: Camila Jones, Chair of the Business Association, you're in contact with the cruise ship liners and tour operators who bring visitors to the port. Would you mind telling us what can be done to strike a balance between attracting visitors and keeping residents happy?

CJ: So your question is, how do we achieve a balance between growing the economy and having a city for the people? Let me say, the two concepts are not mutually exclusive.

CB: I'm not sure I understand what you mean.

CJ: Ah, let me put it another way. If we hadn't developed tourism in the last 20 years, this city wouldn't be on the map today. We wouldn't have attracted international events, and we wouldn't have become a major tourist destination. At the Chamber of Commerce we are doing everything possible to mediate with the local community and support new businesses, but also maintain our international reputation in tourism. We've become a major port; sure, we need to know how to manage it better, and treat both our visitors and our residents with respect, but I'm afraid we can't turn the clocks back.

CB: José, what are the problems with tourism for people in the city? Does your Neighbourhood Association just want to turn the clocks back?

JM: No, no, no. Basically, we're fed up! The city doesn't belong to us anymore. It's been exploited by a handful of rich businessmen, hotel chains, airlines and tour operators. We don't have anything against tourists, but we would like our politicians to take a more sustainable approach. We could introduce a higher tourism tax, for example, as in some other countries. That way we'd attract a different type of tourist. Not the kind who are going to get drunk on the beach, be sick on our streets, and walk naked in our shops! The people of this city pay taxes for the council to clean up our streets and beaches. But, finally, we have a Mayor who is prepared to do something about it!

CB: That was José, Representative of the local Neighbourhood Association and one of the key members on the Committee for Sustainable Tourism. As we've heard, there are obviously two sides to this story. Big business and central government want to continue to promote this port as one of the top destinations in the world. Whereas the City Council and its local residents are fighting to preserve their home city, which they are extremely proud of. Charlotte Baker, Business News.

BSA3.1.11
Extract 1

JM: Minister, you say the previous mayor and local businesses have made this city a more profitable one. I completely agree, but unfortunately it's been at the expense of the people. We pay taxes to clean up the streets, the police are busy arresting young tourists who are misbehaving, the city beach is overcrowded, and local residents aren't able to go shopping in the market anymore because of the high number of cruise passengers walking around.

MT: First of all, let me say, I'm all for sustainable tourism. However, I think the Mayor is in a better position to answer these local issues.

Extract 2

MA: I think José has raised some interesting points. What would you all say to introducing a higher tourism tax?

MT: How would that help exactly?

MA: It would attract a better kind of tourist, we would avoid mass tourism and the city would still profit. But we really need to prevent our city centre from turning into some kind of massive theme park.

MT: Can I ask, how much do you have in mind?

MA: Erm … well, it could be, erm, say, five to ten euros per person per day, but we'd need to consult with the Ministry of Tourism.

MT: Ten euros a day! A family of four on holiday paying ten euros per day would have to pay an extra forty euros a day! Imagine they stay for five nights – they'd end up paying an additional two hundred euros. We'd lose the kind of people that we want to attract.

Extract 3

CJ: As the Minister pointed out, you can't turn the clocks back …

JM: But we're not saying that!

CJ: If I could just finish, please. The Mayor has put a number of projects on hold, namely, the construction of new hotels and other tourism businesses. In the meantime, investors are losing time and money. And now you want to ban the cruise ships! If the City Council continues to ignore the needs of the local and international business community, this city is going to lose its position as a major destination, we won't be able to create new jobs, it'll be a disaster for the economy and we'll end up living in the Middle Ages! At this point, I really don't think we can work together.

JM: Fine, why don't you just leave then? It'll make it a lot easier for us to reach an agreement.

Extract 4

MA: If I could just come in here. Camila, we've all spent the last few weeks working hard to bring this committee together. It's very positive that we are sitting here today and everyone's prepared to discuss the future of our city. We have a number of proposals on the agenda, so I suggest we look at them one by one. Would you like to continue with the discussion, Camila?

CJ: As long as we can have a professional discussion and take into account the needs of businesses …

JM: But you're the one who's being disruptive by …

MA: Hang on a minute, José. We'd be happy to hear from you in a moment. Camila, I'd like to know if you are staying for the meeting or not.

CJ: Of course.

MA: Good. First on the agenda then is the number of people sub-letting their flats to tourists, which is a concern for both residents and hotels. Let's go round the table. José?

BSA3.1.12

1
MT: With all due respect, Charlotte …

2
CB: Would you mind telling us what can be done to strike a balance between attracting visitors and keeping residents happy?

3
CJ: If we hadn't developed tourism in the last 20 years, this city wouldn't be on the map today.

4
CJ: We wouldn't have attracted international events, and we wouldn't have become a major tourist destination.

5
MT: I think the Mayor is in a better position to answer these local issues.

6
MA: What would you all say to introducing a higher tourism tax?

7
MA: It would attract a better kind of tourist, we would avoid mass tourism and the city would still profit.

8
MA: Erm … well, it could be, erm, say, five to ten euros per person per day, but we'd need to consult with the Ministry of Tourism.

9
CJ: At this point, I really don't think we can work together.

10
MA: Camila, we've all spent the last few weeks working hard to bring this committee together.

11
MA: Hang on a minute, José. We'd be happy to hear from you in a moment.

12
MA: Camila, I'd like to know if you are staying for the meeting or not.

3.2 INTERVIEWS

BSA3.2.13 (T = Tim)

T: So you've submitted your application and managed to get a first interview. We all get nervous at this stage. Well, you can prepare for most questions ahead of time. There's a limit to how many questions interviewers can ask and you can look online for ideas on most. What's the worst thing they can ask you? Well, there's one question that comes up more than any other: 'What's your biggest weakness?' I get so many questions about this one in the classes I teach at WinTech. It's easier to answer when you realise that weaknesses are only really the downside to other, more positive things – in other words, your strengths. So, for example, if your strength is that you're organised and good at managing large quantities of information at the same time, your weakness might be that you're not so good at taking time to check up on the others in your team to see if they need help or support. So, when they ask you this, start reminding them of one of your strengths, then go on to mention the downside of this. The final stage is to make sure you explain to the interviewer the steps you've taken to correct this problem. In other words, describe a solution that keeps everyone happy.

BSA3.2.14

1
I have a very strong work ethic. I believe in working hard and doing my best in everything I do. In the past, this has meant that I've been less patient with people who aren't as committed as me to their job. I've learnt that in a team, not everybody's motivated by the same thing and, to get the best from people, I have to try different approaches – and I'm working on that.

2
My biggest weakness is that I'm too much of a perfectionist. I like to do jobs well and I never leave the office until a job is finished. I get disappointed with myself when a job is anything less than perfect.

3
I'm very loyal to the people I work for and the people I work with. But the downside of that is that sometimes I find it hard to let go of ideas or ways of working. I've started trying to look at things more objectively and these days I have a system for evaluating the effectiveness of ways of working, technology – anything, really. I still try to avoid letting things go if possible, but I'm definitely getting quicker at realising when it's time to give up and move on now.

4.1 PRESENTATIONS

BSA4.1.15 (P = Presenter)

P: We all know what it's like to go shopping these days. The sheer volume of choice that consumers face is overwhelming. This hit me again recently when my husband and I wanted to buy a new sofa. The showroom was enormous; the sofas came in a range of sizes, colours and coverings. And as if that wasn't enough, the salesman produced half a dozen catalogues with yet more sofas that could be made to order. My jaw dropped, my mind froze. I wasn't sure I could do this. But I took heart from the fact that I am not alone.
Let me tell you about one famous experiment by American psychologists Mark Lepper and Sheena Iyengar. They found that customers offered an array of six new jam varieties were much more likely to buy one than those offered a choice of 24. In fact, what they discovered was that the smaller selection led to ten times more purchases. Professor Iyengar's follow-up studies have also found that there are circumstances in which adding options reduces the likelihood that people will select anything at all.

This counter-intuitive finding led psychologist Barry Schwartz to write his best-selling book, *The Paradox of Choice*. He argues that what too many options can do is make shoppers unhappy and frustrated by the whole process of comparing, contrasting and choosing. He says the proliferation of consumer choice often paralyses buyers about making purchasing decisions. Not only that, but inevitably buyers are also more likely to be dissatisfied with their final purchasing decision, because they have the nagging doubt that they haven't made the right choice. Thirdly, he adds that greater choice leads to an 'escalation of expectations'. In other words, adding options can increase the expectations people have about how good those options will be. We come to have higher and higher expectations and what that creates is less satisfaction. Seemingly, abundant choice is more attractive in theory than in practice. Schwartz cites cases of companies that have limited the number of items available for sale in order to reduce costs. Remarkably, this has had unintended consequences – sales have increased and consumers have reported greater happiness with the purchasing decision.

BSA4.1.16 (P = Presenter)

P: Repeat **BSA4.1.15**
So where does this leave sales and marketing today? Some of the top-selling brands in the world have long kept their offering simple – such as Apple's iPhone, which comes in just a few colours. And while our supermarket aisles offer more choice than ever, there are signs that change is afoot. For instance, Procter & Gamble, the world's largest maker of household products, is apparently now reducing its product lines. The Chief Executive, A.G. Lafley, told the *Financial Times* recently that the consumer goods industry is offering people more products than they want. In the article, Mr Lafley says, and I quote, 'Consumers want to keep their life simple and convenient … The majority of consumers, once they've decided on their deodorant or anti-perspirant, tend to stick with it.' So, arguably, we want some choice, but don't give us too much of it. Human behaviour isn't always logical. His comments will inevitably send shockwaves through an industry that has for many years operated on the assumption that giving shoppers more choice encourages them to spend more.
Of course, choice overload doesn't always occur. And it doesn't always affect all people at all times. We don't yet know what factors determine when choice overload will occur and when it won't. That brings me back to the sofa dilemma I mentioned earlier. Once we'd chosen the model we wanted, the salesman could see we were suffering from 'decision fatigue' after pondering far too many fabrics, so he showed us the three colours he said were the most popular. Naturally, that made it so much easier for us to choose.
In conclusion, with the potential for limitless choice today, the take-away lesson is to simplify the decision-making process for our customers. It is tempting to offer more options, but that is not necessarily how to sell. Let's face it, sometimes less is undoubtedly more.

BSA4.1.17

1 Seemingly, abundant choice is more attractive in theory than in practice.
2 Remarkably, this has had unintended consequences.
3 Arguably, we want some choice, but don't give us too much of it.
4 His comments will inevitably send shockwaves through an industry.
5 Naturally, that made it so much easier for us to choose.
6 Let's face it, sometimes less is undoubtedly more.

4.2 TELECONFERENCES

BSA4.2.18 (G = GIANCARLO, M = MARTINA, D = DANIEL, E = ELENA, J = JIM)

G: So, good morning. This is Giancarlo here at head office in Milan, and Martina is here with me.

M: Hello, everyone.

G: Daniel? Are you on the call?

D: Yes, I'm here too.

G: Jim? Hello? Oh, that's strange. OK, what about Elena?

E: Yes, I'm here.

G: I'd like to introduce Elena González, our new Sales and Marketing Manager for Spain and Portugal. You'll get a chance to meet her in person at the sales conference next month.

D: Welcome on board, Elena.

M: Good morning, Elena. How's the weather in Madrid today?

E: Good morning, everyone. Too hot, Martina. Nearly thirty-five degrees. And in Milan?

J: Hello? Can you hear me?

G: Who is that speaking? Is that you, Jim?

J: Yes, sorry I'm late. I had a bit of a problem connecting to the call.

G: I see. You missed the first point on the agenda – introduction of new people. I introduced Elena. Well, let's keep going now that everyone is here. Point 2 on the agenda. So as you know, we are here to discuss the plans for the new website, including the mock-up designs submitted by the designer, and the question of whether we need to translate the site into the different languages of our client countries.

J: Well, you know my views. I really think it's a waste of our budget sinking money into a fancy website. Adverts in trade magazines have always worked for us and I don't see any reason to change our strategy.

G: Jim, we went over this in our last discussion. And we agreed that the first port of call for information in this day and age is the Internet and that our current website projects the wrong image of our company. Let's stick to the points on today's agenda. What I need now is everyone's reactions to the mock-ups. Erm, Martina, do you want to start?

M: Sure. Well, I really like the interactive diagrams of the machines. It's neat the way you can click on the picture and the outside casing disappears so that you can see the inside workings of the machine.

G: Yes, I like them too. Daniel?

D: Well, I also like the way you can strip away the outside of the machine and see a cross-section of the inside, but I ...

J: [Coughs] Sorry about that. I've got a cold.

G: Daniel, go on, please – what were you saying?

D: I don't think it's necessary to look at the machines from different sides and zoom in and out.

J: I agree. My wife buys stuff from fashion sites that work that way. It's a bit over the top for us.

M: Me too. If I was buying clothes online, I might want to see front, back and sides, but you really don't need details of the back of our equipment.

G: Elena, what are your views?

E: Well, maybe it's a bit more detail than needed, but I don't think that's a problem. I don't want to be rude, but ...

G: Go ahead, say what you like. We're looking for opinions.

E: I don't like the colours very much. I think they're ...

D: ... far too bright. It's completely the wrong image for the company.

G: Let Elena finish, please, Daniel.

D: I'm sorry.

E: It's OK. I was going to say the same thing.

J: I agree too. Turquoise and lime green are not suitable for a technical site.

M: I don't know. I found them refreshingly different. Our usual dark brown and beige is rather dull and out of date.

G: I think Martina has a point when ...

BSA4.2.19

G: ... Right. That's clear now, so I shall summarise what we've said. We like the interactive diagrams, but it's enough to see the kilns from the front, both inside and out. We'd like to see a more subtle range of background colours, but still something more lively than our current colour scheme. Martina will get the designer to modify the mock-ups accordingly and submit new designs next week. Finally, we agree that translation is probably not necessary. However, Jim will speak to a translation agency he knows in London and get quotes for translating the site into Italian, French, German, Greek and Spanish before we make a final decision on that.

E: Excuse me, can I comment on that?

G: Of course, Elena.

E: What about Portuguese as well? I don't think we can do all those other languages and leave Portuguese out.

G: Good point. All the languages of the countries we sell to or English only.

J: Fine. I'll add that to the list then.

G: Excellent. So, we will have another meeting next week, when the revised design and the translation quotes are ready. I'll e-mail everyone to set up the time. Thank you all for taking part in the meeting.

M/D/J/E: Goodbye. / Bye. / Bye everyone. / Bye.

1.1 E-mails

(A) SPEAKING

Read the survey results. Can you complete the results with the statements in the box?

– don't respond to e-mails quickly enough – write too many unnecessary e-mails
– don't take time to be polite and so damage relationships – write e-mails which are too long
– make language mistakes that look unprofessional

> ## E-mail – virtue or vice?
>
> A new survey into attitudes to e-mail in business reveals some interesting findings:
>
> | How effective do you think e-mail is as a communication tool? | Respondents who agreed (%)* |
> |---|---|
> | – highly ineffective | 65% |
> | – quite ineffective | 20% |
> | – relatively effective | 10% |
> | – very effective | 5% |
>
> | The main problem with e-mail is that people: | |
> |---|---|
> | .... | 23% |
> | .... | 18% |
> | – don't read e-mails properly, so their reply is 'off topic' and creates more e-mails | 15% |
> | – write unclear e-mails which generate serious misunderstanding | 14% |
> | .... | 12% |
> | – use e-mail as a weapon to blame others in public with CC | 6% |
> | – try to solve problems by e-mail when they should use the phone | 5% |
> | .... | 4% |
> | .... | 2% |
> | – other | 1% |
>
> *200 business professionals interviewed across six countries

(C) READING 2

Read Anita's e-mail to Patrick, sent three weeks after the design work started. Answer the questions below.

> Dear Patrick
>
> I just wanted to put in writing a short report on the project, update you on costs and alert you to a little problem with data migration which we have been experiencing.
>
> Everything has been going well, although we have needed additional time to configure the graphics side of the website and parts of the customer interface. However, the costs of 1.5k are within the 2k additional costs agreed at our meeting three weeks ago.
>
> However, data migration is proving more problematic than we expected. We have had problems with reformatting the data from your current database due to issues which we were *not informed about by your engineers* in advance of the project, when we calculated the timeline. This is likely to cause a delay to go-live which I think you need to be aware of.
>
> We have a conf call at the end of this week, so we can talk things through in more detail then.
>
> Very best
>
> Anita

1 Which two issues does Anita mention in her e-mail?

2 Which of the two problems is seen as more problematic, and why?

3 Why does Anita use italics to indicate the cause of the second problem?

4 Which parts of the e-mail appear informal or casual? Which parts appear more formal?

1.2 Small talk

D SPEAKING 2

Student A
- Break into a conversation.
- Ask for advice on something.

Student C
- Ask someone's opinion of something.
- Suggest keeping in touch with someone.

Student B
- Involve someone else in the conversation.
- Politely leave the conversation.

Student D
- Compliment someone on something.
- Disagree with someone about something.

TASK

Student A
- Create pauses in the conversation.

Student C
- Talk about unsuitable topics.

Student B
- Use unsuitable body language.

Student D
- Change the subject suddenly.

2.1 Presentations

C LISTENING 2

Stress and intonation

◀)) BSA2.1.6 **Listen to the extracts from C Listening 2 Exercise 1 again and practise the pronunciation. Try to achieve the same persuasive effect.**

1 In reality there are many, many talented women out there …

2 … and yet the number of women with boardroom seats remains alarmingly low today.

3 Greater representation at board level will actually help other women climb the executive ladder.

4 It will mean that boards and headhunters have to look for people across the widest possible talent pool.

5 Not only is Norway's solution simple, but it is also effective.

6 So far, nothing else has worked.

2.1 Presentations

TASK Part 1

Team A

Read the information and make a note of the main pros and cons of hot-desking.

Hot-desking

Some experts say that the permanent office desk is a thing of the past. They argue there are many good reasons to embrace this change. For one thing, the positioning of people's desks in offices is nearly always hierarchical. Lower level staff typically have more undesirable desks located near noisy and busy areas, such as coffee machines, toilets and printers. Natural light is also one of the biggest physical factors that makes some desks better than others. In the traditional office, the bosses get the best locations regardless of the amount of time they actually spend at their desks.

Hot-desking is now common in many of the world's top businesses, including GE, Deloitte, and Microsoft. 'Hoteling' technical solutions allow people to pre-book meeting rooms and desks (docking stations) online. Some companies also combine designated desks for some staff with collaborative space for teams to work on projects. It is argued that it is good for people from all disciplines to get a chance to sit next to each other and learn about what they do.

Hot-desking also allows companies to use space efficiently and reduce costs. Staff are often out on visits or working remotely or doing flexitime. According to a recent *Financial Times* report, desks and meeting rooms go unused for at least 30% of the working day in many organisations. With the high cost of office space in major cities (e.g. in London it costs up to £1,698 per square metre a year) this represents a huge waste.

On the other hand, detractors say hot-desking is only a free-for-all in theory. Humans are naturally territorial and so people are very reluctant to give up their own designated desks. In reality, people will often have desks they habitually sit at and that others leave free in deference to them, especially if they are more senior staff. Some people complain that it takes more time to set up work for the day at a docking station that is not their regular designated desk. It also takes time at the end of the day clearing the desk and putting personal possessions in lockers. There are also complaints about more cramped conditions and lower productivity due to more noise and distractions in the hot-desking office.

SOURCE: www.ft.com

TASK Part 1

Team B

Read the information and make a note of the main pros and cons of the paperless office.

The paperless office

The concept of the paperless office was first introduced in a *Businessweek* magazine article back in the mid-1970s. Advocates say with today's technology, it is possible for every business to go paperless.

There are many benefits, they say, of going paperless. Firstly, there are greater benefits of digital tools, especially online platforms for sharing and organising documents.

Furthermore, there will be no more papers stacked on desks or lost documents. Documents in a digital format can be stored on a server or cloud account for easy access and retrieval. This reduces the time it takes to do things, increasing productivity and customer satisfaction.

In addition, the paperless office saves money and resources such as paper, ink cartridges, other stationery, printers and physical filing systems. This means offices are 'going green', i.e. becoming more ecologically sustainable.

Critics of the concept question whether going digital really is greener and more sustainable, since computer systems consume vast amounts of electricity. One study found that the average person uses nearly two and half times more power on a single computer, than the power needed to produce all the paper they would need in a year. Manufacturing computers creates not only substantial amounts of carbon dioxide but also non-biodegradable waste. There is also the cost of dealing with obsolete equipment to consider. E-waste is a serious environmental problem.

Another argument is that while people have become used to reading on screen, certain things are more easily done on paper, such as brainstorming. Studies have shown that paper helps people read faster, creates less fatigue and eyestrain, and enables people to engage with content in a far more thoughtful and creative manner.

A further consideration is the security of IT systems. A company is at risk if an employee's computer, tablet or smartphone is stolen or hacked. Encryption, data handling policies and restrictions are needed, which may be costly. Finally, many organisations, fearing the breakdown of IT systems, still keep back-up hard-copies. The completely paperless office is still rare today. According to latest paper-industry data, paper use is falling but only by 1% per year.

SOURCE: www.ft.com

2.2 Meetings

TASK

Meeting Leader

Your main responsibility is to lead the meeting but you can express your own ideas and agree or disagree with the participants. You need to reach agreement on how to change your company's strategies to reverse the negative situation. Introduce each point emphatically. Summarise the main arguments and decisions after each item has been discussed and give a final summary. Your language should reflect the gravity of the situation.

Human Resources Manager

The company shouldn't have cut the workforce by 20%. It reduced the remaining employees' enthusiasm. It left them over-stretched and reduced the quality of work. A higher rate of absenteeism is not very surprising; employees are probably going for job interviews. Some of the best employees have already moved to work with competitors, who mostly pay higher salaries. You have lost talent and in-house knowledge. Poor quality work is due to teleworkers feeling isolated. There are not enough women employed in the company. The company should look at promoting more women and increase the ratio of female employees.

Marketing Manager

You are sure that your recommendation to update the CRM software was the right one. It enabled you to implement a more aggressive approach to e-mail/telephone marketing. You have been able to target 500% more customers and cut marketing costs by 50%. It saved employee costs, which earned the managers a nice bonus. The Finance Manager shouldn't criticise your marketing strategy – you've heard rumours that there have been irregularities in his department. He should encourage a culture of 'whistle-blowing', to ensure that if there is a problem, it doesn't get out of hand.

Finance Manager

It was right to replace humans with an updated CRM system. Every other company is doing it. There was a redundancy cost last year but this year the payroll savings have been good. Fifty per cent of employees made redundant are now employed by the company on a freelance basis. Teleworking is much more cost-effective. The company makes big savings on office space. Teleworkers (and the environment) benefit from reduced commuting to work. You feel that the marketing campaigns should have targeted more women. They hold the purse strings these days. The rise in customer complaints is mostly about intrusive marketing. The company has now lost a large number of long-term customers. The marketing policy should be changed.

Observer(s)

Watch/Listen to the meeting and note how confidently the Meeting Leader and other participants develop their arguments with appropriate highlighting of significant points and relevant supporting detail. Refer to the Language Reference page 128 for emphasising your point and the lesson objectives. Also consider the clarity and impact of the intonation and body language used.

3.1 Negotiation

TASK Parts 1–3

Student A: Mayor of the city

Negotiation aim	To agree on a five-point sustainable tourism plan that will benefit both residents and the local economy. You will announce the plan to the press at the end of the negotiation.
Your position	**You are the Mayor of the city**. You want to make tourism more sustainable in the city. Businesses (hotel chains, tour operators, airlines and cruise liners) have exploited the city and you want to introduce measures to make it possible for local residents to live and work in the city centre again. You have already put some tourism development projects on hold. You're thinking of introducing a tourism tax to attract a better kind of tourist. You would also like to ban cars from the city centre. Think of some other ideas.
Personal motive	You want to be a very popular Mayor so that you can stand for election as a member of parliament next year, possibly as Minister for Environment – so a good result in this negotiation will help your campaign.
Your secret	When you became Mayor, you gave the President of the Neighbourhood Association a well-paid position in the City Council because you are old friends and went to university together. Now you're not sure if they are the right person for the job. The press aren't aware of this. However, if they find out, you won't be very concerned. There's no such thing as bad publicity, especially in politics!
Additional information	You start the meeting. When you chair the meeting, be prepared to deal with any conflict in a firm but polite and constructive way. Look again at the audio script of the news report on pages iii–iv to help you. Try to use these expressions: *As I said before, …* *Our people feel like second-class citizens.* *If I could just come in here … .*

Student B: Minister for Tourism

Negotiation aim	To agree on a five-point sustainable tourism plan that will benefit both residents and the local economy. You will announce the plan to the press at the end of the negotiation.
Your position	**You are the Minister for Tourism.** Your priority is to maintain the city as a major tourism destination and create new jobs. The new Mayor doesn't understand that the main source of income for the region is tourism. You might want to refer to some figures in the meeting. You could introduce a higher tourism tax but it would have to stay low in order to attract visitors. Meanwhile, local residents are sub-letting their flats to visitors and this is taking away trade from hotels. Think of measures to regulate this and other ideas to make tourism sustainable at the same time as generating more income for the city.
Personal motive	Your personal motive is that the Prime Minister of your country is putting a lot of pressure on you to oppose the new Mayor. He has threatened to throw you out of the Cabinet if you let the Mayor become too powerful.

Student B: Minister for Tourism – *continued*

Your secret	You are in secret talks with the Aviation Authority and you're planning to build a new runway making the city airport an international hub for travellers. This will help your political career, although the new City Council won't like it. You are prepared to negotiate with the Mayor on some points but, in return, you will need support for the runway.
Additional information	When it is your turn to chair the meeting, be prepared to deal with any conflict in a firm but polite and constructive way. Look again at the audio script of the news report on pages iii–iv to help you. Try to use these expressions: *You can't have your cake and eat it!* *If you'd just let me finish … .* *I'm all for sustainable tourism.*

Student C: Chair of the Business Association

Negotiation aim	To agree on a five-point sustainable tourism plan that will benefit both residents and the local economy. You will announce the plan to the press at the end of the negotiation.
Your position	**You are the Chair of the Business Association.** You are very concerned that investors are losing money while some tourism projects have been put on hold by the City Council. You want to know when construction work can resume and how long they are going to take to give out licences to new projects. Local shopkeepers, restaurants and cafés all benefit from the tourism industry as well as big businesses. Think of ideas to make tourism more sustainable at the same time as generating more income for the city, e.g. extending the tram network or building more car parks near stations outside the city centre.
Personal motive	You have plans to stand for Minister for Tourism – you know the Prime Minister is unhappy with the current Minister for Tourism.
Your secret	You are secretly negotiating an important contract with a hotel chain to create a new tourism development in an old industrial area near the city beach. You are looking for international investors. If the project goes ahead, you will make a lot of money. You are prepared to agree with the City Council on some points as long as you can convince the Mayor to develop tourism in the industrial area and give you building permission for the project.
Additional information	When it is your turn to chair the meeting, be prepared to deal with any conflict in a firm but polite and constructive way. Look again at the audio script of the news report on pages iii–iv to help you. Try to use these expressions: *Let me put it another way, …* *We can't turn the clocks back.* *If I could just finish, please.*

Student D: President of the Neighbourhood Association

Negotiation aim	To agree on a five-point sustainable tourism plan that will benefit both residents and the local economy. You will announce the plan to the press at the end of the negotiation.
Your position	**You are the President of the Neighbourhood Association.** The local residents in the city centre and port area are fed up with tourists. You think businesses (hotel chains, tour operators, airlines and cruise liners) have exploited the city and you want to introduce measures to make it possible for local residents to live and work in the city centre in peace again. The Mayor has already put some tourism development projects on hold and you support this measure. You think any new tourist developments should be further up the coast in an old industrial area that could be renovated not far from the city beach, and not in the city centre. You also think it's a good idea to introduce a higher tourism tax. Think of some more ideas – you need to maintain your position in the City Council.
Personal motive	Your personal motive is that you and your family own several flats in the city centre which you regularly rent out to tourists to supplement your income but the press don't know. You don't want more hotels in the area because it will take away some of your business.
Your secret	The Mayor gave you a well-paid job in the City Council because you are friends and went to university together. The press and the other members of the Committee aren't aware of this.
Additional information	When it is your turn to chair the meeting, be prepared to deal with any conflict in a firm but polite and constructive way. Look again at the audio script of the news report on pages iii–iv to help you. Try to use these expressions: *Let me put it another way, …* *We're fed up!* *We don't have anything against tourists but …*

TASK Part 4

Web leaks

The Minister of Tourism is having trouble with the Mayor in our city

Government sources say that the Prime Minister is unhappy with the Minister for Tourism's lack of success in creating new jobs in the region's tourism industry. Soon to be an ex-Minister maybe? According to our secret sources, the Minister for Tourism is attempting to save his job by entering into talks with the Aviation Authority, which is planning a new runway for our airport. Not surprisingly, local environmental organisations are planning a demonstration against this proposal.

The Chair of the Business Association in secret talks with a hotel contractor

Plans to create a new tourism development in the old industrial area near the city beach have been revealed to the press. If the project goes ahead, the Chair of the Business Association will be one of the wealthiest people in the city!

The Chair is also a close ally of the Prime Minister and wants the Minister for Tourism's post in the general elections next year. No wonder a good result in recent negotiations is important!

The President of the Neighbourhood Association owns secret flats!

It has come to light that several flats which are regularly rented out to tourists belong to the President of the Neighbourhood Association. Local residents say it's a disgrace! Sources report that being good friends with the Mayor at university is the only reason the President was given a seat on the City Council! In private, however, the Mayor has expressed concerns that perhaps this was a mistake. It seems the President of the Neighbourhood Association isn't the easiest person to work with. We've also recently heard that the Mayor hopes to become the next Minister for the Environment! Hmm, are all these plans for sustainable tourism real or just a way to win votes?

3.2 Interviews

⊙ SPEAKING 2

Student A

1   You are the interviewer. Look at the scenario below. Role-play the questions you need to ask to get the candidate's version of this. You do NOT need to role-play the other parts of the interview.

The candidate has applied for a job in sales. You have received a reference from his/her previous employer saying that he/she was excellent at working with clients and regularly had the highest sales figures. However, they also mentioned that he/she often made promises that the other departments couldn't meet, such as impossible delivery times.

2   You have applied for a job in IT. Look at the scenario below and be prepared to answer Student B's (the interviewer's) questions on this.

You are good at your job and very efficient. You have been running the entire computer system for your company for the last five years, and things have gone smoothly. You're prepared to stay late if necessary to get the job done. However, you disliked attending social functions with other workers because you worked alone, and never got to know them. This was constantly a problem for you.

TASK

Dear ....,

Please ¹*accept this letter* as a register of my interest in the position of ² .... in your company. My solid background as a(n) ³ ...., knowledge of ⁴ .... and my ⁵ .... qualifications have permitted me to develop the skills that I believe can be used by your organisation.

With this application, I ⁶ .... my full CV, in which you can see that I can also offer:

- ⁷ ....
- ⁸ ....
- ⁹ ....
- proven ability to ¹⁰ ....

My CV lists my experience, additional skills and areas of expertise. To discuss my qualifications further, please ¹¹ ...., and I would be happy to attend an interview at your convenience.

Sincerely,

....

4.1 Presentations

TASK Part 1

How **NOT** to retain customers	How **NOT** to manage to staff
1 Don't get to know your customers Customers are not going to like businesses that treat them like just another client. What does it matter if people like to be known and understood?	**1 Keep morale low** If you want to decrease morale and experience a high turnover, all you have to do is bully and intimidate employees. Constantly threaten to fire people over unsatisfactory work, berate them for their performance, or criticise the personal traits of employees in order to create a negative work environment.
2 Rush them to make decisions Many psychological studies show that people do not like to feel rushed or ignored when doing business or making a purchasing decision. By not taking time to understand the customer needs and creating that sense of a real relationship, you are sure to lose repeat business.	**2 Micro-manage** Do not teach employees what's expected and do not help them make it happen. Withhold vital information. Get involved in every aspect of your employees' jobs, then you can expect team members to resent you for not giving them responsibility.
3 Don't deliver on promises Make sure your goods arrive late and do not communicate what is happening to customers. Make sure the quality is below customer expectations. Have a few surprises up your sleeve, such as hidden delivery costs.	**3 Do not be sensitive to their feelings** Ignore the feelings of staff. If they need time off because their baby is sick, make them feel guilty for the problems this causes you.
4 After-sales service A truly awful, unresponsive after-sales service is guaranteed to stop your customers from ever coming back for more.	**4 Sack someone in public for nothing** Fire staff in front of others for totally arbitrary reasons – it will intimidate everyone. Tim Armstrong, boss of AOL, fired an employee in front of 1,000 others simply because he had had the nerve to take a photograph. He said: 'You're fired – out', and waited a couple of seconds for the offender to leave.
5 Handle customer feedback badly Consumer research shows that making it difficult for clients to complain or give you feedback is one way to go. Bombarding them with unsolicited email surveys is another. According to experts, the old-style approach of turning feedback into scores, percentages, and averages is a waste of time. While multiple-choice questions are convenient for the company to process and analyse, they restrict customers. This is much less useful than a system that allows customers to address issues they want to in plain English.	**5 Talk down to staff** Talk in a monologue and do not allow anyone to interrupt you or welcome their ideas. Tell people in a bullying tone of voice that if they don't agree with you they can leave the company right away. Be as nasty as you like and brag constantly about your successes. SOURCE for AOL fact: www.ft.com

3.2 Interviews

D SPEAKING 1

Student B

1   You have applied for a job in sales. Look at the scenario below and be prepared to answer Student A's (the interviewer's) questions on this.

You are confident that you have an excellent track record in sales. You brought in more business than anyone else on your team for three years running. However, you weren't very popular with colleagues in other departments because you often had to make promises to clients to get the sales. Production often couldn't meet the orders and customer services were constantly on the phone to you. You didn't get on that well with your former boss either, and you suspect she's put this in the reference they requested.

2   You are the interviewer. Look at the scenario below. Role-play the questions you need to ask to get the candidate's version of this. You do NOT need to role-play the other parts of the interview.

The candidate has applied for a job in IT. You have received a reference back on him/her and although he/she has an excellent record in solving computer problems, the reference describes this person as antisocial and unwilling to participate in team-bonding activities with the others in the company.

4.2 Teleconferences

TASK

Student A

Sales and Marketing Manager

You are the Sales and Marketing Manager for the school (or other institution). You have invited three people – your assistant, an external consultant on web marketing and one of the school's international agents – to comment on the website and suggest changes. You keep forgetting people's names.

Student B

External consultant on web marketing

You are an external consultant on web marketing. You want to make a lot of changes to the website of the school (or other institution). You experience difficulties hearing what other participants are saying during the call.

Student C

Sales and Marketing Assistant

You are the Sales and Marketing Assistant for the school (or other institution). You conducted a focus group among students at the school and want to report your findings. Halfway through the call you experience technical problems.

Student D

Agent in _____ (choose a country)

You are an overseas agent. You send students from your country to a range of schools and colleges abroad. You have been invited to join this meeting to give your views on the website of the school (or other institution) from an international perspective. You keep interrupting the call and find turn-taking difficult.

Pearson Education Limited
Edinburgh Gate, Harlow, Essex CM20 2JE, England and Associated
Companies throughout the world.

www.pearsonelt.com
© Pearson Education Limited 2016

The right of Iwonna Dubicka and Margaret O'Keeffe to be identified as
authors of this Work has been asserted by them in accordance with the
Copyright, Designs and Patents Act 1988.

First Edition first published 2000

Third Edition first published 2012

Third Edition Extra first published 2016
Second impression 2016

ISBN: 978-1-292-13473-4

Set in Meta OT 9.5/12pt

Printed in Slovakia by Neografia

Acknowledgements
The publishers would like to thank the following authors for writing the
Business Skills lessons: Margaret O'Keefe, Clare Walsh, Iwona Dubicka,
Lizzie Wright, Bob Dignan, Sara Helm and Fiona Scott-Barrett.

The authors would like to thank the following for their invaluable help during
the project: Santiago García Nuez, Elena Gutierrez, Raquel García, and our
students at Giesecke & Devrient Ibérica, Albert Prades and family, Walerian
Dubicki and the Dubicki-Pipers.

The authors would also like to thank Bill Mascull for writing the Teacher's
Resource Book, John Rogers for writing the Practice File and Lewis Lansford
for writing the Test File.

The authors and publishers are very grateful to the following people who
agreed to be interviewed for some of the recorded material in this book: Dr
Bernd Atenstaedt, David Bowen, Ian Brinkley, Philippa Foster Back, Anneliese
Guérin-LeTendre, Angus McCrone, Charles Middleton, Dr Jonathan Reynolds,
Marjorie Scardino, Peter Sirman, Mike Southon, Tom Taylor. Special thanks
from the authors to Chris Hartley for his great work on the interviews.

The publishers and authors are very grateful to the following advisers
and teachers who commented on earlier versions of this material and
contributed to the initial research: Ian Duncan, Andrew Nathan, Nancy
Pietragalla Dorfman, Dr Petra Pointner, Michael Thompson, Benjamin White,
Aukjen Bosma, David Kadas, Hans Leijenaar, Sabine Prochel, Ulrich Schuh
Robert McLarty.

The authors are very grateful to David Cotton, David Falvey and Simon Kent
for their very helpful comments on earlier drafts of this material.

We are grateful to the following for permission to reproduce copyright material:

Logos
Logo (p66) from Triodos Bank, reproduced with permission; Toyota logo
(p84) reproduced with permission from Toyota (GB) plc; logo (p84) from The
Procter & Gamble Company, reproduced with permission; logo (p84) from
Google, reproduced with permission; Amazon logo (p84) copyright © 2010
Amazon. com, Inc.

Text
Extract on p.7 adapted from "Personal communication" by Celeste Sulliman,
PhD. Assistant Professor, Communication, University College of Cape Breton,
Source: Merriam-Webster Collegiate Webster Dictionary (Online), www.
effectivemeetings.com - a website managed by SMART Technologies Inc.;
Extract on p.9 from "Establish contacts" by Mike Southon, *The Financial
Times*, 20/08/2009, copyright © Mike Southon; Extract on p.16 from
"Training leaders to connect the dots" by Donald Sull, *The Financial Times*,
19/05/2009, copyright © Donald Sull; Extract on p.29 adapted from
"California Utility Expands Rebates for Power Efficiency" by James Niccolai,
www.pcworld.com, 13/08/2009, copyright © IDG News Service; Extract in
unit 4 adapted from "Marketing To Women: What Women Really Want!" by
Robert Craven, http://www.robert-craven.co.uk/article-marketing-to-women-
what-women-really-want.php, copyright © 2001-2010 The Directors' Centre
Ltd; Extract in unit 4 from "Dr. Philip Kotler Answers Your Questions on
Marketing" by Professor Philip Kotler, www.kotlermarketing.com, copyright
© 2001-2010 Kotler Marketing Group, Inc. All rights Reserved; Extract on
p.46 adapted from "UK recession: And what don't you do for a living?"
by Judith Woods, *The Telegraph*, 15/04/2009, copyright © Telegraph
Media Group Limited 2009; Extract on p.55 adapted from "The corporate
conscience: Sherron Watkins, Enron whistleblower" by Leslie Curwin,
The Guardian, 21/06/2003, copyright © Lesley Curwen; Extract on p.55
adapted from "Drug Whistleblower Collects $24M, Pfizer Makes Payment
To Scientist Who Exposed Wrongdoing" by Denise Lavoie, *CBS News*,
13/05/2004. Used with permission of The Associated Press, copyright
© 2010. All Rights Reserved; Extract on p.68 adapted from "Innumerate
bankers were ripe for a reckoning" by Martin Taylor, *The Financial Times*,
15/12/2009, copyright © Martin Taylor; Extract on p.74 adapted from 'Top
Ten Things You'll Never Hear from your Consultant', www.workjoke.com,

copyright © Work Joke; Extract on p.77 adapted from 'Day in the life of a
management consultant (client version)', http://managementconsulted.
com/2008/12/15/day-in-the-life-of-a-management-consultant-client-
version/, copyright © Kevin Gao; Extract on p.108 adapted from
"Managing Cashflow Guides, 7. Chasing payment", first published by The
Institute of Credit Management in its 'Managing Cashflow' series at www.
creditmanagement.org.uk, copyright © The Institute of Credit Management;
Extracts in unit 12 adapted from "Project plans: 10 essential elements" by
Trevor Roberts, 2009, www.projectsmart.co.uk, copyright © Trevor Roberts;
Extract in unit 12 adapted from "33 Tips For Using Teleconferencing for
Meeting Preparation" by Susan A. Friedman, CSP, The Tradeshow Coach,
www.corbinball.com, copyright © Susan A. Friedmann, Author of 'Meeting
& Event Planning for Dummies' (Wiley); Extract in unit WAC 4 adapted
from "Bridge the culture gap - and enjoy success when working with your
overseas colleagues and partners", 16 February, 2005, www.canning.com,
copyright © Canning School Ltd; Extract on p.130 adapted from "Japan:
Land of Green Gizmos" by Mark Litke, *ABC News*, 28/04/2007, copyright ©
2010 ABC News Internet Ventures, http://abcnews.go.com.

The Financial Times
Extract on p.25 from "Helge Lund: 'The danger of losing touch with reality'"
by Ed Crooks, *The Financial Times*, 13/10/2009; Quote in unit 4 from
"Household Goods - Up to 100 brands to go as P&G declutters" by Barney
Jopson, *The Financial Times*, 01/08/2014; Extract on p.39 adapted from "Is
the customer always right? Yes, she is" by Jonathan Birchall, *The Financial
Times*, 24/09/2009; Extract on p.99 from "The new corporate firefighters"
by David Gelles, *The Financial Times*, 22/01/2009; Extract on p.106 from
"Go the distance with a one-trick pony" by Jonathan Moules, *The Financial
Times*, 29/06/2009; Extract on p.132 adapted from "Right or wrong, the
customer always matters" by Michael Skapinker, *The Financial Times*,
22/03/2010; Extract on p.133 from "Living strategy and death of the
five-year plan" by Stefan Stern, *The Financial Times*, 26/10/2009; Extract
adapted from "A harsh lesson from Tim Armstrong, AOL's very unappealing"
by Lucy Kellaway, *The Financial Times*, 17/05/2015, copyright © The
Financial Times Limited, 2009, 2010, 2014, 2015. All rights reserved.

In some instances we have been unable to trace the owners of copyright
material, and we would appreciate any information that would enable us to
do so.

Photos
The publisher would like to thank the following for their kind permission to
reproduce their photographs:
(Key: b-bottom; c-centre; l-left; r-right; t-top)

© 2010 Amazon.com, Inc. or its affiliates: 84l, 85tr, 84l, 85tr; **Alamy
Images:** Image 100 59, Jose Luis Pelaez / Blend Images 116tl, Mike
Broughton 117cr, Uppercut Images / Paul Aresu 43c; **Corbis:** Ashley Cooper
6t, Bettman 74t, Chris Collins 46, Gareth Brown / Comet 77, Lester Lefkonitz
96t, Nasa / Reuters 112t, Ocean 31b, 99cr, 102t, Ocean 31b, 99cr, 102t,
Ocean 31b, 99cr, 102t, Peter Ginter / Science Faction 88-89, Schlegalmilch
121b, Scott Stulberg 104t, William Whitehurst 44t, Zhang Jun / Xinhua
Press 61b; **Courtesy of Procter & Gamble UK:** 84bl; **Courtesy of Toyota (GB)
Ltd:** 84cl; **Daniel Pudles:** 68c; **Fotolia.com:** Inferno189 10tl, Pumba A13bl;
FT.com: Charlie Bibby 166; **Geek & Poke/ Oliver Widder:** Oliver Widder 76t;
Getty Images: Altrendo Images 50t, Anderson Ross / Stockbyte 48, Andy
Ryan / Image Bank 42, Bloomberg 39b, Bloomberg / Dimas Ardian 120bl,
Caiaimage / Paul Bradbury A5bl, Chris Hondros 12b, Christoph Wilhelm /
Photographers Choice 40tl, Christopher Polk 13b, David Woodfall / Riser
61tr, Domino / Stone 102bl, Ekaterina Monakhova / iStock Exclusive 58,
Hola Images 78, Image Source 29b, Janet Street / Stock Illustration Source
100t, Joe McNally 86tl, Jupiter Images / Comstock 18tl, Matthius Tunger /
Stone 70tl, Michael Cogliantry 7cl, Siri Stafford / Lifesize 73tr, Steve Bloom /
Taxi 41c, Thomas Northcut / Photodisc 102cr, Thomas Schmidt / Riser 60bl,
Workbook Stock / Jupiter Images 101tl; **Photo courtesy Google UK:** 84tl;
Intel: 83l; **Mandy Haberman:** 106c; **Mercadona:** 83cl; **Pearson Education
Ltd:** Rob Maidment 6bl, 14cl, 22bl, 36b, 44bl, 49cl, 52bl, 67tl, 75tl, 82bl,
97tl, 100cl, 105cl, 113cl,; **Photolibrary.com:** Age Fotostock 39t, Age
Fotostock / Greg Griffith 14t, Chad Ehlers 119, Creatas 15bl, Larry Williams
81tr, Mike Kemp 82t, Nonstock 43cl, 43r, Nonstock 43cl, 43r, Novastock
91, Transworld Photos 118; **Reuters:** Claro Cortes 16c, Luke Macgregor
66t, Win McNamee 55tr; **Shutterstock.com:** Alexander Raths 110b,
Ansar80 20cr, Auremar 15cl, 20r, Auremar 15cl, 20r, Clawan 51, Kharidehal
Abhirama Ashwin 15tl, Perati Komson 36t, Michaeljung A3-A4, Monkey
Business Images A5-A6, A7-A8, A13-A14, Myimagine A1-A2, Outsider 21b,
Paul Barnwell 113tr, Pi-Lens 22t, Andrey Popov A15-A16, Pressmaster
A7b, A9-A10, Serge64 28br, StockLite A11-A12, Szefei 20cl; **Statoil:**
Harald Petterson 25; **The Kobal Collection:** Appian Way / Paramount 52t;
Thinkstock: Brand X Pictures 57, Comstock 73tl, Comstock / Jupiter Images /
Getty Images 116tr, Digital Vision / Photodisc 43l, George Doyle / Stockbyte
8tl, Hemera 23c, 90tl, 90tr, Hemera 23c, 90tl, 90tr, Hemera 23c, 90tl, 90tr,
iStockphoto 15t, 20c, 23t, 28b, 71tl, 73tc, 76cl, 80-81, 108tl, Martin Poole
/ Digital Vision / Getty 101cr, Photographers.com / Jupiter Images / Getty
Images 72bl, Siri Stafford / Digital Vision 90tc, Stockbyte 72b, 79tl, 111cl,
115tr, Todd Warnock 23b; **Triodos:** 66bl; **www.CartoonStock.com:** Royston
26tl; **www.worldvisionphotos.co.uk:** Dianna Bonner 9c

All other images © Pearson Education

Video
© Pearson Education